Law and Society in the Ibāḍī Communities of North Africa and Oman

Studies in Islamic Law and Society

VOLUME 59

The titles published in this series are listed at *brill.com/sils*

Law and Society in the Ibāḍī Communities of North Africa and Oman

History and Critical Assessment

By

Ersilia Francesca

BRILL

ISSN 1384-1130
ISBN 978-90-04-37766-0
ISBN 978-90-04-76576-4 (PDF)
DOI https://doi.org/10.1163/9789004765764

Library of Congress Control Number: 2026940939

Brill and Koninklijke Brill BV are part of De Gruyter Brill.
www.degruyterbrill.com

Questions about General Product Safety Regulation: productsafety@degruyterbrill.com

To all my Ibāḍī friends and colleagues
who shared their love of knowledge with me

•••

To Alessandro
who always encourages me to exceed my limits

∵

Whoever travels a path in search of knowledge, God will make easy for him a path to Paradise.

Prophetic *ḥadīth*

• • •

All acts of devotion, the *jihād* on the way of God, enjoining the right and forbidding the wrong are but a spit in the sea compared to the quest for knowledge.

al-Kudamī, 10th–11th century

Contents

Acknowledgements

Writing this book has been a long journey filled with enthusiasm, hard work, challenges and continuous ups and downs, mirroring life's unpredictable path. It has been many years in the making and has become a reality through the endless support of a large community of people to whom I am deeply indebted. The book project has developed through conversations and exchanges with a number of different colleagues. I cannot name them all, but I am grateful for their role in making this book possible.

I would like to express my sincere gratitude to the individuals and organisations whose support and contribution have been invaluable in the creation of this book. Foremost, I am deeply grateful to the former Minister of Awqaf and Religious Affairs of the Sultanate of Oman, HE Shaykh Abdullah Bin Mohammed al-Salmi and to Dr Abdulrahman al-Salimi; without their support this book would have been unthinkable. Dr Abdulrahman al-Salimi's support extended beyond professional collaboration to genuine friendship; he not only sent me books and provided useful information, but he also smoothed the way for me to access manuscripts and books collection in the Wizārat al-Turāth al-Qawmī wa ʾl-Thaqāfa, and in several other private and public libraries in Oman.

Many colleagues and friends from the Ibāḍī studies community assisted me in the various stages of my research and were fundamental in the conceptualization and making of this book. I will surely forget many names here, and to them I apologize. My thanks go to John Wilkinson, Valerie Hoffman, Amal Ghazal, Angeliki Ziaka, Paul Love, Cyrille Aillet, Augustin Jomier, Salah Bahmani, Enki Baptist, Mandana Limbert, Werner Schwartz and many others. My gratitude goes out also to the late professors Joseph van Ess, Wilferd Madelung, Heinz Gaube and to the late Dr Myklos Muranyi, our conversations during conferences dedicated to Ibāḍī studies and beyond have been a constant source of inspiration for me over the years.

I presented my ongoing research during several conferences and workshops. It is my duty and pleasure to thank the organizers and the participants for their helpful comments that gave new impetus to my work. They are too many to name, but I extend special thanks to Robert Gleave, who invited me to a series of workshops on Shiʿi and Ibāḍī legal systems, which strengthened my awareness that by broadening the evidence base to the whole Muslim legal tradition, one can try to develop a more comprehensive view of Islamic studies. I'm also indebted to Mohammed-Hocine Benkheira who invited me to the role of visiting professor at EPHE in Paris in 2018, giving me the opportunity to discuss the initial results of my research with him and his classes.

It remains for me to register my profound gratitude to many helping hands without whom the publication of this book would not have been possible. I extend my heartfelt thanks to the association Ibadica (Paris), and particularly to Slimane Tounsi and Soufien Mestaoui who gave me valuable insights into the life of the Ibāḍī communities, both in the Maghrib and in the French diaspora. Moreover, Soufien provided me with endless assistance in finding rare Ibāḍī sources.

Special appreciation goes to Augustin Jomier for reading Chapter 7 of this book and providing me with useful suggestions for improving it.

Gratitude is also due to Nienke Brienen-Moolenaar, my editor at Brill, for her assistance in the editing process, and to Sarah Campbell for her careful and accurate review of the English language. I also wish to acknowledge the anonymous reviewers for their constructive comments and suggestions which greatly enhanced the final version of this volume. Finally, I take full responsibility for any remaining errors in this book.

I extended my heartfelt thanks to SOAS in London, where I was visiting scholar in 2015, and to Cambridge University Library for providing me with a peaceful workspace and a rich book collection, which I could enjoy during the long months I spent in Cambridge (UK) over recent years.

Finally, I am deeply grateful to my family for their unwavering support and understanding, in particular I thank my husband, Alessandro, whose support got me through the inevitable rough patches of writing.

Note on Transliteration and Dates

I have followed the Arabic transliteration guidelines set forth in Brill's general guidelines for manuscript submission and preparation. I did not transliterate well-known words such as "Islam" or "Quran" and the most commonly used toponyms. Double dates are used for the classical era.

Consonants

ʾ	d	ḍ	k
b	dh	ṭ	l
t	r	ẓ	m
th	z	ʿ	n
j	s	gh	h
ḥ	sh	f	w
kh	ṣ	q	y

Vowels

Long	Short	Diphtongs
ā	a	aw
ū	u	ay
ī	i	

Introduction

The field of Islamic law has been flourishing in Western academia over the past century, since Ignaz Goldziher (1850–1921) and Joseph Schacht (1902–1969) started questioning its origins and early development. Goldziher was among the first scholars to explore the foreign elements assimilated by the Islamic faith,[1] while Schacht, following in his footsteps, analyzed in detail the development of Muslim legal theory, reaching – in his opinion – its culminating point with al-Shāfiʿī. He tackled the role of traditions, consensus and analogy in the emerging schools of law and the tendency to accept into the schools tradition the influence of Jewish and Roman rules. Along with these external influences, popular as well as administrative practices played a fundamental role in what would become Islamic law.[2] From the beginning, Joseph Schacht's theories have provoked continuous vivid debates, which have engaged generations of scholars, passionately accepting or rejecting his conclusions.

In recent decades, scholarship on Islamic law has grown exponentially thanks to access to new sources, historiographical advances and data science tools. Interdisciplinary approaches have provided productive critical lenses and model studies for dating early legal dicta, which are potentially fruitful for reconstructing the early history of Islam. Recent research has demonstrated that traditions were collected and transmitted in the early 8th century and possibly much earlier. At the same time scholars have started exploring the idea of the "beginnings" of Islamic law (instead of "origins"), thus highlighting the sense of continuity between Islamic juridical praxis, local custom and extant legal systems, which Islam encountered over the course of its spread from the Arabian Peninsula into other regions of the ancient Near East. The degree of outside influence on early Islamic law is highly debated. Wael Hallaq argues that "the ingenious process of assimilation, systematization and Islamization managed to dissipate all the indigenous features of legal institutions and to recast them in a fashion that is not in the least reminiscent of older institutions".[3]

It makes sense to assume that Muslim jurists took inspiration from their counterparts in other legal systems in order to find solutions to difficult problems. It thus seems more sensible not to state a direct influence of such systems

1 Goldziher, *Mohammed and Islam* chapter 2.
2 Schacht, *The Origins*; idem, *An Introduction to Islamic Law*.
3 Hallaq, The Use and Abuse of Evidence: The Question of Provincial and Roman Influences on Early Islamic Law 90.

 | HTTPS://DOI.ORG/10.1163/9789004765764-002

on Islamic law, but rather to assume that both these systems and Islamic law stem from a common patrimony of legal praxis and religious and socio-cultural values. Elements of Roman law survived in what Patricia Crone called "Roman provincial law", and it is possible that they resurfaced in early Islamic legal discourse; but this cannot be regarded as constituting an influence of external legal practices on the development of Islamic law.[4] A more suitable interpretation, as argued convincingly by Lena Salaymeh, is that the conventional models of comparative legal studies, which assume clear boundaries between legal systems, do not correspond to the historical fluidity and porousness of the legal systems of the Ancient Near East. The interplay between tradition and innovation had lasting echoes in Islamic jurisprudence. Generations of Muslim scholars interpreted scripture and precedents in ways that simultaneously renewed and perpetuated already existing legal traditions. They created a dialectic of Islamic law with parallel legal systems where an amount of syncretism and legal continuity was both inevitable and necessary.[5]

By moving beyond Goldziher's and Schacht's critiques of the origins of Islamic law, academia has recently opened promising avenues of research that moved away from the last century's early methodologies and inquires, evolving into an increasingly dynamic and multifaceted intellectual scene. One of the new tendencies in the field of Islamic legal studies is the recognition of the sub-fields of non-Sunni (in particular Shiʿi) legal systems.[6] As Robert Gleave argued, by broadening the evidence base to the whole Muslim legal tradition, one can try to develop more comprehensive answers to the principal research questions that might be addressed in the field. Nonetheless, he noticed "that the field continues to be locked into the habit of treating some traditions as afterthoughts or marginal offshoots, rather than part of a wider, richer Muslim legal history".[7]

The main challenge here is to go beyond the approach which considers the non-Sunni legal systems (Shiʿi as well as Ibāḍī) somehow exotic birds requiring particular knowledge and skills to be studied, or worse, the overlooked Cinderellas to their Sunni counterpart, to which only scant attention should be given. On the contrary, the academic debate would be enriched by acknowledging the valid contribution Shiʿi and Ibāḍī schools made to the development of the theological and legal debate as well as the level of interchange there was among scholars belonging to different schools. Today academia reflects

4 Crone, *Roman, Provincial and Islamic Law*.
5 Salaymeh, *The Beginnings of Islamic Law* 1–14.
6 Siddiqui (ed.), *Locating the Sharīʿa*, introduction by the editor, 1–9.
7 Gleave, Sectarianism and Integration, in Siddiqui (ed.), *Locating the Sharīʿa* 30.

the same Sunni pressure which worked – in particular from the 10th century onwards – to marginalize Shiʿites and Ibāḍīs by establishing a belief system impinging on the social and political structure and restricting Islamic religious discourse to only the "orthodox" *madhhab*s.[8]

However, as Devin Stewart argued,

> the threat which faced them, that of exclusion from the community by the Sunni juridical *madhhab*s, presented one of the most formidable challenges within the intellectual history of Islam. It is this challenge, more than any other, which brought about the formation of the Twelver Shiʿite *madhhab* and the establishment of a legal system based on the authority of the jurists. The Twelvers succeeded in creating a *madhhab* that is essentially functionally equivalent to the Sunni *madhhab*s that has persevered from the 10th until the present century with remarkable intellectual vigor.[9]

Likewise – as I will prove in this book – for the Ibāḍīs this Sunni pressure was a catalyst, pushing them toward greater doctrinal consistency and activating a latent rationalizing force, which enabled the survival of the school under the leadership of the religious elites as its cultural champions.

Recent decades have witnessed a remarkable growth in interest in the legal traditions and intellectual history of Shiʿi Islam, with a growing number of articles and books devoted to the subject and the publication (and in many cases the translation) of several classical works which constitute the intellectual foundations of this extraordinarily diverse tradition.

Notwithstanding an increasing interest in Ibadism over last years and an extensive publication activity that has made available to academics handful of Ibāḍī primary sources, sustained engagement with Ibāḍī legal theory remains in its infancy. Yet it was the many unanswered questions about Ibāḍī law and jurisprudence that prompted me to write this book with the aim of contributing to filling some gaps in our understanding of this particular *madhhab*, and perhaps of Islamic legal theory and history in general.

Arguably, the Ibāḍī *madhhab* is one of the oldest medieval *madhhab*s, producing an incredibly rich patrimony of literature spanning two continents (Africa and Asia) and including several languages, notably Arabic, Berber and Swahili. That is why I believe it is groundbreaking to explore the experiences of this often overlooked group in Islamic legal history. Examination of the Ibāḍī tradition shows how this legal system functioned over time, maintaining its

8 Ibidem, 34.
9 Stewart, *Islamic Legal Orthodoxy* 252–253.

own character but at the same time creating a large degree of similarity with the other schools of law.

This book provides an opportunity to chart alternatives to the dominant and largely Sunni-centric (and secondarily Shiʿi-centric) narratives on Islam. Abandoning the typical habit of viewing Islamic history "from the centre",[10] that is, focusing mainly on Sunni sources, I aim at offering a more comprehensive view of the historical evolution of Islamic society. The Sunni/"orthodox" mainstream and the sectarian/"heterodox" Islam concurred in elaborating historical readings, which are conflicting but, at the same time, simultaneous and interdependent.

A broader perspective on the Islamic tradition's underrepresented sources also runs the risk of creating an academic silo in which, for example, Shiʿism or Ibadism becomes a subfield of Islamic studies rather than actually breaking into mainstream Islamic studies per se. In the face of such a challenge, there is also a unique third position, which entails a more holistic approach to studying Islam and Muslim sources. The point of emphasis here is to not see Sunni sources as determinative of the categories of Islamic studies, or other important Muslim traditions such as the Shiʿi as a distinctive and therefore confined sub-unit of Islamic studies. Rather, we should view Sunni, Shiʿi and Ibāḍī approaches as all informative, and thus (to the extent possible) normative expressions of the Islamic tradition's vast pre-modern heritage. Approaching the Islamic tradition in this manner is sure to yield promising results for the field, especially for the scholars of the formative period of Islam, whose research has often been adversely affected by scarcity of sources.

Ibāḍī sources provide us with abundant raw data for analyzing the Ibāḍī jurists' contribution to the development of Islamic law. Therefore, a thorough analysis of Ibāḍī material may add new dimensions to our understanding not only of the development of the movement, but also of the whole history of Islam. Ibāḍī legal theory develops early on in Islamic history in parallel with – not as a derivative of – any comparative Sunni theories. It is possible to unearth some of this material from the early Ibāḍī sources, allowing for a reconstruction of both early Ibāḍī legal theory and its contribution to the development of Islamic legal thought.

The formative period of the Ibāḍī school in the 2nd/8th century epitomizes the recasting of the Ibāḍī/Khārijī piety into a distinctive pattern of legal rationality. Ibāḍī moralistic conception of Islamic community had unparalleled influence on the formation of Ibāḍī law: moral ideals shaped the growth and the internal dynamics of the school, and their implementation affected Ibāḍī

10 Aillet, *L'archipel ibadite* 5–9; idem, L'ibâḍisme, une minorité au cœur de l'islam 13–36.

relations with other Muslims and contributed to the construction of their own group identity. The *ʿulamāʾ* played a key role in the survival of the school from the outset, shaping and reshaping the legal tradition to adapt to new circumstances. The first three Ibāḍī leaders and jurists, Jābir b. Zayd, Abū ʿUbayda and al-Rabīʿ b. Ḥabīb, not only shaped the organization of the movement, but laid the foundations of the legal debate from which the Ibāḍī law would emerge – sometimes in opposition to, sometimes in cooperation with their Sunni counterparts. They became mythicized figures of an Ibāḍī Golden Age in Basra, especially when the community split into two main branches: one settled in Oman and another in the Maghrib.

From the 4th/10th century onward, Ibāḍī jurists responded to Sunni pressure through a process that John Wilkinson calls "rationalization" of law and jurisprudence, meaning converting the primitive form of Ibadism into a model *madhhab*.[11] In Oman this process coincided with a resurgence of the imamate after the collapse of the first imamate. In the Maghrib, where the institution of the imamate had disappeared to give rise to the more secret organisation of the *ḥalqat al-ʿazzāba* (circle of elders), the process of normalisation emerged probably in reaction to Maliki influences.

The "rationalization/normalization" process allowed the Ibāḍīs to participate in the Sunni system as peers, through the creation of a *madhhab* parallel to those of the Sunnis. The Ibāḍī legal system was anchored in the authority of the jurists as a restricted category of learned men. Religious knowledge (*ʿilm*) and mastery of scholarly skills necessary for attaining an understanding of the law defined their leading role within the community. Some elements are relevant to this point. In particular, the fact that "the doors of *ijtihād*" were never sealed among the Ibāḍīs. The high-ranking jurists might exercise independent interpretation (*ijtihād*) of the sources and question the opinions of earlier jurists. The parallel act of *taqlīd*, on the contrary, entailed a decision to live in accordance with the system of authority by following a *mujtahid*'s doctrine rather than by going directly to the scriptural texts for guidance.

The deposition of the *imām* al-Ṣalt ibn Mālik in 886 was a major turning point in the history of Oman, providing the Ibāḍī scholars with the impetus to reflect on a detailed theory of the imamate and on their own role in relation to (and in competition with) political power. An analogous turning point in North Africa was the fall of the Rustumid imamate following the Fatimid victory in 909, which implied a definitive renunciation of the imamate as a centralized and hierarchized structure and the switch to a political organization based on the power of the *ḥalqat al-ʿazzāba*. Within Maghribi Ibadism, the

11 Wilkinson, *Ibāḍī Ḥadīth* 253–259.

rule of the elders – along with the rule of the chiefs of the tribes – militated against the emergence of permanent and tyrannical rulers, thus enabling the Ibāḍī communities to escape the ephemeral life of the imamates which had characterized their past history. The merit of the system was to provide balance against tyranny and political ambitions, its corresponding weakness was the ultimate renunciation of the unity of the Ibāḍī communities scattered throughout the Maghrib. Jurists' role was paramount in this context where no single state or overarching power ruled supreme. Their presence was vital to the maintenance of social stability as well as to the internal understanding of Ibāḍī knowledge transmission at a time when North African Ibāḍī communities were exposed to an increased interaction with the Maliki school, with which, excepting some episodes of violent confrontation, they managed to live together peacefully.

As I will argue in this book, understanding the development of Ibāḍī law and jurisprudence goes hand in hand with an analysis of the social role and political agenda of the intellectual elite, as represented by *fuqahā'* and *'ulamā'*.

In the last part of the book, I will explore the development of Ibāḍī law within the Ibāḍī reform movement, which anticipated and partially paralleled the better known *nahḍa*, "renaissance", in the Sunni intellectual milieu. The Ibāḍī intellectuals began to advocate for significant legal reform and for a rapprochement with the Sunnism in the name of the common fight against colonial power. One eventual result was a pragmatic eclecticism that involved crossover and borrowing between the several schools of law. Two personalities stood out in this context: the Mzabi Muḥammad Aṭfayyish (1820–1914) and the Omani Nūr al-Dīn al-Sālimī (1869–1914). They both make it clear that mastering the Ibāḍī heritage meant knowing its various aspects but also recognizing its relativity and historicity. Therefore, these authors referred to the search for an Ibāḍī identity in modernity, which can blossom only where there are no bans on innovation and rethinking. *Ikhtilāf* (difference of opinion) was a source of intellectual wealth that ought to be utilized for the benefit of the whole community, and *tarjīḥ*, or preponderance, provided the epistemic and methodological starting point for choosing the epistemologically most sound or weighty opinion among different views on a single matter. *Ijtihād* and *talfīq* (the derivation of rules from various schools of law) were fundamental means to reform Islamic law. Aṭfayyish and al-Sālimī argued passionately in favour of *ijtihād* to respond to the intellectual and practical problems of the modern age and of *tajdīd* (renewal) in the interpretation of legal texts. Although couched in scholarly terms, this paradigm sanctioned the pursuit of political goals under the aegis of religion.

The efforts by the Ibāḍī reform movement to modernize the Islamic law – along with the efforts of many other activists in the Muslim world – was almost contemporary with the process of progressive abandonment of the *sharīʿa* with the adoption of codes modelled on those of Europe in many Muslim countries. In a vast realm of civil, criminal, commercial and constitutional law, secular codes replaced the religious law at an unprecedented speed, with the significant exception of the law of personal status, which still today remains the last stronghold of the *sharīʿa*.

Ibāḍī reformers tried to resist the replacement of the *sharīʿa*, arguing that planting European institutions and laws in the Arab countries could not harmonize with their juridical environment and, because nobody understood these imported laws, nobody would respect or obey them. They represented the last effort to implement Ibāḍī law and institutions. In the Maghrib, Ibāḍī tradition was sidelined by French colonization. In Oman and Zanzibar, the multiethnic and multireligious empire of the Āl Bū Saʿīdī dynasty was built over successful trading and a multicultural approach to politics and religion.

CHAPTER 1

Theories on the Origins of Ibāḍī Law and Jurisprudence

1.1 The Origins of Ibadism

Ibāḍīs took their name from ʿAbd Allāh ibn Ibāḍ, an almost obscure figure about whom Ibāḍī historiography provides little information. According to Sunni historical sources he was among the group of Khārijī dissidents who left Basra under the leadership of Nāfiʿ b. Al-Azraq in 63/683, and moved to Mecca to defend ʿAbd Allāh b. al-Zubayr (624–692) against the assault of the Umayyad army. Later he broke with the radical Khārijī trend, represented by Nāfiʿ b. Al-Azraq and ʿAbd Allāh b. al-Ṣaffār, over their attitude towards other Muslims, whom he refused to consider as "polytheist" (*mushrikūn*).[1]

Today Ibāḍīs make up the majority of the population in Oman, while tiny Ibāḍī minorities are dispersed between Zanzibar (East Africa) and the traditional North African strongholds of the Mzab Valley and the Oasis of Warjla (Algeria), Jerba Island (Tunisia) and Jabal Nafūsa (Libya).

Ibāḍīs emerged from the nebula of the *Muḥakkima* movement, which was born as a protest against the acceptance of anything other than a divine settlement for the conflict that had evolved around the question of leadership between the followers of ʿAlī and the supporters of Muʿāwiya after the murder of ʿUthmān in 656. Once ʿAlī accepted Muʿāwiya's proposal to settle the war through arbitration, which finally ended in Muʿāwiya's favour, a group of extremist supporters of ʿAlī broke away, shouting the slogan "*la ḥukm illā li-Allāh*" ("the Judgement belongs to God alone"). This formula could be applied not only to ʿUthmān but also to every other ruler who deviated from the right path. The Khawārij used it against ʿAlī to withdraw from his party. Their argument was not weak: ʿAlī had made an unjust pact with Muʿāwiya and then was unwilling to break it. He had surrendered God's right which had caused the struggle against ʿUthmān and Muʿāwiya and had signed a treaty with men who did not recognize that right.[2]

1 Madelung, Abd Allāh Ibn Ibāḍ and the Origins of the Ibāḍiyya 52–57; van Ess, *Theologie und Gesellschaft* ii, 187–189; Wilkinson, *Ibâḍism* 150–154.

2 Hoffman, Ibāḍism: History, Doctrines, and Recent Scholarship 297–307.

 | HTTPS://DOI.ORG/10.1163/9789004765764-003

The root meaning of Khawārij is "those who go out", although its precise significance is disputed: some interpret it to mean "seceders", i.e. those who seceded from ʿAlī's army, while others say that it meant those who went out in battle to perform the sacred duty of struggle in the path of God (*jihād*).

The proto-Ibāḍis were part (and today are the only survivors) of the *Muḥakkima* movement, sharing with them the principles that rule on earth belongs to God alone and that the authority of leaders is annulled by sin. However, the Ibāḍis are very distant from the Khawārij on other political as well religious matters. Muslim heresiographical works divide the Khawārij into three main groups: the Azāriqa, followers of Nāfiʿ ibn al-Azraq, who are viewed as the most extreme branch, denouncing their opponents as unbelievers or polytheists (*mushrikūn*) deserving of death; the Ibāḍīs/Ibāḍiyya, followers of ʿAbd Allāh ibn Ibāḍ/Abāḍ, who are seen as the most moderate of the Khawārij; and the Ṣufrīs, followers of ʿAbd Allāh ibn al-Aṣfar or al-Ṣaffār, the origin of whose name is obscure, but who are seen as falling somewhere between the two groups.[3]

Ibāḍī scholars, especially from the *nahḍa* (renaissance) period (end of the 19th–beginning of the 20th century) onwards, question the Khārijī origins of the movement, distancing themselves from alleged Khārijī violence and developing their own narrative of an Ibāḍī identity based on a quietist attitude and tolerance, entirely different from that which fell from the pens of medieval heresiographers.[4] This narrative represents Ibāḍī Islam as the purest form of God's message, preserved against corruption by Muslim ascetics and martyrs (*shurāt*),[5] a group of whom settled in Basra under the leadership of Ibn

3 Recent scholarship has questioned the narrative of the three main groups of Khawārij whose patronymic names imply a colour (in Arabic, *azraq* is blue, *abyaḍ* is white and *aṣfar* is yellow). See for example: Cook, *Early Muslim Dogma* 64; Lewinstein, Making and Unmaking a Sect 75–96; Fierro, Al-Aṣfar 169–181; idem, Al-Aṣfar again 196–213. Wilkinson (*Ibâḍism*, 150–160) underlines the tribal dimension in the spreading of Ibadism in the Arabian Peninsula: the early Ibāḍīs were 'southern' (Yamanī) Arabs, whereas other Khārijī groups were 'northern' (Nizārī) Arabs. Thus Ibadism became a vehicle of Yamanī resistance to Nizārī domination. Omanis and other Yamanī tribes embraced Ibadism only after the crushing of the non-Khārijī Yamanī uprisings of Ibn al-Ashʿath al-Kindī (699–701) and Yazīd ibn al-Muhallab al-Azdī (720–721), which gave new opportunities to the moderate Khawārij to spread their propaganda among the defeated.

4 Baptiste and Gaiser, Early Ibāḍī Historiography 52–70; Ennami, *Studies* 16–31 (online edition); Gaiser, *Sectarianism in Islam* 57–61; al-Bārūnī, *Mukhtaṣar tarīkh al-ibāḍiyya* 16–17, 65–75; al-Sālimī, *Lumʿa* 5–7; Muʿammar, *Ibāḍīyya fī mawkib al-tārīkh* I, 19–35; idem, *Ibāḍīyya bayna firaq al-islāmiyya* 425–434.

5 The word *shurāt* denotes the "martyrdom-seekings"; its literal meaning indicates purchase or exchange, because the lives of the rebels (*shurāt*) were purchased by God, or they exchanged

Ibāḍ. The term early Ibāḍīs used for themselves, namely *Muslimūn* (while the "others" were *ahl al-qibla* or *mukhālifūn*, dissidents) or *ahl al-istiqāma* (people of rightness),[6] underlines their understanding of their community as the most virtuous and accurate, and themselves as the sole remaining righteous heirs of the true Islam. Ibāḍīs developed this idea of belonging into the notion of a "communal pedigree", a patrimony of belief constituting the *āthār* (tradition, practice) of the community, going back, through a continuous line of pious forebears, directly to the Prophet, thus attesting the soundness of Ibāḍī Islam.[7]

As early as 1952, the Italian scholar Laura Veccia Vaglieri tried to bypass the standard narrative of violence, bloody and barbaric acts, depredation and arson committed by the Khārijīs using material from inside the Ibāḍī movement. She challenges the childish reconstruction that the sources make of the arbitration and its immediate consequences, posing a series of research questions: What were the Kharijites' intentions? Did they want to fight ʿAlī or Muʿāwiya? Did they want to proclaim independence and elect a new Caliph? Was the battle of Nahrawān before or after the meeting between the two arbiters? Was Muʿāwiya really proclaimed Caliph given that until that time he had advanced no claims? She based her pioneering study on the struggle between ʿAlī and Muʿāwiya on the *Kitāb al-Jawāhir* by Abū 'l-Faḍl Abū 'l-Qāsim b. Ibrāhīm al-Barrādī (14th–15th century), the *Kitāb al-Siyar* by al-Shammākhī (second half of 15th–beginning of 16th century) and the *Kashf al-ghumma* by an unknown Omani scholar from the 18th century. The sources she used referred to ancient materials, in particular to *Kitāb al-Nahrawān*, whose main transmitter seems to have been ʿAbdallāh b. Yazīd al-Fazārī. Laura Veccia Vaglieri provides political interpretation to the Khārijī secession: their idea since the time of Ḥarūrā' had been that it was possible to be without a Caliph for a period of time, while waiting for a committee of wise men to choose the most suitable person. It is probable – she maintains – that from that very time the theory that any Muslim could become Caliph if he had the right qualities was first mooted, which would later become a firm Khārijī principle. The Khārijīs did not intend to attack ʿAlī but rather were sickened by his behaviour and, hoping for a ruler who respected divine right, distanced themselves from

---

their lives for God's reward. See Gaiser, *Shurāt Legends, Ibāḍī Identities*; Higgins, *The Qur'anic Exchange of the Self in the Poetry of Shurāt (Khārijī) Political Identity*.

6 Apparently the first reference to the Ibāḍīs referring to themselves with this label is recorded in the book *al-Daynūna al-ṣāfiya* by the Maghribi scholar ʿAmrūs al-Fatḥ al-Nafūsī (d. 283/896). Al-Nafūsī, *al-Daynūna al-ṣāfiya* 68.

7 Gaiser, *Ballaghanā ʿan an-Nabī* 437–448.

him. The rise of the Khārijīs forced the Muslim community to define its own position on who was to be considered Muslim and who an infidel.[8]

Legal or proto-legal factors were crucial during the first civil war. Issues like the succession to Muḥammad, the right to rebel against an unjust leader and, on the contrary, the kin's right to take revenge for the murder of a caliph instigated and dominated the strife, with each side appealing to the Quran and claiming to be right. The victory of Muʿāwiyya did not settle the dispute nor prevent the development of different factions, with the fiercely egalitarian Khawārij at one end of the spectrum, and the legitimist party (*shiʿa*) championing the rights of the descendants of ʿAlī and Fāṭima, the Prophet's daughter, at the other.[9]

The question of the qualifications of the leader of the Muslims (*khalīfa* or *imām*) split the community. For the Ibāḍīs, bloodline and lineage had no value: only the most deserving Muslim should be elected, whatever his ethnic origins might be. Leadership stemmed from personal excellence, and the confidence which the community placed in its *imām* constituted his authority.

According to the standard Ibāḍī narrative, the Ibāḍīs settled in Basra under a series of *imāms* operating in secrecy (*kitmān*), beginning with Jābir ibn Zayd (*c.*642–711), who is said to have organized the Ibāḍī community, and followed by Abū ʿUbayda Muslim ibn Abī Karīma (d. probably during al-Manṣūr caliphate between 767 and 775), who sent out missionaries (*ḥamalat al-ʿilm*) to establish imamates in various provinces, from Khurāsān to the Ḥaḍramawt and the Maghrib.

This early phase of the movement was crucial to its development, as well as to the history of Islam as a whole, as we shall see over the course of the next chapters, for Basra and Kufa were the centres of the major legal and theological debate out of which Islamic theology and law would emerge.

The basic Ibāḍī strategy of survival in a hostile environment took the form of an alliance with the Muhallabid family. The pragmatic relations of the Ibāḍīs and the Muhallabis were based on their common interest in trade. This association remained intact through the turmoil of the Abbasid revolution and provided the means by which the Ibāḍīs could survive during a time of great uncertainty.[10]

The Ibāḍī quest for alliance was already underlined as early as 1953 by Roberto Rubinacci in his study on relations between ʿAbd al-Malik b. Marwān (r. 65–86/661–680) and the Ibāḍīs, based on two letters from Ibn Ibāḍ to the

8 Veccia Vaglieri, Il conflitto ʿAlī-Muʿāwiya e la secessione khārijita 65–67, 71.

9 Arjomand, *Sociology of Shiʿite Islam* 2–3.

10 Savage, *A Gateway to Hell, a Gateway to Paradise* 40–41.

caliph, preserved in *Kitāb al-Jawāhir* by al-Barrādī and in *Kashf al-ghumma*.[11] According to Rubinacci, the significance of the split from the Khārijī extremists did not escape ʿAbd al-Malik; a lasting neutrality would have highly benefitted the Umayyad cause. Ibāḍī chronicles (he consulted the *siyar* by al-Shammākhī) agree on the good relations between the caliph ʿAbd al-Malik b. Marwān and ʿAbdallāh b. Ibāḍ.

The two letters are a summa of early Ibāḍī belief and political agenda; even if they do not articulate a creed, already constitute a coherent body of doctrine on the principles of the imamate, the status of the sinner and his final fate.[12]

The attribution of the two letters to ʿAbd Allāh b. Ibāḍ is disputed. The second letter is generally considered spurious, but also the authenticity of the first one is challenged in modern scholarship. Michael Cook suggests that the letter was written rather by Jābir b. Zayd to the Muhallabid governor ʿAbd al-Malik b. al-Muhallab. According to John Wilkinson the letter was addressed to ʿAbd al-Malik, the son of the caliph ʿUmar II, and, due to the militant tone of the letter, Jābir b. Zayd could not have been its author but most likely one of early militant leader of the movement, such as Bisṭām b. ʿUmar al-Ḍabbī, Sālim b. Dhakwān or perhaps Ḍumām b. al-Sāʾib.[13] Wilferd Madelung maintains that the first letter is an authentic letter of ʿAbd Allāh b. Ibāḍ addressed to the son of ʿUmar II, but he suggests that the alleged founder of the Ibāḍiyya was not ʿAbd Allāh b. Ibāḍ but Ibāḍ b. ʿAmr, presumably his father, who was the leader of the moderate Muḥakkima in Basra. ʿAbd Allāh b. Ibāḍ was an Ibāḍī scholar contemporary of Abū ʿUbayda Muslim b. Abī Karīma.[14]

1.2 The Ibāḍī Role in the Development of Islamic Law: the State of the Art

1.2.1 Setting the Field: the Beginning of Studies on Ibadism

Studies on Ibadism were first carried out during the European colonial period in Africa and in the Middle East when French (A. Imbert, M. Morand, M. Mercier, E. Zeys) and German (E. Sachau) scholars began to examine

11 Rubinacci, Il califfo ʿAbd al-Malik b. Marwān e gli Ibāḍiti 99–121.
12 Cuperly, *Introduction* 26.
13 Cook, *Early Muslim Dogma* 51–67; Wilkinson, *Ibâḍism* 202–205.
14 Madelung tentatively identifies the founder of the movement with Ibāḍ b. ʿAmr (presumably the father of ʿAbd Allāh b. Ibāḍ) following a single heresiographical source: Al-Malaṭī *Kitāb al-tanbīh wa l-radd*. Madelung, The Authenticity of the Letter of ʿAbd Allâh b. Ibāḍ to ʿAbd al-Malik 37–43. See also Madelung, ʿAbd Allāh Ibn Ibāḍ's Second Letter to ʿAbd al-Malik 7–17.

some legal documents of the Ibāḍī communities in Algeria, East Africa and Zanzibar.[15] R. Basset's research, published in 1886, reporting the existence of a number of treatises on Ibāḍī law in the Algerian Mzab libraries, generated interest in Ibadism in northern Africa.[16] In the same year, A. Motylinski published a translation of the catalogue of texts drawn up by the Ibāḍī historian Abū ʾl-Qāsim al-Barrādī at the end of his *Kitāb al-Jawāhir*.[17] Al-Barrādī indicated the existence of legal treatises attributed to the school's authorities from the 2nd/8th and 3rd/9th centuries.[18]

The 20th century Italian 'Orientalists' (Laura Veccia Vaglieri, Carlo Alfonso Nallino, Mario Martino Moreno and Roberto Rubinacci, together with Vanna Cremonesi and Generosa Crupi La Rosa) were among the first scholars to underline that the Ibāḍis made an important contribution to Islamic thought and to the whole formation of Islamic culture. As Rubinacci states in his work on ritual purity among the Ibāḍīs, they had a dominant role in developing both the law and the dogma, as they were driven by a particularly strict ethical code, inflamed by an intense religiosity. The early definitions of the Khārijīs and the points they brought up for discussion may have provided the first impulse for the formation of the oldest juridical schools as well as spurred the debate from which the Muʿtazilī dogma originated. What is certain is that in the field of dogma as well as in the legal field, the Ibāḍīs elaborated a system of their own.[19]

In the early Ibāḍī legal studies by Western scholars, the principal aim of the researchers seems to have been to make the legal texts of this religious minority available to the colonial rulers. An academic reconstruction of Ibāḍī law was first attempted by Joseph Schacht in *The Origins of Muhammadan Jurisprudence*.[20] Schacht assumes that the Khārijī and Shiʿite groups were in

15 Imbert, Le droit abadhite chez les musulmans de Zanzibar et de l'Afrique orientale 5–29; Morand, *Études de droit musulman algérien*; Morand, *Avant-Projet de Code Présenté à la Commission de Codification du Droit Musulman Algérien*; Mercier, *Étude sur le waqf abadhite et ses applications au Mzab*; Zeys, *Législation mozabite, son origine, ses sources, son présent, son avenir*; Zeys, *Droit mozabite – le Nīl*; Sachau, Mohammedanisches Erbrecht nach der Lehre der Ibaditischen Araber von Zanzibar und Ostafrika 159–210.

16 Basset, *Les manuscrits arabes des bibliothèques des Zaouias de ʿAin Madhi et Temancin, de Ouargla et de ʿAdjadja* 35–65.

17 Al-Barrādī, *Kitāb al-Jawāhir*. On al-Barrādī and his work Rubinacci, Il Kitāb al-Ǧawāhir di al-Barrādī 95–110.

18 Motylinski, Bibliographie du Mzab 15–72 (no. 7, 8, 10, 12, 13, 15, 16). See also Smogorzewski, Essai de bio-bibliographie Ibadite-Wahhabite, Avant-propos 45–57; Rubinacci, Notizia di alcuni manoscritti ibāḍiti 431–438; Schacht, Bibliothèques et manuscripts abadites 375–398; Ennami, A Description of New Ibāḍī Manuscripts 63–87; van Ess Untersuchungen 25–63; van Ess, Nachträge 1–4.

19 Rubinacci, La purità rituale 1–41.

20 Schacht, *The Origins* 260–261 (chap. 8: *Khārijī Law*).

contact with the Sunni community during the first centuries of Islam, and they merely adopted the Islamic law already developed in the schools of law, introducing marginal modifications intended to adapt it to their own political lines and dogma. Furthermore, he is rather sceptical concerning the attribution of the origin of Khārijī doctrine in the Ṣufrī and Ibāḍī tradition to two followers, respectively ʿImrān b. Ḥiṭṭān and Jābir b. Zayd. Their names appear among the transmitters of the traditions recognized by the Sunnis. Consequently, their presence in the chain of transmitters is not in itself sufficient to establish the Khārijī origin of a doctrine.

Schacht's position on Khārijī law has been challenged by several scholars. In his study on Ibāḍī ritual purity, based on *Kitāb al-waḍʿ fī ʾl-furūʿ* by *shaykh* Abū Zakariyyāʾ Yaḥyā b. al-Khayr al-Jannāwunī, who lived in Jabal Nafūsa in the first half of the 6th/12th century, Roberto Rubinacci contests the Schacht's assumption that the Khārijīs merely adopted the legal system of the orthodox schools. Rubinacci, on the contrary, believes that

> the Khārijīs had a dominant role in developing the Law, as they were driven by a particularly strict ethical code that was inflamed by an intense, on occasion exaggerated, religiosity. Rather, it is not improbable – as was certainly the case for Muʿtazilī dogma, originating in Basra in the first half of the 2nd century AH – that in the case of law, too, it was the first declarations by the Khārijīs, the points they proposed for discussion, that spurred the formation of the Iraqi school.[21]

In the course of the 2nd century AH, as the political and religious importance of the sect faded, the active participation of the Khārijīs in forming law slowly diminished. Yet, there was a development of Khārijī doctrine in parallel to the Sunni doctrine, the same questions were discussed by both sides, as the Khārijīs were in contact with the orthodox community for a long period in the 2nd and 3rd centuries. Evidence for Rubinacci's theory can be found in the fact that the Ibāḍīs had their own scholars in Basra at the time of the ancient schools of law, like Jābir b. Zayd, and Abū ʿUbayda al-Tamīmī, his pupil and successor, at the leadership of the Ibāḍī community. These scholars continued writing political and doctrinal works. Concerning the contacts with the orthodox legal schools, Rubinacci cites the case of al-Rabīʿ b. Ḥabīb (d. *c.*170/796) who attended courses by Ibāḍī scholars in Basra, like Abū ʿUbayda, and Sunni scholars, like Qatāda b. Diʿāma, Abū ʿAwāna and Ḥammād b. Salāma. Rubinacci's studies on the Ibāḍī *madhhab* demonstrated that, contrary to what Schacht averred, the Ibāḍīs took a detached line from the beginning.

---

21 Rubinacci, La purità rituale 37.

Given that the early schools of law were driven by the deep spiritual requirements of Muslim law and the need to define ritual norms, and that in this context Ibāḍī behaviour is significant, he provides several examples of divergences between Ibāḍīs and Sunnis on ablution. Other elements are shared with orthodoxy and they agree with one or another of the schools on varying points. Rubinacci concludes that these are the result of original thought, rather than the passive acceptance of principles drawn up elsewhere. However, the decisive argument against the late derivation of the Ibāḍī legal system from the Sunni system, according to Rubinacci, is the fact that, had the Ibāḍīs adopted a system already defined by the schools of law at the end of the 2nd/8th century, they would have reproduced it along the lines of the Sunni books of the time. This notion of Ibāḍīs reproducing a Sunni system can be excluded given the specific structure of the *Kitāb al-waḍʿ*, where the chapter on the *tawḥīd*, the summary of beliefs, precedes the *ʿibādāt*. The characteristic structure is reaffirmed during the work through the emphasis given to the spiritual content of the rite, in particular the prayers that accompany the single gestures, intended to exalt the concept of reward and divine punishment. The efforts in *Kitāb al-waḍʿ* to weave ethical elements into the law lead Rubinacci to conclude that they resemble a unitary conception of dogma, law and ethics, like that inspiring the first learned scholars of Islam. The *Kitāb al-waḍʿ* should be considered the codification of a long oral tradition, which can be traced back through the *silsilat al-dīn*, to Abū ʾl-Zājir Ismāʿīl b. Darrār al-Ghadāmsī, one of the five scholars who were trained in Basra at the school of the famous Abū ʿUbayda al-Tamīmī, and then transferred to the Maghrib in the first half of the 2nd/8th century.[22]

Rubinacci challenges some of the examples used by Schacht to demonstrate the inexistence of an ancient Khārijī legal system as follows:

1. Concerning the Ibāḍī opinion, in contrast with Najadāt opinion, according to which women and children would receive no share of the booty from army incursions but only remuneration, there is nothing to prove that the Ibāḍīs, who differed from the Najadāt in many parts of dogma, could not have professed a different doctrine concerning war from the very beginning of their separation from the latter group.

2. The coincidence concerning Ibāḍī doctrine of 5 *dirham* as the minimum fine for the application of the *ḥadd* punishment for theft, with the same analogical reasoning (*qiyās*) as the Iraqi school of the first half of the 2nd/8th century, can be easily explained considering that both schools acquired a

22 Rubinacci, La purità rituale 40–41. See also Crupi La Rosa, I trasmettitori della dottrina ibāḍita 123–139.

local practice followed in their shared centre, Basra, rather than proving any relationship of dependence.

3. The anachronism found by Schacht in al-Ashʿarī's[23] affirmation – according to which some Khārijīs recognized *ijtihād al-raʾy*, namely the use of systematic reasoning, while others rejected it, following a literal interpretation of the Quran – that predates a successive development of the legal theory to the 1st/7th century – could imply, according to Rubinacci, merely the wrong use of terms. Indeed, although there is no doubt that *ijtihād al-raʾy* acquired its technical meaning only at a later stage, this does not rule out the practical use of *raʾy* (personal reasoning) among the *Najadāt* – especially since such reasoning is attested in the rulings of the earliest Sunni judges.[24]

4. As an argument to support this theory, Schacht discusses the question of the *masḥ ʿalā ʾl-khuffayn*, that is the wiping of one's shoes instead of washing one's feet as part of the lesser ritual ablution under certain conditions, which became a distinctive point of difference between the Khārijīs and the Shiʿites, who rejected it, and the Sunnis, who considered it to be valid. Schacht argues that this was not yet the case in the second half of the 2nd/8th century because the *masḥ* is not mentioned in the *Fiqh Akbar* by Abū Ḥanīfa, where other points of difference between Sunnis and non-Sunnis are debated. He concludes that the discussion about the *masḥ* started between the Sunni traditionalists and the adherents of the ancient Medinan school and only later, in the early 3rd/9th century, did the rejection of this procedure become an essential feature of both Khārijī and Shiʿite doctrine in opposition to the Sunnis.[25] Rubinacci casts serious doubt on Schacht's conclusion. He suggests that the *Fiqh Akbar* does not talk about the *masḥ ʿalā ʾl-khuffayn* as mentioning the points of divergence between Sunnis and non-Sunnis, because the Sunni position on the question was still unsettled during the 2nd/8th century. Only when the institution was definitively acknowledged as obligatory could the Sunni polemic against the Khārijīs and the Shiʿites start.[26]

In assuming that the Khārijīs and the Shiʿites derived their doctrines from the orthodox schools of law, Schacht deals only with Sunni literature. The Ibāḍī sources show that the discussion on the validity of the *masḥ* started earlier than he assumed. The first *fatwā* concerning this question is preserved in the *Futyā al-Rabīʿ b. Ḥabīb,* where ʿAbd Allāh b. ʿAbd al-ʿAzīz and Abū ʾl-Muʾarrij ʿAmr al-Sadūsī, Ibāḍī jurists from the second half of the 2nd/8th century, were

---

23 Ashʿarī, *Maqālāt* i, 105.
24 Rubinacci, La purità rituale 38–39.
25 Schacht, *The Origins* 263–264.
26 Rubinacci, La purità rituale 33.

questioned about the status of the Ibāḍī who wipes over his shoes instead of washing his feet. They were inclined to put him in an intermediate state between that of the true believer and that of the unbeliever, because the question of the *masḥ* was still debated among the Ibāḍī authorities.[27] Some decades later, the Ibāḍī jurists would decide to consider him an unbeliever.

Rubinacci's studies on the Ibāḍī *madhhab* demonstrate that, contrary to what Schacht averred, the Ibāḍis took a detached line from the beginning.

Rubinacci's conclusions on ritual purity are confirmed by his research on the invitation to prayer, in use among the Ibāḍis of western Africa, in which he points out similarities of Ibāḍī doctrine with the Sunni schools as well as some divergences.[28]

Further doubts on Schacht's historical reconstruction of law have been mooted by Noel J. Coulson in his *A History of Islamic Law*.[29] Concerning Schacht's thesis on Khārijī and Shiʿite doctrine, Coulson contests Schacht's claim that they "do not differ from the doctrines of the orthodox or Sunni schools of law more widely than these last differ from one another".[30] According to Coulson, this could be said for Khārijī law, while Shiʿite law has characteristics that are in clear contrast with the Sunni and Khārijī systems. Moreover, the Khārijīs too, despite disagreeing with the Sunni schools on secondary issues and accepting, in general, the norms of one or the other school, have a legal system that is in line with their own spirit and character. They, like the Shiʿites, have a *corpus* of traditions that are quite distinct from the Sunni one and that respond to their probative criteria. The most important criteria being the presence of the names of the authorities they recognize in the *isnāds* (the chains of transmitters).[31]

1.2.2 Ennami and the New Trends in the Ibāḍī Studies

In 1971, ʿAmr Khalīfa Ennami (al-Nāmī) defended his PhD thesis at Cambridge University, entitled *Studies in Ibāḍism*, which can be considered a milestone in research on Ibāḍī dogma and law. In the chapter on jurisprudence, he confutes Schacht's theory on the late derivation of Ibāḍī law compared to the Sunni schools by showing that the Ibāḍīs contributed to the process of the formation

27 Ibn Khalīfa (ed.), *Futyā* 135–137 (Ms. 40_{14}). See also Abū Ghānim, *al-Mudawwana al-kubrā* i, 24 (henceforth *Mudawwana*).
28 Rubinacci, L'aḏān presso gl'Ibāḍiti 279–290.
29 Coulson, *A History of Islamic Law*.
30 Schacht, *The Origins* 260.
31 Coulson, *A History of Islamic Law* 109.

of Islamic law, developing their own legal system which differed in several ways from the Sunni system.[32] Ennami's study is based on his own research on Ibāḍī manuscripts, which led him to study works that scholars had not previously consulted from the first centuries of Islam. Therefore, Ennami could demonstrate that the Ibāḍīs began to draw up their own law treatises at the same time as the ancient schools of law. If credence can be given to the Ibāḍī historian Abū Zakariyyā' al-Warjlānī on the existence of the *Dīwān* (collection of works) of Jābir b. Zayd, Ibāḍīs were the first to put the traditions of the companions and followers of the Prophet into writing.

According to Ennami, the primary sources for the early Ibāḍī jurisprudence are preserved in the following works:

1. *al-Jāmiʿ al-Ṣaḥīḥ* of al-Rabīʿ b. Ḥabīb;
2. *al-Mudawwana* of Abū Ghānim Bishr b. Ghānim al-Khurāsānī;
3. *al-Dīwān al-Maʿrūḍ ʿalā ʾl-ʿulamāʾ al-Ibāḍiyya*, which contains a number of works relating to Ibāḍī authorities as well as tradition from different authorities of Kufa, Basra and Medina;
4. *Riwāyāt Ḍumām*, composed by Abū Ṣufra ʿAbd al-Malik b. Ṣufra, around the beginning of the 3rd century AH;
5. *Futyā al-Rabīʿ b. Ḥabīb*, a collection of traditions by al-Rabīʿ b. Ḥabīb and other Ibāḍī authorities from the 2nd century AH;
6. *K. Nikāḥ al-shighār* of ʿAbd Allāh b. ʿAbd al-ʿAzīz;
7. The books and the correspondence of the first two *imāms* of the Ibāḍī school, Jābir b. Zayd and Abū ʿUbayda.

Ennami provides a detailed analysis of the structure and contents of these works, concentrating in particular on the contribution of the Ibāḍī authorities to the collection of traditions. The Ibāḍīs, he writes: "contributed to the field of *Ḥadīth* by preserving and recording their own collection of *Ḥadīth*. All early authorities, who founded the Ibāḍi school, were eminent traditionists such as Jābir b. Zayd, Abū Nūḥ Ṣāliḥ b. Nūḥ al-Dahhān and Ḥayyān b. al-Aʿraj [...]".[33]

The Ibāḍīs, just as they had their own *tafsīr*, had their own collections of traditions. The most important of these was *al-Jāmiʿ al-Ṣaḥīḥ* or *Musnad al-Rabīʿ b. Ḥabīb*. Ennami concludes

> Ibāḍi jurisprudence during its long history depended only on Ibāḍi material reported by Ibāḍi authorities. The other collections of traditions by Sunnis were not used at any stage. In fact, the first Ibāḍi scholar of North Africa to mention Sunni collections of *ḥadīth* in his works was Abū Yaʿqūb al-Warjlānī of the 6th/12th century. Up to the time of al-Barrādī, Ibāḍīs discouraged the use of the

32 Ennami, *Studies* 72–104 (chap. 3) (online edition).
33 Ennami, *Studies* 76–77 (online edition).

> Sunni collections of *ḥadīth*. In his treatise, *al-Ḥaqā'iq*, al-Barrādī advised Ibāḍī students as far as possible not to read them. Thus the Ibāḍī legal system was derived from the material reported by Ibāḍī authorities only.[34]

Furthermore, Ennami maintains that the Ibāḍīs did not derive their legal system from that formed by the orthodox schools, but rather established it prior to the Sunni system. When Jābir b. Zayd, the founder of the Ibāḍī school, died, Mālik b. Anas (d. 795) was only three years old, and Abū Ḥanīfa about twelve (d. 767). The similarities between the Sunni and Ibāḍī legal systems can easily be explained by the fact that both referred to the same sources. The divergences come from a diverse interpretation of the Quran and the *sunna*.[35]

As regards the question of the origin of Ibāḍī law, the middle ground between Schacht and Ennami was taken by J.C. Wilkinson. He does not agree with Ennami on Jābir b. Zayd's contribution to the formation of the Ibāḍī legal system.[36] The role the sources give to Jābir in the formative phase of Ibāḍī law is the fruit of a process of "rationalization", through which the successive generations of Ibāḍī lawyers have legalized some norms, attributing their genesis to him. According to Wilkinson, the role of Jābir has been exaggerated in some ways. In particular:

1. Stressing his relationship with Abū Bilāl Mirdās, leader of the moderate wing of Khārijīs in Basra. They both accepted the repentance (*tawba*) of 'Ā'isha for her role in the fight against 'Alī. Abū Bilāl also consulted Jābir before launching the rebellion in Arabia. When this exploded, however, Jābir was absent, and the sources mention his position in deliberately vague terms.

2. Overstating the dangers encountered by Jābir at the time of the persecution of Ziyād Ibn Abīhi and al-Ḥajjāj against the Ibāḍīs. In truth, as Wilkinson notes, while during the governorate of al-Ḥajjāj, the real heads of the Ibāḍī movement, Abū 'Ubayda Muslim and Ḍumām b. al-Sā'ib, were imprisoned in Basra, Jābir was exiled to Oman. This very circumstance appears rather dubious as, according to Abū 'Ubayda, Jābir would die in Basra in the same year as Anas b. Mālik, that is to say, two years before the death of al-Ḥajjāj and the liberation of the Ibāḍī leaders. To overcome this anachronism, the sources progressively postponed the reported death of Jābir to year 96–97 or 100 AH. The manipulation of Jābir's date of death is also linked to the emphasis placed by Ibāḍī sources on the role of Jābir as teacher of Abū 'Ubayda, his successor as leader of the community. Abū 'Ubayda, according to Wilkinson, however,

34 Ennami, *Studies* 79–80 (online edition).
35 Ennami, *Studies* 91 (online edition).
36 Wilkinson, The early development of the Ibāḍī movement in Baṣra 133–136. See also Wilkinson, Ibāḍī theological literature 33–39.

was only one of Jābir's younger pupils, while Ibāḍī historiography affirms that his principal teachers were Ḍumām b. al-Sā'ib, Ja'far b. al-Sammāk and Ṣuḥār al-ʿAbdī.[37]

In a later study on Ibāḍī *ḥadīth* entitled "*Ibāḍi Ḥadīṯ: an Essay on Normalization*",[38] Wilkinson refers again to the theory on the process of "normalization" through an analysis of the development of Ibāḍī jurisprudence. He summarizes the various phases in its development:

> The Ibāḍī legerdemain of rationalizing the development of their school consisted of building up Jābir b. Zayd with his Meccan connections into the founding figure; of more or less suppressing the uncoordinated middle generation of Ḍumām and other "proto"-Ibāḍīs, who often had their own individual *majlis*; and of making the activist Abū ʿUbayda the direct successor to the unified community supposedly developed by Jābir. Al-Rabīʿ, who was in fact a contemporary of Abū ʿUbayda, albeit perhaps a few years younger, is in turn made a 'pupil' of Abū ʿUbayda, the master of the movement, and his own inheritance from their common teacher, Ḍumām (and others of the generation), played down. Al-Rabīʿ thus inherits (*ḥamal* or *rafaʿ al-ʿilm*) and sets down the basics of his learning from Abū ʿUbayda, who in turn received it from the great scholar Jābir b. Zayd in the same way as the 'Imamate' of the community passed along this same line.[39]

According to Wilkinson, the *Musnad* by al-Rabīʿ b. Ḥabīb, which has been transmitted in the edition (*tartīb*) by Abū Yaʿqūb Yūsuf al-Warjlānī (d. 570/1174), is the fruit of this normalization through which Ibadism attempted to attain the level of development of the orthodox schools. In the first two sections, there are 742 *ḥadīth*, mostly to be found also in Sunni collections, passed down through the chain of transmission Jābir – Abū ʿUbayda – al-Rabīʿ b. Ḥabīb, which seems like the result of a later manipulation.

Wilkison summarizes his theories on origins and development of the Ibāḍī school in his book *Ibâḍism: Origins and Early Development in Oman* (2010). He deconstructs the standard accounts of the origins of Ibadism, arguing that the movement's evolution into a *madhhab* can only be understood in a wider historical perspective taking in tribal and regional dimensions. The historical, geographical, economic and social context is essential for understanding the

---

37 Al-Shammākhī, *Siyar* (1883), 79, 81.

38 Wilkinson, Ibāḍi *Ḥadīth* 231–259.

39 Wilkinson, Ibāḍi *Ḥadīth* 235. See also Wilkinson, *The Imamate Tradition of Oman*, 177–199; Wilkinson, Ṣuḥar (Sohar) in the early Islamic period 889–905. The early development of the Ibāḍī school is summarized in Wilkinson, *Ibāḍism* 122–210 (chaps. 5 and 6).

juridical evolution of Ibadism. The ability to adapt to different situations, the pragmatic rulings concerning agriculture, trade, mining and, for the Omanis, the capacity to expand their commerce in the Indian Ocean, ensured the survival of the movement to the present day. In parallel, the convergence towards Sunnism, the assimilation of Prophetic *sunna* into the tradition of the community, and even the production of their own *ḥadīth* were all factors giving the Ibāḍī legal system a flexibility that ensured its survival both in Oman and North Africa.[40]

1.2.3 The Turning Point in the Ibāḍī Studies

The last quarter of the 20th century and the first two decades of the 21st century witnessed a turning point in studies on Ibadism. The publication of a number of early Ibāḍī sources by the Ministry of National Heritage and Culture in Oman, by Ibāḍī associations (such as Ibadica in Paris) and by individual scholars fuelled research focusing on the early development of Ibāḍī law and dogma by academics like Crone-Zimmermann, Cook, van Ess, Madelung, Wilkinson, Abd al-Rahman al-Salimi, Muranyi and myself. The Ministry of Religious Affairs' patronage of a series of international conferences devoted to Ibadism, and the publication of the proceedings by Olms Verlag represent a further step forward in the development of Ibāḍī studies.[41]

At the same time the work of Adam Gaiser attempts to correct some common scholarly misperceptions of the Khawārij and Ibāḍīs as anomalous cases in Islamic history. In *Muslims, Scholars, Soldiers: The Origin and Elaboration of the Ibāḍī Imāmate Traditions* (2010) he focuses on the Ibāḍī theory of imamate showing how the idea of personal merit shaped the pre-Islamic institution of the *sayyid*, and that the advent of Islam associated the merits of the tribe's leader with Islamic piety. The early Khawārij adopted the notions of piety and moral rectitude that were perceived to be part of the Prophet's leadership and of the early Caliphs of Medina (Abū Bakr and ʿUmar). The Ibāḍīs, in turn, adapted the Khārijī institutions of authority to their own institution of *imām al-ẓuhūr*, the *imām* of manifestation, who can rule with full authority during a time when the Ibāḍīs can openly practise their faith.

In his next book, *Shurāt* (2016), Gaiser focuses on the early period, when the Ibāḍīs emerged from among the masses of the quietists in Basra constructing their own sense of uniqueness over and against the militant Khawārij. In accordance with how early Muslims conceptualized group affiliation, the

40 See also Wilkinson, Contextualizing the Development of Ibadi Fiqh 15–23.

41 See https://www.ibadistudies.org/index.php and https://www.olms.de/search/result.aspx?q=Ibadism.

Ibāḍīs elaborated the principle of *walāya* and *barāʾa*, association and dissociation, expanding these notions into a complex theological–legal doctrine, which continues to distinguish their creed to this day.

As recent studies have demonstrated, Ibāḍīs took an independent line from the Sunni schools from the start, with independent authorities and jurists. They have a rich literary heritage stretching back to the formative period, which is of great potential importance.[42]

In this book I will show that we can sift through this literary material to unearth some "gems" of historical truth which can help to depict the development of Islamic law and jurisprudence. This study is primarily one of legal theory and institutions. It is based on analysis of juridical texts as well as on chronicles and on biographical works. Historically, it covers the period from the 8th until the early 20th century. Geographically, it concentrates on the areas of Iraq, Oman and the Maghrib, for these were the foremost centres of Ibāḍī learning, where the formative works in the legal tradition were produced.

My abundant literary sources were written in the 8th century CE (maybe even at the end of the 7th century at the earliest) and often in the 9th and 10th, and span until the early 20th century, the time of the Ibāḍī renaissance, which constitutes the last serious attempt to revitalize the Ibāḍī law. Often the Ibāḍī authors had their particular agendas which can be depicted and analyzed. Some of the late Ibāḍī sources draw upon earlier written materials that can be tentatively reconstructed; some of them prove an advanced state of sophisticated and self-conscious legal expertise and thus the emergence of jurists and their legal literature as an essential feature of the mature historical existence of the Ibāḍī *madhhab*. The Ibāḍī *madhhab* clearly represents one of the schools in which the *sharīʿa* was articulated, a tradition among the traditions that together constituted Islamic law as a historical phenomenon. As jurists, the Ibāḍīs have a lengthy and distinguished, if lesser known, history. Early segments of this history involved individuals active in Iraq in lesson circles of teachers and students, which were an interpretative community in microcosm. Beyond the specific issue of the role of Ibn Ibāḍ, the formative period of Ibadism was distinctive in other ways. Jābir b. Zayd was highly reputed for his scholarship; his writings as well as those of other early authorities are understood to have initiated the Ibāḍī *madhhab*. The interpretative project of this group of early scholars was later fleshed out by subsequent generations of jurists, who elaborated the conceptual bases and extended the substantive coverage of the school, thereby contributing to its systematization and consolidation.

42 Custers, *Al-Ibāḍiyya, a Bibliography*. Vol. 1: *Ibāḍīs of the Mashriq*; vol. 2: *Ibāḍīs of the Maghrib*; vol. 3: Secondary Literature.

CHAPTER 2

The Early Beginnings of Ibāḍī Jurisprudence in Basra

2.1 Introduction

In this chapter, and in the one that follows, I will discuss the origins and early development of Ibāḍī law. I will show that, in this period, a number of features emerged in Ibāḍī law that diverged from Sunni law. Among the features that differ between Ibāḍī and Sunni law are the rejection of *masḥ ʿalā ʾl-khuffayn* (wiping shoes instead of washing feet as part of *wuḍūʾ*); the ruling that property of a client (*mawlā*) who has no relatives is to be inherited by his people and not by his patron; and the impediment to marriage between an unmarried man and an unmarried woman who have committed fornication.

Some traditions transmitted by the early Ibāḍī jurists support doctrines that are rejected in later legal works. Typical of this group of "unsuccessful" traditions are those assuming that exchanges of precious metals involve no usury unless there is a time lag in the transaction (absolute equality in quantity is not demanded) and those allowing the sale of *umm al-walad* and *mudabbar* slaves.

There is no easy way to affirm the authenticity of the ancient sources of Islamic law. The risk of having been manipulated is high, but the arguments in favour of the genuineness of the content of the sources I used for this study are convincing. As I will show in the next two chapters, my assumption is based on the analysis of both the structure and the contents of the ancient sources of Ibāḍī law.

These sources show a primitive structure: they deal with *aqwāl* (*dicta*) of certain *fuqahāʾ*, on occasion supported by an incomplete *isnād* going back to the Companions. Reports are brought together under convenient chapters in which they are not arranged according to their prestige, namely with traditions from the Companions preceding the *aqwāl*. Traditions from the Prophet appear sporadically and are supported by an elementary *isnād*: "*al-Rabīʿ ʿan ʿUthmān anna al-nabiyya suʾila ʿan*" or just introduced by expressions such as: "*yuqālu inna Rasūla Allāh*", "*balaghanā inna Rasūla Allāh*".[1]

---

1 See, for example, Ibn Khalīfa (ed.) *Futyā* 119 (Ms. 36_{26}). For the incidence of Prophet's traditions in the early Ibāḍī sources see Francesca, La fabbricazione degli *isnād* nella scuola ibāḍita 51–53. See also Schwartz, *Die Anfänge der Ibaditen in Nordafrika* 45–46.

 | HTTPS://DOI.ORG/10.1163/9789004765764-004

Reports tracing back to the Companions or Successors, and the Prophet's sayings, are scattered in the *Mudawwana* by Abū Ghānim al-Khurāsānī. Their opinions are quoted without *isnād* as follows: "*ḥaddathanī rajul min ahl Khurāsān rafaʿa ʾl-ḥadīth ilā Anas b. Mālik*", or just "*jāʾa min al-nabī*". Reports referring to Ibāḍī authorities are mentioned in a personal style: "I asked …" or by narrating them by hearsay (*samiʿtu, akhbaranī,*). The early Ibāḍī sources follow a dialogue scheme, with legal cases introduced by expressions like: "*Saʾaltu Abā al-Muʾarrij ʿan* [followed by a brief illustration of the problem]. *Qāla: saʾaltu ʿan dhālika Abā ʿUbayda fa-qāla* […]". If there is conflicting opinion on the question, it is followed by: "*wa-kāna al-Rabīʿ yaqūlu* […]". On other occasions, the norms are introduced by a brief *isnād*: "*al-Rabīʿ ʿan Abī ʿUbayda*".

The concept of *sunna* comprising the exemplary behaviour of the Prophet is conspicuously absent in the works compiled by the early Ibāḍī jurisprudents as in the early Sunni sources. The old *fuqahāʾ* relied on the authorities whose opinion they had arrived at; they rarely had it from the Prophet and even in that case they mostly conveyed what they conceived of as Prophetic wisdom.[2]

In the correspondence of Jābir, the term *sunna* occurs in a letter addressed to the Omani Mālik b. Usayd (no. 12) meaning "your regional custom (*sunnat arḍikum*) on which there is a general agreement". Moreover, in the letter addressed to ʿUnayfa (no. 5), Jābir said that any matter that contradicts the *sunna* can be rejected, a reference to the *imām* who did not respect the rule concerning the ritual prayer.[3]

The themes treated in the Ibāḍī manuscripts reflect the legal debate that was ongoing during the first two centuries of Islam, and the solutions which the Ibāḍī lawyers propose for the legal cases are often primitive. The debate reflects two opposing trends, which may be identified in the formative phase of Islamic law: on the one hand the continuation of local legal traditions and, on the other, the efforts of the first lawyers to find solutions that conform to Islam.

An example of the archaism of the questions discussed in the ancient Ibāḍī manuscripts can be seen in the condemnation of the sexual promiscuity of female slaves, which was frequently repeated.[4] This reflected the will (on occasion only theoretical) of the ancient lawyers to oppose a widespread practice

2 Juynboll, Some Notes on Islam's First *fuqahāʾ* 289; idem, *Muslim Tradition* 30–39; idem, Some New Ideas 97–118.

3 Al-Jaʿbīrī (ed.), *Rasāʾil* 122, 109 (Ms. $73B_{17}$, $70A_{26}$). See also Ennami, *Studies* (online edition) 48.

4 See Jābir's legal opinions in al-Salimi (ed.), *Aqwāl* 353, 405 (Ms. 92_{24}, 111_2), and al-Jaʿbīrī (ed.), *Rasāʾil* 125 (Ms. $72B_4$), Ms. $65B_3$ (letter addressed to Rāshid b. Khaytham, missing in the edition by al-Jaʿbīrī), and al-Rabīʿ's legal opinions in al-Salimi (ed.), *Aqwāl* 405 (Ms. 113_{15}). See also Ibn Khalfūn, *Ajwibat* 50ff.

in the 1st century AH.[5] The problem of female slaves' sexual promiscuity became much less important once the schools had defined the rules of concubinage. From the 3rd/9th century on, it was no longer discussed in legal texts, whether Sunni or Ibāḍī.[6]

Yet another example of the archaism of the problems discussed concerns the sale of free men as slaves.[7] According to Islamic law, Muslims could not sell themselves or their children as slaves, nor could they be sold to creditors. However, the first lawyers' insistence that it was forbidden to sell free men as slaves gives credence to the suspicion that this custom continued even after the death of the Prophet.[8]

According to the ancient Ibāḍī lawyers, it was permissible to buy the children of *ahl al-ḥarb* as slaves if they were sold because their parents were not able to support them, whilst the children of *ahl al-dhimma* sold by their parents had to be freed. The council of the community took this decision during the imamate of Abū ʿUbayda al-Tamīmī (first half of the 2nd/8th century). According to the Ibāḍī scholar al-Shammākhī (d. 792/1389), Abū ʿUbayda had to judge the following case: a member of the community had purchased a woman of the *ahl al-dhimma* who had been offered for sale by her own father, and he had had children by her. How should he now behave? Abū ʿUbayda gathered the members of the community and they decided that the man had to free the woman and then marry her. Abū ʿUbayda's behaviour, which was unlike his reaction when judging legal questions in other situations, shows that at the time there cannot yet have been a unanimous doctrine concerning the cases in which parents sold their children. This was proved by the fact that he was not able to

5 See the *responsa* by Ibn Ṭāwūs and ʿUmar b. ʿAbd al-ʿAzīz in ʿAbd al-Razzāq, *al-Muṣannaf* vii, no. 12850–12855.

6 Motzki, *Anfänge* 232.

7 According to Santillana, the widespread pre-Islamic custom of selling free persons as slaves was greatly modified by Islamic law. See Santillana, *Istituzioni di Diritto Musulmano Malichita* i, 142–143. Irene Schneider claimed that there are hardly any sources which can prove the existence of this pre-Islamic custom. See Schneider, *Kinderverkauf und Schuldknechtschaft*, in particular chap. iii, 279–350. For a critical evaluation of Schneider's thesis and arguments for the pre-Islamic custom of selling free persons, see Motzki, Der Prophet und die Schuldner 50–61.

8 In the *Muṣannaf* by Ibn Abī Shayba there are numerous traditions which reiterate the fact that the sale of free men as slaves is null and void (vii, no. 2879–2881, 3046, 3391–3396). One of these, a document attributed to the caliph ʿUmar b. ʿAbd al-ʿAzīz, forbids the sale of a bankrupt debtor to pay his creditors, a sign that this practice had not completely disappeared by the time of the Umayyad Caliphate (no. 3046). Also among the Shiʿites the question was discussed until about the end of the 2nd/8th century. See al-Ṭūsī, *al-Istibṣār* iii, ii part, 83.

find a solution to the question himself, but rather was forced to present it to the council of the community.

> With regard to the *ahl al-dhimma*, it is reported from Abū ʿUbayda in the chronicle of Abū Sufyān:
>
> A Muslim [i.e. an Ibāḍī] named Mukhlis Abū Rūḥ, said that he had bought the daughter of a man from the *ahl al-dhimma*, whom her father had put up for sale because of the hunger that afflicted them, and he had children by that woman. While Abū Rūḥ was sitting next to Abū ʿUbayda, a man came and questioned the latter about the same matter that was troubling him. Abū ʿUbayda said: "This is not lawful". When it was Abū Rūḥ's turn again, Abū ʿUbayda asked him: "What do you have in your possession now?" He replied: "Umm Rūḥ and Rūḥ my son, their story is this and this".[9] Abū ʿUbayda said: "Gather your companions". He gathered the elders of the community who were present that day, and when they were assembled, Abū ʿUbayda told them his story and asked: "What do you think?" Some of them said: "Now you must free her, oh Abū Rūḥ, and marry her". Abū ʿUbayda did not utter a word, and when he found that they all agreed on this fact, he said: "Oh Abū Rūḥ! If you have enjoyed the woman lawfully, be satisfied with what you have obtained from her up to now; if you have enjoyed her unlawfully, go no further, separate yourself rather from her and set her free".[10]

Jābir prohibited the sale of free men as slaves; in the *Futyā* al-Rabīʿ was asked about the case of a man who was sold as slave on the basis of his own assertion. He deemed the contract invalid: the buyer owned the price from the seller and, in case he didn't find him, he could impose that the slave acquire his freedom by work.[11]

Al-Rabīʿ's *fatwā* shows a primitive reasoning: first he acknowledges the man's affirmation of being slave, which had no juridical relevance according to the later development of both Sunni and Ibāḍī doctrine. This recognizes freedom immediately to the free person sold as slave,[12] finally al-Shaybānī declares void the sale of free men.[13]

A further interesting case is discussed in the *Rasāʾil* by Jābir, where he is asked about a man who bought a slave girl having been deceived that she was a

9 Probably he had already sold the other children.

10 Al-Shammākhī, *Kitāb al-īḍāḥ* iii, 80–81.

11 Al-Jaʿbīrī (ed.), *Rasāʾil* 123 (Ms. 72A4); Ibn Khalīfa (ed.), *Futyā* 171 (Ms. 484).

12 Ibn Abī Shayba, *Muṣannaf* vii, no. 3391–3396. This was also the teaching of the Ibāḍī authorities in the generation after al-Rabīʿ. See Abū Ghānim, *Mudawwana* ii, 198–199.

13 Al-Shaybānī, *Kitāb al-aṣl*, part i: *Kitāb al-buyūʿ wa ʾl-salam* 86, no. 4.

free woman. Only after the woman bore him children (thus acquiring the rights of being an *umm al-walad*), her true status was disclosed to him. Jābir says that the children are free and that the man should separate from the woman, to whom, however, neither a *ṣadāq* nor a consolatory gift (*niʿma*) was due.[14]

In conclusion, unlike forged documents dating back to early centuries of Islam, the Ibāḍī legal sources I will present in this chapter do not deal with matters of great doctrinal momentum, nor does their overall tone contain any political emphasis. Nor it is based on a well-known pool of fixed phrases and motifs. On the contrary, they reflect a definite historical conjunction and give us a fresh glimpse into the past. Moreover, they shed light on the methods of knowledge transmission among early Muslim scholars.

In the following paragraphs I will discuss the most relevant early Ibāḍī legal works and I will present the leading figures of the beginnings of the Ibāḍī law and jurisprudence in Basra, in particular the first three *imāms* of the school, Jābir b. Zayd, Abū ʿUbayda and al-Rabīʿ b. Ḥabīb, who authored works that prove fundamental to reconstructing the early steps of the Ibāḍī law, and Abū Ghānim al-Khurāsānī, the author of the first compilation of legal cases in the history of Ibadism. Throughout the entire 2nd/8th century, Basra was the spiritual centre of Ibadism in the East. However, even during the last years of al-Rabīʿ's life (he died between 180/796 and 190/806), the city's role began to decline with the formation of the imamate in Oman, where the community could have greater chances of survival. Al-Rabīʿ's successor, Abū Sufyān Maḥbūb b. al-Ruḥayl (or al-Raḥīl, d. 260/874) decided to definitively settle in the region, which became, along with the Maghrib, one of the spiritual and political centres of Ibadism.

2.2 Jābir ibn Zayd

Abū ʾl-Shaʿthāʾ Jābir b. Zayd was born in 18/639 or 21/642 in Nizwā, (or Firq, near Nizwā) in Oman, and took the leadership of the Ibāḍī community of Basra upon the death of ʿAbd Allāh b. Ibāḍ (d. 89/708). Like the latter, Jābir b. Zayd maintained good relations with the Umayyad rulers, but, towards the end of the 1st/7th century, he was exiled, with other Ibāḍī leaders, to the southern part of the Arabian Peninsula due to political disagreement with the powerful Umayyad governor, al-Ḥajjāj (r. 74–95/694–714). The date of Jābir b. Zayd's death is uncertain (93/711–712, 96/714–715, 103/721–722, or 104/722–723).

14 Letter no. 1 addressed to Rāshid b. Khaytham, Ms. $64B_{11}$.

In Basra he had enjoyed an enormous prestige as a man of learning and he was a personal friend and follower of Ibn ʿAbbās. According to a tradition related in the *Āthār al-Rabīʿb. Ḥabīb*, when Anas b. Mālik (d. *c.*712), who was one of Jābir's teachers, heard the news of Jābir's death, he commented "The most knowledgeable of God amongst the people died. May God have mercy on Jābir b. Zayd".[15]

Jābir trained the first jurists of the movement: Abū Nūḥ Ṣāliḥ al-Dahhān,[16] Ḥayyān al-Aʿraj,[17] Ḍumām b. al-Sāʾib,[18] Jaʿfar b. al-Sammāk,[19] and Abū ʿUbayda al-Tamīmī.[20] Jābir's teaching was crucial in the formation of the Ibāḍī legal thought. Nevertheless, some Sunni sources cast doubt on Jābir's membership in the Ibāḍī movement.[21] Such statements were partially due to the attempt to justify Jābir's appearance among the transmitters of tradition acknowledged by the Sunnis. Moreover, in this initial phase, the first Ibāḍīs (or perhaps it is better to speak of proto Ibāḍīs) kept in close contact with the Sunni community. They lived in places where Islamic law began to develop, namely in Basra and Kufa, but also in the Ḥijāz, in close contact with the learned experts of the time with whom they exchanged opinions and teachings. Al-Ḥasan al-Baṣrī and Ibn ʿAbbās were teachers as well as personal friends of Jābir, and the first Ibāḍīs recognized the authority of the Sunni traditionists who were

15 Al-Kharusi (ed.), *Āthār* 68, 123. See Francesca, Jābir b. Zayd, EI THREE. See also Nāṣir and Shaybānī, *Muʿjam aʿlām al-ibāḍiyya. Qism al-Mashriq al-Islāmī*, 79–82; Wilkinson, *Ibâḍism* 183–205.

16 Abū Nūḥ Ṣāliḥ b. Ibrāhīm al-Bāhilī al-Dahhān lived in Basra, where he studied with Jābir b. Zayd and cooperated with Abū ʿUbayda in the diffusion of the Ibāḍī teachings. Traditions from Abū Nūḥ are preserved in the *Kitāb Nikāḥ al-Shighār* by ʿAbd Allāh b. ʿAbd al-ʿAzīz. See al-Shammākhī, *Siyar* (1883) 88, 104; al-Darjīnī, *Ṭabaqāt* i, 154–155, ii, 276. For the biographies of Ibāḍī scholars/authorities, see also the biographical dictionaries *Muʿjam aʿlām al-ibāḍiyya min al-qarn al-awwal al-hijrī ilá al-ʿaṣr al-ḥāḍir* by Bābāʿammī (2000) and Nāṣir and Shaybānī (2006).

17 Al-Shammākhī, *Siyar* (1883) 89; Darjīnī, *Ṭabaqāt* ii, 275; Ennami, *Studies* 62 (online edition).

18 Ḍumām b. al-Sāʾib al-Nabdī came from Nabd in Oman; in Basra he was one of Jābir's pupils and teacher of Abū ʿUbayda, with whom he was imprisoned and released after al-Ḥajjāj died. See al-Shammākhī, *Siyar* (1883) 87–88, 96; al-Darjīnī, *Ṭabaqāt* ii, 246–247.

19 Al-Darjīnī, *Ṭabaqāt* ii, 232.

20 Abū ʿUbayda Muslim b. Abī Karīma al-Tamīmī, *mawlā* of the tribe of the Tamīm, was the first true political leader of the Ibāḍī movement, until his death during the al-Manṣūr Caliphate (136/754–158/775). See al-Darjīnī, *Ṭabaqāt* ii, 238–248; Shammākhī, *Siyar* (1883), pp. 83–86.

21 Ibn Saʿd, *Ṭabaqāt* vii, 32; Abū Nuʿaim, *Ḥilyat* iii, 89.

among Jābir's pupils: Qatāda b. Diʿāma, ʿAmr b. Harim, ʿAmr b. Dīnār, Tamīm b. Khuwayṣ and ʿUmāra b. Ḥayyān.[22]

As discussed in the first chapter, John Wilkinson refutes Jābir's role as founder of the Ibāḍī school. The formation of the school was chiefly the work of later men who worked up the eponym's ideas into a body of authoritative doctrine. I agree with Wilkinson that Jābir, just like other teachers around whom schools formed, did not intend to found a school. Nevertheless, his teaching was crucial in the formation of the Ibāḍī school, and his works are among the most ancient Islamic legal sources, predating many Sunni sources. That is why I accept the traditional Ibāḍī designation of Jābir as the first Ibāḍī *imām* and founding father of the school.

The Ibāḍī sources even preserve Jābir's legal opinions, which were later abandoned, such as:

1. *Zakāt* must be paid on olives. Jābir's opinion coincides with those of Ibn ʿAbbās and al-Zuhrī.
2. The master can sell his female slave *umm al-walad*.
3. The slave can leave a legacy of his estate if his master agrees.[23]

When expressing his legal responses, Jābir used the Quran and *sunna*; *raʾy* (individual reasoning) was admissible only when confirmed by a tradition from the Prophet's Companions.[24] A great deal of information on the methods used by Jābir can be deduced from the *Jawābāt*. In these, the term *sunna* indicates the local tradition or a practice generally accepted by the community.[25] From Jābir's assertions, it is clear that he did not distinguish between the legal speculation of the Companions and what they passed on from the Prophet, as the two concepts were identified in the generic *sunna*. The names of the authorities on which Jābir based his judgements are only occasionally quoted. At the

22 Al-Dhahabī, *Tadhkirat* i, no. 67; Ibn Ḥajar, *Tahdhīb* i, no. 61; Abū Nuʿaim, *Ḥilyat* iii, no 213; al-Ḥārithī, *al-ʿUqūd* 103. Abū ʾl-Mundhir Tamīm b. Ḥuwayṣ al-Azdī al-Ahwāzī relates from Ibn ʿAbbas and Abū Zayd al-Anṣārī, from him relate Shuʿba and Nūḥ b. Qays. In the Ibāḍī works, Tamīm relates from Jābir b. Zayd and Ḥayyān al-Aʿraj, from him relates Ḥāzim b. ʿUmar. In the *Āthār al-Rabīʿ* he is quoted as b. Khuwayṣ o Ḥuwayḍ. See al-Dhahabī, *Tārīkh* v, 50; Ibn Khalfūn, *Ajwibat* 113, no. 20. ʿUmāra b. Ḥayyān was an orphan under Jābir's guardianship. See al-Shammākhī, *Siyar* (1883), 95–96; al-Dhahabī, *Mīzān* i, no. 6022.

23 Al-Jaʿbīrī (ed.), *Rasāʾil* 153 (Ms. $90A_2$); al-Salimi (ed.), *Aqwāl* 144 (Ms. 123_6); Ibn Khalīfa (ed.), *Futyā* 152 (Ms. 42_{19}); Ḥārithī, *ʿUqūd* 102.

24 See Francesca, La fabbricazione degli *isnād* nella scuola ibāḍita 51–52.

25 Al-Jaʿbīrī (ed.), *Rasāʾil* 109, 122 (Ms. $70A_{26}$, $73B_{17}$). During the first two centuries of Islam, *sunna* meant "precedent", "way of life", only later acquiring the restricted meaning of precedent set by the Prophet (*sunnat al-nabī*). The early texts contain numerous traces of the ancient meaning of *sunna*, see, for example, Ḥasan b. Muḥammad b. al-Ḥanafiyya, *Kitāb al-irjāʾ* 21–25; *Risāla* by Abū Ḥanifa to ʿUthmān al-Battī (d. 143/760) 36f.

end of the 1st century AH, the concept of an authority on which a doctrine was based was only just developing, and the learned cited the Companions of the Prophet, whom they had known personally, or those who the local common tradition recognized as authorities.[26]

Jābir cites Ibn ʿAbbās, who had been his friend and teacher, and occasionally Ibn ʿUmar and ʿIkrima, *mawlā* of Ibn ʿAbbās. In his reply to ʿAbd al-Malik b. al-Muhallab, he sets out where the Muslim community should look for the solutions to its problems and gives priority to opinions delivered by the Companions.[27] On the contrary, personal opinion (*raʾy*) seems to have a lesser value; in the letter addressed to ʿUnayfa, Jābir said: "There is nothing of that except what people narrate from each other expressing personal opinions. We attach a reduced value to the *raʾy*".[28]

When the Companions differ from each other, Jābir retains the right to choose from their opinions whichever he prefers. In such cases he usually follows the opinion of his teacher Ibn ʿAbbās, whose superiority he admitted even in cases where he was in disagreement. For example, in the case of a woman divorced by a seriously ill husband before the consummation of the marriage, Ibn ʿAbbās considered that she had to await the recovery of the man before the recognition of the right to her nuptial gift and inheritance. Jābir, after having related his master's opinion, said:

> Had the question not been examined by Ibn ʿAbbās, I would have decided that the woman should keep all her rights [both to the nuptial gift and to the inheritance] even if she married while her husband was dangerously ill, as long as her portion of the inheritance had not been lost.[29] But the systematic reasoning of those who have preceded us must take preference over ours. The juristic speculation (*raʾy*) of those who were before us is better than the opinions we hold. Yet again the successor recognizes the superiority of his ancestor. The most deserving of such a right are the emigrants who accompanied the Prophet of God (*muhājirūn*) and those who followed them in good-deeds for they have witnessed and learned. It is our duty to follow in their footsteps and to follow their tracks.[30]

26 van Ess, *Anfänge muslimischer Theologie* 122.

27 See footnote 63. Al-Jaʿbīrī (ed.), *Rasāʾil* 152 (Ms. 89 B_{13}).

28 Al-Jaʿbīrī (ed.), *Rasāʾil* 107 (Ms. 69B_{23}).

29 The meaning of the last sentence is obscure. Jābir probably refers to the accidental loss of the husband's estate after paying his debts including the nuptial gift, or to the circumstance that the debts are equal or exceed the assets of the estate, therefore the wife, as well as all the legitimate heirs, doesn't receive the inheritance.

30 Al-Jaʿbīrī (ed.), *Rasāʾil* 152 (Ms. 89B_8). Trans. also in Ennami, *Studies* (online edition) 48–49.

According to Ibāḍī historical sources, Jābir composed a *Dīwān*, a collection of traditions and *fatwās*, which was available in the library of the Abbasid Caliph Hārūn al-Rashīd. A Sunni source, the *Kashf al-ẓunūn* by Ḥājjī Khalīfa, also mentions a *Dīwān Jābir b. Zayd*, but it doesn't give any further details about the work and nor does it quote the source of his information about it.[31] Al-Wisyānī relates that the *Dīwān* was in possession of Abū ʿUbayda, then in possession of al-Rabīʿ b. Ḥabīb, then in possession of Abū Sufyān, then in possession of his son Muḥammad. A copy of the *Dīwān* arrived also in Jabal Nafūsa. The circumstance is wrapped in legend: the Ibāḍī sources relate of an encyclopaedic work, divided into ten books, which needed ten camels to be transported.[32]

The primary sources for Jābir's legal responses (*fatāwā*) and traditions (*riwāyāt*) are as follows:

1. The *Jawābāt Jābir Ibn Zayd*. This is a collection of letters written by Jābir to his friends and followers in which he gives his legal response on several questions. This collection is the oldest Ibāḍī legal document.[33]
2. The *Āthār al-Rabīʿ b. Ḥabīb* and *Futyā al-Rabīʿ b. Ḥabīb*.[34]

---

31 Ḥājjī Khalīfa, *Kashf al-ẓunūn* i, 781.

32 Al-Wisyānī, *Siyar*, 120. On the *Dīwān* see also al-Warjlānī, *Kitāb siyar al-aʾimma* 95–97 (trans. Masqueray, *Cronique d'Abou Zakariya* 138); al-Shammākhī, *Siyar* (2009) i, 182–189.

33 Jābir's letters were edited in 2013 by al-Jaʿbīrī (Jaabiri), *Rasāʾil al-imām Jābir bin Zayd al-Azdī* (henceforth *Rasāʾil*). Some letters were already edited in 1984 by al-Kharūṣī, *Min jawābāt al-imām Jābir b. Zayd.* My research is based on the printed books and a manuscript coming from the library *al-Bārūniyya* (Jerba, Tunisia). Description: 28 folios (two pages to the folio), 23–25 lines to the page; old Maghribi hand; it is undated. This MS is a part of a collection of letters by Ibāḍī *imāms* (ff. 64–91). At its end, the following is written: "*tamma mā wujida wa-'l-ḥamdu li-llāhi min Jawābāt Abī 'l-Shaʿthāʾ Jābir b. Zayd*". A collection of letters by Jannāw b. Fatā and other Ibāḍīs from Fezzān follows immediately after. This would seem to indicate that this is a fragment of *Kitāb jawābāt al-aʾimma* by Ismāʿīl b. Mūsā al-Jayṭālī (d. 750/1349–50), see al-Shammākhī, *Siyar* (1883) 556–557. On the manuscript see Ennami, A Description of New Ibāḍī Manuscripts 65–66; van Ess, Untersuchungen 27–31; Darwīsh, *Ḥayāt min ajl al-ʿilm*, 145–158. I borrowed the copies of the Ibāḍī manuscripts I used for this book from Dr Werner Schwartz, to whom I am deeply indebted.

34 The *Āthār al-Rabīʿ b. Ḥabīb* was edited by al-Kharusi in 2016 (henceforth *Āthār*); the *Futyā al-Rabīʿ b. Ḥabīb* was edited by Ibn Khalīfa in 2017 (henceforth *Futyā*). My research is based on the printed books and on the MS *al-Bārūniyya, Fiqh Ibāḍī* (without number). Description: 49 folios, 29 lines to the pages; clear Maghribi hand of Ṣāliḥ b. Sālim b. Sulayman al-Sidrīnī; part of MS of mixed contents called *al-Dīwān al-maʿrūḍ ʿalā ʿulamāʾ al-ibāḍiyya*, a collection of books relating to Ibāḍī authorities concerning different topics of jurisprudence. The MS follows the *Aqwāl Qatāda b. Diʿāma*. It is entitled: "*hādhā al-juzʾ al-awwal min āthār al-Rabīʿ ʿan Ḍumām ʿan Jābir b. Zayd*". It concludes at f. 32: "*tamma bi-ḥamdi 'llāhi wa-ḥusni ʿawnihi wa-tawfīqihi*". Dated: 23 *Shawwāl* 1191/25 Nov. 1777. Part II (ff. 32–49) titled: "*al-juzʾ al-thānī min futyā al-Rabīʿ b. Ḥabīb*", dated: 29 *Shawwāl* 1191/1 Dic. 1777. In this part the text is divided into 25 chapters. The MS is also known as *Kitāb Ḍumām* or *Kitāb Abī Ṣufra*, from the name of Abū Ṣufra ʿAbd al-Malik b. Ṣufra, who

3. The traditions reported by ʿAmr b. Dīnār and ʿAmr b. Harim in parts V and VI of the *Aqwāl Qatāda b. Diʿāma*.[35]
4. The *Kitāb al-ṣalāt* transmitted by Ḥabīb b. Abī Ḥabīb al-Jarmī from ʿAmr b. Harim from Jābir, included in some manuscripts after in the last part (VII) of the *Aqwāl*.
5. The *Kitāb al-nikāḥ* which is a collection of Jābir's legal opinions on marriage. The collator of the work is unknown, but as it is included in the same manuscript as the *Kitāb nikāḥ al-shighār* by ʿAbd Allāh b. ʿAbd al-ʿAzīz, it was presumably narrated by the latter.[36]

The abovementioned works, with the exception of the *Jawābāt Jābir b. Zayd*, are part of a collection of Ibāḍī manuscripts known as *al-Dīwān al-maʿrūḍ ʿalā al-ʿulamāʾ al-ibāḍiyya*, which is the principal source for information on Ibāḍī jurisprudence in the first centuries of Islam.[37] The traditions and legal responses of Jābir have been transmitted to us through an Ibāḍī line (Ḍumām b. al-Sāʾib, Abū ʿUbayda, Abū Nūḥ Ṣāliḥ, Ḥayyān al-Aʿraj and others) and a Sunni line (Qatāda, ʿAmr b. Dīnār, ʿAmr b. Harim).[38] Only a few copies of *al-Dīwān al-maʿrūḍ ʿalā ʿulamāʾ al-ibāḍiyya* have survived; the one found in the *Dār al-Kutub* in Cairo was probably obtained from the Ibāḍī collection of

---

collected the material towards the beginning of the 3rd/9th century. See Ennami, A Description of New Ibāḍī Manuscript 68–69, where he describes the MS under the title *Riwāyāt Ḍumām*; Sezgin, *Geschichte* i, 93; van Ess, Untersuchungen 36–37.

35 The *Aqwāl Qatāda b. Diʿāma* was edited by al-Salimi in 2017 (henceforth *Aqwāl*). My research is based on the printed book and on a manuscript from the library *al-Bārūniyya*. Description: 140 pages; 29 lines to the pages; clear Maghribi hand of Ṣāliḥ b. Sālim b. Sulayman al-Sidrīnī; dated: 15 *shawwāl* 1191/17 Nov. 1777; it is part of *al-Dīwān al-maʿrūḍ ʿalā ʿulamāʾ al-ibāḍiyya*. It contains narrations from Jābir b. Zayd, al-Rabīʿ b. Ḥabīb, the chief scholars of the Ibāḍī sect, and mainly from the "successor" Qatāda b. Diʿāma, who was one of the best friends and teachers of Jābir b. Zayd. See Ennami, *Studies* 83–84 (online edition); van Ess, Untersuchungen 31–32 and Nachträge 2.

36 *Al-Dīwān al-Maʿrūḍ*, Ms *al-Bārūniyya, Fiqh Ibāḍī* (without number). The *Kitāb al-ṣalāt* and the *Kitāb al-nikāḥ* have been recently edited by A. al-Salimi under the title *Early Islamic Law in Ḥadīth Text from Basra. The Book of Prayer and the Book of Marriage by Jābir b. Zayd (d.c. 93/712–3)* (Brill 2026). The complete edition of *al-Dīwān al-Maʿrūḍ* will be published in 2027: A. al-Salimi (ed.) *Early Islamic Law in Kufa. Al-Dīwān al-maʿrūḍ ʿalā al-ʿulamāʾ al-ibāḍiyya* (Brill 2027).

37 According to Ennami, the Ibāḍī scholar Abū Ghānim al-Khurāsānī (second half of the 2nd/8th century) recorded the *al-Dīwān al-maʿrūḍ*. Ennami, *Studies* 83.

38 The transmission lines "Qatāda from ʿAmr b. Harim from Jābir" and "Qatāda from ʿAmr b. Dīnār from Jābir" are attested by the Sunnī sources. See Abū Nuʿaim, *Ḥilyat* iii, 85; al-Dhahabī, *Tadhkirat* I, 67; Ibn Ḥajar, *Tahdhīb*, i 38, viii, 68, 113, 351. Ibāḍī biographical sources ignore Qatāda but cite ʿAmr b. Harim and ʿAmr b. Dīnār among those who had transmitted from Jābir. See al-Shammākhī, *Siyar* (1883) 121.

manuscripts known as *Wakālat al-Jamūs*, an endowment (*waqf*) established for Ibāḍī students who study at Azhar University.[39]

2.3 The *Jawābat Jābir b. Zayd*

The work at the basis of this analysis contains 18 letters written by Jābir to the following pupils or friends:
1. Rāshid b. Khaytham – 2. Ṭarīf b. Khulayd – 3. Ghiṭrīf b. ʿAbd al-Raḥmān[40] – 4. al-Ḥārith b. ʿAmr – 5. ʿUnayfa – 6. Nāfiʿ b. ʿAbd Allāh – 7. Yazīd b. Yasār – 8. ʿAbd al-ʿAzīz b. Saʿd[41] – 9. Sālim b. Dhakwān – 10. Nuʿmān b. Salama – 11. Mālik b. Usayd – 12. ʿUthmān b. Yasār – 13. ʿAbd al-Malik b. al-Muhallab – 14. Khayra bint Ḍamra.

Jābir b. Zayd furnishes all kinds of details, sometimes secondary, on the addressees of his letters: a collection of individuals, almost obscure traditionists or jurisprudence experts, with no relation between them, but constituting together a group faithful to its teacher.

The problem of the identification of the addressees of the letters is by no means simple to resolve. Many of them are not mentioned in the Ibāḍī historical sources nor in the Sunni historiography or heresiography. Therefore, it seems likely that they are shadowy figures (proto Ibāḍīs or Khārijīs), who lived in border regions (in one case, it appears from Jābir's reply that the addressee lived in Khurāsān, in another three cases they are from Oman) and who are not recorded in the sources. In some cases, identification is doubtful due to homonyms and lack of information on the addressees. However, in at least three cases the addressee can be identified with certainty:

ʿAbd al-Malik b. al-Muhallab (letter no. 17), brother of more well-known Yazīd b. al-Muhallab, enemy of the powerful governor of Iraq, al-Ḥajjāj. ʿAbd al-Malik, was first governor of Khurāsān, then of Iraq; he was implicated in his family's power struggles in the latter region and fled to Khurāsān, where he would meet his death together with his family (102/721).[42]

39 Al-Salimi, *Early Islamic Law in Kufa*, introduction (iv: manuscripts).

40 Ennami reads ʿAbd al-Salām. Ennami, A Description of New Ibāḍī Manuscripts 65.

41 Ennami, A Description of New Ibāḍī Manuscripts 65; van Ess reads ʿAbd Allāh b. Saʿd. van Ess, Untersuchungen 29.

42 Al-Ṭabarī, *Annales* ii, 1100, 1141, 1182 and *passim*; al-Balādhurī, *Futūḥ al-buldān* 540; Crone, *Slaves on Horses* 133.

Khayra bint Ḍamra al-Qushairyya (letter no. 18), wife of al-Muhallab b. Abī Ṣufrā (d. 81 or 82/701–2),[43] enjoyed notable social prestige in Basra, thanks to her wealth. The Ibāḍī sources refer to other cases of direct contact between the exponents of the sect and women from Muhallabi families, such as the case of Ḥalbiyya who lived in Mecca around the 2nd/8th century and after converting to Ibadism, supported Abū Ḥamza's revolt, providing food and aid to the rebels.[44] In the case of another Muhallabi woman who also converted to Ibadism, ʿĀtīqa bint Abī Ṣufra, sister of Yazīd b. al-Muhallab, Ibāḍī sources report that she consulted Jābir b. Zayd concerning questions of the cult and doctrine.[45]

Letter no. 9 (no. 15 in the printed edition) is addressed to Sālim b. Dhakwān, an obscure Sīstānī figure of the 2nd/8th century who is credited with a polemic epistle on questions relating to the Ibāḍī dogma and doctrine, which is not mentioned in the Jābir's letter.[46]

In a further two cases the identification of the addressee is uncertain:

Al-Ḥārith b. ʿAmr (letter no. 4, no. 5 in the printed edition) is identified by Ennami as one of the Ibāḍīs from Kufa who died during the caliphate of Yazīd b. Muʿāwiya (60–64/680–683). Jābir's recommendation at the end of the letter: "[…] You are in a country where I would not to be named so I beg you not to pass on anything I have written" led Ennami to deduce that the letter had been written during the governorship of Ziyād ibn Abīhi, who died in Kufa in 56–57/*c.*673.[47] Jābir, however, arrived in Basra after the death of Abū Bilāl Mirdās in 60–61/680–681, as there is no evidence of his participation in the revolt led by the latter.[48] Moreover, he took on the leadership of the Ibāḍī community only towards the end of the 7th century. As shown by the fact that Ibn Ibāḍ, as head of the community, corresponded with the caliph ʿAbd al-Malik b. Marwān in about 695–696. These facts make Ennami's hypothesis appear improbable. On the contrary, van Ess's hypothesis seems more likely: he believed that the addressee was al-Ḥārith b. ʿAmr al-Ṭāʿī, who had been

43 Al-Ṭabarī, *Annales* ii, 1034; al-Balādhurī, *Futūḥ*, 454.
44 Al-Shammākhī, *Siyar* (1883) 88, 117.
45 Al-Darjīnī, *Ṭabaqāt* ii, 255; al-Shammākhī, *Siyar* (1883) 88–89.
46 The epistle was edited by Crone – Zimmermann in 2001 under the title *The Epistle of Sālim Ibn Dhakwān*. On the author, see 11–14.
47 Al-Jaʿbīrī (ed.), *Rasāʾil* 102 (Ms. 68B$_{22-24}$); Ennami, *Studies* 46 (online edition).
48 Al-Shammākhī, *Siyar* (1883) 67, 72.

nominated governor of Balqā' (Transjordan) by 'Umar II (99–101/717–720) and who had fought in Armenia in 107/725–726.[49]

Nāfiʿ b. ʿAbd Allāh, the addressee of letter no. 6 (no. 7 in the printed edition), could well be the traditionist Nāfiʿ b. ʿAbd Allāh b. Kathīr al-Ḥijāzī, handed down by the Medinan Abū Ḍamra Anas b. ʿIyāḍ (104/722–200/816).[50]

Jābir's letters start with the obligatory *taḥmīd,* which turns into the *waṣiyya bi-'l-taqwā* (enjoinder to piety), a *topos* in the early doctrinal epistles. It regularly appears in the letters and speeches originating from Iraq: thus the first letter of ʿAbd Allāh b. Ibāḍ to the caliph ʿAbd al-Malik, the *Kitāb al-Irjā'* by Ḥasan b. Muḥammad b. al-Ḥanafiyya (d. around 100/718), the *Risāla ilā ʿUthmān al-Battī* by Abū Ḥanīfa (d. 150/767), the *Kitāb al-ṣafwa* by Zayd b. ʿAlī (d. 122/740).

After the expression *amma baʿdu* which signals that the preliminaries have finished, the author continued with generic recommendations to the addressee to be cautious and prudent in order to avoid danger from the enemies, but he did not deal with specific Khārijī issues here. Then the formula "*wa-ammā-'l-ladhī dhakarta min* […]", with a short summary of the question introduces his *responsa,* in which he frequently uses Quranic expressions.[51]

- Letter no. 1[52] (addressed to Rāshid b. Khaytham) – (Ms ff. 64A–65A; missing in *Rasā'il* where the first letter is a fragment with no mention of the author and the addressee corresponding to letter no. 13 in *Rasā'il*): Jābir provides legal responses (*responsa*) to questions regarding slaves, marriage, adultery, the false accusation of adultery (*qadhf*), and the ban on sexual relations between a father and the concubine slave of his son.

---

49 Van Ess, Untersuchungen 29.

50 Al-Dhahabī, *Mīzān* no. 8993; Ibn Ḥajar, *Tahdhīb* x, no. 730. On Abū Ḍamra, s. Ib. i, no. 689; Ibn Saʿd, *Ṭabaqāt* v, 323.

51 See for example the introduction of letters to ʿUnayfa, ʿAbd al-ʿAzīz b. Saʿd, Sālim b. Dhakwān, Nuʿmān b. Salama, Ṭarīf b. Khulayd. In other cases the Qur'ān is not quoted literally, see for example: "*Fa-inna 'llāha mūfī al-ṣābirīna ajrahum bi-ghayri ḥisābin*", which corresponds to Cor., XXXIX, 10: "*Innamā yuwaffā 'l-ṣābirūna ajrahum bi-ghayr ḥisābin*", al-Jaʿbīrī (ed.), *Rasā'il* 97 (Ms. $68A_1$) – "*Alladhī balaghaka 'llāhu min al-fiqh fī 'l-dīn*" (see Cor., IX, 122: "*Li-yatafaqqahū fī 'l-dīn*"), *Rasā'il* 98 (Ms. $68A_{11}$) – "*Fa-inna 'llāha lā yughnī ʿalayka shay'an min dhālika*" (see Cor., XII, 66: "*wa-mā ughnī ʿankum mina 'llāhi min shay'in*"), *Rasā'il* 127 ($72B_{24}$) – "*Illā an tataṭawwaʿa bi-khayrin fa-inna 'llāha shākirun ʿālimun*" (see Cor., II, 158: "*wa-man taṭawwaʿa khayran fa-inna 'llāha shākirun ʿālimun*"), *Rasā'il* 141 ($87B_3$).

52 The epistles' as well the manuscripts' pages/folios numbering is mine.

- Letter no. 2 (addressed to Ṭarīf b. Khulayd) – (Ms ff. 65A–67A; no. 3 in Rasāʾil no. 3, 82–90): Replies to eleven questions concerning heredity, sale, ritual purity and prayer.
- Letter no. 3 (addressed to Ghiṭrīf b. ʿAbd al-Raḥmān) – (Ms ff. 67A–67B; in *Rasāʾil* no. 4, 91–96): Replies to four questions relating to the *salaf*, Friday prayers, the problem of a couple who had committed illegal sexual intercourse before converting to Islam and pilgrimage.[53]
- Letter no. 4 (addressed to al-Ḥārith b. ʿAmr) – (Ms ff. 67B–69A; in *Rasāʾil* no. 5, 97–102): Replies to nine questions relating to ritual purity, prayer and *salaf*.[54]
- Letter no. 5 (addressed to ʿUnayfa) – (Ms ff. 69A–70B; in *Rasāʾil* no. 6, 103–110): Replies to ten questions concerning illegal sexual intercourse, repudiation provided that the mother breastfeeds the infant for two years, the marriage pact (*mīthāq*) stipulated while the woman is still under *ʿidda* (the waiting time), compensation for injury (*diya*), prayer, *zakāt*, the slave *umm al-walad* who has had illegal sexual intercourse and a slave owned by two men.
- Letter no. 6 (addressed to Nāfiʿ b. ʿAbd Allāh) – (Ms ff. 70B–71A; in *Rasāʾil* no. 7, 11–114): It contains six Jābir's *responsa* relating to the bequest for pilgrimage, marriage, compensation (*diya*) due in the case of an injury caused by a beast of burden, the effects of the conversion to Islam on marriage and the *ʿidda* of a repudiated slave.
- Letter no. 7 (addressed to Yazīd b. Yasār) – (Ms ff. 71A–71B; in *Rasāʾil* no. 8, 115–117): Replies to four questions concerning the rent of land and business contracts when one partner provides the land and the other his work, the *salaf*. Yazīd b. Yasār must have had an official post in Oman as Jābir praises his honesty (Ms 71B6–14; *Rasāʾil* 116).
- Letter no. 8 (addressed to ʿAbd al-ʿAzīz b. Saʿd) – (Ms ff. 71B–71A; in *Rasāʾil* no. 9, 118–119): In the manuscript only the introduction is preserved. In the *Rasāʾil* it contains the answer to a single question regarding taxation.
- Letter no. 9 (addressed to Sālim b. Dhakwān) – (Ms ff. 72A–72B; in *Rasāʾil* no. 11, 124–126): Jābir's *responsa* deal with the ban on marrying two sisters at the same time, even if foster-sisters, or to have two sisters as concubines, and the ban on an owner having sexual intercourse with the same slave that had had intercourse with one's father.
- Letters no. 10 and 11 (addressed to Nuʿmān b. Salama) – (Ms ff. $72B_{11-26}$ and $72B_{26}$–$73A_{19}$; in *Rasāʾil* no. 12, 127–128 and no. 13, 129–133): Both letters deal

53 The epistle was edited by Darwīsh, *Ḥayāt min ajl al-ʿilm* 183–185.
54 The epistle was edited and translated by Naggar, *Fatwā von Jābir an al-Ḥārith b. ʿAmr*.

with the question of collecting the land tax (*kharāj*) and poll tax (*jizya*) from subject populations.

- Letter no. 12 (addressed to Mālik b. Usayd) – (Ms ff. 73A–73B; in *Rasāʾil* no. 10, 120–123): This letter contains only two *responsa* by Jābir (the third question is incomplete) concerning the payment of *mahr* (the nuptial gift).
- Letter no. 13 (there is no addressee) – (Ms ff. 74A–75A; in *Rasāʾil* no. 1, 74–76): The addressee, probably from Oman in the light of a brief reference by Jābir, received *responsa* from Jābir about sale and rental contracts.
- Letter no. 14 (addressed to ʿUthmān b. Yasār): Only the "enjoinder to piety" (Ms f. 75A) remains of this letter; the successive page bears the words "*hādhā ʾl-wajh bāṭil*". The following page (76A) is a letter without any addressee that may not be by Jābir, followed by an epistle by the Maghribi *imām* Jannāw b. Fatā al-Madyūnī.

Jābir's correspondence continues on f. $86A_{11}$ with the letter no. 15 (addressed to Ṭarīf b. Khulayd – see let. no. 2; in *Rasāʾil* no. 14, 134–136): The *responsa* concern the *salaf*, a case in which the owner – who is apparently the addressee's father – causes *umm al-walad* (*walīda*) abortion, and ritual purity. In one of these questions, (Ms $86B_{8-14}$; *Rasāʾil* 136), Ṭarīf (who must have had an official post) asks Jābir if the acceptance of gifts is permitted. Jābir advises him to beware of any gift made with an intent to corrupt and accept only those offered in good faith (*bi-ʾl-maʿrūf*).

- Letter no. 16 (addressed to Mālik) – (Ms. ff. 86B–87B; in *Rasāʾil* no. 15, 137–142 where only "Mālik" as the addressee's name is mentioned): According to Ennami, the addressee of this letter is Mālik b. Usayd (see also letter no. 12).[55] The letter provides interesting information on the internal relations of the Ibāḍī community. Mālik b. Usayd must have been a wealthy member of the Ibāḍī community in Oman, as can be deduced from Jābir's reply to his question on pilgrimage. He wrote: "I do not believe that you are held to make donations in favour of the pilgrimage (*ḥajj*) which you have asked permission for, unless you do so spontaneously as a good act" (Ms. $87B_{3-4}$; *Rasāʾil* 116). In fact, the financing of pilgrimages of the poor by the wealthy was a custom of the sect and considered highly worthy. The sources contain many references to this. Abū Sālim, one of the Ibāḍīs imprisoned by al-Ḥajjāj together with Abū ʿUbayda, made his camels available to allow the *shaykh* of the community to complete his pilgrimage. Abū ʾl-Ḥurr b. al-Ḥusayn, a rich merchant from Basra, arrived in Mecca with a gold ingot

55 Ennami, A Description of New Ibāḍī Manuscripts 65.

that he shared among the poor (a half), and (Ibāḍī) Muslims he wanted to help (a quarter), keeping only a quarter for himself. Yet another merchant, al-Naẓar b. Ma'mūn, offered 40 *dīnār* to al-Rabīʿ so that the needy learned of the community could go Mecca.[56]

The other *responsa* of the letter concern how to pay the *zakāt* on the harvest in the scattered villages, prayer and fasting when travelling, the exchange of camels for sheep and the *diya* (compensation) for mortal injury.

- Letter no. 17 (addressed to ʿAbd al-Malik b. al-Muhallab) – (Ms. ff. 87B–90A; in *Rasāʾil* no. 16, 143–149 and no. 17, 150–155): On the letter heading, in deference to authority, the name of ʿAbd al-Malik precedes that of Jābir (*li ʿAbd al-Malik ibn al-Muhallab min Jābir ibn Zayd*). The *fatāwā* pronounced by Jābir, in reply to ʿAbd al-Malik's questions, mainly deal with problems linked to waiting period (*ʿidda*), repudiation and slaves (the lack of a hereditary vocation between owner and freedman). In the manuscript the first letter to ʿAbd al-Malik b. al-Muhallab is interrupted on f. 89A (question no. 195 in *Rasāʾil*) and resumes on f. 89B with the second letter (question no. 208 in *Rasāʾil*).
- Letter no. 18 (addressed to Khayra bint Ḍamra) – (Ms. ff. 90–91; in *Rasāʾil* no. 18, 156–158): The *responsa* given by Jābir concern the ritual purity of women, slaves and the conditions for restoring marital intercourse after the vow of abstinence.

2.4 Abū ʿUbayda

Abū ʿUbayda, a *mawlā* of the Tamīm tribe, was the second Ibāḍī *imām* in Basra. He took over the leadership after being released from prison along with other early Ibāḍī authorities, following the death of the Umayyad governor al-Ḥajjāj (95/714). He died probably after 150/767,[57] but the exact date of his death is unknown as the Ibāḍī historical sources only record that he died during the al-Manṣūr caliphate (136/754–158/775).[58]

---

56 Al-Shammākhī, *Siyar* (1883) 96, 101–102, 103.

57 Abū ʿUbayda seems to have died after 150/767, as that year he ordered the killing in Sistan of Maʿn b. Zāʾida al-Shaybānī who was guilty of the murder of Zājir al-Ḥaḍramī. Al Salimi, Identifying the Ibāḍī/Omani *Siyar* 127 no. 59.

58 al-Darjīnī, *Ṭabaqāt* ii, 238–246; al-Shammākhī, *Siyar* (1883) 83–86; Nāṣir and Shaybānī, *Muʿjam aʿlām al-ibāḍiyya. Qism al-Mashriq al-Islāmī* 445–447; van Ess, *Theologie und Gesellschaft* ii, 193. Jāḥiẓ quotes Abū ʿUbayda among the Khārijī authorities twice in his *al-Bayān wa-ʾl-tabyīn* stressing that he was a very learned scholar (i, 331; iii, 227).

The Ibāḍī authors describe him as a pious man, a brilliant orator, an excellent teacher, a great scholar, covering the fields of theology, jurisprudence and traditions, and, finally, as an excellent political leader. Abū ʿUbayda studied under the first Ibāḍī *imām* Jābir b. Zayd (although his learning from Jābir stemmed mainly indirectly via Ḍumām b. al-Sā'ib)[59] and other teachers, such as Jaʿfar b. al-Sammāk, Suḥār al-ʿAbdī and also ʿUrwa b. ʿUdayya, the first to reject arbitration and fight against ʿAlī, who should have strongly influenced him.[60]

Abū ʿUbayda was a skilful political leader and the true organizer of the Ibāḍī movement. He provided the basis for the diaspora which has allowed the survival of Ibadism until today, creating teams of missionaries (*ḥamalat al-ʿilm*) who left Basra for the outer regions of the Islamic Empire with a proselytizing intent to create Ibāḍī centres. The missionaries' activity was entwined with merchant activity, exploiting their ability to organize long-distance journeys, their knowledge of routes and their freedom of movement in an age when this was regarded with some suspicion by the authorities.

The activities of the movement in Basra took place within meetings (*majālis*) which were held in secret in the members' houses. The sources describe three types of *majālis*: the first open to all members in which doctrinal and legal questions were discussed; a second reserved for the elders to organize propaganda (*daʿwa*), and a third intended for the training of missionaries.

The development of the Ibāḍī doctrine, the growth of their organization and the rapid expansion of their movement in Yemen, Oman, Khurāsān and North Africa is undoubtedly due to Abū ʿUbayda. Under his imamate, the movement entered into an expansionist stage with revolts which broke out in several regions. At the end of the Umayyad period, a short-lived imamate was established in South-Western Arabia under the guidance of Ṭālib al-Ḥaqq (ʿAbd Allāh b. Yaḥyā) who succeeded in taking possession of the Holy Cities. An imamate survived for a short time in Ḥaḍramawt, while further imamates were created in both North Africa and Oman, which held out under alternate circumstances for quite a long time.[61]

---

59 Wilkinson, *Ibâḍism* 166–170.

60 Ennami, *Studies* (online edition) 57–78.

61 According to the *Kitāb Abī Sufyān* by Abū Sufyān Maḥbūb b. al-Raḥīl (or al-Ruḥayl), the last Basran *imām* (d. *c.*210/825) the revolts of ʿAbd Allāh b. Yaḥyā in Yemen, of Abū 'l-Khaṭṭāb and ʿAbd al-Raḥmān in North Africa and al-Julanda b. Masʿud in ʿUmān were all organized by Abū ʿUbayda. Kāshif (ed.), *al-Siyar wa 'l-jawābāt* ii, 265.

During Abū ʿUbayda's imamate – once the attempts at reconciliation with the Sunni authorities had conclusively failed – there was a progressive radicalisation of the Ibāḍī movement. Not only did the Ibāḍīs take a firm position on some questions of dogma which were debated at the time (in particular, the *qadar* and the question of a created or uncreated Quran), but they began to develop doctrines within the creed that would come to characterize the movement. Abū ʿUbayda wanted a pure Ibāḍī organization and firmly opposed any contact with non-Ibāḍīs; even the marriage of an Ibāḍī woman with non-Ibāḍī man, although it was lawful, was disapproved of.[62] The validity of prayers performed with a non-Ibāḍī *imām* was also discussed at length at that time; in contrast, Jābir was said to have performed the Friday prayer under the guidance of the Umayyad governor al-Ḥajjāj.[63]

In delivering legal judgement Abū ʿUbayda gave priority to the Quran. According to al-Darjīnī, Abū ʿUbayda said: "The Quran has been presented to the people, whoever thinks he is able to learn something by himself [without making recourse to It], God shall alienate him as he has alienated himself from Him".[64]

If there was no ruling to be derived from the Quran, recourse should be made to the *sunna* of Companions. Abū ʿUbayda claims the authority of the following Companions for the Ibāḍī school: Ibn ʿAbbās, Ibn Masʿūd, ʿAbd Allāh b. Sallām. He describes them as being firmly rooted in knowledge. He further says: "We walked in their steps, followed their sayings, relied on their conduct and emulated their methods".[65] He describes them as being "firmly rooted in knowledge" (*al-rāsikhūna fī ʾl-ʿilm*). He also states that "those who had intelligence and understanding would not be interested in views and opinions which emerged after the time of the Companions; it is the aim only of those who became lax in their worship to be interested in what happened after the Companions".[66]

However, Abū ʿUbayda did not oppose individual judgement in forming legal opinions on matters, which were not dealt with by Quran and *sunna*

62 Related by Abū ʾl-Muʾarrij in Abū Ghānim, *Mudawwana* ii, 12.

63 Al-Kharusi (ed.), *Āthār* 68 (Ms. 16_{5-7}); Ibn Jaʿfar, *al-Jāmiʿ* ii, 395; al-Ḥārithī, *al-ʿUqūd* 97; al-Kindī, *Bayān al-Sharʿ* xv, 6. This dispute is also quoted in the *sīra* of Abū Sufyān Maḥbūb b. al-Raḥīl addressed to the people of Ḥaḍramawt concerning the question of Hārūn b. al-Yamān, and gave rise to the question of the true *sunna* of the Baṣran movement. See Kāshif (ed.) *al-Siyar wa ʾl-jawābāt* i, 307; Wilkinson, Ibāḍī *Ḥadīth* 252.

64 *Ṭabaqāt* ii, 241.

65 Abū ʿUbayda, *Masāʾil* quoted in Ennami, *Studies* (online edition) 56.

66 Ennami, *Studies*, p. 98.

and he recognized the value of the lawyers' prudent systematic reasoning: "In deciding, they apply their prudent systematic reasoning (*wa-ijtahidū ra'yahum fīhi*), based on what God has ordered concerning the distribution (of the tithes) among those who he has ordered shall receive them".[67]

2.5 Abū 'Ubayda's Epistle on *Zakāt*

Abū 'Ubayda's epistle on *zakāt* – the *Risālat Ibn Abī Karīma fī 'l-zakāt li-'l-imām Abī 'l-Khaṭṭāb al-Ma'āfirī* (henceforth *risāla*) – was probably addressed to the Maghribi Ibāḍī *imām* Abū 'l-Khaṭṭāb between 757 and 761.[68] The letter is a reply (*jawāb*) from Abū 'Ubayda on questions concerning the payment of *zakāt* (the obligatory almsgiving) as well as other matters relating to both law and dogma.

In the epistle I have noted points in which Abū 'Ubayda was asked about significant legal matters beside secondary questions or details, such as questions related to the payment of the *zakāt* on partnerships, the constitution of a *waqf* (trust) using the *zakāt* funds, the *zakāt* payment for a landowner who has properties in more than one village.

This work is of particular importance for the understanding of Abū 'Ubayda's way of legal reasoning. It includes *fatwās* which reveal the opinions of Abū 'Ubayda as well as of other Ibāḍī authorities, who are referred to by name (as Jābir b. Zayd) or by the general term "*aṣḥābunā*" (our companions) or "*jamā'at al-muslimīn*" (the board of Muslim – i.e. Ibāḍī – authorities).[69]

Moreover, the *risāla* offers valuable insights into the relationships between the Ibāḍī community in Basra and the Ibāḍīs in the Maghrib. As Abdulrahman al-Salimi argued, epistles (generally called *sīra*, pl. *siyar*) are among the most important historical and intellectual sources for reconstructing the early development of the Ibāḍī movement. The Ibāḍīs of North Africa depended very much on the scholars of Basra in whatever problems they faced on legal and theological issues. It became necessary to consult the Basran authorities since there was no original codified Ibāḍī doctrine the community could refer to.

67 *Risāla* 4.

68 The edition by Sālim b. Muḥammad al-Ḥārithī (Muscat 1982) is based on the Ms. Dār al-Kutub al-Miṣriyya (no. Ib. 215882). The text is made up of 26 pages. See Khulaifāt (Khleifat), *Nash'at al-ḥaraka al-ibāḍiyya* 149; Francesca, Law and Politics in the Early Ibāḍī Communities, 72–88.

69 van Ess, *Theologie und Gesellschaft* ii, 193.

These contacts were particularly effective during the time of the "bearers of learning" (*ḥamalat al-ʿilm*), who were trained in Basra under the tutorship of Abū ʿUbayda and were to spread the teaching of the movement in North Africa, where Ibadism took root thanks to their proselytizing activities. The *siyar* prove the leading role of the Basrans and shed light on their attitude towards the Ibāḍī community in diaspora. In particular, *siyar* were a way to provide the members of the missionary network with instructions on their policies, enlightenment on controversial issues of the Ibāḍī doctrines and suggestions to produce solutions to events that arose unexpectedly.

Abdulrahman al-Salimi credited Abū ʿUbayda with several letters addressed to other early Ibāḍī scholars.[70] In his epistles, Abū ʿUbayda sometimes encouraged his followers to continue their work and activities in a more discrete way; he also discussed political, theological and legal issues, such as reward and punishment earned by human actions, free will and predestination, the principle of *walāya* (association), *barāʾa* (dissociation) and *wuqūf* (suspended judgement). The epistles by Abū ʿUbayda are an essential source if one is to draw a comprehensive picture of the history of early Ibadism as they are often elicited by specific historical events. For instance, epistle no. XXVI alludes to an obscure episode of early Ibadism in North Africa. It was addressed by Abū ʿUbayda and another Basran authority, Abū Mawdūd Ḥājib al-Ṭāʾī (d. between 136/753 and 148/764), to the Tripolitanian Ibāḍīs in order to explain the main doctrinal implication of the of *walāya/barāʾa* principle, but its primary aim seems to be advising the community to remain united and to abstain from division and sectarianism.[71] In fact it refers to the tragic death of two Ibāḍī propagandists, al-Ḥārith (or al-Ḥāris) b. Tulayd al-Ḥaḍramī and ʿAbd al-Jabbār b. Qays al-Murādī, who took the leadership of the Ibāḍī revolt in Tripolitania after ʿAbd Allāh b. Masʿūd al-Tujībī (who had seized Tripoli in 743–744) had been arrested and beheaded. Their joint leadership, supported by the powerful Hawwāra tribe, proved short-lived and the two *imāms* (or more likely, one an *imām* and the other a judge or visir) fought each other to the death (748–749). They were found in the same house, each with the opponent's weapon stuck in his body. The community was divided over how to judge the incident: both al-Ḥārith and ʿAbd al-Jabbār were reliable Ibāḍī leaders who merited *walāya* for their activity in propagating and defining the true religion. Against whom

---

70 Identifying the Ibādī/Omani *Siyar* 127–130, *siyar* no. xvii, xviii, xix, xxvi, xxvii, xxviii. The latter, addressed to the second Rustumid *imām*, ʿAbd al-Wahhāb b. ʿAbd al-Raḥmān (168–208/784–823), is probably spurious. On the *siyar*'s contents see Al Salimi, Themes of the Ibādī/Omani *Siyar* 475–514.

71 Al Salimi, Identifying the Ibāḍī/Omani *Siyar* 129, no. xxvi.

should the community declare *barā'a* (dissociation) as guilty of unjust murder? This tragic story is alluded to by Abū ʿUbayda and Abū Mawdūd Ḥājib in their epistle where they instructed the Maghribi Ibāḍīs to adopt the *wuqūf* (suspended judgement) with regard to both of them and to refrain from evoking their memory.[72]

Among the extant epistles by Abū ʿUbayda to the Maghribi Ibāḍīs there is his treatise on *zakāt* which he apparently wrote to the *imām* Abū 'l-Khaṭṭāb al-Maʿāfirī. Sālim b. Aḥmad b. Sulaymān al-Ḥārithī, who edited the *risāla* in 1982 using a manuscript from the Dār al-Kutub al-Miṣriyya (Cairo), designated Abū 'l-Khaṭṭāb as the recipient of the letter, although he is not expressly mentioned in the beginning/incipit of the letter.[73]

On the contrary, according to Ennami, Abū ʿUbayda wrote the epistle to Ismāʿīl b. Ziyād al-Nafūsī. He describes a manuscript of the *risāla* coming from Jerba (al-Maktaba al-Bārūniyya), which is part of a larger manuscript collecting several Ibāḍī works, dated 30 Muḥarram 1211/August 1797. The *risāla* was copied immediately after the *Kitāb al-ṣalāt* by Jābir b. Zayd. The beginning of the epistle studied by Ennami shows some differences in comparison to the edition by al-Ḥārithī.[74]

Abū 'l-Khaṭṭāb al-Maʿāfirī and Ismāʿīl b. Ziyād al-Nafūsī were both leading figures of early Ibadism in North Africa. At the initial stage, the Ibāḍī movement was strictly bound to tribal politics and took the form of an association with the Berber tribes, whose opposition to the Umayyad central authority was channelled through Ibāḍī claims that faith, religious knowledge and political power went hand in hand. The Ibāḍī doctrine rejecting the authority of the caliph in favour of one elected from the community was extremely appealing for the Berbers and represented the movement's strength, but it was also the basis on which the Ibāḍī *imāms* came to be challenged.

The complex interweaving of tribal, political and religious interests led to the widespread rebellions of the 740s. In 743–744, ʿAbd Allāh b. Masʿūd al-Tujībī, supported by the Hawwāra, seized Tripoli but was killed shortly thereafter; he was succeeded by al-Ḥārith and ʿAbd al-Jabbār, who killed each other in 748–749. The temporary political vacuum was filled by Ismāʿīl b. Ziyād

72 *Bi-'l-kaff ʿan dhikhrihumā*, s. al-Warjlānī, *Kitāb siyar al-a'imma* 64. The epistle is also quoted in the later Ibāḍī historical sources: al-Darjīnī, *Ṭabaqāt* i, 24–25; al-Shammākhī, *Siyar. Al-juz' al-khāṣṣ bi-tarājim ʿulamā' al-Maghrib* 25–26.

73 *Risāla* 26. He bases his statement also on Khulaifāt (Khleifat), *Nash'at al-ḥaraka al-ibāḍiyya* 149.

74 Ennami, A Description of New Ibāḍī Manuscripts 67; idem, *Studies*, 73.

al-Nafūsī who was elected *imām al-difāʿ* (*imām* of defence) in the same year.[75] His death took place soon after his election near the town of Qābis (Gabès) in an encounter with the troops of ʿAbd al-Raḥmān b. Ḥabīb, the Arab Governor of Qayrawān. The Ibāḍī state of Tripolitania collapsed but the population, though it found itself leaderless again, remained Ibāḍī.

Ten years later, in the years after 140/757, the legendary team of missionaries (*ḥamalat al-ʿilm*) arrived, sent by Abū ʿUbayda to Tripolitania with the aim of forming an Ibāḍī imamate. The team was formed of Āṣim al-Sadrātī, Abū Dāwūd al-Qibillī, Ismāʿīl b. Darrār al-Ghadāmsī, ʿAbd al-Raḥmān b. Rustum – of Persian origins – and Abū ʾl-Khaṭṭāb al-Maʿāfirī – a *mawlā* of the tribe of the Maʿāfira.

The Ibāḍī team met with great success and a new Ibāḍī imamate came into being in 140/757–758. Abū ʾl-Khaṭṭāb was elected *imām* by six Berber chiefs of the tribes of Hawwāra, Nafūsa and Zanāta.[76] Commanded by the new *imām*, they conquered the whole of Tripolitania under the rallying cry *lā ḥukm illā li-llāh wa lā ṭāʿa illā ṭāʿat Abī ʾl-Khaṭṭāb* (No rule but God's rule and no submission except to Abū ʾl-Khaṭṭāb).[77] Tripoli became the residence of Abū ʾl-Khaṭṭāb. In Ṣafar 141/June-July 758, Abū ʾl-Khaṭṭāb took Qayrawān and appointed ʿAbd al-Raḥmān b. Rustum governor of the town. The result of Abū ʾl-Khaṭṭāb's conquest was the creation of an Ibāḍī state comprising Tripolitania, Tunisia and the eastern part of Algeria. He also had a certain influence over the Ṣufrites of Sijilmāssa.

The new imamate would not last long. Abū ʾl-Khaṭṭāb died during the battle of al-Tawargha between the Ibāḍī forces and the Abbasid army led by the governor of Egypt, Muḥammad b. al-Ashʿath al-Khuzāʿī (Ṣafar 144/May-June 761), which turned into a great massacre of the Ibāḍī population of Tripolitania.[78] After the Abbasid reconquest, Ibadism experienced a new flowering with

75 Schwartz, *Die Anfänge der Ibaditen in Nordafrika* 124; Prevost, *L'aventure ibāḍite dans le Sud tunisien* 60; Savage, *A Gateway to Hell, a Gateway to Paradise* 45.

76 Al-Warjlānī, *Kitāb siyar al-aʾimma* 61–75; al-Darjīnī, *Ṭabaqāt* i, 22–36; al-Shammākhī, *Siyar. Al-juzʾ al-khāṣṣ bi-tarājum ʿulamāʾ al-Maghrib* 23–35, Ibn al-Ṣaghīr, *Akhbār al-aʾimma al-rustumiyyīn* 30–31; Ibn Sallām, *Kitāb Ibn Sallām* 139–143, 150. The author's grandfather fought in the Abū ʾl-Khaṭṭāb's army (see 140, 150). See also Lewicki, *Ètudes ibāḍites nord-africaines* 112–114; Motylinski and Lewicki, EI2, s.v. Abū l-Khaṭṭāb ʿAbd al-Aʿlā al-Maʿāfirī; Schwartz, *Die Anfänge der Ibaditen in Nordafrika* 145–188; Prevost, La deuxième scission au sein des ibadites 29–63.

77 Al-Warjlānī, *Kitāb siyar al-aʾimma* 64.

78 Prevost, *L'aventure ibāḍite dans le Sud tunisien* 63; idem, ʿAbd al-Raḥmān ibn Rustum al-Fārisī. Une tentative de biographie du premier *imam* de Tāhart 46–49.

ʿAbd al-Raḥmān b. Rustum who was proclaimed *imām* in 160/776–777 or 162/778–779. Under his reign, the Ibāḍī influence in North Africa developed considerably.

Coming back to the question of the addressee of the *risāla* by Abū ʿUbayda, I agree with al-Ḥārithī's statement that the *risāla* was addressed to Abū ʾl-Khaṭṭāb, basing my opinion on the following arguments. The sources do not credit Ismāʿīl b. Ziyād al-Nafūsī with any connection to the Basran community; moreover his imamate was very brief. Abū ʾl-Khaṭṭāb's imamate was also short-lived, only four years, but the Ibāḍī sources praised him as the ideal *imām*, the best Muslim elected by the community, the formidable military chief due to his bravery and personal prestige. His knowledge originated in the heart of the community and he was appointed *imām* by Abū ʿUbayda himself, thus representing the junction through which the Basran legacy passed into the Maghribi community.[79] Therefore, it seems more likely that he was the one who corresponded with Abū ʿUbayda.

Abū ʾl-Khaṭṭāb's capabilities as a political leader may be also inferred from his correspondence with the caliph al-Manṣūr (754–775) through an intermediary, Yazīd b. Ḥātim al-Muhallab, active in Egypt. At this early stage, Ibāḍī thought was not yet considered politically dangerous or subversive and it seems probable that the caliph welcomed the infusion of a moderate Khārijī element, at that time still friendly to the Abbasids, among the turbulent Berber population. As is well known, the Ibāḍīs' attempt at an allegiance with the Abbasids quickly failed and it took ten years for the Abbasid army to seize control of the Maghribi provinces from the Ibāḍī chiefs.[80]

2.6 al-Rabīʿ ibn Ḥabīb

After Abū ʿUbayda's death, his pupil Abū ʿAmr al-Rabīʿ b. Ḥabīb (d. between 180/796 and 190/806)[81] became the key figure of the movement: he was both a *muftī* and an activist involved in the organization of missionary activity in

79 Savage, *A Gateway to Hell, a Gateway to Paradise* 46.

80 Savage, *A Gateway to Hell, a Gateway to Paradise* 38–39.

81 Al-Rabīʿ b. Ḥabīb al-Baṣrī was the last Ibāḍī *imām* who lived in Basra, after his imamate the community, under the leadership of Abū Sufyān Maḥbūb b. al-Ruḥayl, immigrated to Oman. Ibn Jaʿfar, *al-Jāmiʿ* ii, 395; al-Ḥārithī, *al-ʿUqūd* 97; al-Kindī, *Bayān al-Sharʿ* xv, 6; Nāṣir and Shaybānī, *Muʿjam aʿlām al-ibāḍiyya. Qism al-Mashriq al-Islāmī*, 152–153. According to Brockelmann, al-Rabīʿ died in about 170/786 (G.A.L., Suppl., II, p. 823); Cook (*Early Muslim Dogma* 56) Wilkinson (Ibāḍī *Ḥadīth* 233f.), Nāṣir and Shaybānī (2006) agree

North Africa and in Oman. He was also responsible for the first moves within Ibadism towards the collection of the *ḥadīth*. At the end of his life, having handed over the leadership of the movement in Basra to Abū Ayyūb Wā'il al-Ḥaḍramī, he moved to Oman, where he died at his home at Ghaḍfān, near Ṣuḥār.[82] In Oman he charged a certain Abū 'l-Mundhir Bashīr al-Mundhir al-Nazwānī, one of the missionaries, with the task of spreading his traditions.[83] Al-Rabīʿ's traditions and legal responses, together with those of the other Ibāḍī authorities of the 2nd/8th century can be found in the *Āthār*, in the *Futyā al-Rabīʿ* and in the *Aqwāl Qatāda b. Diʿāma* (2nd, 3rd and 4th parts). A *Musnad*, known as *al-Jāmiʿ al-ṣaḥīḥ*, which has been attributed to al-Rabīʿ, has survived in the *tartīb* of Abū Yaʿqūb b. Ibrāhīm al-Warjlānī (d. 570/1174).

Al-Rabīʿ followed the path of his teachers in providing his legal judgement. In his *Ṭabaqāt* al-Darjīnī states that he claimed to have been a pupil of Abū ʿUbayda, Abū Nūḥ and Ḍumām, and that he based his legal advice on their teaching.[84]

For the whole of the 2nd/8th century, Basra was to remain the spiritual centre of Ibadism in the East. However, even during the last years of al-Rabīʿ's life, the city's role began to decline with the formation of the imamate in Oman, where the community could have a greater chance of survival. Al-Rabīʿ was the last Ibāḍī *imām* who lived in Basra; his successor, Abū Sufyān,[85] decided to settle permanently in Oman.[86] From the beginning of the 3rd/9th century, Basra's role in the development of Ibāḍī doctrine declined, as from then on the two spiritual and political poles of Ibadism would be Oman and the Maghrib (in particular the regions of Jabal Nafūsa, Fezzan, Mzab and Jerba Island).

---

with him. On the contrary, van Ess fixes the date of al-Rabīʿ's death between 180/796 and 190/806, see Untersuchungen 32–33; *Theologie und Gesellschaft* ii, 199.

82 Wilkinson, The Ibāḍī Movement in Baṣra 142.

83 van Ess, *Theologie und Gesellschaft* ii, 199; idem, Untersuchungen, 33 and footnote 21; Lewicki, al-Ibāḍiyya, 651–652.

84 *Ṭabaqāt* ii, 276; al-Shammākhī, *Siyar* 104.

85 Abū Sufyān Maḥbūb b. al-Ruḥayl (or al-Raḥīl) was among the Ibādī jurists of the second half of the 2nd/8th century. He studied in Basra with Abū ʿUbayda and al-Rabīʿ. See al-Darjīnī, *Ṭabaqāt* ii, 278–290; al-Shammākhī (1883), *Siyar* 117; Crone and Zimmermann (eds.), *The Epistle of Sālim Ibn Dhakwān* 309–315.

86 Al-Darjīnī, *Ṭabaqāt* ii, 273–277; al-Shammākhī, *Siyar* (1883) 102–105.

2.7 The *Āthār* and the *Futyā al-Rabīʿ b. Ḥabīb*

Al-Rabīʿ's traditions and legal responses, together with those of other Ibāḍī authorities of the 2nd/8th century, can be found in the *Āthār*, in the *Futyā al-Rabīʿb. Ḥabīb* and in the *Aqwāl Qatāda b. Diʿāma* (2nd, 3rd and 4th parts). A *Musnad* or *al-Jāmiʿ al-ṣaḥīḥ* which has survived in the arrangement by Abū Yaʿqūb b. Ibrāhīm al-Warjlānī (d. 570/1174), has been attributed to al-Rabīʿ but this is probably spurious.

Ibāḍī sources refer to the *Āthār* as *Kitāb Ḍumām* or *Kitāb Abī Ṣufra*.[87] The name of the latter appears only once right at the beginning of the first *riwāya*: *ḥaddathanā Abū Ṣufra ʿAbd al-Malik b. Ṣufra, qāla: ḥaddathanā al-Haytham ʿan al-Rabīʿ b. Ḥabīb ʿan Ḍumām b. al-Sayib* (sic) *ʿan Jābir b. Zayd al-Azdī*, followed by the first question and answer.

Later on, the transmission line becomes shorter: *al-Rabīʿ b. Ḥabīb ʿan Ḍumām ʿan Abī ʾl-Shaʿthāʾ* (Jābir b. Zayd al-Azdī). Jābir's opinion on legal as well as religious matters is reported in an extremely abridged way, sometimes almost on a yes–no basis, and a reason is never given for the opinion.

Ibāḍī *rijāl* works provide little information about Abū Ṣufra. He belonged to the last generation of Ibāḍī *ʿulamāʾ* from the old Basran school, bridging the period between the last years of the Basran leadership and the settlement of the Ibāḍī community in Oman.[88] The *Bayān al-Sharʿ* of Muḥammad al-Kindī (end of the 5/11th century) preserves a reply written by Abū Ṣufra concerning the creation of the Quran. He addressed it from Iraq to the two sons of Abū Sufyān Maḥbūb b. al-Ruḥayl – Abū ʿAbd Allāh Muḥammad and Sufyān – between 230/845–237/851.[89] The epistle refers to a controversy on the creation

87 Al-Barrādī, *Kitāb al-jawāhir* 218; al-Sālimī, *al-Lumʿa* 19; Ennami, A Description of New Ibāḍī Manuscripts 69; Ibn Khalīfa (ed.), *Futyā* 36.

88 Al-Darjīnī, *Ṭabaqāt* ii, 416; al-Shammakhī, *Siyar* (1883) 119; According to al-Kharusi he was born around 160H and died around 230H, Kharusi (ed.), *Āthār* 140–142.

89 Al-Kindī, *Bayān al-Sharʿ* i, 152–154, 182–185; Wilkinson, Ibāḍi *Ḥadīth* 243–244. Abū ʿAbd Allāh Muḥammad was Abū Sufyān's most famous son. He was *qāḍī* of Ṣuḥār from 249/863 until his death in 260/873 and was involved in the controversy over the creation of Quran. He backed this doctrine and therefore he was almost expelled from Oman, since his contemporary Omani fellows opposed the speculative *kalam* theology (See introduction by al-Salimi and Madelung, eds., *Early Ibāḍī Literature* vii). Abū ʿAbd Allāh is credited with a collection of *fatwās* called *Jāmiʿ* which has not survived although one section was still extant in the Maghrib at time of al-Barradī (second half of the 14th century) who quotes it in his *Kitāb al-Jawāhir*. A number of epistles by Abū ʿAbd Allāh Muḥammad are preserved

of the Quran between Abū ʿAbd Allāh and the Ibāḍī *ʿulamāʾ* in Oman during the imamate of Muhannā b. Jayfar (226/840–237/851). Abū Ṣufra mentions the opinion of Abū ʿAlī Mūsā b. ʿAlī (d. 230/845) on the Quran's creation and says that he discussed the issue with some Ibāḍīs from Baghdad, amongst whom there was Jaʿfar b. Yaḥyā b. al-Rabīʿ (perhaps al-Rabīʿ b. Ḥabīb's grandson). The *terminus ante quem* the letter was written is the end of Muhannā's imamate, on the other hand the *terminus post quem* for dating the epistle is 845, the year of Abū ʿAlī Mūsā's death, as Abū Ṣufra refers to him using the past tense. Moreover, he quotes authorities from two generations after al-Rabīʿ.[90]

In the same period, or shortly before, at the beginning of the 9th century, Abū Ṣufra wrote down the *Āthār*, containing the teaching of the old Basran masters in order to preserve it because there was no continuity provided by the central organisation.

Ibāḍī biographical sources pay no attention to al-Haytham, who transmitted to Abū Ṣufra from al-Rabīʿ. He is presumably al-Haytham b. ʿAbd al-Ghaffār al-Ṭāʾī, who in the *Kitāb al-ʿilal wa maʿrifat al-rijāl* by Aḥmad b. Ḥanbal (d. 241/855) is mentioned as having transmitted from Ḥammām[91] and from "a man whose name was al-Rabīʿ b. Ḥabīb" from Ḍumām from Jābir. Presumably because of his Ibāḍī connections, ʿAbd al-Raḥmān b. Mahdī (d. 198/813–814), teacher of Ibn Ḥanbal, did not consider al-Haytham a reliable transmitter.[92] Kharūṣī agrees with my hypothesis building on Ibn Ḥajar al-Asqalānī (*Lisān al-mīzān* vi, 208) and al-Khaṭīb al-Baghdādī (*Tārīkh Baghdād* xiv, 55) who credited al-Haytham as "the most knowledgeable of Jābir's opinion".[93]

On the contrary, according to Wilkinson, he was al-Haytham b. ʿAdī (d. *c.*206/821), who transmitted the Ibāḍī version of Ibn Ḥamza al-Mukhtar's famous sermon after taking the Holy Cities in the name of Ṭālib al-Ḥaqq (746–747).

---

in the Ibāḍī sources. Kāshif (ed.), *al-Siyar wa ʾl-jawābāt* ii, 223–268; Wilkinson, Ibāḍī *Ḥadīth* 254; Crone and Zimmermann (eds.), *The Epistle of Sālim Ibn Dhakwān* 309–314. The controversy about the creation of Quran and other matters of speculative theology reverberates in the Omani epistles edited by al-Salimi, *Ibadi Texts in Oman from the 3rd/9th Century* (in particular epistles no. 5–7).

90 Wilkinson, Ibāḍī *Ḥadīth* 243–244. On early Ibāḍī theology see the editions of the *kalām* tests written by al-Fazārī (d. *c.*190s/805–815) by al-Salimi and Madelung (eds.), *Early Ibāḍī Theology* and al-Salimi (ed.), *Early Ibadi Theology*.

91 Ḥammām b. Yaḥyā is quoted among Qatāda's transmitters in Ibn Ḥajar, *Tahdhīb* viii, 352.

92 Ibn Ḥanbal, *Kitāb al-ʿilal* i, 254 no. 1455. See my Investigating Early Ibāḍī Jurisprudence 243.

93 Kharusi (ed.) *Āthār* 144–145.

Al-Haytham b. ʿAdī is also mentioned in *al-Bayān wa ʾl-tabyīn* by Jāḥiẓ, along with Abū ʿUbayda in a list of Khārijī authorities.[94]

Ḍumām b. al-Sāʾib, who appears in the *isnād* in second place after Jābir, belonged to the first generation of Ibāḍī *ʿulamāʾ*. He studied under Jābir and transmitted his teaching to Abū ʿUbayda.[95]

The latter, according to Ibāḍī *rijāl* works, heard Jābir as a young man (a fact which would help the idea – later developed – that the great *imām*'s mantle fell on him), but his teachers were actually Ḍumām and Abū Nūḥ. By the lineage of al-Rabīʿ-Ḍumām the majority of Jābir's opinions are related. Occasionally the intermediary is Abū Nūḥ and, at times, both Ḍumām and Abū Nūḥ are quoted as sources. On p. 54 (f. 16 of the manuscript) this lineage stops and we get other pupils of Jābir emerging: ʿUmāra b. Ḥayyān, Tamīm b. Khuwayṣ, ʿAbbās b. al-Ḥārith and others. From p. 65 (f. 18 of the manuscript) Ḥāzim b. ʿUmar and not al-Rabīʿ becomes the source of Jābir's opinions, recording them directly, via Tamīm b. Khuwayṣ or Ḍumām. Similarly on p. 68 (no. 316; manuscript f. 20) ʿUmāra b. Ḥabīb relates from Jābir via his father. The final two sources, Jumayl al-Khawārizmī and Abū Ayyūb, authorities from the final quarter of the 8th/2nd century, record traditions from Ibn ʿAbbās with the transmission line: al-Rabīʿ b. Ḥabīb – Abū ʿUbayda – Jābir.

The work edited by al-Kharūṣī ends here with a tradition from Ibn ʿAbbās, transmitted by Jumayl, on the fifth (*khums*) on the spoil of war (*ghanīma*). On the contrary, in the manuscript (folios 21_4–32), the *Āthār* continues with *dicta* and *responsa* introduced by the formula "I asked him" (*saʾaltuhu*), as in the section on Abū Sufyān (pp. 53–56; fols. 13–15), which al-Kharūṣī considers a spurious interpolation.[96]

The style of the work changes dramatically, with the material roughly divided into chapters as follows:

1. *bāb ghusl al-janāba*
2. *bāb ṣalāt al-khawf*
3. *bāb ṣalāt al-fiṭr wa ʾl-aḍḥā*
4. *masāʾil fī ʾl-ḥayḍ*
5. *bāb ṣalāt al-musāfir*
6. *bāb al-ṭalāq*.

94 Wilkinson, Ibāḍī *Ḥadīth* 243; al-Jāḥiẓ, *al-Bayān wa ʾl-tabyīn* i, 331. S. Leder (1991) analyzed the contribution of al-Haytham b. ʿAdī to the transmission of historical traditions, but he did not point out his contribution to the transmission of Ibāḍī teachings as well.

95 See Darjīnī, *Ṭabaqāt* i 246–247; Shammakhī, *Siyar* 87–88, 96; Siyābī, *Ṭalaqāt al-maʿhad al-riyāḍī fī ḥalaqāt al-madhhab al-ibāḍī*, Oman 1400/1980, 30.

96 Kharusi (ed.) *Āthār* 53 footnote 369.

The authorities to whom the questions are addressed are mentioned occasionally: Abū Ayyūb Wā'il b. Ayyūb al-Ḥaḍramī, Abū Sufyān, Abū Bakr al-Mawṣilī, Jumayl al-Khawārizmī, Abū Saʿīd ʿAbd Allāh b. ʿAbd al-ʿAzīz and al-Rabīʿ himself.[97] They are quoted in the *Mudawwana* by Abū Ghānim Bishr b. Ghānim al-Khurāsānī (who lived between the end of the 2nd/8th century and the first decades of the 3rd/9th century) as pupils and transmitters of Abū ʿUbayda. Therefore, I would suggest that the interpolation is probably due to the hand of Abū Ghānim, who is credited with the collection *al-Dīwān al-maʿrūḍ ʿalā al-ʿulamāʾ al-ibāḍiyya*, of which the *Āthār* and the *Futyā al-Rabīʿ b. Ḥabīb* were originally part.

The personal style, "I asked him" or "He was asked"/ "He said" or "He told me", continues in the *Futyā al-Rabīʿ*, which in the manuscript follows the *Āthār*. The source (probably Abū Ghānim) was asking al-Rabīʿ directly, and occasionally other authorities: Abū 'l-Mu'arrij ʿAmr al-Sadūsī, ʿAbd Allāh b. ʿAbd al-ʿAzīz, Abū Ayyūb. The *fatwā*s are quite long and are roughly divided into 28 chapters dealing mainly with issues related to commerce, taxation, lands, slaves, marriage and repudiation, and adultery.[98] As in the *Muddawana* by Abū Ghānim al-Khurāsānī the style is that of a dialogue between a teacher (al-Rabīʿ) and his pupils and followers on everyday juridical matters. In a few words, the *Āthār* and *Futyā* are drawing on the teachings of early Basran Ibāḍī authorities. In this respect Abū ʿUbayda, who succeeded Jābir at the head of the Ibāḍī community in Basra, appears as a minor direct source recording Jābir's opinion only in few cases.

The *Āthār* and *Futyā al-Rabīʿ b. Ḥabīb* pose a problem to both the editors of the manuscripts and the scholars dealing with them, as they are respectively titled "*hādhā al-juzʿ al-awwal min āthār al-Rabīʿ ʿan Ḍumām ʿan Jābir b. Zayd*" and "*al-juzʾ al-thānī min futyā al-Rabīʿ b. Ḥabīb*". Ibāḍī sources do not mention any second part of the *Āthār* nor any first part of the *Futyā*, so we must conclude that it was a typo or a misinterpretation by the copyists of the manuscript *al-Dīwān al-maʿrūḍ*.[99]

---

97 For a short biography of Abū Ayyūb and Jumayl (or Jamīl) al-Khawārizmī, and in general of the transmitters quoted in the *Āthār*, see Kharusi (ed.) *Āthār* 137–151.

98 Ibn Khalīfa (ed.), *Futyā* 57–64.

99 There are three extant copies of *al-Dīwān al-maʿrūḍ*, two from Jerba and one from Dār al-Kutub in Cairo, which are almost identical, though there are slight differences in the order in which the various parts are copied. Kharusi (ed.) *Āthār* 5–7; Ennami, *Studies* (online edition) 83–8; Salimi, *Early Islamic Law in Kufa* (forthcoming).

However, since other parts of *al-Dīwān al-maʿrūḍ* have a similar title (first part of … second part of …), we can infer that the entire work gathers together fragmentary materials, which Abū Ghānim collected in Basra and Kufa and put together in a sort of "compendium" of early Ibāḍī law.

2.8 A Source in between: the *Aqwāl Qatāda b. Diʿāma*

Qatāda b. Diʿāma al-Sadūsī (about 60/680–117/735) was a celebrated successor, famous for his prodigious memory and his expertise in Quranic exegesis and *ḥadīth* transmission. He transmitted the *ṣaḥīfa* by Jābir b. ʿAbd Allāh, while his Quranic teachings were written down by Saʿīd b. Bashīr (d. 168/784–85). In Basra, where he spent almost all his life, he was the pupil of Ibn Sīrīn, Jābir b. Zayd and Ḥasan al-Baṣrī, whom he succeeded as the head of his teaching circle. He was associated to the Muʿtazila movement, to which he is said to have given the name, and inclined in theology to the doctrine of free will (*qadar*) which he abandoned in later life.[100] It is probably due to his close relationship with his teacher, Ḥasan al-Baṣrī, that a collection of legal traditions and opinions known as *Aqwāl Qatāda* became part of the Ibāḍī legal literature.[101]

The *Aqwāl Qatāda* has repeatedly attracted particular interest among modern scholars, as it raises questions concerning the early development of the Basran Ibāḍī community.[102]

It is a unique document because it attests to the existence of a scholarly link between Sunnis and Ibāḍīs during the early development of Islamic law. The fact that the legal responses and traditions of Qatāda are part of an Ibāḍī collection, in which the traditions of Jābir have been transmitted through ʿAmr b. Harim and ʿAmr b. Dīnār, proves that the Ibāḍī lawyers of the first generations considered Qatāda to be a faithful upholder of Jābir's doctrine. Qatāda's legal responses corresponded to those of the first Ibāḍī authorities, thereby explaining why the collator of the *Aqwāl Qatāda* (probably Abū Ghānim al-Khurāsānī) included them in an Ibāḍī manuscript. This affinity is attested by brief annotations at the foot of Qatāda's traditions and legal responses where the collator

100 Abū ʾl-Khaṭṭāb Qatāda b. Diʿāma b. Qatāda al-Sadūsī. See Pellat (1978), s.v. Ḳatāda b. Diʿāma, EI2, iv: 748; Vitestam, Qatāda b. Diʿāma as-Sadūsī et la Science du Ḥadīth, in *Actes du Ve Congrès International d'Arabisants et d'Islamisants*, Bruxelles, 1970, Publications du Centre pour l'étude des problèmes du monde musulman contemporain 489–498.

101 Madelung, Ibāḍiyya and Muʿtazila 24; al-Salimi (ed.), *Aqwāl* 25–30.

102 Francesca, The Formation and Early Development in the Ibādī *madhhab* 264; idem, Investigating Early Ibāḍī Jurisprudence 234–236; al-Salimi (ed.), *Aqwāl* 3–15.

emphasizes the fact that Qatāda's opinion coincides with those of an Ibāḍī authority (al-Rabīʿ, Abū ʿUbayda, Jābir).[103]

Abū Ghānim probably related the *Aqwāl* from al-Rabīʿ b. Ḥabīb, as proved by the expression "*wa-ḥaddathanī bi-hādhā al-Rabīʿ*", which we find on occasion in the manuscripts. This explains why the *Aqwāl* preserves also *responsa* from al-Rabīʿ (II, III, IV part) and traditions related by al-Rabīʿ from Abū ʿUbayda and Jābir (mainly in parts I and II).

The work is dived into 7 parts.

Part I: (*Aqwāl* 25–120; Ms. ff. 1–27) This contains *dicta* and *responsa* from Qatāda dedicated to the ritual purity of women and prayer.

Part II: (*Aqwāl* 121–183; Ms. ff. 27–46) This bears the title: "*al-juzʾ al-thānī min qawl Qatāda fī ʾl-zakawāt wa-qismati ʾl-ghanīma*", and begins with traditions on the raising of *zakāt* and division of the spoils; it then deals with fasting (*bāb al-ṣiyam*), the vote (*bāb al-nadhr*), atonement for having broken a vow (*bāb kaffārat al-yamīn*) and the ban on alcoholic beverages (*bāb al-ashriba*). A series of *responsa* by Qatāda follow on slaves. On p. 178 (Ms. 44_{19}) the following is written: "*bāb al-khiyār mimmā suʾila ʿanhu al-Rabīʿ min bāb al-ṭalāq*", introducing the *responsa* of al-Rabīʿ b. Ḥabīb on the right of a wife to obtain the dissolution of the marriage vow in certain cases. Finally, there are other *responsa* by Qatāda on the *kaffārat al-yamīn* and repudiation (*ṭalāq*).

Part III: (*Aqwāl* 185–255; Ms. ff. 46–67) *Responsa* by Qatāda on marriage, divorce, repudiation (*bāb al-ẓihār*), exchange (*ṣarf*), sale (*bayʿ*), *salaf* and society (*shirka*); it is followed by (p. 219; Ms. f. 56_{24}): "*mā suʾila ʿanhu Abū ʿAmr al-Rabīʿ*". Al-Rabīʿ b. Ḥabīb gives his legal opinion on prayer, purity, voting and hunting. Other *responsa* follow by Qatāda on compensation (*diya*), punishments (*ḥadd*) and heredity.

Part IV: (*Aqwāl* 257–338; Ms. ff. 67–87) In the first half, the *responsa* deal with problems relating to morals and customs, as well as the ban on alcohol, ritual butchery and hunting (in the latter two cases, Jābir b. Zayd, Abū ʿUbayda and al-Rabīʿ's opinion is referred to). *Responsa* follow on giving evidence (*shahāda*), punishment (in particular for theft, adultery and fornication), heredity and bequest (*bāb al-mīrāth wa ʾl-waṣiyya*), the contract for freeing a slave (*bāb al-kitāba*), marriage and repudiation.

Part V: (*Aqwāl* 339–395; Ms. ff. 88–105) This part includes traditions from ʿAmr b. Harim from Jābir relating to marriage and *zakāt*.

103 For example, after a responsum by Qatāda about the *ṣalāt al-khawf*, we find: "*wa hādhā qawl al-Rabīʿ ʿan Abī ʿUbayda wa-huwa qawl Jābir b. Zayd wa Ḍumām*", al-Salimi (ed.), *Aqwāl* 61 (Ms. 10_{23}).

Part VI: (*Aqwāl* 387–465; Ms. ff. 121–122) This contains traditions from ʿAmr b. Dīnār from Jābir on the subject of pilgrimage, ablutions, *salaf* (a special kind of sale involving the ordering of goods to be delivered later for a price paid immediately), and repudiation; and from ʿAmr b. Harim concerning inheritance and repudiation.

Finally, part VII (*Aqwāl* 467–494; Ms. ff. 131–140) contains tradition from Qatāda on prayer and ablution. According to an annotation of the copyist, the majority of the manuscripts include the *Kitāb al-ṣalāt* by Jābir b. Zayd from Ḥabīb b. Abī Ḥabīb al-Jarmī al-Baṣrī (d. 162/778) in this part.

As I have already mentioned, the *Aqwāl Qatāda* are a unique source in both the Sunni and Ibāḍī context, as they prove the existence of close relationships and intellectual exchanges among jurists from different schools in Basra in the 2nd/8th century. Following developments in the Ibāḍī school and the progressive radicalisation of the movement, with the resulting tendency to base legal norms solely on the authorities of the school, overshadowed hybrid sources such as the *Aqwāl Qatāda*, which therefore didn't become part of the legal Ibāḍī heritage in Oman and in the Maghrib.

2.9 The First Compendium of Ibāḍī Law: the *Mudawwana* by Abū Ghānim al-Khurāsānī

Abū Ghānim Bishr b. Ghānim al-Khurāsānī, a prominent Ibāḍī scholar and jurist from Khurāsān, lived between the second half of the 2nd/8th century and the early decades of the 3rd/9th century. Missionaries (*ḥamalat al-ʿilm*) dispatched by the *imām* Abū ʿUbayda Muslim b. Abī Karīma at the beginning of the 2nd/8th century brought Ibāḍī doctrine to Khurāsān, where they succeeded in converting to Ibadism a number of scholars, who preserved and propagated Ibāḍī doctrine. One of these scholars was Abū Ghānim, who studied under the students of Abū ʿUbayda in Basra where, towards the end of the 2nd/8th century, he composed his major work, the *Mudawwana*. Ibāḍī biographical sources pay only scant attention to Abū Ghānim, reporting that he travelled to Tahert with a copy of his work, which he offered to the second Rustumid *imām*, ʿAbd al-Wahhāb b. ʿAbd al-Raḥmān b. Rustum (168–208/784–823), for his library, the famous *al-maktaba al-maʿṣūma*, which contained other books sent to the Maghrib by the Eastern Ibāḍī communities. The library was destroyed by fire in 296/909 when Tahert fell to the Fatimid army.

According to the Ibāḍī historical sources, the *Mudawwana* has only survived thanks to a copy made by the Ibāḍī scholar Abū Ḥafṣ ʿAmrūs b. Fatḥ, who Abū Ghānim reportedly met in Jabal Nafūsa on his way to the *imām* ʿAbd al-Wahhāb. In fact, however, Abū Ḥafṣ died in 283/896, about 73 years after ʿAbd al-Wahhāb, during the battle of Mānū in which the Aghlabid army defeated the Ibāḍī Berber tribe of the Nafūsa which supported the Rustumid state. Abū Ḥafṣ ʿAmrūs probably did not make his copy of the *Mudawwana* until the middle of the 3rd/9th century, when he was appointed *qāḍī* in Jabal Nafūsa during the imamate of Yūsuf b. Muḥammad b. al-Aflaḥ (deposed *c.*281/894).[104]

The *Mudawwana* is also quoted as *Ghānimīyāt* or *Dīwān Abī Ghānim*.[105] In modern times, the famous Ibāḍī scholar Muḥammad Aṭfayyish (d. 1332/1914) produced an expanded version (*tartīb*) of the text, called *al-Mudawwana al-kubrā* to distinguish it from the original text, known as *al-Mudawwana al-ṣughrā*. The two works are identical, except for the editor's comments in the *Mudawwana al-kubrā*, which are easily identified by the expression "*wa-qāla ʾl-murattib*". Both texts were published in Oman in 1984. More recently, two updated versions of the *Mudawwana* have been published, by Ibrāhīm b. Muḥammad al-ʿAsākir and Muṣṭafā b. Sāliḥ Bājū, in 2006 and 2007, respectively.

Al-ʿAsākir's edition is based on five manuscripts, including a copy made by the well-known Omani scholar al-Nabhānī which includes two unique supplements: one known as *Kitāb Ibn ʿAbbād* (by Ibn ʿAbbād al-Miṣrī, one of Abū Ghānim's main sources) and the other entitled *Kitāb al-ribā*, by an unknown author. The three-volume edition by Muṣṭafā b. Ṣāliḥ Bājū follows the arrangement and commentaries by Aṭfayyish and is based on nine manuscripts including small fragments; it is the main source of Miklos Muranyi's book on *Mudawwana*. A manuscript called *Kitāb al-Barbariyya* preserves a Berber version of the *Mudawwana*.[106] In this book I used the 1984 and the 2006 Bājū edition of the *Mudawwana al-kubrā* (quoted as *Mudawwana*).

One of the most significant collections of works relating to early Ibāḍī authorities, a large Ibāḍī manuscript called *al-Dīwān al-maʿrūḍ ʿalā ʿulamāʾ al-Ibāḍiyya*, can also be attributed, in all probability, to Abū Ghānim. Although the compiler of the manuscript is unknown, Ennami suggested that it was put together by Abū Ghānim because many of the authorities who transmitted the texts contained in the compilation are identical to the authorities mentioned in the *Mudawwana*.[107]

104 On the *Mudawwana*, see Muranyi, *The First Compendium of Ibadi Law*.

105 Al-Barrādī, *Kitāb al-Jawāhir*, trad. Motylinski, Bibliographie du Mzab no. 12; Schacht, Bibliothèques et manuscrits abadites no. 16; Sezgin, *GAS* i:586.

106 Ms. BINA, INALCO, Paris, available online at https://bina.bulac.fr/search/results?fulltext_search=كتاب+البربرية. On the Berber version of the *Mudawwana* see Brugnatelli, The Original Format of Abū Ghānim's *Mudawwana*.

107 *Studies in Ibāḍism*, 94.

Ibāḍī scholars pay great attention to the *Mudawwana* as it gives a clear account of the development of Ibāḍī jurisprudence in its early times. The *Mudawwana* is divided into fourteen chapters:

1. *Kitāb al-ṣalāt* – 2. *Kitāb al-zakāt* – 3. *Kitāb al-ṣawm* – 4. *Kitāb al-nikāḥ* – 5. *Kitāb al-ṭalāq* – 6. *Kitāb al-buyūʿ* – 7. *Kitāb al-hiba wa ʾl-niḥla* – 8. *Kitāb al-iʿtāq* – 9. *Kitāb al-waṣāyā* – 10. *Kitāb al-shahādāt* – 11. *Kitāb al-aḥkām wa ʾl-aqḍiyya* – 12. *Kitāb al-ashriba wa-ʾl-ḥudūd* – 13. *Kitāb al-ḥudūd* – 14. *Kitāb al-diyāt*.

These books follow a dialogical scheme that is similar to that of *Āthār* and *Futyā al-Rabīʿ*: legal cases are introduced by expressions like: "*Saʾaltu Abā ʾl-Muʾarrij ʿan* [followed by a brief illustration of the problem]. *Qāla: saʾaltu ʿan dhālika Abā ʿUbayda fa-qāla* […]". If there is conflicting opinion on the question, it is followed by: "*wa-kāna al-Rabīʿ yaqūlu* […]". On other occasions, the traditions are introduced by a brief *isnād*: "*al-Rabīʿ ʿan Abī ʿUbayda*". Abū ʿUbayda's teachings are handed down by jurists who were his pupils:

1. al-Rabīʿ b. Ḥabīb
2. Abū ʾl-Muʾarrij ʿAmr al-Sadūsī
3. Abū Saʿīd ʿAbd Allāh b. ʿAbd al-ʿAzīz
4. Abū Ghassān Makhlad b. al-ʿAmarrad
5. Abū ʾl-Muhājir Hāshim b. al-Muhājir
6. Abū Ayyūb Wāʾil b. Ayyūb al-Ḥaḍramī
7. Ḥātim b. al-Manṣūr
8. Abū Sufyān Maḥbūb b. al-Ruḥayl.

They were of different origins and later settled in different places working on Ibāḍī propaganda: Abū ʾl-Muhājir Hāshim b. al-Muhājir was from Ḥaḍramawt and settled in Kufa; Abū Ayyūb Wāʾil b. Ayyūb was from Ḥaḍramawt too; Ibn ʿAbbād al-Miṣrī came from Egypt and, after completing his studies in Basra, went back to Egypt and settled there.

The *Mudawwana* mainly hands down ʿAbd Allāh and Abū ʾl-Muʾarrij's legal opinions. They supported a freer use of rational criteria (*raʾy* and *qiyās*) and personal reasoning and, along with Shuʿayb b. al-Maʿrūf, were part of a widespread dissident current within the Ibāḍiyya, called Shuʿaybiyya, which originated in Basra in the late Umayyad age when a group of young scholars among Abū ʿUbayda's disciples openly dissented from the religious and legal teaching of their master.[108] They were reprimanded and expelled from the Abū ʿUbayda's clandestine teaching circle and only reaccepted after a public repentance. After Abū ʿUbayda's death, they resumed promoting their dissident views in defiance of al-Rabīʿ b. Ḥabīb.

108 Al-Shammākhī, *Siyar* (1884) 104, 119–121.

The juridical tradition of the Nukkār in North Africa inherited from the Shuʿaybiyya much more than the legal literature of the Omani as well as the North African Wahabī Ibāḍīs. It preserved a wide range of legal opinions of ʿAbd Allāh b. ʿAbd al-ʿAzīz and Abū ʾl-Muʾarrij al-Sadūsī, though it does not include opinions by Shuʿayb.[109]

109 Madelung, *Aqwāl Qatāda* and the Shuʿaybiyya and Nukkār 25–30.

CHAPTER 3

Unveiling Ibāḍī Law in the Formative Period

3.1 Introduction

In this chapter, I provide an overview of early Ibāḍī law, together with an analysis of some case studies that are significant for reconstructing the ongoing legal debate and the peculiarities of Ibāḍī law. One of the main features that emerges in this early period, in particular during the imamates of Abū ʿUbayda and al-Rabīʿ b. Ḥabīb, is the progressive radicalisation of the Ibāḍī school. Though the sources describe Abū ʿUbayda as quietist, under his imamate the movement entered into an expansionist stage with revolts breaking out in several regions. Ibadism took the form of an intellectual religious movement distinct from the other emerging schools. This development became apparent through doctrines concerning the states of association (*walāya*) and dissociation (*barāʾa*) within the community, as well as through rules that drew a clear boundary between the community and the "others", such as the ban on marriage between an Ibāḍī woman and a non-Ibāḍī man, and the discussion on the validity of prayer performed with a non-Ibāḍī *imām*. Jābir was said to have performed the Friday prayer led by the Umayyad governor al-Ḥajjāj, but a generation later, scholars held that praying with a non-Ibāḍī *imām* was worthless and that the prayer should be offered again.

The case studies I analyze in this chapter concern, in particular, fornication and adultery, the prohibition of usury and the payment of almsgiving, which are examples of juridical matters in which the Ibāḍī jurists developed their own vision. Moreover, they are significant for reconstructing the legal debate that took place during the formative phase of Islamic law.

One of the main difficulties scholars face in reconstructing the history of early Islamic schools of law is the very uneven survival of texts by ancient authorities. In the case of the Ibāḍī school, an added difficulty is associated with the ignorance of its literary patrimony, which has become available to scholars only recently. Moreover, the extent to which we may single out early rules focusing on the surviving juridical sources remains a vexed question. Scholars shift from very optimistic stands to very critical ones. Among the first group, we can quote Harald Motzki, who allegedly reconstructed early Meccan law focusing on the *Muṣannaf* of the Yemeni ʿAbd al-Razzāq al-Ṣanʿānī (d. 211/826).[1]

1 Motzki, *Anfänge*.

 | HTTPS://DOI.ORG/10.1163/9789004765764-005

On the other hand, according to Norman Calder – to take but one example of the sceptical attitude towards ancient Islamic legal documents – the actual doctrine of early jurists is virtually irrecoverable.[2] He regards early legal writings as "organic texts", which were not fixed during the lifetime of their authors, but underwent a lengthy process of editing and compilation over generations. Such a process resulted in substantial changes in the text, as followers added new material to an extent that it is quite impossible to extract the opinion of the original author.[3]

However, taking all these circumstances and elements into account, I argue that a careful analysis of single traditions proves valid in dating early material to a degree of reasonable approximation. The ancient Ibāḍī sources I have examined so far demonstrate that a certain form of legal writing existed among the Ibāḍīs as early as the end of the 1st/7th century, in the generations of Jābir b. Zayd. Although this assumption does not prove that an "Ibāḍī" *madhhab* already existed by that time, nor that Jābir intended to build up a school of law, we cannot overlook the doctrinal indebtedness of the succeeding generations of Ibāḍī scholars to their master. Their loyalty to Jābir is consciously articulated by accepting his teachings and following the same intellectual methods. As we have seen in the previous chapter, Ibāḍīs were embedded into the intellectual *milieu* of Basra which, along with Kufa, the other garrison city in Iraq, vigorously participated into the formation process of Islamic law and theology. However, the early Ibāḍī sources do not hint at the presence of any local practice that we can label as Basran and/or Iraqi. On the contrary, in many cases –, due to Jābir's connections with Ibn ʿAbbās and other Meccan transmitters, in particular ʿIkrima and ʿAmr b. Dīnār – they favoured Hijazi authorities.[4]

The formative stage of the Ibāḍī school challenges the generally accepted assumption that the 8th century schools of law depended on a geographically based collective doctrine. Almost a century later, they turned from regional schools into personal schools, which coalesced around the authority of a scholar, whose teaching was upheld by his pupils and followers (mid-8th–9th century).[5] This notion of transformation of schools from regional to personal ones is problematic due to the scarcity of evidence substantiating the very existence of legal opinions that can be explicitly attributed to a collective

2 *Studies in Early Muslim Jurisprudence*.

3 Brockopp, *Early Mālikī Law* 67–68.

4 Motzki, *Anfänge* 178–181.

5 Schacht, *The Origins* in part. chapters 4 and 5; idem, The Schools of Law 28–84; Makdisi, *Ṭabaqāt*-Biography 371–396; Melchert, *The Formation of the Sunni Schools of Law* 32–47, idem, How Ḥanafism Came to Originate in Kufa 318–347.

regional doctrine. On the contrary, numerous circles of masters and pupils existed already at the beginning of the 8th century, constituting the core from which personal schools developed into doctrinal ones.[6]

The early Ibāḍī juristic repertoire derives from an allegiance to individual authorities. Jābir received from Ibn ʿAbbās and other scholars operating within and outside Basra and Iraq, who had in turn received from the Successors and the Companions. They constitute the individual voices on which a consensus could be based. We can label these jurists alternatively as "Basrans", "Kufans", "Meccans", "Medinans" but there is no indication that they culled their doctrine from a local anonymous legal practice, which had a degree of geographically based uniformity.[7]

Early Ibadism possessed a vast corpus of opinions attributed to Jābir, its founding father and to his immediate successors, relying on scriptural sources – mainly the Quran – and on traditions from other earlier authorities, but also on analogy and other rational methods taken from Basran Muʿtazilite circles. As is well known, Muʿtazilite rational theology had a greater impact on Ibāḍīs, and on Imami Shiʿites, than on the Sunni mainstream.[8] The struggle between whether to rely on "tradition" or on rational criteria was very sharp in the generations of Abū ʿUbayda and al-Rabīʿ, and extended well beyond disagreement over juridical problems, to include also the polemic on Quran creation and free will.

The formative period of the Ibāḍī school epitomizes the recasting of Ibāḍī/Khārijī piety into a distinctive pattern of legal rationality. The Ibāḍī moralistic conception of Islamic community had unparalleled influence on the formation of Ibāḍī law: moral ideals shaped the growth and the internal dynamics of the school, and their implementation affected Ibāḍī relations with other Muslims and contributed to the construction of their own group identity.

Early Ibāḍī juristic sources form a cogent complete *corpus* whose legal injunctions represent actual practice, rather than standardized legal arguments and cases. They provide a view of an era when legal categories were fluid and legal debates aimed at the resolution of real problems rather than at discussing matters of doctrine. Hence, they provide us with an undistorted mirror of daily life in early Islamic society.

6 Hurvitz, Schools of Law and Historical Context 37–64; Hallaq, From Regional to Personal Schools of Law? 1–26.
7 Hallaq, From Regional to Personal Schools of Law? 16.
8 Arjomand, *Sociology of Shiʿite Islam* 17–18.

3.2 Early Ibāḍī law

Towards the end of the 1st/7th century, or at the beginning of the 2nd/8th century, some of the doctrines which were to characterize Ibāḍī law began to be defined. This includes the recurrent impediment to marriage between a man and a woman who have fornicated, which is ascribed to Jābir; the principle that usury (*ribā*) does not exist in the simultaneous exchange of precious metals, and the fixation of the *niṣāb* (taxable limit) for pasturing oxen at 5 head, as it was for pasturing camels. Conversely, Sunni law applies a taxable limit of 30 head of oxen, less than 30 being *zakāt*-free. The Ibāḍīs based their theory on two traditions containing the Prophet's and ʿUmar b. al-Khaṭṭāb's instructions in this connection. I will discuss these cases in more detail below.

On the other hand, the later Ibāḍī jurists abandoned some of the teachings that the ancient Ibāḍī lawyers had sustained. In particular, this is the case of the right of the slave-owner to sell the *umm al-walad*, that is, the slave-girl who has borne her master a child. According to the oldest Ibāḍī sources, the position of the *umm al-walad* was not privileged; a number of *dicta* and *responsa* from Jābir and al-Rabīʿ insist on considering her as a slave who could be sold or otherwise alienated by her master.[9]

Slavery is a constant in human history, but Islamic normative systems devoted particular attention to the whole matter and especially to the enslaved girls and women who, being licit sexual partners for their male owners, raised a number of issues concerning sexuality, family law and ownership rights. Such issues cast light on the multifaced interaction among slavery, women's rights and the lawmaking process in Islam across the centuries. Two widely cited books, *Marriage and Slavery in Early Islam* by Kecia Ali and *Concubines and Courtesans: Women and Slavery in Islamic History*, edited by Matthew S. Gordon and Kathryn A. Hain, examine the ubiquitous presence of female slaves in medieval Muslim worlds. Slave girls and women landed in Muslim society through capture and physical transfer during the 7th century Islamic conquests, or through slave commerce, which reached its peak during the first Abbasid period (750–950). In urban households they provided labour and could become a more or less willing sexual partner to their owners according to Quran 4:24 that grants the masters access to the bodies of their female slaves. As is well known a significant number of elite children were born to concubine mothers and their free owners. During the Umayyad caliphate in particular there was a progressive shift from a negative attitude toward

9 Al-Kharusi (ed.), *Āthār* 29 no. 37, 36 no. 103 (Ms. 3_{14}, 6_{10}); Ibn Khalīfa (ed.), *Futyā* 152 (Ms. 43_{23}); Abū Ghānim, *Mudawwana* ii, 193–194.

concubine unions and their offspring towards a more lenient position. Thanks to the fundamentally egalitarian nature of Islam and the increasing number of non-Arab Muslims, Muslim society began looking at non-Arab mothers as a neutral or even positive circumstance and, by the end of the Umayyad era, Yazīd III (r. 744) was the first concubine-born caliph.[10]

Muslim jurisprudence carefully elaborated a normative framework regulating the institution of concubinage; in particular the *umm al-walad* played an important role in the development of Islamic conceptions of sexuality, household and religious authority.[11] Over centuries Muslim jurists struggled to define the *umm al-walad*'s status and her right to be manumitted upon the master's death. A vexing question concerns the right of the master to alienate his *umm al-walad*. In the first century of Islam the sale of the *umm al-walad* was considered to be valid. When the discussion on her status started, we find on one side the tendency to set her free at the death of her master – with the provision that she could not be sold before – expressed in traditions ascribed to ʿUmar, and on the other the conservative resistance to this innovation, expressed in traditions from ʿAlī.[12] Because the resistance to an improvement in the status of the *umm al-walad* happened to be expressed by ʿAlī, Shīʿa law insists on considering her a slave who could be ceded, whilst the other schools of law accepted the opposite view.[13]

According to J. Brockopp, evidence from the early Maliki practice suggests that the children of enslaved women and free men were generally freed, while the mothers were kept as slaves. Any emancipation, even at the death of the master, was considered discretionary. The tradition attesting that the Prophet freed his slave Māriyya after she gave birth to Ibrāhīm must be regarded – according to Brockopp – as an exceptional act. Conversely, by the mid-8th century, the position of the *umm al-walad* changed dramatically from that of an ordinary slave to a slave with special rights and an expectation of emancipation. Only at that time did the Maliki school start considering her a special slave who cannot be alienated from her master and who is freed, along with her children, at her master's death. It is also possible to discern an intermediate position, in which the *umm al-walad* is freed upon the death of her master only if she is still in his possession. A parallel development of the status

10 Robinson, Statistical Approaches to the Rise of Concubinage in Islam 12.

11 Gordon, Introduction 1–10. See also Mirza, Remembering the *Umm al-Walad* 297–323.

12 Schacht, *The Origins* 264–266; Motzki, *Anfänge* 88. For traditions on the sale of the *umm al-walad*, see Abū Yūsuf, *Kitāb al-āthār* no. 872; al-Shaybānī, *Muwaṭṭa'-Sh.* 282 no. 799, ʿAbd al-Razzāq, *Muṣannaf* vii, no. 13210–13211.

13 Zayd b. ʿAlī, *Musnad* 276–277; al-Nuʿmān, *Daʿāʾim al-Islām* ii, 314, no. 1192; al-Ṭūsī, *al-Istibṣār* iii (ii part), 11–12, no. 34–36.

of the *umm al-walad*'s children is harder to trace. Brockopp underlines three options among the early Malikis: first, that they are freed immediately in cases where the master declared his will to establish his children by his female slave as his heirs; second, the master could deny the paternity of his slave's children; and third, in absence of any such statement, the female slave became an *umm al-walad* and her children were freed upon her emancipation.[14]

The improvement in the *umm al-walad*'s status, as it can be depicted in early Sunni law, mirrors a parallel development within early Ibāḍī law. Early Ibāḍī texts address two specific areas of concern: the *umm al-walad*'s status and her manumission. Looking first at her status, Ibāḍī texts emphasize that she is considered to be a slave (*ama*) and, as such, the master can sell her:

> Al-Rabīʿ – Ḍumām – Abū Shaʿthāʾ [Jābir b. Zayd]: It is permitted to sell the *umm al-walad*, as well as to buy and to manumit her.[15]

Without a formal act of emancipation, the *umm al-walad* has no special status, and therefore her testimony is regarded as the testimony of a slave. If she commits a tort (*jināya*), the owner becomes liable for her as for any act of his slaves.[16] In the case that the master dies before she gives birth, she is entitled to receive maintenance (*nafaqa*) in virtue of the child she is bearing. However, if the child dies before birth, she must return the maintenance to the master's heirs, who have the right to take it or to remit it.[17]

The fact that the rights of the *umm al-walad* depended on her child can be also inferred from a further tradition attesting that the master can make a legacy (*waṣiya*) in her favour, but she loses her right to take possession of it if her child dies.[18]

The master can make any marriage arrangements for his *umm al-walad*, and he is entitled to receive her dowry (*ṣadāq*). Moreover, according to a tradition from Jābir, if the master dies before his *umm al-walad*'s husband has paid the full dowry, the remaining amount is due to his heirs.[19]

Having borne a child to her master does not imply that the *umm al-walad* is automatically freed. The ancient Ibāḍī sources equate her emancipation to

14 Brockopp, *Early Mālikī Law* 155, 192–203. See also Mattson, *A Believing Slave*.

15 Kharusi (ed.), *Āthār* 36 no. 103 (Ms. 6_{10}).

16 Al-Salimi (ed.), *Aqwāl* 247, 405; Kharusi (ed.), *Āthār* 36 no. 101 (Ms. 6_7). The tradition is transmitted with the *isnād*: al-Rabīʿ – Ḍumām – Abū Shaʿthāʾ.

17 Al-Salimi (ed.), *Aqwāl* 316.

18 Al-Kharusi (ed.), *Āthār* 39 no. 127 (Ms. 7_9).

19 Al-Kharusi (ed.), *Āthār* 36 no. 102; 37 no. 116 (Ms. 6_8; 6_{25}).

the manumission of a slave, and in cases where such act of will is issued during a mortal illness (*marḍ*), it is valid only if the sick master does not die of it.[20] This opinion expressed by Jābir b. Zayd shows some inconsistency with further traditions inferring that the *umm al-walad* has an overall right to be freed on her master death:

> Al-Rabīʿ – Ḍumām – Abū Shaʿthāʾ [Jābir b. Zayd]: [he was asked] about a man who died leaving a pregnant *umm al-walad*. He said: She is manumitted from the full estate (*min jāmiʿ al-māl*).[21]

The circumstance in which the *umm al-walad* is manumitted, that is, whether during the lifetime of her master or after his death, affects the duration of her waiting period (*ʿidda*), which is respectively three monthly periods or four lunar months and ten days. In both case the length of her waiting period is matched significantly to that required to a free divorced woman or a free widow.[22]

In contrast to the earlier Ibāḍī texts, the *Mudawwana* by Abū Ghānim al-Khurāsānī offers a more nuanced view on the status of the *umm al-walad*. Here Abū Ghānim goes against Ibn ʿAbd al-ʿAzīz on the admissibility of the sale of the *umm al-walad*, supporting the opposite opinion that once a woman has borne her master a child, she acquires the special status of *umm al-walad* and must be freed upon the death of her master. In this respect, he quotes the tradition stating that the Prophet, after his slave Māriyya bore him Ibrāhīm, said: "Her son manumitted her", meaning that she could not be regarded as a slave anymore.

The interpretation of the Prophet's statement raises some inconsistencies regarding when the *umm al-walad* must be released: upon the birth of her child or after her master's death? Ibn ʿAbd al-ʿAzīz argues that there is no agreement among the jurists about this point, and he concludes that the most appropriate way to understand the Prophet's tradition is the prevailing view among the Ibāḍīs that the *umm al-walad* is freed only upon the master's death.[23]

•••

20 Al-Kharusi (ed.), *Āthār* 38 no. 118 (Ms. 6_{29}).

21 Al-Kharusi (ed.), *Āthār* 30 no. 52 (Ms. 4_5).

22 Al-Salimi (ed.), *Aqwāl* 186, 336. On the several contending views about the *ʿidda* of the *umm al-walad*, see Spectorsky, *Sunnah* in the Responses of Isḥāq b. Rāhwayh 57–58.

23 Abū Ghānim, *Mudawwana* ii, 193–194. See also Muranyi, *The First Compendium of Ibadi Law* 78–80.

By the mid-8th century, the separation of the Ibāḍī movement from the Sunni community was clear in the tendency to set principles aimed at emphasizing their status as a group apart. In this vein, we find the ban on attending the Friday prayers in the mosque with the other faithful, as this would imply recognizing the authority of an unjust *imām*. This doctrine was expressed in the generation of Ibn ʿAbd al-ʿAzīz and Abū ʾl-Muʾarrij and became one of the reasons for the religious dispute between Abū Sufyān and Hārūn b. al-Yamān, which arose during the imamate of Muhannā b. Jayfar in Oman (226–237/841–851).[24]

A further example of the increasing strictness in the Ibāḍī *madhhab* is given by the doctrine of association (*walāya*) and dissociation (*barāʾa*), that is to say, the solidarity towards their coreligionists and the greater or lesser militant enmity towards non-Ibāḍīs or reprobate Ibāḍīs which began to form at this time. In conformity with the *barāʾa* principle, sinners could be banished and admitted again after their public repentance. On the other hand, the *walāya* principle imposed the distribution of alms (*zakāt*) only among poor Ibāḍīs who were considered true believers. Moreover, some scholars held that the poor impious Ibāḍī is entitled to *zakāt* before the upright learned non-Ibāḍī Muslim. On the question of *ʿadāla*, only an "associate" is *ʿadl* and his testimony is admissible in all cases.

The doctrine of *walāya* and *barāʾa* started to be developed during the imamate of Abū ʿUbayda. At that time, the Ibāḍīs actively debated the question of whom they would accept as a member of their community and whom to reject. They progressively abandoned the quietist behaviour of the preceding generation when they deemed it lawful to treat other Muslims as coreligionists and held it lawful to intermarry with them, inherit from them and eat the meat slaughtered by them. This quietist attitude to the other Muslims is expressed by early Ibāḍī authorities, such as ʿAbd Allāh b. Ibāḍ and Sālim b. Dhakwān, who are both credited with epistles on the Ibāḍī creed.[25]

---

24 Al-Shammākhī (1884), *Siyar* 104; Ibn Jaʿfar, *al-Jāmiʿ* ii, 401; Wilkinson, The Omani Manuscript Collection 205; idem, The early development of the Ibāḍī movement in Basra 244 note 25. The letter of Abū Sufyān to the people of Oman and to the people of Ḥaḍramawt concerning the dispute with Hārūn b. al-Yamān and Hārūn b. al-Yamān's letter to Muhannā b. Jayfar have been published in Kāshif, *al-Siyar wa ʾl-jawābāt* i, 273–336. This dispute is quoted also in the *sīra* of Abū Sufyān Maḥbūb b. al-Raḥīl addressed to the people of Ḥaḍramawt concerning the question of Hārūn b. al-Yamān, and gave rise to the question of the true *sunna* of the Basran movement. See Kāshif (ed.) *al-Siyar wa ʾl-jawābāt* i, 307; Wilkinson, Ibāḍī *Ḥadīth* 252. See al-Darjīnī, *Ṭabaqāt* ii, 273–277; al-Shammākhī, *Siyar* 102–105.

25 Crone and Zimmermann (eds.), *The Epistle of Sālim b. Dhakwān* 196–197.

On the contrary, according to a tradition related by Abū ʾl-Muʾarrij ʿAmr al-Sadūsī, Abū ʿUbayda strongly censured the case of an Ibāḍī who gave his daughter in marriage to a non-Ibāḍī man, justifying this decision by the fact that he was wealthy.[26] The doctrinal effect of this tradition is significant: the Ibāḍīs regarded forbidding wrongdoing as a matter of overriding importance for the welfare of the community and imposed unhesitating and unquestioning obedience to the principles of the movement on their members.

The *walāya* and *barāʾa* doctrine assured the growth of the movement as it was both a tool for cohesion and a means of control over its members. There is much in the Ibāḍī sources relevant to the early application of *walāya* and *barāʾa* dynamics. For example, such dynamics emerged during the controversy between Abū ʿUbayda and Ḥamza al-Kūfī on the matter of divine decree (*qadar*), the latter having accepted the thesis of Ghaylān al-Dimashqī that good comes from God while evil comes from man. First, Ḥamza al-Kūfī was invited to the house of Ḥājib al-Ṭāʾī to discuss the matter. Both Abū ʿUbayda and Ḥājib al-Ṭāʾī, who opposed the Qadarite ideas, tried to convince him to abandon this dogmatic position but, afterwards, when they heard that Ḥamza continued asserting his view, they called the members of the movement to a general meeting in which Abū ʿUbayda declared *barāʾa* from Ḥamza and his followers and expelled them from the community.[27]

3.3 Peculiarities of Ibāḍī Law

From the beginning the Ibāḍīs developed a cohesive legal system, which preserves its internal consistency even when the solutions given to the legal cases coincide (totally or partially) with those provided by the other schools of law. Ennami, who devoted a long chapter to Ibāḍī Jurisprudence, argued that:

> As the Ibāḍīs have derived their legal system from the same sources as other schools, i.e. Quran, *sunna* and *ijmāʿ*, and have used almost the same methods of juristic speculation in formulating opinions, which were not dealt with in the previous sources, the differences, which appeared between their legal system and those of other Islamic schools, were limited to *furūʿ*. The differences occurred in cases where Ibāḍīs possessed Traditions narrated by their authorities, which the other schools did not approve of and vice versa. It also resulted

26 Abū Ghānim, *Mudawwana* ii, 12.

27 Al-Darjīnī, *Ṭabaqāt* ii, 241–242; al-Shammakhī (1884) *Siyar* 85. See Ennami, *Studies* 211–212; Wilkinson, *Ibâḍism* 221–223.

> from the difference of opinion in interpreting either of the two principal sources, Quran or *sunna*.[28]

In the same chapter, Ennami provided a list of the most relevant points of difference between Ibāḍī and Sunni law.[29] These are summarized below.

3.3.1 Ablution

The most distinctive element in this regard is that Ibāḍīs refuse the permissibility under certain circumstances of the wiping of leather socks/sandals during ablution (*masḥ ʿalā ʾl-khuffayn*) instead of washing the feet. Ibāḍīs share this doctrine with the Shiʿites. Jābir b. Zaid argued, concerning this matter: "How should I wipe, while God orders us to wash the very limb [i.e. the feet]?"[30]

In the *Futyā al-Rabīʿ b. Ḥabīb* we find a tradition conveying the opinion of ʿAbd Allāh b. ʿAbd al-ʿAzīz and Abū ʾl-Muʾarrij ʿAmr al-Sadūsī on the status of the believer who wipes his shoes instead of washing his feet as part of the ablution (*wuḍūʾ*). They were inclined to not declare dissociation (*barāʾa*) from him, but rather to suspend any judgement against him:

> I asked ʿAbd Allāh [b. ʿAbd al-ʿAzīz] and ʿAmr [Abū ʾl-Muʾarrij ʿAmr al-Sadūsī] about the one who wipes over his legs [instead of washing them]. He answered: "We don't consider him as a true Muslim [i.e. an Ibāḍī]". I said: "And if he wipes over his shoes, do you dissociate from him (*yabraʾuna minhu*)?". He said: "No, we don't, because *ḥadīth* and *riwāya* relate that the Messenger of God practised the *masḥ*". I said: "But this happened before the revelation of the *sūrat al-māʾida*.[31] The revelation of the *sūrat al-māʾida* abrogated the wiping over the shoes and the Messenger of God didn't practise it anymore". He said: "ʿAmr told me that the Quran can abrogate only the Quran and it can be abrogated only by the Quran.

28 Ennami, *Studies* (online edition) 91.

29 Ennami, *Studies* (online edition) 91–98.

30 Quoted in Ennami, *Studies* (online edition) 92. See Ibn Khalfūn, *Ajwibat* 39; al-Sālimī, *Ḥāshiyat al-Jāmiʿ al-Ṣaḥīḥ* i, 177–179. The question of wiping over the shoes instead of the washing the feet as part of *wuḍūʾ* is discussed in detail by Schacht as a distinctive point of difference between the Shiʿites, who rejected it, and the Sunnis who, on the contrary, considered it as valid. Schacht, *The Origins* 263–264.

31 See Quran 5:6: "O you who have believed, when you rise to [perform] prayer, wash your faces and your forearms to the elbows and wipe over your heads and wash your feet to the ankles. And if you are in a state of *janāba* [major ritual impurity], then purify yourselves. But if you are ill or on a journey or one of you comes from the place of relieving himself or you have contacted women and do not find water, then seek clean earth and wipe over your faces and hands with it […]".

> He also told me that as the *masḥ* is not mentioned in the Quran, therefore it could not be abrogated by the *sūrat al-māʾida*. Hence, I prefer to suspend judgement (*waqafa*) concerning the one who wipes over his shoes, instead of dissociating from him (*barāʾa*), because the question is not clear".[32]

Some decades later the Ibāḍī jurists would decide to dissociate from him.

The tradition reported in the *Futyā* raises the question of the hierarchy of sources within Islamic law comparing the *sunna* of the Prophet with the normative authority of the Quran. Abū ʾl-Muʾarrij's opinion on the prohibition of the *masḥ ʿalā ʾl-khuffayn* is confirmed in the *Mudawwana* by Abū Ghānim relating his saying that Quran can be abrogated by Quran only. Therefore, any tradition supporting the practice of the *masḥ* must be considered void.[33]

3.3.2 *Adhān*

The Sunni version of the call (*adhān*) for the Morning Prayer has an added phrase which says: "Prayer is better than sleep". They recommend it as *sunna*. The Ibāḍīs and Shiʿites disagree with the Sunnis on this point; the Shiʿites went as far as calling it an innovation (*bidʿa*).[34]

3.3.3 Prayer

Regarding prayer, there are three main points of difference between Sunnis and Ibāḍīs. First, Ibāḍīs hold that only the *Sūrat al-Fātiḥa* (the Quran's opening chapter) must be recited in the first two and the second two *rakʿa*s of the *ẓuhr* and *ʿaṣr* (midday and afternoon) prayers, which are considered "silent" prayers. This assumption is based on an analogy with the silent parts of other prayers, such as the third *rakʿa* of the *maghrib* (sunset) prayer and the second *rakʿa* of the *ʿishāʾ* (night) prayer, where only the *Fātiḥa* is recited. This opinion is ascribed to Jābir b. Zaid.

Second, with respect to the prayer when travelling (*ṣalāt al-safar*), the Ibāḍīs consider its shortening (*qaṣr*) during a journey of at least two *farsakhs* (about six miles) to be compulsory (*farḍ*). The Hanafites also dictate that prayers should be abbreviated during a trip, but most of them maintain that the shortening applies for a distance of at least three days' travel. They ascribe

---

32 Ibn Khalīfa (ed.), *Futyā* 135–137 (Ms. 40_{14}).

33 Abū Ghānim, *Mudawwana* i, 24. See also Muranyi, *The First Compendium of Ibadi Law* 103.

34 Modarresi, Common Ibāḍī/Shīʿite Legacy: Examples from the Ritual Law 111–112; Rubinacci, L'aḏān presso gl'Ibāḍiti 279–290.

the opinion to Abū Ḥanīfa and Ibn Masʿūd. On the contrary, the Malikis hold that abbreviated prayers are not mandatory but a matter of personal choice or practice (*sunna*). Moreover, the Ibāḍīs allow the traveller to perform the *ṣalāt al-safar* even in case of a long stay in the place to which he journeyed, unless he adopted it as a homeland or, according to Abū ʿUbayda, he owns a house in it. They base their opinion on traditions reporting that Ibn ʿUmar sojourned in Azerbaijan for six or seven months performing abbreviated prayers.[35]

Conversely, Sunnis allow the shortening of the prayer only for sojourns of less than four days (Malikis and Shafiʿis) or fifteen days (Abū Ḥanīfa and Sufyān al-Thawrī).

Finally, Ibāḍīs reject the practice of *qunūt* during the ritual prayers, which both Sunnis and Shiʿites consider as valid. Ibāḍīs base their opinion on traditions ascribed to Jābir b. Zayd who considered *qunūt* an innovation.[36]

As is well known, the interpretation of the term *qunūt* is controversial: literally, it means being obedient or the act of standing and it is connected with a supplication made while standing during the morning and evening prayers, as well as during the *witr* prayer (Night Prayer).[37] It is also interpreted as "cursing" God's enemies. According to some traditions, the Prophet Muḥammad appealed to God during the Morning Prayer (*ṣalāt al-ṣubḥ*) for a month against the tribes of Riʿl and Dhakwān, as they were accused of slaying a group of *qurrāʾ* (Quranic reciters) at a place called Biʾr Maʿūna.[38]

In the early Ibāḍī sources we find both interpretations of the word "*qunūt*". The episode of the murder of the *qurrāʾ* is referred to in the *Aqwāl Qatāda*. A tradition transmitted by Qatāda on the authority of Anas b. Mālik relates that the Prophet sent seventy Quranic reciters from the Anṣār to the tribes of Banū Ḥayān, who had converted to Islam, to bring them the Word of God, but they were all killed at Biʾr Maʿūna. When the news reached the Prophet, he recited the *qunūt* in the *ṣalāt al-ṣubḥ*. This was the only case of the Prophet practising

35 Ennami, *Studies* (online edition) 93–94; Abū Ghānim, *Mudawwana* i, 172–176.

36 Al-Kharusi (ed.), *Āthār* 15–16; Abū Ghānim, *Mudawwana* i, 109.

37 *Witr* is a night prayer performed after *ʿishāʾ* or before *fajr* (dawn prayer). Al-Tirmidhī (*al-Jāmiʿ al-Ṣaḥīḥ* ii, *abwāb al-witr*, bāb 10) provides a formula for the *qunūt al-witr*: "O Allah, lead me amongst those whom Thou guidest, and pardon me among those for whom Thou pardonest, and care for me among those for whom Thou caresst". Quoted in Wensinck, Ḳunūt, EI2, v 395.

38 Wensinck, Ḳunūt, v, 395. Ennami translates *qunūt* as "the imprecation against political enemies during the ritual prayers" (*Studies* – online edition – 93), but Hoffman argues that it means blessing, see Hoffman, *Essential of Ibadi Islam*, 43. On *qunūt* see Bashear, *Qunūt* in *Tafsīr* and *Ḥadīth* Literature 36–65.

qunūt. In a further tradition, transmitted again by Qatāda on the authority of Anas b. Mālik, *qunūt* is understood as "standing" during the prayer.[39]

3.3.4 Fasting

As far as fasting is concerned, Ibāḍīs differ from the Sunnis in that they require the believer to be in the condition of major ritual purity to perform fasting as for praying. They rely on traditions reported from Abū Hurayra and al-Faḍl b. ʿAbbās that the Prophet said, "Who gets up in the morning in the state of major ritual impurity has broken his fasting".[40]

Moreover, Ibāḍīs consider that grave sins impact on fasting causing its breaking. They infer this opinion from the tradition of the Prophet stating that calumny breaks both fasting and minor ritual ablution (*wuḍūʾ*). Based on an analogical reasoning (*qiyās*), they held that lies, perjury and similar sins break the fast as well. Finally, Ibāḍīs maintain that compensatory fasting days, e.g. the fasting days needed to recover those not fasted in Ramaḍān, must be kept successively. On the contrary, the Sunnis state that the believer is free to perform the compensatory fasting days in succession or not.

3.3.5 *Zakāt*

Concerning *zakāt*, Ibāḍīs state that the *niṣāb* (taxable limit) for cows or bulls is five head, as it is for camels, in spite of 30 head as established by the other schools of law. Moreover, they distribute the *zakāt* funds to needed people who are in the state of association (*walāya*) that means mainly to the poor pious Ibāḍīs.

3.3.6 Adultery and Fornication (*zinā*)

In the case of pre-marital or extramarital intercourse, Ibāḍīs affirm that such a relation constitutes a permanent impediment to a subsequent marriage between the guilty partners.

I will deal with both *zakāt* and *zinā* in more details in the next paragraphs.

---

39 Al-Salimi (ed.), *Aqwāl* 77–78; 80. On the early Ibāḍīs authorities rejecting *qunūt* as an innovation (*bidʿa*) and on the meaning of the words, see Muranyi, *The First Compendium of Ibadi Law* 72–73.

40 Ennami, *Studies* (online edition) 95; Muranyi, *The First Compendium of Ibadi Law* 33.

3.3.7 Inheritance

In the field of inheritance law, Ibāḍīs opposed the doctrine claiming that the manumitter took the estate of his freedman who died without heirs. In contrast, according to the other schools of law, in this situation, the manumitter was his heir; if he was not alive, his relatives had a claim on the freedman's estate, and if also the latter could not be found, the public treasury (*bayt al-māl*) took the freedman's property.[41] The Ibāḍīs held that only the freedman's kinfolk (*qawn*) had a claim on his estate, and not his patron. The Ibāḍī doctrine of the lack of a hereditary title between the slave-owner and the freed slave dates back to Jābir b. Zayd and it based on a tradition from ʿAbd Allāh b. ʿUmar, who refused to inherit from his manumitted slave who died without heirs, preserved in the *Aqwāl Qatāda*:

> ʿAmr (b. Harim) said: Jābir b. Zayd was asked about a man who had manumitted a slave who died without leaving, as far as known, a son or a relative from the female line (*dhū raḥim*). Does the master (*mawlā*) who manumitted him inherit? [Jābir] said: No, except if he [e.g. the manumitted slave] bequeathed in his favour part of his property and even all his property. This is allowed. But if he died without legitimate heir and he did not leave any bequest in favour of the master or of someone else, his property must be given as alms. He said: They claimed that a manumitted slave of ʿAbd Allāh b. ʿUmar b. al-Khaṭṭāb died leaving 10,000 *dirham*. Ibn ʿUmar asked if he had a son or a relative from the male line (*dhū qarāba*) as far as known, or if there was a Muslim among the people of his village (*min ahl qariyatihi*). But they did not find any relative from the male or from the female line, nor someone of those was asked about. Ibn ʿUmar found it reprehensible (*karaha*) to inherit from him, therefore he bought with his money slaves and freed them saying to each of them: This is God's slave, this is God's property.[42]

The later Ibāḍī jurisprudence further developed Jābir's doctrine, providing that the inheritance of a manumitted slave belongs to the people of his same stock/race (*jins*), if he does not leave any heirs. If one cannot prove that he belongs to a certain stock, his inheritance must be given as alms.[43]

---

41 On the inheritance of the *mawlā* who dies with no heirs, see Crone, *Roman, Provincial and Islamic Law* 36–37; Mitter, Unconditional Manumission of Slaves 119.

42 Al-Salimi (ed.), *Aqwāl* 444–445. Jābir provides a similar *responsum* in his letter addressed to ʿAbd al-Malik b. al-Muhallab. Al-Jaʿbīrī (ed.) *Rasāʾil*, 153–154 no 216 (Ms. 90A$_{2-8}$).

43 Al-Bisiyānī, *Mukhtaṣar*, 157; Aṭfayyish, *Sharḥ Kitāb al-Nīl* viii, 392f.; Sachau, Mohammedanisches Erbrecht 181. For a full discussion of the inheritance of a manumitted slave according to Ibāḍī law, see Cilardo, *Teorie* 211 and *Diritto ereditario islamico* 475–476. See

3.3.8 Penal Law

A central feature that characterizes Ibāḍī penal law is the assumption that *ḥudūd* punishments (with the exception of the death penalty, excluding stoning) could not be imposed during the state of secrecy (*kitmān*), when weakness forced Ibāḍīs to live under the rule of their opponents concealing their true belief. Embedded in this view is the assumption that living in secrecy the Ibāḍī community could not elect an *imām al-ẓuhūr*, an *imām* with full authority who only had the right to administer *ḥudūd* punishments.

A further peculiarity to be mentioned here is that Ibāḍīs established fixed sums to be paid for minor injuries, whereas the other schools of law left such cases to the decision of the arbiter. Moreover, in case of retaliation (*qiṣāṣ*), Ibāḍīs sustained that if a man should be killed in retaliation of a woman, the *walī* of the latter should pay back half of the blood money to the relatives of the man. The Twelver Shiʿites sustain the same doctrine.

As Ennami argued, apart from the abovementioned examples, Ibāḍī law shows commonalities with one or another of the Sunni schools. In some points, it resonates with Shiʿite law, but also in this case there are fundamental features of disagreement. In particular, concerning *mutʿa* marriage (temporary marriage), Ibāḍīs concur with both Sunnis and Zaydīs in prohibiting it, while the Imami Shiʿites consider it lawful.[44]

Further research on Ibāḍī law will depict more instances of commonality and disagreement between the Ibāḍī and the other Islamic schools, thus shedding light on the general development of Islamic law.

A closer analysis of some legal cases, which I present in the following paragraphs, will help in mapping out more clearly the early development of Ibāḍī law. Moreover, I want to stress the paramount importance of carrying out further research on Ibāḍī law, focused both on the texts that have been published so far and on still unexplored manuscript collections.

The case of *zināʾ* as permanent impediment to a subsequent marriage between the culprits, which I will analyze in detail, is useful to scrutinize the differences between the Quran's teachings and the earliest legal sources. It also provides us with useful insights into the role of outside influences on early Islamic jurisprudence.

The early Ibāḍī debate on the application of *ribā* sheds light on one of the most problematic parts of Islamic law. According to Hiroyuki Hanagihashi, the prohibition of excess *ribā* (*ribā al-faḍl*) in gold-for-gold, silver-for-silver

---

also Crone, *Roman Provincial and Islamic Law* 36–37; Francesca, La fabbricazione degli *isnād* nella scuola ibāḍita 43–44.

44 Ennami, *Studies* (online edition) 97.

exchanges arose as a consequence of Umayyad monetary reform. In the 70s/690s, the Umayyad Caliphate issued their own coins, which they exchanged at face value in return for the older, heavier coin, without taking into consideration the difference in weight. Moreover, they collected a commission for the minting in the exchanges of the new coins in return for bullion and spurious coins. Iraqi jurists seem to have welcomed the Ummayad monetary policies, while Medinans were strongly opposed. Traditions both in favour of and against unequal exchanges of precious metals were put into circulation. The latter came to be generally accepted and represented the prohibition of excess *ribā* as understood by the later jurists.[45]

Finally, the case of the *zakāt* law provides an excellent opportunity for analyzing the role of Abū ʿUbayda in political activism and in developing early Ibāḍī law. It is also an attempt to assess the relationship between Eastern and Western Ibāḍī communities.

3.4 Ibāḍī Family Law: Adultery and Fornication

Family law is a locus of investigation of crucial importance within Islamic law, as well as within other legal systems, providing insights into wider structures of social organization, and into the way communities constructed their own identities. Islam promoted new attitudes towards sexuality and the household, which spread throughout the Muslim world, also influencing Middle Eastern Christian communities.[46] The Islamic conception of marriage and the household recognized the overall contours of the structure of the family in pre-Islamic Arabian Peninsula; however, it introduced a number of radical changes in order to secure the stability of the institution of marriage and strengthen women's and children's rights. New sexual and reproductive mandates emerged in the Quran, creating a social order based on marriage, which, along with concubinage, became the only permitted framework for male and female sexuality. Islam defined a gender-based division of roles in marriage and sex relations, identifying women with passivity and men with activity. In fact, only men could exercise the right of "ownership" (*milk*) in marriage and concubinage. Men were the ones who married (*nakaḥa*) women and who took concubines (*milk yamīn*). The exclusive control held by men over marital ties is synthetized in the concept of men being "in charge of" (*qawwāmūn ʿalā*) women expressed in Q. 4:34. Based on this Quranic verse, Muslim jurists

45 Yanagihashi, *A History of the Early Islamic Law of Property* 294–297.

46 Weitz, *Between Christ and Caliph* 8–9.

emphasized women's subalternity in family law and their incapability to exercise control over a sexual relationship.[47] Polygamy, concubinage, the husband's right to physical chastisement against insolent wives, and to disband the marriage contract at will represented further elements of gender inequality in marriage. Such privileges, symbolizing patriarchal authority, were only partially mitigated by the *qāḍī*s jurisdictions acting to protect women's rights within the marriage.

Early Muslim sources abound with traditions and judgements concerning marriage and repudiation, which provide a crucial vantage point from which to view how early scholars confronted with the wide range of questions and problems arising from the effort of regulating sexuality and family life according to the Islamic principles.

Without going into detail, it suffices here to say that the cases concerning marriage discussed in early Ibāḍī sources resemble those preserved in the Sunni ones.[48] Marriage was a contract established by mutual agreement and with the intention of founding a stable family; hence, the consent of both parties was the main pillar of its conclusion. Any free male in his majority and of sound mind had an overall control over his marriage, whereas a free female not only should be assisted by her guardian (*walī*), but also the way of expressing her consent varied. Silence was a valid expression of consent for a virgin girl (*bikr*), while a woman who had attained puberty and discretion ("who possessed her own affairs", *malakat amraha*), and the one who was *thayyiba* (no virgin) had to express her consent verbally.[49]

According to a tradition by Abū 'l-Mu'arrij, preserved in the *Mudawwana* by Abū Ghānim al-Khurāsānī, a father could marry off his daughter (the source does not specify if she is a virgin or not) without asking her permission with the caveat that it should be a suitable match. But, in the case that the daughter didn't agree upon the arranged marriage, Ibn ʿAbd al-ʿAzīz, Abū Ghassān and other early Ibāḍī authorities accorded her the right to ask for an annulment (*fiskh*).[50]

47 Ali, *Marriage and Slavery in Early Islam* 176–184.

48 Abū Ghānim, *Mudawwana* ii, 3–16 (see also idem, *al-Mudawwana al-ṣughrā* ii, 271–278). On marriage in early Ibāḍī law, see Kondo, The Development of Ibāḍī Jurisprudence in Oman 81–91.

49 Abū Ghānim, *Mudawwana* ii, 15. On woman's capacity/incapacity to contract a marriage by herself, see Yanagihashi, *Studies in Legal Hadith* chap. 5 "Marriage and Guardianship", 262–338. On prepubescent marriage and compulsion, see Baugh, *Minor Marriage in Early Islamic Law*.

50 Abū Ghānim, *Mudawwana* ii, 8–9.

An important element of the marriage contract was the nuptial gift (*mahr*), usually paid in cash, and divided into an advance and a deferred portion. The marriage contract, which testified to the validity of a marriage, recorded the dowry pledged by the groom. In cases where the parties agreed upon a certain dowry keeping it secret, and then the marriage was contracted on the basis of a different dowry, whose amount was attested only by witnesses, Ibn ʿAbd al-ʿAzīz held that the first *mahr* was valid, though the prevailing doctrine within the school, based on al-Rabīʿ's view, considered valid the second one.[51] Ibāḍī marriage law presents two main elements of distinctiveness in comparison to Sunni law, concerning on one hand the prohibition on an Ibāḍī woman marrying a non-Ibāḍī Muslim man and on the other hand the permanent impediment to marriage for people who have committed *zinā*. Both rules are connected with the idea of a moral impurity that is transmitted to a sexual partner carnally and to offspring genealogically.

Early Ibāḍī jurists put barriers to unions involving a woman of their own faith (*muslima*) and a non-Ibāḍī Muslim man (*rajul min qawminā min al-munāfiqīn*). Abū 'l Muʾarrij considered such a marriage reprehensible (*makrūh*) and advised Ibāḍī men not to allow their daughters or sisters to marry outside the community. He narrated that Abū ʿUbayda got extremely angry and left the meeting to calm down, after hearing than an Ibāḍī man married off his daughter to a rich non-Ibāḍī man because of his wealth.[52] The episode meant that Ibadism was one of the criteria to assert suitability or equality (*kafāʾa*) of a bridegroom. This discourse was gendered: early Ibāḍī authorities specified that Ibāḍī women should not marry across religious boundaries. As for men, marriages with Christian or Jewish women were permitted, although discouraged. In the *Kitāb al-Nikāḥ* attributed to Jābir b. Zayd, several traditions report that the caliph ʿUmar b. al-Khaṭṭāb discouraged such unions and required their dissolution unless the woman converted to Islam.[53] In the *Mudawwana* by Abū Ghānim, Abū ʿUbayda narrates that the caliph ʿUmar b. al-Khaṭṭāb called upon Ḥudhayfa b. al-Yamānī (d. 656), one of the Prophet's companion, to divorce the Christian woman he had married at Seleucia-Ctesiphon (al-Madāʾin), on the basis that such interfaith mingling was not in line with his superior status as *ṣāḥib Rasūl Allah*.[54]

51 Abū Ghānim, *Mudawwana* ii, 15 (see also idem, *al-Mudawwana al-ṣughrā* ii, 271).

52 Abū Ghānim, *Mudawwana* ii, 12–13. See also, Kondo, The Development of Ibāḍī Jurisprudence in Oman 82–83, 85.

53 Al-Salimi (ed.), *Early Islamic Law in Ḥadīth Texts from Basra* 130–132.

54 Abū Ghānim, *Mudawwana*, ii, 13.

Significantly, Abū 'l-Mu'arrij did not understand the episode to prohibit marriages with Christian or Jewish women, but as a precedent for restricting Ibāḍī women's potential husbands to those within the Ibāḍī community. In fact, in a mixed marriage, the principle of the superiority of the male gender came into conflict with another hierarchy setting the purity of Ibāḍī faith above any other faith. Marrying a non-Ibāḍī Muslim, the Ibāḍī woman was subject to a man of another faith, thus being irreconcilable with her "superior status" as member of a "chosen" community. According to the same reasoning, the offspring of an Ibāḍī woman would inherit the "inferior" faith of their father.

These rules mirror the standard assumption, characteristic of patriarchal societies, that only the husband/father defines the religious identity of his family. For a man an interfaith marriage means to bring this woman into his community. But, if a woman marries outside the community's boundaries, both her reproductive power and her material property are siphoned away from her original group in favour of a foreign one. Essentially any legal system has the necessity to formulate norms concerning intermarriages as part of the process of self-definition of the group subjected to its rule, because such norms have consequences for procreation, and they work to manage and ensure the survivance of the group itself across time. Sexual boundaries constitute an important parameter in order to measure the degree of interaction between groups. According to a similar logic, different ideas about purity led to different views on intermarriage.[55]

In medieval Islam marriage was first and foremost an alliance between two households, which implied also the transfer of property through the dowry paid by the groom to the bride as well as through inheritances and donations. Islamic law encoded a patrilineal social organization built upon patriarchal families organized around securing female material and reproductive potential. The community aimed at controlling its women and their offspring. The religion of children was that of the father, so it became a delicate issue in case of mixed marriages, and one of the main points that brought the Muslim jurists to maintain a consistent theological principle of opposition to these forms of interreligious contact.

Among the Ibāḍīs the issue of mixed unions played a much more important part than among the Sunnis, due to the fear that intermarriage could be a tool of their assimilation as a minority group into the majority.

---

55 On the mechanisms of controlling intermarriage in late antiquity and early Islam, see Weitz, *Between Christ and Caliph* 203–219; Zorgati, *Pluralism in the Middle Ages* in part. 171–178.

Legal discourse prohibiting intermarriage among Ibāḍī women and non-Ibāḍī Muslim men may be understood as a boundary-maintaining mechanism, aiming to define who belonged to the community and who was excluded from it. As is well known, according to Islamic law, Muslim women were not allowed to marry outside their faith, but this "religious endogamy" became absolute for the Ibāḍī women who were discouraged from marrying outside their community. Clear-cut boundaries aimed at upholding the exclusiveness of Ibadism in its early days, along with other key markers of Ibāḍī identity, such as the *walāya/barā'a* dynamic, which were also important elements in the subjective self-understanding as a group distinct from the "others". Two main elements concurred in defining an Ibāḍī identity: the idea of moral-religious purity and a genealogical one. The emphasis on genealogical purity defined the degree to which the community boundaries were impermeable to external influences.[56] This emphasis on purity emerged even more clearly in the Ibāḍī legal discourse on adultery and fornication, as we shall see in the following paragraphs.

3.4.1 Adultery in the Early Ibāḍī Sources

Chastity, and in particular women's chastity, emerged in the Quran as a fundamental virtue, which guarantees the legitimacy of the lineage (*nasab*). There is a clear ban in the Quran concerning sexual relations with a married woman, as she is deemed inviolable to any man other than her husband: "And [also forbidden to you are] married women, except what your right [hands] own" (4:24).

The Quran shows an increasing severity in punishing fornication and adultery, both of which are referred to by the noun *zinā'*. Verse 4:15 commands that women who commit unlawful sexual intercourse (*fāḥisha*), which can be either adultery or fornication, attested by four witnesses, must be confined in their home "until death takes them or God makes a way for [dealing with] them". The following verse (4:16) prescribes an unspecified punishment or deterrent (*adhā*) to prevent the culprits from committing illegal sexual intercourse.[57] Both the adulteress [and the fornicatress] and her partner are guilty, but if they repent and correct themselves, the Quran orders to "let them be" (4:16), in particular if they erred due to "ignorance, [and] then turn [in repentance] soon after" (4:17).

56 Purity and impurity, holiness and profaneness are powerful, value-laden terms used to construct identities. On similar mechanisms among Jewish communities, see Hayes, *Gentile Impurities and Jewish Identities*.

57 Berjak, Injury 299.

Most interpreters maintain that detention in the home as punishment for *zinā*, as laid down by Q. 4:15, was abrogated by Q. 24:2, which stipulates that culprits must be punished with one-hundred lashes if witnessed by four competent men (24:4). Jurists who do not admit the existence of abrogation in the Quran maintain that verses 4:15–16 refer to homosexuality.

The flogging is to be administered in public, and spectators cannot show any compassion. If the offender is a female slave, her punishment will be half that of a free woman (Q. 4:25). The repudiated wife, who commits adultery during the waiting period (*ʿidda*), will be turned out of her home where she would otherwise be entitled to remain for three months (Q. 65:1).[58]

The false accusation of adultery/fornication (*qadhf*) is categorized as a Quranic offence as well, and thus those who accuse others of having committed *zinā* without providing sufficient evidence for their claim are punished with 80 lashes (Q. 24:4). This provision, along with the need to present four witnesses who can testify to the act of penetration, partially neutralizes the penalty for adultery/fornication, as the evidence required seems to be prohibitive. As a result, *ḥadd* punishment for *zinā* proves to be almost inapplicable.

Despite the fact that the Quran provides quite mild penalties for the culprits and makes them difficult to apply, jurists and interpreters normally understand Q. 24:2 as referring to non-*muḥsan*, i.e. non-married individuals, only. Conversely, for the *muḥsan* (married) adulterers they enforce the death penalty by stoning (*rajm*) which is not mentioned in the Quran, though it is attested in the earliest Islamic legal corpora. According to al-Ṭabarī, not only does Q. 24:2 abrogate verse 4:15, but the "way" mentioned in Q. 4:15 is flogging and banishment for the fornicators and stoning for the adulterers, "because of the validity of the report that the Messenger of Allah (ṣ) stoned and did not flog". Al-Ṭabarī's shift towards the enforcement of stoning is meant to endorse this form of punishment as part of God's revelation. According to Pavlovitch it is also indicative of the fact that the dispute regarding the appropriate penalty for *zinā* still persisted well into the third quarter of the 3rd/9th century.[59]

Due to the lack of scriptural reference, the legitimacy of stoning as punishment (*rajm*) remains highly debated in Islamic law. In the 2nd/8th and 3rd/9th century, Muslim scholars still engaged in lengthy discussions about the exact conditions for its imposition, developing several arguments supporting its enforcement. The main arguments advocated the sunnaic provenance of the penalty, thus posing the sensitive question about the exact relationship

58 Abu Zahra, Adultery and Fornication, EQ i, 28–29; Peters, Zinā, EI2.

59 *Tafsīr al-Ṭabarī* vi, 494–496, quoted in Pavlovitch, The Islamic Penalty for Adultery 482–483.

between *sunna* and Quran within the framework of the evolving concept of abrogation (*naskh*).[60]

Commenting on Q. 24:2, the Ibāḍī Omani jurist Abū 'l-Ḥawārī (3rd/9th century), who authored a *Tafsīr* of the verses dealing with legal matters, states that the verse abrogates the previous verse, 4:17, as the other "way" mentioned in this verse refers to the subsequent revelation of verse 24:2, which imposes one hundred lashes to be administered to both the man and woman who have been found guilty of committing fornication or adultery. Though the verse mentions flogging irrespective of the marital status of both culprits, Abū 'l-Ḥawārī supports the prevailing view among Muslim jurists differentiating between married (*muḥsan, thayyib*) adulterers, who deserve lapidation, and unmarried adulterers (*bikr*), who must be flogged. He quotes a widespread tradition stating that ʿAlī flogged in accordance with the Book of God and lapidated in accordance with the *sunna* of the Prophet.[61]

Punishment by stoning is clearly attested in the early Ibāḍī sources. These grapple with the hotly debated issue of the relationship between the *sunna* and the Quran with respect to abrogation, by discussing whether the *muḥsan* must be first flogged and then stoned. The proponents of this view relied on a narration from ʿAlī, which states that he flogged the culprit on Thursday following the Quran and stoned him/her on Friday following the *sunna* of the Prophet. Abu 'l -Mu'arrij and Ibn ʿAbd al-ʿAziz support the opposite opinion, which prevailed within the school, rejecting any double punishments: only stoning should be imposed on the *muḥsan* adulterer, while the non-*muḥsan* fornicator, punished with one-hundred lashes, should not be sent into exile as additional punishment. These jurists ascribe this opinion to the earlier Ibāḍī authorities: Jābir b. Zayd, Abū ʿUbayda, al-Rabīʿ b. Ḥabīb, Wā'il b. Ayyb and Maḥbūb b. al-Ruḥayl.[62]

Ibāḍī sources also discuss the question of whether the status of *muḥsan* (and thus the punishment of stoning) should apply to a man married to a Christian or Jewish woman or to a female slave. According to Abū 'l-Mu'arrij, Abū ʿUbayda and Jābir supported the opinion that it should; the opposite view,

60 Pavlovitch, The Stoning of a Pregnant Adulteress 1–62; idem, The Islamic Penalty for Adultery 473–497; Kara, *Integrity of the Qur'an*, part ii (Searching for the stoning penalty in the Book of God) 77–170.

61 Abū 'l-Ḥawārī, *al-Dirāya* 127–129, 132, 145. Lapidation is also attested in al-Salimi (ed.), *Aqwāl* 374–375 and in Abū Ghānim, *Mudawwana* ii, 278–279.

62 Abū Ghānim, *Mudawwana* ii, 279. See also al-Salimi (ed.), *Aqwāl* 251. On the question of double punishment for *zinā* see Pavlovitch, The Islamic Penalty for Adultery 492–496.

ascribed to the followers of Ibrāhīm al-Nakhaʿī (the Kufans), is held by Abū ʾl-Ḥawārī.[63]

Early Ibāḍīs offer a coherent legal reconstruction of the rules concerning witnesses in case of adultery, and discuss them at length. In particular, they underline that, when one or more eyewitnesses retract or cannot confirm that the act of penetration took place, the ones who thus "falsely" accused the woman are guilty of defamation (*qadhf*) and must be punished with eighty lashes, while the accusation of *zinā* is dropped. In the same vein, when one of the four witnesses happens to be the husband of the adulteress, his testimony is void due to the conflict of interest. Consequently, also the wife may not act as witness against her adulterous husband.

According to a tradition attributed to Jābir b. Zayd, reported in the *Āthār al-Rabīʿ b. Ḥabīb,* the Quranic punishment of eighty lashes for the false accusation of *zinā* is not applicable to a free man who falsely accuses a female slave, even if she is married to a free man. Conversely the Kufans (probably early Hanafite jurists) differentiate between female slaves who are known for their righteousness and those who are not, and they maintain that if false accusations are moved against the former, the accuser must be imprisoned if he comes from a prominent family (*in kāna min ahl al-muruwwa*), or beaten if he is an individual of humble origins.[64] According to a tradition preserved in the *Muṣannaf* by ʿAbd al-Razzāq, Ibn ʿUmar may have held a similar opinion. Yet there is also a third opinion attributed to Ibn ʿUmar and ʿUmar b. ʿAbd al-ʿAzīz, stating that the accuser should be punished with eighty lashes exactly as if he had accused a free woman.[65]

If a husband or wife confesses to their spouse that he/she has committed adultery and then claims that it was a joke, the statement has no effect on the marriage. However, if the wife witnesses her husband committing adultery, she may dissolve the marriage (even if she does not produce the four witnesses required for the accusation of *zinā*). This was al-Rabīʿ's opinion. A similar case is discussed in Jābir's letter addressed to ʿUthmān b. Yasār, in which Jābir states that if the wife sees her husband committing adultery, it is reprehensible for her to remain in the marriage.[66]

---

63 Abū Ghānim, *Mudawwana* ii, 272; Abū ʾl-Ḥawārī, *al-Dirāya* 131.

64 Al-Kharusi (ed.), *Āthār* 38 no. 117 (Ms. 6_{25}); see also Ib. 47 no. 192 (Ms. 10_{24}) on the false accusation against the slave *Umm al-walad.*

65 Al-Kharusi (ed.), *Āthār* 93–94 (comment to no. 117); ʿAbd al-Razzāq, *Muṣannaf* vii, 439 no. 13800.

66 Ibn Khalīfa (ed.), *Futyā* 175 (Ms. 49_{1-6}); al-Jaʿbīrī (ed.), *Rasāʾil* 80.

Ibāḍī jurists are aware that the Quranic teachings make it practically impossible to prove adultery. They therefore offer ample scope to the casuistic concerning *liʿān* (mutual cursing) that takes place in cases where the husband accuses his spouse of adultery but lacks the corroborating witnesses to prove his allegations, while the wife denies their validity. In such cases, *liʿān* is suggested in order to bring about separation and eventually deny the paternity of the child borne by the wife. The husband is required to swear four times that he is telling the truth, and in a fifth oath to invoke God's curse on himself if he is lying. The wife can defend herself from the accusation by undertaking a solemn oath that her husband is telling a lie and invoke God's anger on herself if her husband is telling the truth (Q. 24:6–10). Ibāḍī sources provide us with a glimpse into the multifaceted casuistic deriving from the *liʿān* procedure. For example, if the procedure is interrupted by the death of one of the partners, Jābir's opinion is that both husband and wife are entitled to inherit from one another.[67]

Liʿān can also be a process of contesting the paternity of a child, but only if a husband has never recognized the child as his own offspring. On the contrary, according to Jābir, if the father accepted the paternity, even for a moment, he can no longer employ *liʿān*. *Liʿān* is annulled also if the procedure is interrupted by the death of the husband.[68]

In cases where the husband withdraws his false accusation of unchastity (*kadhdhaba nafsuhu*) against his wife before the waiting period (*ʿidda*) has elapsed, Jābir argues that he cannot restore the marital ties with his wife anymore, as the marriage is deemed definitively dissolved, but the paternity of the child is his. Conversely, according to the Kufans, he is allowed to resume the marital relationship after undergoing the *ḥadd* punishment for the false accusation of adultery.[69]

As we have seen so far, control over sexuality (particularly female sexuality) involved the question of purity and impurity and set clear boundaries for the sense of belonging to the Ibāḍī community. Let us now turn to another

---

67 Al-Kharusi (ed.), *Āthār* 24 no. 1 (Ms. 1_1) and 74 (comment to no. 1). See also al-Salimi (ed.), *Aqwāl* 374–375; ʿAbd al-Razzāq, *Muṣannaf* vii, 107–109.

68 Al-Kharusi (ed.), *Āthār* 51 no. 220; 53 no. 231, 233 (Ms. 12).

69 Al-Kharusi (ed.), *Āthār* 47 no. 193 (Ms. 10_{25}); 51 no. 216 (Ms. 12_9). The majority of Ibāḍī scholars approved the same opinion of Jābir b. Zayd mentioned in this tradition (see Abū Ghānim, *al-Mudawwana al-sughrā* 276). However, there seems to be another Ibāḍī point of view similar to that ascribed to the Kufan here. This latter opinion is also ascribed to the Hanafite. Malikite and Shafiʿite are of the first opinion. See al-Kharusi (ed.), *Āthār* 104 (comment on no. 193).

distinctive element of Ibāḍī law dealing with both purity and control over sexual behaviours, namely the question of *zinā* as impediment to marriage.

3.4.2 The Question of *zinā* as Impediment to Marriage

3.4.2.1 The Quranic Background

A controversial issue concerning *zinā* punishment was raised by the Quranic provision that the adulterous/fornicators could only marry individuals who have committed the same sin: "The adulterous man shall marry no one but an adulterous woman (*al-zānī lā yankiḥu illā zāniyatan*) or an idolatrous woman (*mushrika*), and the adulterous woman (*al-zāniyya*) – no one shall marry her but an adulterous man or an idolatrous man (*mushrik*). That is forbidden (*wa ḥurrima dhālika*) to the believers" (Q. 24:3). According to this verse, the Quran assumes that unchaste individuals are unacceptable marriage partners (see also Q. 2:221; 60:10). A similar concept is also expressed in Q. 24:26: "The bad women for the bad men, and the bad men for the bad women. And the good women for the good men, and the good men for the good women", where *khabīth/a* (bad man/woman) means *zānī/zāniyya* and *ṭayyib/a* (good man/woman) means *muḥṣin/a*.[70]

Nonetheless, this verse does contain some ambiguities, as it seems to allow for marriage with polytheists. Exegetes have solved the question by arguing that the verse states that it is forbidden for pious Muslim men and women to marry people who are known to possess an immoral character.[71] This prohibition applies to those men and women who persist in their evil behaviour and not to those who repent and reform themselves, for after repentance they will no longer be regarded as fornicators/adulterers.[72] The verse does not validate the marriage of an adulterous Muslim with an idolatrous woman and of an adulterous Muslim woman with an idolatrous man, as such a marriage is forbidden. It simply warns against *zinā*, by declaring it a sin peculiar to unbelievers, and declares that the person who commits it while being a Muslim makes himself unfit for contracting marriage with a pious partner.

Quran exegetes offer specific historical evidence for why verse 24:3 was revealed. According to Muqātil b. Sulaymān (d. 767), the alleged author of the oldest complete *Tafsīr*, some *muhājirūn*, due to their economic hardship, asked the Prophet's permission to marry Medinan women, from the People

70 Motzki, *Wal-muḥṣanātu mina n-nisā'i* 197–198.
71 I discussed Q. 24:3 in Francesca 'Put the ocean between them' 101–137.
72 Al-Ṭabarī, *Tafsīr* v, 394–395.

of the Book or from the people of *shirk*, in order to live off the money they earned practising prostitution. The Prophet disapproved of such marriages and thereafter the verse was revealed. The last part of the verse "*wa ḥurrima dhālika*" refers notably to the prohibition for Muslims of marring prostitutes and women committing *zinā*.[73]

The *Tafsīr* by al-Ṭabarī endorses this exegesis of the verse 24:3.[74]

3.4.2.2 The Pre-Islamic Context

In his article "Adultery as an impediment to marriage in Islamic and Canon law", Joseph Schacht argues that the doctrine of permanent impediment to marriage for those who have committed fornication spread in Kufa and was put into circulation by a group of traditions, which remained unsuccessful among the Sunnis but were adopted by both Shiʿites and Ibāḍīs. According to Schacht, the doctrine was well known to the Canon law of Eastern Churches, which developed an idea of Roman law originating in the *Lex Julia de adulteriis coercendis*. This law, issued by the emperor Augustus in about 18 BC, called on the husband to repudiate his adulterous wife and prohibited the woman who had been repudiated for adultery or convicted of fornication from entering into a subsequent marriage with anybody.[75]

In my article "'Put the ocean between them': fornication as permanent impediment to marriage in early Ibāḍī Islam", I argued that Schacht's thesis of a parallel to adultery as an impediment to marriage in Eastern Canon law is not accurate, and neither are some other parallels with Roman law, which he outlined, such as the maxim *al-walad li-l-firāsh* (the offspring belongs to the owner of the bed).[76]

Things are far too complex to allow for such a simplistic option in favour of the allegedly Canon law strata within Islamic law. Islam's peculiar relationship to the historical, religious and cultural context in which it originated is a core issue here. Elements of Roman law survived in what Patricia Crone called "Roman provincial law", and it is possible that they resurfaced in early Islamic legal discourse. But this cannot be regarded as an influence of Roman over Islamic law, either directly or indirectly through the medium of the Eastern Churches' Canon law. Rather, as Lena Salaymeh proves, the conventional

---

73 Muqātil b. Sulaymān, *Tafsīr* 160.

74 Al-Ṭabarī, *Tafsīr* v, 394–395.

75 On the *Lex Julia de adulteriis coercendis* see Fayer, *La familia romana* 252, 260–264. On a critical assessment of Schacht's theory, see Francesca 'Put the ocean between them'.

76 Rubin, *Al-Walad li-l-Firāsh* 6.

models of comparative legal studies, assuming clear boundaries between legal systems, do not correspond to the historical fluidity and porousness of the legal systems of the Ancient Near East. The interplay between tradition and innovation had lasting echoes in Islamic jurisprudence. Generations of Muslim scholars interpreted scripture and precedents in ways that simultaneously renewed and perpetuated already existing legal traditions. They created a dialectic of Islamic law with parallel legal systems where an amount of syncretism and legal continuity is both inevitable and necessary.[77] Hence, a more plausible answer to the question of the relationship between Islamic law and foreign legal systems concerning adultery and fornication can be found in the common cultural and social background they shared, which refracted in the Jewish and Christian legal tradition down to the eve of the rise of Islam.

An analysis not only of Christian but also of Biblical sources shows both commonalities and substantial points of difference among them and the Islamic sources. Regarding the impediment to marriage, Canon law refers mainly to adulterous fornication as an impediment to marriage, and the case of pre-marital sexual relationships is not referred to explicitly. The same happens in Jewish law.

The early Christian Church, following the council of Verberie in 756, allowed the betrayed spouse to dissolve the marriage and remarry. However, this rule could not be maintained once the principle of the indissolubility of marriage had been established. A further sensitive question is whether the marriage between the guilty spouse and his accomplice is permitted once the former has become free. Muslim legislation easily solves the problem as it establishes the death penalty for adultery, but in Canon law, which punishes this crime with mild penalties, a problem arises that is not easy to deal with. By simply allowing the marriage of the adulterer with the adulteress one could allow an easy rehabilitation of the culprits. On the other hand, a perennial impediment runs the risk – without any real social and religious benefit – of preventing the restoration of legality.[78]

In the 9th century the Church debated whether the accomplice – or any other man – could marry the adulteress, the courtesan, the woman *praegnans ex fornicatione*, or the woman who had previously been a concubine. Gratianus (Chiusi or Ficulle, about 1075/80–Bologna, 1145/47), who examines only the case of the adulterous woman and the courtesan, does not present a definite

77 Salaymeh, *The Beginnings of Islamic Law* 1–14.
78 Esmein, *Le mariage en droit canonique* i, 374–393.

doctrine: he only says that the marriage is lawful when the guilty woman repents and returns to the right path.[79]

As far as Jewish law is concerned, outside the Decalogue it is especially Leviticus 20:1ff. and Deuteronomy 22:22ff. that deal with adultery. From this scriptural material, as well as from the rabbinical speculation, it is clear that the old Jewish scholars consider "adultery" only the illicit sex committed with a married woman or betrothed girl, an offence punishable by death under certain circumstances. Sexual intercourse with an unmarried woman does not fall under the category of adultery but under that of fornication. A married woman who voluntary submits to a man other than her husband, be he married or unmarried, commits adultery; both she and her partner are equally guilty and both are forbidden by the *Halakah* to continue any relationship. Moreover, the husband must divorce his adulterous wife because she becomes prohibited to him forever. According to the Talmud (*Sotah* 5:1), the married women accused of adultery is forbidden to both her husband and her paramour. Special marriage restrictions are imposed by the Torah on the members of the priestly family, *kohanim*: "They shall not marry a woman that is a harlot (prostitute) or profaned, nor shall they marry one divorced from her husband; for they are holy to their God" (Lev. 21:7).[80]

3.4.2.3 The Early Ibāḍī Sources

The question of impediments to marriage in the case of unlawful intercourse is often discussed in Ibāḍī sources offering original and consistent responses to the problem. Ibāḍī scholars consider forbidden sexual activities, including adultery and fornication, rebellion against God. Hence, their rule against fornication is not vaguely against sexual irregularities of any sort but against men and women engaging in sexual intercourse outside of God's ordinance system. They reinforced the outward dichotomy between permissible and forbidden sexual activities as a distinctive edge that separated them from the rest of the Muslim community.

---

79 Esmein, *Le mariage en droit canonique* i, 208–211; Bernardus Papiensis, *Summa de matrimonio* in idem, *Summa Decretalium* 151.

80 A harlot is the English version for the Hebrew *zonah*, but the Sages have interpreted it to include both a woman who had sexual intercourse with a prohibited partner or a female converted to Islam. The profaned woman is a daughter of a union between a Kohen and a woman prohibited only to kohanim (e.g. the daughter of a Kohen married to a divorcé). Lewittes, *Jewish Marriage* 24; Guggenheimer (ed.), *The Jerusalem Talmud, Tractate Yebamot* 398–399, 449; *Tractates Sotah and Nedarim*, Sotah v, 198; Maimonides, *Leyes sobre el matrimonio* 289–290 no. 24–25; Lewittes, *Jewish Marriage* 15, 24, 176–178.

The Ibāḍīs were stricter than the Sunnis in the sexual norms they promoted, as proved by the textual evidence of some *responsa* by Jābir b. Zayd quoted in the *Aqwāl Qatāda*. The first of these *responsa* put in a different light a famous statement from Ibn ʿAbbās: "What begins as fornication can end up as marriage" (*awwaluhu sifāḥ ākhiruhu nikāḥ*), reported in the early Sunni sources. Indeed, permission to get married is restricted to the fornicators who had illicit sex before converting to Islam. Jābir was asked about the case of unlawful intercourse committed by unbelievers, and he decreed that both culprits are acquitted if they convert to Islam and marry. He founds his opinion on the aforementioned maxim from Ibn ʿAbbās.

> [ʿAmr b. Harim] said: Jābir b. Zayd was asked about a man who committed *zinā* with a woman as they were infidels (*fī ʾl-shirk*). Is it permissible for him to marry her after conversion (*fī ʾl-Islām*)? He said: This is what Ibn ʿAbbās said: "What begins as fornication can end up as a marriage".
>
> ʿAmr [b. Harim] said: Jābir b. Zayd was asked about a man who committed *zinā* with a woman in Islam. Is it permissible for him to marry him after that? He said no.
>
> ʿAmr said: Jābir b. Zayd was asked about her daughters, are they lawful to him? He said: No, and ʿIkrima also said that.
>
> ʿAmr said: Jābir b. Zayd was asked about a man who touched a woman, and put his hands or his sexual organ on her vagina, or watched her vagina, but he didn't penetrate her. Is it permissible for him to marry her? He said no.
>
> ʿAmr said: Jābir b. Zaid was asked about a married woman who went out to the "people of war" with the "people of religion" and married one of them. Then returned to the land of Islam, is it allowed to a Muslim [i.e. an Ibāḍī] to marry her after that? He said: No, it is forbidden for every Muslim to marry her after she has done so.
>
> ʿAmr said: Jābir b. Zayd was asked about a woman who used to have sexual intercourse with both women and men. Is it permissible to marry her if she repents from that? He said: I do not see that a Muslim may marry her after she did that.[81]

A further judgement, reported in the part 6 of *Aqwāl Qatāda*, relates to with people who had illicit sexual intercourse and then decide to marry:

---

81 Al-Salimi (ed.), *Aqwāl* 357–358. A similar discussion concerning the impediments to marriage for those who have committed fornication is found in al-Salimi (ed.), *Early Islamic Law in Ḥadīth Texts from Basra* 127–130 (*Kitāb al-nikāḥ*), particularly in traditions nos. 102, 103, 104, 107 and 108.

> [al-Rabīʿ b. Ḥabīb] was asked about a man who after having illicit sex with a woman wants to marry her. [He answered that] Jābir b. Zayd said: "He may never marry her. Rather put the ocean between them. This is our opinion".[82]

The part 6 of *Aqwāl Qatāda* preserves two more traditions on the same subject. In the first Jābir b. Zayd states that the marriage of the man who commits adultery with his sister-in-love must be dissolved,[83] and in the second al-Rabīʿ b. Ḥabīb expands the impediment arising from illicit sex upon the relations with slaves:

> He was asked about a man who committed *zinā* with a slave-girl of another man and then bought her. He said: He may not include her among his concubines (*milk al-yamīn*).[84]

In the same vein, Ibāḍī jurists condemn the sexual promiscuity of female slaves and prohibit the master to put them to the sexual use of his male relatives, in particular his son and his father.[85]

Ibn ʿAbbās's maxim: "What begins as fornication can end up as marriage" is quoted in two further Ibāḍī sources. The first is a letter by Jābir b. Zayd addressed to Ghiṭrīf b. ʿAbd al-Raḥmān, preserved in the *Jawābāt Jābir b. Zayd*, where Jābir decides that polytheists who committed fornication before converting to Islam may legally marry after the *ḥadd* punishment for *zinā*. He derives his judgement from the Ibn ʿAbbās's maxim.[86] The second source is a *responsum* by al-Rabīʿ, who allows their marriage relying on the same statement but without mentioning the *ḥadd* punishment for the culprits. Al-Rabīʿ's *fatwā* clarifies that the decisive point is the conversion to Islam: if a man commits *zinā* with a Zoroastrian woman (or a woman from *ahl al-ḥarb*) before converting, the marriage after conversion is lawful. Conversely, if he commits *zinā* with such a woman after conversion, the marriage is forbidden forever, thus according to Jābir's opinion.[87]

Given this background, what is noteworthy here is that the early Ibāḍī authorities have no doubts in understanding Ibn ʿAbbās's maxim as exclusively

82 *Al-baḥr al-akhḍar* (the green sea, the deep sea), it was one of the name medieval Arabs used for the Atlantic Ocean. Glick et. al., *Medieval Science* 365; al-Salimi (ed.), *Aqwāl* 404. The Jābir's tradition is also quoted in Ibn Khalfūn, *Ajwibat* 42.

83 Al-Salimi (ed.), *Aqwāl* 397.

84 Al-Salimi (ed.), *Aqwāl* 405.

85 See *infra* p. 24 and footnote 4. See Francesca, Investigating Early Ibāḍī Jurisprudence 254.

86 Al-Jaʿbīrī (ed.), *Rasāʾil* 96.

87 Ibn Khalīfa (ed.), *Futyā* 173–174 (Ms. 48_{20-25}).

referring to illicit sex committed before conversion. On the other hand, *zinā* committed by Muslims constitutes a permanent impediment to marriage, as proved by Jābir's saying "Put the ocean between them". Moreover, by a strict analogy with a legal marriage, the illicit sexual relations create impediments to marriage with the female ascendants and descendants of the woman with whom a man committed *zinā*.

The *Tafsīr* by Abū 'l-Ḥawārī Muḥammad b. al-Ḥawārī al-ʿUmānī (second half of the 3rd/9th century) understands verse 24:3 as referring to the banning of marriage with prostitutes and women indulging in illegal sex. It substantiates the doctrine of the early Ibāḍī authorities by referring to a tradition from Ibn ʿAbbās forbidding the marriage of the two fornicators/adulterers. It also reports a tradition relating that the caliph Abū Bakr was called to judge the case of a man and a woman from Quraysh, both unmarried, who had committed *zinā*. He ordered to fustigate them and to part them from each other forever.[88]

Occasionally the solution by analogy with parallel cases could lead to extremely strict decisions. The Ibāḍī historian al-Darjīnī (d. 1271–72) relates that Abū ʿUbayda was asked about a man who had put his hands under the clothes of a free woman but she was able to defend herself against the attempted rape. Might the man marry the woman? Abū ʿUbayda held this marriage to be unlawful. Upon his arrival in the meeting where Abū ʿUbayda was together with his students and companions, Abū Nūḥ, another early Ibāḍī scholar, was approached with the same question. He disputed Abū ʿUbayda's statement but he did not invalidate his decision, and he warned the companions not to ask him when Abū ʿUbayda was present. The episode is evidence of the debate surrounding the entire doctrine regulating impediments to marriage at about the mid of 2nd/8th century, but it also sheds light on power dynamics inside the early Ibāḍī community.[89]

Abū Ghānim al-Khurāsānī admits that Jābir's opinion is sound; nonetheless he prefers the opposite view, allowing the marriage between the fornicators.[90]

Jābir's opinion was also not taken over by the Rustumid *imām* Aflaḥ b. ʿAbd al-Wahhāb (208/835–258/872), who comments on the verse 24:3 by saying that the fornicators may marry each other after being flogged.[91] This view

88 Abū 'l-Ḥawārī, *al-Dirāya* 166–172.

89 Al-Darjīnī, *Ṭabaqāt* ii, 239. Al-Shammākhī adds that Abū Nūḥ contradicted Abū ʿUbayda's decision on the basis of an opinion expressed by Jābir b. Zayd, see *Siyar* (1884) 89–90.

90 Abū Ghānim, *Mudawwana* ii, 28.

91 The *imām* Aflaḥ's opinion is reported in his *addenda* to the *Musnad* al-Rabīʿ b. Ḥabīb 260, no. 904.

supporting the prevailing Sunni doctrine remains unsuccessful among the majority of the Ibāḍīs, who approve of Jābir's teaching.

A key concern in early Ibāḍī sources involves promiscuous women due to the risk that Muslim men could marry them after having illicit sex with them. This protectionist attitude is evident in the case of a woman who had sexual intercourse with both men and women reported in the *Aqwāl Qatāda*. A similar case is also referred to in a letter by Jābir b. Zayd addressed to ʿUnayfa, though here Jābir considers marrying her to be reprehensible and not forbidden:

> As far as the question if the *ḥadd* penalty should be applied to a woman who had illegal sexual intercourse with both a man and a woman at same time, and if it is allowed to marry her in case she repented and avoided indulging in illicit sex anymore, [my opinion is that] the *ḥadd* penalty must be imposed upon all three [guilty] persons and it is reprehensible (*akrahu*) for all Muslim men to marry the woman.[92]

The danger of promiscuity results also if a woman abandons her Ibāḍī spouse to move to the *dār al-ḥarb* where she remarries. May she marry again if she comes back to the Ibāḍī land? As we have seen in the tradition reported in the *Aqwāl Qatāda*, such a marriage is absolutely forbidden as the woman makes herself *ḥarām* for any Ibāḍī man having had sexual activity with a religiously alien spouse. A similar episode, concerning a married woman from Khurāsān, is reported in the epistle by Jābir b. Zayd addressed to ʿUnayfa. After stating that it is forbidden for any Muslim (i.e. Ibāḍī) to marry her even if she had repented, Jābir adds that "he doesn't like to be asked about such cases".[93]

What is noteworthy in both cases is that they mention the "people of war/ the *dār al-ḥarb*" with the "people of religion/people of the *qibla*", the latter being the way the Ibāḍīs designated the non-Ibāḍī Muslims. It is likely that both traditions arose from historical episodes during the great Ibāḍī revolts in the late Umayyad age, which broke out mainly in the peripheral regions of the Muslim empire.

Unlike other more radical Kharijite groups, Ibāḍīs consider the non-Ibāḍī Muslims not as polytheists, but as "infidels by ingratitude" (*kuffār al-niʿma*) and their territory as *dār al-Islām* with the exception of the regions where they were fighting against an illegitimate government. Nevertheless, it was illicit to

92 Al-Jaʿbīrī (ed.), *Rasāʾil* 107.
93 Al-Jaʿbīrī (ed.), *Rasāʾil* 107.

intermarry with non-Ibāḍī Muslims as well as to inherit from them. This rule facilitates rebellion of Ibāḍīs against other Muslims and allows them to not completely integrate into the Muslim community.[94]

The early Ibāḍī jurists tend to characterize the eligible spouses not only by their personal and ethnic status, but also by their religious conduct. The dishonour of women having sexual activity with a non-Ibāḍī man is regarded as a "sexual apostasy" and therefore absolutely prohibited as other forms of fornication. Such relation is immoral not because it is extramarital (in fact both episodes mention the women having "married" a non-Ibāḍī from the *dār al-ḥarb*) but because it represents a religiously mixed marriage that breaks the community endogamy rule.

Several early Muslim traditions depict fornication between unmarried partners as a tolerated, though morally censured, behaviour – especially when it did not constitute a blatantly defiant act proven through testimony, pregnancy, or voluntary confession. Though it was clear in early Islam that wives committing adulterous fornication must be stoned to death, scholars adopt a more lenient stance, under several circumstances, toward fornication committed by unmarried persons. They are not put to death, but rather encouraged to marry each other, generally after showing repentance and being flogged. Marriage, in their view, turns an illicit action into a legal one.

The impediment to marriage became a sectarian issue between Sunni on one side and Shiʿites and Ibāḍīs on the other side, only after that the Sunni jurists agreed to reject any doctrine aiming at declaring *zinā* a permanent impediment to a subsequent marriage between the guilty parties, while also rejecting the extension of the prohibited degrees for marriage to the ascendants and descendants of a woman with whom a man committed *zinā*.

The Ibāḍīs intensify sexual austerity in a way that regulates sexual behaviour in discontinuity with their Sunni counterparts. They identify any forbidden sexual activity as a threat to the security and integrity of the community, and even if they are not excessive in punishing the unmarried fornicators, they use strong arguments and express intense loathing and intolerance of the transgressors by not allowing them to get married. Their highly restrictive sexual ethics rely on some ancient traditions, which echo elements of a syncretic patrimony of juridical speculation in the Near East.

94 Madelung, *Religious Trends* 72–73.

3.5 "There Is No Usury Except in Delay": the Application of *Ribā* in the Ibāḍī Sources

The Quran censured the practice of *ribā* very early on and denounced it in unprecedentedly strong terms (Q. 30:39; 3:130; 2:275–280). It seems, however, that at some stage the Quranic account of *ribā* was held as inadequate in that just one form of *ribā* was considered. Consequently, jursits felt the need to extend the *ribā* ban to other forms of transactions. Over the course of time a vast and expanding *ḥadīth* literature accumulated on the subject.

What the Quran intended was to avoid the increase in capital obtained through continuous redoubling (*aḍʿāfan muḍāʿafatan*, III, 130). The historical sources called this practice *ribā al-jāhiliyya*.[95]

By a common development of doctrine, the schools of law extended the law of usury to all exchanges of gold, silver, wheat, barley, dates and salt; besides, they demanded not only the immediate delivery of the two lots, which were being exchanged, but also absolute equality in quantity if the two lots belonged to the same kind. In a famous *ḥadīth*, the companion Abū Saʿīd al-Khudrī reports the Prophet as saying:

> Gold is to be paid for by gold, silver by silver, wheat by wheat, barley by barley, dates by dates and salt by salt like for like (*mithl bi-mithl*), payment being made hand for hand (*yadan bi-yad*). If someone gives more or asks for more, he has dealt in *ribā*.[96]

Ribā is thus, in general, any unjustified increase of capital for which no compensation or return is given. The whole prohibition is directed against speculation in food and against any transaction that is tantamount to giving or taking interest. The subjects of such an injunction are the essential commodities of basic needs, which were in common use during the early period of Islam. Dates, barley and wheat formed the staple food of the people. In barter trade, these commodities were widely exchanged.

---

95 Relying on the authority of Zayd b. Aslam, Mālik's *Muwaṭṭaʾ* states: "In the pre-Islamic days (*jāhiliyya*) *ribā* operated in this manner: if a man owed another a debt, at the time of its maturity the creditor would ask the debtor: 'Will you pay up or will you increase (*am turbī*)?' If the latter paid up, the creditor received back the sum; otherwise the principal was increased on the stipulation of a further term". Al-Zurqānī, *Sharḥ ʿalā Muwaṭṭaʾ* ii, 324; also al-Ṭabarī, *Tafsīr* iv, 22–24.

96 The *ḥadīth* is quoted in almost all juridical sources dealing with *ribā*. See, for example, al-Sarakhsī, *Kitāb al-Mabsūṭ* xii, 110.

The *ribā* described above is known by the technical name of *ribā al-faḍl* (*ribā* of excess). Some eminent companions of the Prophet, like Usāma b. Zayd, Zayd b. Arqam and ʿAbd Allāh b. ʿAbbās, were unaware of it and held that there could be no usury unless there was a time-lag in the transaction. This doctrine, formulated in the maxims "there is no *ribā* except on loans" and "there is no *ribā* when the payment is made on the spot", was ascribed to the Prophet.

The *Aqwāl Qatāda b. Diʿāma* records from Ibn ʿAbbās as following:

> Usāma b. Zayd and Zayd b. Arqam were making exchange transactions in which broken gold (*al-tibr al-munkasar*) was sold for an inferior quantity of gold bullion. Anas b. Mālik disapproved of that. Then Usāma asked the Prophet whether this involved *ribā*. The Prophet said: "Was the exchange from hand to hand (*yadan bi-yad*)?". Usāma replied that this was the case and the Prophet authorized such exchange transactions.[97]

The *Mudawwana* of Abū Ghānim al-Khurāsānī substantiates this doctrine, relating that the Prophet had no objection to the exchange of one *dīnār* for two, or one *dirham* for two, if both lots were delivered immediately. He only objected to it if the delivery of one lot was postponed. According to the *Mudawwana* of Abū Ghānim, Ibn ʿAbbās said:

> Usāma b. Zayd reported God's Messenger as saying: "There is no objection to the exchange of gold and silver, two for one, because usury is on loans".[98]

From the tradition of Usāma b. Zayd, the Ibāḍīs derived their doctrine that there is no *ribā* in the simultaneous exchange of different quantities of gold, silver and other commodities. That the ancient Ibāḍīs supported this doctrine is confirmed by a Sunni source, the *Kitāb al-Mabsūṭ* of al-Sarakhsī, where the doctrine is attributed to Jābir b. Zayd.[99]

The prohibition of giving an increased quantity of one commodity in exchange for another in transactions involving precious metals is unanimously agreed upon by the Sunni jurists. Nevertheless, they were aware of what was reported about Ibn ʿAbbās, who allowed increase in the exchange of gold and silver provided they were exchanged simultaneously. The glaring contradiction between *ḥadīth*s dealing with the "*ribā* of excess" (*ribā al-faḍl*) and those related to the "*ribā* of credit" (*ribā al-nasīʾa*) could not be overlooked. The

97 Al-Salimi (ed.), *Aqwāl* 423 (Ms. 116_{28}–117_{11}).
98 Abū Ghānim, *al-Mudawwana al-ṣughrā* ii, 182–183; Id, *al-Mudawwana al-kubrā* ii, 246–247.
99 Al-Sarakhsī, *Mabsūṭ* xii, 111–112.

early traditionists tried to solve it. A number of *ḥadīth*s were put in circulation supporting the fact that Ibn ʿAbbās had retracted from his opinion.[100] But how Ibn ʿAbbās showed penitence is narrated in a contradictory manner. Such contradictions show the increasing strictness of the jurisprudence in the law concerning *ribā*. Moreover, some early sources did not relate the change in his view.

According to the *Musnad* of al-Ṭayālisī (d. 203/818–819), Abū Saʿīd al-Khudrī, who strongly opposed the conception that *lā ribā illā fī ʾl-nasīʾa*, met Ibn ʿAbbās and asked him whether he had heard anything about it from the Prophet or whether it reflected his personal opinion (*raʾy*). Ibn ʿAbbās replied: "I didn't hear it from the Prophet, but I see no objection if the exchange is from hand to hand".[101] The opposing teachings of Ibn ʿAbbās and Abū Saʿīd al-Khudrī were set against each other in a tradition recorded by ʿAbd al-Razzāq (d. 211/826):

Ibn ʿAbbās relates from Usāma b. Zayd that he heard the Prophet saying: "Usury exists only in delay (*al-ribā fī ʾl-nasīʾa*)". Abū Saʿīd replied that he heard from the Prophet: "Gold is to be paid for by gold like for like (*mithl bi-mithl*), silver by silver like for like (*mithl bi-mithl*)".[102]

Other sources relate the *ḥadīth* in variant versions.

Bukhārī records from Abū Ṣāliḥ:

> I heard Abū Saʿīd al-Khudrī saying: "*Dīnār* be exchanged for *dīnār*, *dirham* for *dirham*, like for like. One who gives an increase or seeks an increase earns *ribā*". I told Abū Saʿīd that Ibn ʿAbbās held the opposite view. Abū Saʿīd said that he had met Ibn ʿAbbās and asked him whether he found anything in the Prophetic tradition or in the Quran in support of his opinion. Ibn ʿAbbās replied that he had not heard it from the Prophet, nor had he found it in the Quran, but it had been related to him by Usāma b. Zayd who said that the Prophet declared that *ribā* was in *nasīʾa*.[103]

---

100 Yanagihashi, *Studies in Legal Hadith* 354–357, 380–382, 410. The author offers a thorough analysis of *ḥadīth*s dealing with *ribā al-faḍl* and *ribā al-nasīʾa*. In his previous work *A History of the Early Islamic Law of Property*, he also dealt with the prohibition of *ribā*, drawing on early legal sources, in the chapter titled "On the origins and early development of prohibition of usury in early Sunnī schools", 213–246.

101 Al-Ṭayālisī, *Musnad* ii part 269.

102 ʿAbd al-Razzāq, *Muṣannaf* viii, 117–118 no. 14546.

103 Al-Bukhārī, *Ṣaḥīḥ* iii, 694, *buyūʿ, bāb al-dīnār bi ʾl-dīnār nasīʾatan*; al-Qasṭallanī, *al-Irshād* iv, 78; al-Tirmidhī, *al-Jāmiʿ al-Ṣaḥīḥ* iii, *kitāb al-buyūʿ, bāb* 24 (*mā jaʿa fī ʾl-ṣarf*); al-Nawawī, *Sharḥ* vii, 12; al-Bayhaqī, *Kitāb sunan al-kubrā* v, 460–461.

Furthermore, ʿAṭāʾ b. Abī Rabāḥ relates that Ibn ʿAbbās asserted that he hadn't found any evidence in the Quran and the *ḥadīth*. He added that, regarding the sayings of the Prophet, Abū Saʿīd was more knowledgeable than he. Usāma b. Zayd told him that the Prophet had said that *ribā* was in *nasīʾa*.[104]

Other traditions claim that, in his later life, Ibn ʿAbbās rejected the doctrine that there is no *ribā* except on loans and accepted the general condemnation of the "*ribā* of excess".[105] The growing strictness of the prohibition of *ribā al-nasīʾa* is clearly stated in this sequence of *ḥadīth*.

Only the Ibāḍī sources have preserved the full narration of the *ḥadīth* reported by Usāma b. Zayd. Just a part of it is contained in the Sunni sources, relating in general terms that the Prophet was asked about the bullion exchange (*ṣarf*) and he said "*al-ribā fī ʾl-nasīʾa*" or "*lā ribā illā fī ʾl-nasīʾa*".[106] The use of the word *ṣarf*, which in early Islam meant both the exchange of gold for gold and silver for silver and the exchange of gold for silver, brings some ambiguity to the *ḥadīth*. Therefore, some scholars suggested that the question pertained to the barter (*mubādala*) of precious metals of different types. Thus, they overlooked the fact that it was unanimously accepted that the exchange of commodities of different varieties was not subject to the prohibition of *ribā al-faḍl* but only to that of *ribā al-nasīʾa*. Therefore, the controversy between Ibn ʿAbbās and Abū Saʿīd al-Khudrī would not have arisen.

In the *Sunan* by al-Dāraquṭnī (d. 385/995) we can find a further way of interpreting the *ḥadīth* "*al-ribā fī ʾl-nasīʾa*":

> ʿAmr b. Dīnār heard Abū Minhāl saying that a companion of his sold dirham on credit. He disapproved this practice but the other replied that he performed the transaction on the market and nobody disapproved. Abū Minhāl asked Barāʾ b. ʿĀzib, who said: "The Prophet arrived as we were dealing in such a way and he said: Hand to hand exchange is valid, exchange on credit (*nasīʾa*) is illegal".[107]

The most famous and popular attempt to explain the *ḥadīth* of Usāma comes from al-Shāfiʿī, who writes:

---

104 Muslim, *Ṣaḥīḥ* i, *buyūʿ, bāb bayʿ al-taʿām mithlan bi-mithl*; al-Bayhaqī, *Kitāb sunan al-ṣaghīr* ii, 244–245.

105 ʿAbd al-Razzāq, *Muṣannaf* viii, 118 no. 14548–49.

106 Abū Ḥanīfa, *Musnad* 158 no. 329; Bayhaqī, *Kitāb sunan al-kubrā* v, 460–461.

107 Al-Dāraquṭnī, *al-Sunan* iii part, 16–17. See also Bukhārī, *Ṣaḥīḥ, buyūʿ, bāb bayʿ al-wariq bi ʾl-dhahab nasīʾatan*.

> It is possible that Usāma found that the people had questioned the Prophet regarding hand-to-hand exchange with excess of different commodities, for example the exchange of gold with silver, of dates with wheat and likewise other articles with those of a different kind. The Prophet replied, according to Usāma's report, that *ribā* concerns an exchange of commodities on credit. It is also possible that the questioner may have explained this at the time when he put the question and he received this reply from the Prophet. Then Usāma related only the reply but forgot to relate the question as well. It is also possible that he may have some doubts regarding this matter, because the *ḥadīth* related by him does not contain anything which is incompatible with these propositions.[108]

Thus, the inconsistency and contradiction between the *ḥadīth* of Usāma b. Zayd and all the others on the same subject could be resolved.

Al-Shāfiʿī's proposal brings about the problem of the authenticity of the tradition of Usāma b. Zayd as reported in the Ibāḍī sources. But a careful study of the ancient juridical sources suggests that it represents an earlier stage with regard to the doctrine that prevailed in the Iraqi and Medinan schools. In his *Kitāb ikhtilāf Mālik wa ʾl-Shāfiʿī*, al-Shāfiʿī discusses the Medinan custom of allowing the exchange of unmanufactured gold for a smaller amount of coins of the same metal in order to cover the minting expenses.[109] This is a serious infringement of the general rules for the exchange of precious metals, which was ascribed to Mālik, to Ibn al-Qāsim and to Muʿāwiya.[110] Schacht proved that this decision must be seen not as an exceptional concession, but rather as original Medinan doctrine. According to Schacht, the deliberate obliteration of these transactions from most of the old sources shows the growing strictness in the enforcement of the prohibition of usury. This strictness prevailed in the generation after Mālik (d. 179/ 795).[111]

In the Umayyad period, the prohibition of usury was avoided through the exchange of unmanufactured gold for the same amount of coins and by paying at the same time a minting fee.[112]

As parallel cases of the survival of the old custom, there were exceptions to the rules concerning *ribā* in the exchange of objects which could be measured or weighed, which was allowed in early Islam, such as the sale of meat for meat,

---

108 Al-Shāfiʿī, *Risāla*, 126; al-Sarakhsī, *Mabsūṭ* xii, 111–112.

109 Quoted in Schacht, *The Origins* 67.

110 Mālik b. Anas, *Muwaṭṭa*ʾ ii, 633 no. 31; al-Ṭabarī, *Ikhtilāf al-fuqahā*ʾ 62–64; Abū ʾl-Walīd al-Bājī al-Andalusī, *Kitāb al-muntaqā* iv, 261–263; Ibn Rushd, *Kitāb bidāyat al-mujtahid* 119; ʿAbd al-Razzāq, *Muṣannaf* viii, 125–126 no. 14574–76.

111 *The Origins*, p. 67.

112 Al-Balādhurī, *Futūḥ* 575.

bread for bread, eggs for eggs, in equal quantities estimated without weighing. These transactions were called "our generally agreed practice" by Mālik.[113]

The rules concerning the exchange of food and sale on credit, as they were developed by the ancient schools of law, are conflicting and contradictory: on the one hand they were carefully developed to avoid any usurious transactions, on the other they allowed a number of legal devices to receive and give interest. One consisted of a double sale, of which there were many variants.[114] For instance, the (prospective) debtor sells goods for cash to the (prospective) creditor, and immediately buys them back from him for a greater amount payable at a future date; this amounts to a loan with the goods as security and the difference between the two prices represents the interest.

Another infringement to the general rules concerning the prohibition of usury and aleatory transactions was the re-sale of goods before taking possession, which the ancient lawyers allowed as no direct risk of usury was involved.[115]

It seems likely that the acceptance by the Ibāḍīs of the maxim "*al-ribā fī 'l-nasī'a*" when gold was sold for gold and silver for silver, represents the survival of an ancient custom, which was born out of the logic of economics since it acknowledged the higher value of gold and silver coins in relation to unmanufactured metal. The Sunni *ḥadīth* collections testify a growing strictness in the *ribā* law, which constitutes the result of the jurists' effort to bring extensive and complex spheres of economic life within the logic of the *ribā* prohibition. Although the Ibāḍīs attached a strong moral censure to the practice of *ribā*, they did not take the prohibition of usury to its extreme, namely including those transactions that they did not perceive as illegal. Thus, their behaviour was affected by the values of merchant capitalism and the accumulation of wealth, which were clearly a part of the ethos of Ibadism.

From the 3rd century onwards, the Ibāḍīs made a great effort to specify all illicit *ribāwī* transactions in loans and exchanges, but at the same time, they continued to consider the *ḥadīth* of Ibn 'Abbās from Usāma b. Zayd as well authenticated (*thābit*). They even justified it theoretically by assuming that the

113 Quoted in Schacht, *The Origins* 67.

114 The legal devices (*ḥiyal*, sing. *ḥīla*) were not confined to the prohibition of taking interest but covered other subject matters as well. The schools of law showed some differences of degree in the attitude towards the *ḥiyal*. The Ḥanafīs were the most favourably inclined. See al-Shaybānī, *Kitāb al-makhārij fī 'l-ḥiyal*; al-Khaṣṣāf, *Kitāb al-ḥiyal wa 'l-makhārij*. The device of the double sale was permitted by the Ibāḍī scholar Jābir b. Zayd, Al-Kharusi (ed.), *Āthār* 50 no. 214 (Ms. 12_4).

115 Schacht, *The Origins* 108, 200 f., 296, 313.

Sunni had rejected it deliberately.[116] Only at the end of the 19th century did the eminent Ibāḍī scholar and reformist, Muḥammad Aṭfayyish (d. 1332/1914) recognize the inconsistency of this *ḥadīth* and replace the Ibāḍī theory of *ribā al-nasīʾa* with the Sunni reasoning, arguing that Ibn ʿAbbās had recanted his opinion late in life. Moreover, the *ḥadīth* should be interpreted as referring to the exchange of commodities of different types.[117]

In dealing with the *ribā* prohibition, we can point out a further incongruity of the Ibāḍī law. As stated above, money exchange and, in general, dealing in precious metals demanded the immediate delivery of the two lots that had been exchanged. This doctrine was generally accepted, but among the Ibāḍīs, the Omani scholar Ibn Baraka stated that the exchange of gold for silver on credit is allowed, as saying: "The exchange on credit is valid (*thābit*) if it is based on the individual's responsibility (*dhimma*)".[118]

A corresponding doctrine, ascribed to the *imām* Abū ʿAbd Allāh Jaʿfar al-Ṣādiq (d. 148/765), was also put into circulation among the Shiʿites around the end of the 2nd/8th century by ʿAmmār b. Mūsā al-Sābāṭī. Like the Ibāḍī doctrine of Ibn Baraka, that of Jaʿfar al-Ṣādiq remained unsuccessful and did not become part of the school's teachings.[119]

This doctrine may be regarded as a survival of the original Medinan custom, in that some traditions quoted by Muslims reported that during the Prophet's life people in Medina used to exchange gold for silver on credit.[120] Although such a custom was overshadowed by the growing strictness in the enforcement of the prohibition of *ribā*, during the caliphate of ʿUmar b. al-Khaṭṭāb transactions of precious metals on credit were still performed, earning the caliph's disapproval.[121]

---

116 Ibn Baraka, *al-Jāmiʿ* ii, 320–321; al-Bisiyānī, *Mukhtaṣar* 119–120; Ibn Qays, *Mukhtaṣar al-khiṣāl* 132–133; al-Shammākhī, *Īḍāḥ* iii, 13–19.

117 Aṭfayyish, *Sharḥ Kitāb al-Nīl* xi, 38–39, xii, 112.

118 *al-Jāmiʿ* ii, 340.

119 Al-Ṭūsī, *Istibṣār* ii, ii part 94–95. The Kufan traditionist Abū ʾl-Faḍl ʿAmmār b. Mūsā al-Sābāṭī was a companion of the Shiʿite *imām* Mūsā al-Kāẓim (d. 183/788). See Abū ʾl-Qāsim, *Muʿjam rijāl al-ḥadīth* xii, 260–264; al-Kishshī, *Kitāb rijāl* 218 no. 130.

120 Muslim, *Ṣaḥīḥ* i, 693 (*bāb al-nahī ʿan bayʿ al-waraq bi-ʾl-dhahab dayyinan*).

121 Al-Shāfiʿī, *al-Umm* iv, 30.

3.6 The *Zakāt*

In this paragraph I will focus mainly on Abū ʿUbayda's epistle on *zakāt*: the *Risālat Ibn Abī Karīma fī ʾl-zakāt li-ʾl-imām Abī ʾl-Khaṭṭāb al-Maʿāfirī*, which I have already dealt with in Chapter 2.

The issues arising from Abū ʿUbayda's letter can be summarized as follows.

1. **The collection and distribution of the *zakāt* funds:** According to Abū ʿUbayda, the task of the collection of the *zakāt* must be assigned to trusted men (*rijāl umanāʾ*). They must make their decisions (*ijtāhidū raʾyhim*) on the basis of what God ordered in His Book, acting justly. Alms are collected from the best goods of those who have to pay them and should be distributed to the poor in every village. As well as to the poor, they may be distributed to wayfarers (*ibn al-sabīl*), those who are in bondage and those in debt (*ghārim* and *riqāb*), if present. The community (*jamāʿa*, i.e. the Ibāḍī authorities) shall decide who is to be considered poor in case of controversy.[122]

A poor man who has the right to be maintained by a relative (father, son, brother) cannot receive *zakāt*. If his family refuse to maintain him, Abū ʿUbayda passes the decision to the *imām al-ẓuhūr* (the *imām* of manifestation),[123] even if according to tradition (*sunna*), he would not have any right to *zakāt*.[124]

Referring to the question of whether the *zakāt* must be distributed among the eight categories of beneficiaries quoted in the Quran (9:60), or if it could be primarily used for the relief of the members of the community in distress, Abū ʿUbayda inclined to the latter view. He based his view on traditions from Abū Bakr and ʿUmar b. al-Khaṭṭāb. Moreover, the *zakāt* collectors (*saʿāt*) are not entitled to receive a share from the *zakāt* but only a remuneration (*ujr*) and upkeep for their mount. The same was true for the governor (*wālī*).[125]

When asked whether the clergy of the community (*ahl al-faḍl fī ʾl-dīn*) had privileged rights to the *zakāt*, Abū ʿUbayda replied by citing Abū Bakr – who did not give them any privileges but distributed *zakāt* only considering poverty – and ʿUmar who, on the other hand, took into consideration some questions of merit: faith, knowledge of law, years of conversion, and so on. He said: "this is what we prefer and we shall follow this".[126]

---

122 Abū ʿUbayda, *Risāla* 4–6, 12.

123 He represented the ideal leader among the Ibāḍīs ruling when they fully controlled the territory in which they were located and could practice their faith without fear of persecution. Gaiser, *Muslims, Scholars, Soldiers* 19–47.

124 Abū ʿUbayda, *Risāla* 14.

125 Abū ʿUbayda, *Risāla* 4–8.

126 Abū ʿUbayda, *Risāla* 10.

One of the questions referred to Abū ʿUbayda concerned the case of a man who converted to Ibadism. Should he pay his *zakāt* again? According to Abū ʿUbayda, he does not have to pay it again, but if an Ibāḍī gives his *zakāt* to a non-Ibāḍī (*ahl al-khilāfa*) – deliberately or by mistake – he must pay it again. The same is true for an Ibāḍī who joins the "*ahl al-khilāfa*" and later repents and returns to the bosom of the community (*rajaʿa ilā ʾl-ḥaqq*).[127]

A similar case is discussed in the *Futyā al-Rabīʿ*: according to two pupils of Abū ʿUbayda, ʿAbdallāh b. ʿAbd al-ʿAzīz and Abū ʾl Muʾarrij, a newly converted follower cannot give *zakāt* to his people (*qawmuhū*). If he does, he must give it again to the Ibāḍīs. If he continues to give *zakāt* outside the Ibāḍī community, should *barāʾa* (dissociation) be declared towards him? ʿAbdallāh b. ʿAbd al-ʿAzīz and Abū ʾl Muʾarrij declare a state of *wuqūf* (suspension of judgement) in this case. According to al-Rabīʿ he should give the *zakāt* again, but he made no statement on his status.[128]

Whoever has given his goods due as *zakāt* to a trustee (*amīn al-qawm bi-raʾy-him*) and they have suffered a loss or been destroyed, must also give *zakāt* again. If the trustee has hidden them, he is responsible.[129]

Following the opinion of some Ibāḍī authorities (*baʿḍ aṣḥābinā*), food and goods given to support the "soldiers of our people" (*ʿasākir qawminā*) are considered *zakāt*.[130]

2. The right of the Ibāḍī *imām* to receive from the *zakāt* funds: Abū ʿUbayda answers that he is not entitled to accept the *zakāt* unless he is in the category of the poor and destitute. Moreover, the *imām*'s intermediation in the levying of the *zakāt* depends on his effective capacity to rule over a region, otherwise people are not obliged to send him their *zakāt*.[131]

The funds from the *zakāt* cannot be used for any reason other than those given by the Quran, such as building a mosque or other public works.

The epistle also discusses the right of the Ibāḍī *imām* to receive from the spoils of war (*fayʾ*). Abū ʿUbayda states that he has no right unless he fought against a people in the name of justice (*bi-ʾl-maʿrūf*). Furthermore, he cites traditions referring to the first two caliphs Abū Bakr and ʿUmar, who he stressed would both take the spoils only when it was strictly necessary to

127 Abū ʿUbayda, *Risāla* 18.

128 Ibn Khalīfa, *Futyā* 134–135 (Ms. 39_{26}). Translated by Schwartz in *Die Anfänge der Ibaditen in Nordafrika* 60–61. See also Ibn Khalīfa, *Futyā* 147 (Ms. 42_{15}).

129 Abū ʿUbayda, *Risāla* 9.

130 Abū ʿUbayda, *Risāla* 12.

131 Abū ʿUbayda, *Risāla* 8–9.

keep themselves and their families. Furthermore, when ʿUmar was dying, he ordered his son ʿAbd Allāh to give his money to the central treasury (*bayt al-māl*). However, this model of a sober and modest lifestyle for the leader of the community was soon abandoned and the *imāms* were given privileges to the detriment of the other Muslims.[132]

3. **The question of *walāya* and *barāʾa*:** An important point discussed in the *risāla* is connected to the conduct of the person to whom *zakāt* should be given. Only the poor Ibāḍīs in the state of association (*walāya*) deserve a share of the *zakāt* funds. Anyone who has lost the status of "association" due to, for example, a false testimony, a false accusation of adultery or because he has drunk *nabīdh*,[133] is not entitled to receive from the *zakāt*. He is considered *fāsiq*, and *barāʾa* should be declared against him.

The *risāla* by Abū ʿUbayda also tackles the case of a man who sees a person in authority (*amīn*) excommunicating someone (*ḥarrama*) without clear evidence and gives him *zakāt*, notwithstanding that the man is in the condition of *barāʾa*. According to Abū ʿUbayda, if the man has been banned on the basis of the prudent judgement of the community (*raʾy al-jamāʿa baʿd ijtihādihim*), then the judgement of the community is binding and he is not entitled to receive from the *zakāt* funds: "This is the *sunna* and I do not believe that he has the right to contravene the *sunna*. If, on the other hand, the community has made a mistake (*ghalata*), then his opinion is right".[134]

4. **The *zakāt* on the wealth belonging to a minor:** As far as the wealth belonging to a minor is concerned, Abū ʿUbayda maintains that the tutor (*khalīfa*) must pay the *zakāt* due on his property. This is also the opinion held by Jābir b. Zayd, by "all our jurists" (*jamīʿ fuqahāʾinā*), and by some eminent companions, such as ʿAlī, ʿĀʾisha and ʿUmar b. al-Khaṭṭāb. On the contrary, Ibn ʿAbbās and Jābir b. ʿAbd Allāh believe that the minor should not pay any tax until he reaches puberty. Apparently, they base their opinion on Quran 9:103: "Take alms out of their property, you would cleanse them and purify them thereby". This "purification" – they argue – is from the sins committed and the minor has not committed sins.[135]

---

132 Abū ʿUbayda, *Risāla* 6–7, 25.

133 *Nabīdh* is a drink made from raisins/grapes or dates, which becomes intoxicating (mildly or heavily depending on the level of fermentation), if they are left to steep in water for over 12 hours.

134 Abū ʿUbayda, *Risāla* 19–24.

135 Abū ʿUbayda, *Risāla* 24–25. Jābir's opinion on the obligation of *zakāt* on minor's property is confirmed in al-Kharusi (ed.), *Āthār* 61, no. 267 (Ms. 173).

Some of the questions treated in the *Risāla* by Abū ʿUbayda are also found in the epistle by Muḥmmad b. Maḥbūb b. al-Ruḥayl, written to the people of the Maghrib on behalf of the *imām* al-Ṣalt b. Mālik (r. 237/851–272/856). It reflects the real development of the Ibāḍī political views after the centre at Basra dispersed and the community moved to Oman where an imamate was established. The epistle is written in response to questions posed by the Maghribi Ibāḍīs concerning *zakāt*, in particular whether *zakāt* should be paid to a government that offers no protection. According to Abdulrahman al-Salimi, the sender was perhaps from Jabal Nafūsa or Tripoli, where Ibadism had split into several subdivisions, namely the Nukkāriyya, the Naffāthiyya and the Khalafiyya, who opposed the Rustumid *imām*s of Tāhert. The epistle discusses some crucial issues concerning the imamate, in particular the *imām*'s authority, the states' boundaries, the *imām*'s election and the right of the people to elect an *imām* if they are a minority. Concerning *zakāt*, Muḥammad b. Maḥbūb b. al-Ruḥayl advises the people that the *imām* has no right to collect the *zakāt* unless he is able to protect them from oppression and aggression. If he does not satisfy these conditions, but claims to collect *zakāt*, he is considered a "tyrant" and people should rise up in rebellion against him.[136]

3.6.1 The *Zakāt* on Cattle

The fiscal system in the early centuries of Islam was rather uncertain and was subject to different influences. It included not only taxes considered as legal (*zakāt*, *ʿushr*, *kharāj*, *jizya*), but also a series of illegitimate taxes and duties linked to commercial practice, which came to be designated by the term "*maks*". Moreover, the Prophet granted a special taxation regime to several tribes converted to Islam. The very obligation of *zakāt* itself was questioned after the Prophet's death during the revolt of the Arab tribes (*ridda*). Even after the revolt had been crushed and the *zakāt* clearly established as compulsory, many uncertain points concerning its application remained. One of these was the taxable threshold for cattle, which the Ibāḍīs established at 5 head, the same for pasturing camels. On the contrary Sunni and Shiʿite law applied a taxable threshold of 30 head to oxen, less than 30 being free of *zakāt*. The Ibāḍīs based their theory on two traditions reporting the Prophet's and ʿUmar b. al-Khaṭṭāb's instructions.[137]

---

136 Al Salimi, Themes of the (Ibāḍī/Omani) *Siyar* 510–512; idem, Identifying the Ibādī/Omani *Siyar* 136–137, no. LI.

137 Kister, Some reports concerning al-Ṭā'if 11; see also Francesca, Comparing the Ibāḍī and Sunnī Law in Baṣra.

The oldest Ibāḍī account on the *niṣāb* for cattle is preserved in the *Aqwāl Qatāda b. Diʿāma* in the chapter on *ṣadaqāt*. The chapter opens with a tradition, transmitted by ʿAmr b. Harim from Muḥammad b. ʿAbd al-Raḥmān al-Anṣārī, relating that when the caliph ʿUmar b. ʿAbd ʿAzīz (r. 717–720) was elected, he sent him to Medina to look for a document in which Muḥammad had given instructions for the payment of *zakāt* and for a similar document issued by ʿUmar b. al-Khaṭṭāb. The agent found the Prophet's document in the family of ʿAmr b. Ḥazm, the Prophet's companion and governor of Najrān. He also found another writing on charity sent by ʿUmar to his tax collector and kept by the latter's family that was identical to the Prophet's writing addressed to ʿAmr b. Ḥazm. ʿUmar b. ʿAbd ʿAzīz ordered to Muḥammad b. ʿAbd al-Raḥmān al-Anṣārī to copy the writings on *zakāt*.[138] According to these documents, the minimum tax threshold fixed for oxen was five head, as it was for camels.[139]

The tradition attesting that the *niṣāb* for oxen corresponds to that of camels is confirmed also by some Sunni sources. One of them, the *Kitāb al-Amwāl* by Abū ʿUbayd al-Qāsim (d. 223/837), reports a tradition that corresponds, except in a few minor details, to the *Aqwāl Qatāda*. The *Kitāb al-Amwāl* also refers to the Prophet's and the caliph ʿUmar's writings on almsgiving, transmitted by Yazīd b. Hārūn from Ḥabīb b. Abī Ḥabīb, from ʿAmr b. Harim, from Muḥammad b. ʿAbd al-Raḥmān al-Anṣārī.[140]

Regarding the minimum taxable amount for cattle, the *Kitāb al-Amwāl* reports on the authority of Ḥabīb b. Ḥabīb from ʿAmr b. Harim and Muḥammad b. ʿAbd al-Raḥmān al-Anṣārī:

> In the writings of the Prophet (PBUH), and in those of ʿUmar b. al-Khaṭṭāb, it is written that the [tax] levied on cattle is the same than the one levied on camels.[141]

Two further Sunni sources quote the Prophet's and the second caliph ʿUmar b. al-Khaṭṭāb's writings on almsgiving, but they do not mention the minimum amount for cattle. They are the *Sunan* of Abū Dāwūd (d. 275/888), with an *isnād* going back to al-Zuhrī, and the *Sunan* by al-Dāraquṭnī which relates the tradition using the same *isnād* than in the *Aqwāl Qatāda*.[142]

Ibāḍī sources, except the *Aqwāl Qatāda b. Diʿāma*, do not refer to the Prophet's or to ʿUmar's writings on *zakāt*, but they confirm that the amount of

138 Al-Salimi (ed.), *Aqwāl* 378 (Ms. 102).

139 Al-Salimi (ed.), *Aqwāl* 380 (Ms. 103_{25}–104_{3}).

140 Abū ʿUbayd al-Qāsim, *Kitāb al-Amwāl* 497.

141 Abū ʿUbayd al-Qāsim, *Kitāb al-Amwāl* 524.

142 Abū Dāwūd, *Sunan* i, 491; al-Dāraquṭnī, *Sunan* ii part, 116–117.

the *niṣāb* on oxen is 5 head, the same as for camels. The *Mudawwana* of Abū Ghānim al-Khurāsānī states, on the authority of Abū ʿUbayda, that the *zakāt* for oxen is 5 head, like for camels. Moreover Abū ʾl-Muʾarrij refers that "our companions, Abū ʿUbayda and Jābir b. Zayd, did not accept the tradition of Muʿādh", i.e. the tradition stating that the minimum amount for taxable oxen was 30 head.[143]

In the *Jāmiʿ* of Ibn Jaʿfar (3rd/9th century) we find more information about the taxation of cattle:

> For cattle the same amount is taken as for camels, for 5 head 1 sheep is taken, for 10 head 2, for 15 head 3, for 20 head 4, and if the cattle amount reaches 25 head a *jadhaʿa* [a cow in her second year] is taken, as old as a *bint makhāḍ* [a female camel in her second year]; for 36 head of cattle a *thaniyya* [a cow in her third year] is taken, as old as a *bint labūn* [a female camel in her third year]; for 46 head a *rabāʿiya* [a cow in her fourth year], as old as a *ḥiqqa* [a female camel in her fourth year]; for 61 head a *sadas* [a cow in her fifth year] is taken, as old as a *jadhaʿa* [a female camel in her fifth year]; for 76 head, 2 head are taken, of the age corresponding to the camels and so on; for 300 head of cattle, 1 head is taken from every 40.[144]

The correspondence of the minimal amount for cattle and that of camels is also reflected in other Sunni sources, in particular the following.

1. ʿAbd al-Razzāq, *Muṣannaf*: transmitted by al-Zuhrī, from Qatāda, from Jābir b. ʿAbd Allāh:

> For 5 cows a sheep is taken, for 10 cows 2 sheep, for 15 cows 3 sheep, for 20 cows 4 sheep. Al-Zuhrī said: from 20 to 75 cows, 1 cow is taken, from 76 to 120 cows 2 cows and then 1 cow is taken for every 40 cows. This reduction was beneficial to the people of Yaman.[145]

2. Ibn Abī Shayba, *Muṣannaf*:

> According to the tradition related by Ibn Abī Shayba, ʿIkrima b. Khālid, the tax collector of the Banū ʿAkk tribe, said that some *shuyūkh* maintained that the

143 Abū Ghānim, *Mudawwana* i, 246–249.
144 Ibn Jaʿfar, *al-Jāmiʿ* iii, 149. See also al-Kindī, *Muṣannaf* vi, 10–16.
145 ʿAbd al-Razzāq, *Muṣannaf* iv, 24, 25, transmitted on the authority of Maʿmar b. Rashīd, from his master al-Zuhrī.

> *zakāt* on cattle was equal to that on camels, while others claimed that a calf was taken every 30 cows, yet others said that a cow was taken every 40 head.[146]

3. al-Bayhaqī: transmitted by Ma'mar, from Zuhrī, from Jābir b. 'Abdallāh:

> For 5 sheep 1 sheep is taken, for 10 sheep 2, for 15 sheep 3, for 20 sheep 4. Zuhrī said: From 25 to 75 cows, 1 cow, from 76 to 120 cows 2 cows, from 121 head upwards 1 cow is taken every 40. From Ma'mar following al-Zuhrī: The words "a *tabī'* [an uncastrated bull in his second year] every 30 head" refers to a tax reduction in favour of the inhabitants of Yaman.[147]

4. Ibn Ḥazm (4–1064) says that the *niṣāb* of 5 head for oxen was an opinion of the Medinan school.[148]
5. 'Alā' al-Dīn 'Alī al-Muttaqī (888/1472–975/1568):

> It is reported from al-Zuhrī that the Prophet's words "Every 30 cows, 1 calf" should be considered as a tax reduction in favour of the people of Yaman, after which it has become a rule. [...] From Ayyūb: I heard people saying: "Take from us what the Prophet took", and I was surprised until al-Zuhrī told me that the Prophet wrote a document on these taxes, but he died before being able to send it to the tax collectors. The document passed to Abū Bakr who gave it to one to his tax collectors, except the part regarding oxen. [...] From Qatāda, from Sa'īd b. Musayyib, and from Abū Qalāba and others: The *zakāt* on oxen is the same as the *zakāt* on camels.[149]

Contrary to the *niṣāb* for camels, the *niṣāb* for cattle is frequently questioned in Arabic medieval sources. The ambiguity of the sources about the minimum threshold for oxen may come from the fact that the tradition transmitted by Mu'ādh b. Jabal, Muḥammad's tax collector in Yaman, giving 30 head as the minimum tax threshold, was not considered authentic by all jurists.[150]

At the same time, there were discordant opinions also based on instructions given to the tax collectors by the Prophet or by the second caliph 'Umar. Historical sources show that the tax collectors were often free of deciding

146 Ibn Abī Shayba, *Muṣannaf* iii, 127.
147 Al-Bayhaqī, *Kitāb sunan al-kubrā* iv, 168–169.
148 Ibn Ḥazm, *al-Muḥallā* vi, 3–16.
149 Al-Muttaqī, *Kanz al-'ummāl* iii, 306–307.
150 Ibn Rushd, *Kitāb bidāyat al-mujtahid* ii, 517; al-Qaraḍāwī, *Fiqh al-zakāt* i, 192–203.

alone on questions considered as secondary.[151] According to al-Qaraḍāwī, in the case of oxen, the tax collectors could fix the minimum tax threshold on the basis of their effective local value, which could vary greatly given that herds of oxen were much less common than camels.[152]

Another important document provides norms for the payment of *zakāt*: the instructions given to ʿAmr b. Ḥazm by the Prophet when he sent him to Najrān. This document has also been subject to manipulations: while the first versions of the document reported by Ibn Ishāq (d. 150/767) and by Abū Yūsuf (d. 182/798) do not refer to the *zakāt* on cattle, in the definitive version reported by Ibn Hishām (d. 218/833), it is reported in detail.[153] The minimum taxable threshold for oxen is fixed at 30 head.

It is rather significant that many sources do not give the precise minimum taxable threshold for oxen when they deal with *zakāt*. For example, in the *Kitāb al-Kharāj* of Abū Yūsuf, a reference is made to the instructions on *zakāt* left by the Prophet who wrote them and tied them to his sword. In another account, these instructions are mentioned among his last will, which would be realized only after his death. These accounts do not refer to oxen, but only to camels and sheep.[154]

Al-Shāfiʿī refers in his *al-Umm* to a writing of Muʿādh, owned by ʿUmar b. ʿAbd al-ʿAzīz, where it is stated that the minimum taxable threshold for cattle should be 30 head. He also states that there is no discordance (*khilāfa*) on the tradition, a possible clue that the *niṣāb* on cattle was accepted in his time.[155] However, in the *Musnad al-imām al-Shāfiʿī*, a tradition transmitted by Hamr d. Dīnār from Ṭāwus says that Muʿādh had not received precise orders from the Prophet about the *zakāt* on cattle, and that when he came back to Medina to ask whether the *niṣāb* of 30 head for cattle was correct, the Prophet was already dead.[156]

How can the rules concerning the *zakāt* on oxen be interpreted? Leaving apart customary and local practice, the level of the tax threshold was also determined for political reasons. The first rules appear to be a political concession to the people of Yaman, who were ordered to pay the same customary taxes as before the rise of Islam. According to al-Zuhrī (d. 124/742), whose name appears in the tradition reported by Sunni sources, the Prophet's instructions

151 Francesca, Comparing the Ibāḍī and Sunnī Law in Baṣra 55.

152 Al-Qaraḍāwī, *Fiqh al-zakāt* i, 203.

153 Caetani, *Annali dell'Islam* year 23, 317–320.

154 Abū Yūsuf, *Kitāb al-kharāj*, 115. Further Sunni sources attests of the Prophet's writing on *zakāt* without mentioning any minimun amount for cattle: Abū Dāwūd, *Sunan* i, 41; al-Dāraquṭnī, *al-Sunan* ii part, 116–117; Ibn Māja, *Sunan* i, 573.

155 al-Shāfiʿī, *al-Umm* iii, 22.

156 al-Shāfiʿī, *Musnad al-imām al-Shāfiʿī* 187.

fixing the *niṣāb* for pasturing oxen to 30 head were a provisional benefit for the inhabitants of Yaman. They were later abrogated by the rules fixing the *niṣāb* at 5 head.[157]

It is worth mentioning that al-Zuhrī and some of his Medinan pupils appear in traditions about the Prophet's letters concerning fiscal regulation that would have been sent to foreign leaders, or that would have been found tied to his sword after his death.[158] These letters are fictitious: they are so markedly imbued with caliphal ideology that they clearly belong to the caliphal debate of the 8th century.[159] Al-Zuhrī was active in this process, as is clearly demonstrated by his presence in the traditions connected with the Umayyad caliph ʿUmar b. ʿAbd al-ʿAzīz. The latter, who was a former governor of Medina, was also connected with the Medinan practice. As is often the case, his pious position (or alleged position) stands in sharp contrast with that of some of his predecessors and successors. ʿUmar Ibn ʿAbd al-ʿAziz is supposed to have written to the people of Medina in order to find out what was the original practice in the Prophet's time. He apparently felt the need to legitimize new fiscal arrangements for the Muslim empire with reference to Muḥammad's practice. He also tried to further state interests and prevent the imminent breakdown of the Islamic state with the growing development of religious thought. ʿUmar's fiscal legislation can be considered as the consequence of his predecessor's attempts to reform the state.[160]

One of the most important aims of ʿUmar's "Fiscal Rescript" was to reassert the obligatory character of *zakāt*. The Arab expansion and the conquest of the Byzantine and Persian empires undermined the economic significance of the *zakāt* paid by the tribes of the Arabian Peninsula, substituted by a new taxation system based mainly on land taxes, *ʿushr* and *kharāj*.[161] *Zakāt* was no longer the general concern of the Muslim community as a whole but was mainly paid to indigent people. Nonetheless, ʿUmar's fiscal regulation shows a great concern for how *zakāt* was administrated. The alms-tax had to be rigorously but justly taken from all Muslims on their landed properties, livestock and monetary capital, and improper extortion had to be prohibited. The obligatory and fiscal character of the tax was stressed; the tax had to be paid to the provincial treasury against a delivery receipt, apparently in opposition to whoever insisted

157 ʿAbd al-Razzāq, *Muṣannaf* iv, 24–25; al-Qaraḍāwī, *Fiqh al-zakāt* i, 198–199.

158 Ibn Abī Shayba, *Muṣannaf* iii, 131; Abū Dāwūd, *Sunan* 490; al-Tirmidhī, *al-Jāmiʿ al-Ṣaḥīḥ* iii, no. 621 (*bāb* 4); al-Dārimī, *Sunan* i, 466; Ibn ʿUmar, *Musnad* 359–361; Abū Yūsuf, *Kitāb al-kharāj* 115.

159 Simonsen, *Studies in the Genesis* 50.

160 Umar's fiscal legislation is preserved in Ibn ʿAbd al-Ḥakam (d. 214/829), *Sīrat ʿUmar b. ʿAbd al-ʿAzīz*. See also Guessous, Le rescrit fiscal de ʿUmar b. ʿAbd al-ʿAzīz.

161 Løkkegard, *Islamic Taxation in the Classic Period*; Dennet, *Conversion and the Poll Tax*.

on its voluntary character. In the tradition of the minimum tax threshold of 5 oxen, the mention of al-Zuhrī along with the Umayyad caliph ʿUmar Ibn ʿAbd al-ʿAzīz is suggesting that there was an attempt to reaffirm the Medinan practice and to give historical relevance and religious legitimization to the caliphal taxation by making a reference to the rules instituted by Muḥammad and the first caliphs.

The Islamic taxation system must be seen as an attempt of the nascent Medinan polity to extend its political authority and religious message over a tribal society by managing the distribution of booty and charity. Nonetheless, it was mainly a product of the empire, derived from the conquests, and eventually detailed later by statemen in administrative handbooks (like the *Kitāb al-Kharāj* of Abū Yūsuf, d. 182/798, or Qudāma b. Jaʿfar, d. 337/948), and by religious scholars seeking to define imperial administration in Islamic terms (like in the *Kitāb al-Amwāl* of Abū ʿUbayd al-Qāsim).[162]

In this systemization process, the traditions about the *niṣāb* on cattle transmitted by the Ibāḍīs represent an "unsuccessful opinion", which was abandoned by the prevailing doctrine accepted by both Sunnis and Shiʿites. The attempt of al-Zuhrī and ʿUmar b. ʿAbd al-ʿAzīz to reaffirm the "real" (or allegedly real) Medinan practice was minimized by the growth of Prophetic traditions affirming the contrary doctrine fixing the amount of the *niṣāb* on cattle to 30 head. Conflicting doctrines about the *niṣāb* on cattle existed until the 8th century, a fact that can be clearly detected by the analysis and comparison of parallel traditions. In this respect, the ancient Ibāḍī sources, which preserved several "unsuccessful traditions" represent an important field for studying the development of Islamic jurisprudence in the early centuries, along with its interaction with custom, local and administrative practice.

3.7 Conclusion

In this chapter I dealt primarily with the problem of how the early history of Ibāḍī law and jurisprudence can be reconstructed, what sources are available for such reconstruction and how reliable and significant they are. As I discussed in Chapter 2, Ibāḍī law has its roots primarily in the juridical efforts and teaching activities of the first leaders of the movement and of less well-known jurists, such as Abū ʾl-Muʾarrij ʿAmr al-Sadūsī, ʿAbd Allāh b. ʿAbd al-ʿAzīz and Abū Ghānim al-Khurāsānī. The role of Jābir b. Zayd as founding father of the movement should not be undermined. He was really the teacher of a number of

162 Ben Shemesh, *Taxation in Islām*.

scholars who propagated the Ibāḍī law, such Abū Nūḥ Ṣāliḥ al-Dahhān, Ḥayyān al-Aʿraj, Ḍumām b. al-Sāʾib, Jaʿfar b. al-Sammāk and Abū ʿUbayda al-Tamīmī.

The particular importance of the sources attributed to the early Ibāḍī authorities lies in their being not only among the first formulations of Islamic law, but also early evidence of that law as a lived reality rather than a theoretical reconstruction. As we have seen, they provide judgements on practical cases handed down by the early Ibāḍī jurists. To adequately investigate every aspect of the Ibāḍī law in its formative period would be obviously beyond the scope of this volume. Instead, I have chosen to concentrate upon specific case studies highlighting specific aspects of Ibāḍī law. These allow us to uncover "unsuccessful" early strata of the development of Islamic legal tradition as well as to recognize its multi-layered nature. My hypothesis is that a focus on Ibāḍī sources, which preserve ancient material, provides a stronger basis for the study of the early centuries of Islam.

Another question, which is no less important, is that of the substantive development of the Ibāḍī legal discourse in relation to the Sunni schools in the early centuries of Islam. The portrait of Ibāḍī law that I have sketched on the basis of the early Ibāḍī legal literature suggests that its articulation and development were parallel to those of the emerging Sunni schools, with which the early Ibāḍī authorities had numerous exchanges, as is well documented in the *Aqwāl Qatāda*. Nonetheless, as proved by the overview of the early Ibāḍī law in the first part of this chapter, from the start the Ibāḍīs took an independent line from the Sunni schools, with independent authorities and jurists.

In the second part of the chapter, I offered an analysis of some case studies which provide a strong basis for uncovering some dynamics of the first centuries of Islam. Indeed, one of the primary reasons for the focus upon some aspects of the early Islamic debate surrounding fornication and adultery is to uncover the historical dimension of the links between Islamic law and the adjacent legal cultures of the Near East. Islamic conceptions of marital power and of control over female bodies shared commonalities with other Near Eastern legal systems. In particular, the adoption of stoning as punishment for adultery, which is not referred to in the Quran, poses the controversial possibility that the ancient Near Eastern legal background played some role in the emergence of Islamic law. The permanent impediment to marriage between the partners found guilty of fornication, which is a peculiarity of both Ibāḍī and Shiʿite law, is the ideal example of late antique influence on Islamic law, as it echoed elements of a syncretic heritage of juridical speculation in the Near East. In fact, the most plausible answer to the question of the relationship between Islamic law and foreign legal systems concerning adultery and fornication can be found in a common cultural and social background among

Jewish, Christian and Islamic legal tradition. Within the Ibāḍī ethos, which places significant emphasis on the preservation of the community's internal purity, the rule regarding the perpetual impediment to marriage for the fornicators was designed to identify any form of prohibited sexual activity as a potential threat to the purity and integrity of the community. Indeed, the Ibāḍī law was characterized by the establishment of regulatory frameworks that diverged from the practices observed among their Sunni counterparts. This shift was accompanied by the employment of vehement rhetoric, denoting profound aversion and intolerance towards those perceived as transgressors. This stance was further reinforced by the imposition of restrictions that prevented transgressors from entering into marital union with one another.

The other two case studies that I discussed at length concern the restriction of the prohibition of usury to non-contextual exchanges only, and the *niṣāb* on cattle. Both opinions represent "unsuccessful traditions", set aside by the prevailing doctrine accepted by Sunnis and Shiʿites alike. In this respect, the Ibāḍī sources, which preserve ancient material, are an important field for studying the development of Islamic jurisprudence in the early centuries, alongside its interaction with custom, local practice and administration.

CHAPTER 4

Developing the Concepts of *Sunna* and *Uṣūl al-Fiqh*: the *Musnad al-Rabīʿ b. Ḥabīb*

4.1 Introduction

In this chapter I will discusses the development of Ibāḍī law starting from the 9th to 10th century. This period saw a rebirth of the imamate in Oman after its collapse at the end of the 3rd/9th century The Ibāḍī *fiqh* fully took on the form of a *madhhab*, with works of *uṣūl* and *furūʿ*. The development achieved by Ibāḍī jurisprudence is clearly visible in the work of Muḥammad b. Saʿīd al-Kudamī (who lived between the end of the 4th/10th and the beginning of the 5th/11th centuries) entitled *al-Muʿtabar*, which was a critical edition of the *Kitāb al-jāmiʿ* by Ibn Jaʿfar (3rd/9th century). A few years after al-Kudamī's treatise, the *Kitāb al-jāmiʿ* by ʿAbd Allāh b. Muḥammad b. Baraka al-Bahlawī (second half of the 4th/10th century) became a fundamental reference point for the works of Ibāḍī encyclopaedists at the end of the 5th/11th and the beginning of the 6th/12th centuries, in particular, the *Kitāb al-ḍiyāʾ* by Salama b. Muslim al-ʿAwtabī, the *Bayān al-sharʿ* by Muḥammad b. Ibrāhīm al-Kindī (d. 508/1115), the *Kitāb al-kifāya* (of which only a few fragments have survived) by Muḥammad b. Mūsā and the *Muṣannaf* by Abū Bakr Aḥmad b. Mūsā al-Kindī (d. 557/1162).

The *Mukhtaṣar al-khiṣāl* by Abū Isḥāq Ibrāhīm Ibn Qays al-Ḥaḍramī, the last Ibāḍī *imām* of Ḥaḍramawt (r. *c.*443–475/1052–1083, d. about 520/1126), and the *Mukhtaṣar* by Abū ʾl-Ḥasan ʿAlī b. Muḥammad al-Bisiyānī (also al-Bisyawī or al-Basīwī), pupil of Ibn Baraka, belong to the same period as the latter's *Kitāb al-jāmiʿ*.

In North Africa, after the definitive collapse of the Rustumid imamate and a period of stasis, there was a reflowering of the jurisprudence, parallel to that found in Oman. In the first half of the 6th/12th century, Yūsuf al-Warjlānī completed his arrangement (*tartīb*) of a collection of *ḥadīth* attributed to al-Rabīʿ b. Ḥabīb, in which traditions of the Prophet and the Companions were handed down through the *imāms* of the school, known as *Musnad al-Rabīʿ b. Ḥabīb* or *al-Jāmiʿ al-ṣaḥīḥ*.

For the Ibāḍī *madhhab* the *Musnad* fulfils two important functions: that of providing an independent Ibāḍī collection of *ḥadīth* without having to refer to other schools, and that of affirming the pupil-*imām* transmission line from the

 | HTTPS://DOI.ORG/10.1163/9789004765764-006

founder of the *madhhab* Jābir b. Zayd, via his successor Abū ʿUbayda, via the successor of the latter, al-Rabīʿ.

According to Wilkinson, we can take the period between the end of the 4th/10th and the beginning of the 5th/11th century as the starting point for the process of "rationalization" of Ibāḍī jurisprudence, meaning converting the primitive form of Ibadism into a model *madhhab*. In Oman this process coincided with a resurgence of the imamate after the collapse of the first imamate. In the Maghrib, where the institution of the imamate had disappeared to give rise to the more secret organisation of the *ḥalqat al-ʿazzāba* (circle of elders), the process of normalisation likely emerged in reaction to Maliki influences.

This "rationalization" process can be followed through specific thematic complexities such as the development of the concept of the *sunna* starting from the early Ibāḍī sources.

4.2 The Concept of *Sunna* among the First Ibāḍī Authorities

The first Ibāḍī authorities – mainly the first *imāms* of the Basran community, Jābir b. Zayd, Abū ʿUbayda and al-Rabīʿ b. Ḥabīb – gave life to a school which was greatly influenced by traditions from the companions and by the community's own tradition (*āthār*). As we have already seen, in Jābir's letters, the term *sunna* indicates the local tradition or a practice generally accepted by the community.[1] In the letter addressed to al-Ḥārith b. ʿAmr (no. 4), Jābir fiercely refuses to recognize the validity of prayers which were performed without recitation of the Quran, on the argument that this was against a well-founded *sunna* (*fa-innahu qad taraka al-sunna*).[2]

In the epistle by another early Ibāḍī scholar, Sālim Ibn Dhakwān, written before *c.*800 (its precise date is disputed) and directed against Khārijī extremism and Murji'ism, *sunna* appears both as prophetic *sunna* and as "*sunna* of the righteous among God's servants" (*sunnat al-ṣāliḥīn min ʿibād Allāh*), meaning the "Righteously Guided Caliphs" (*al-Khulafāʾ al-Rāshidūn*).[3] This term is used to refer in particular to Abū Bakr and ʿUmar, whereas the third caliph ʿUthmān

1 Al-Jaʿbīrī (ed.), *Rasāʾil* 109, 122 (Ms. $70A_{26}$, $73B_{17}$).

2 Al-Jaʿbīrī (ed.), *Rasāʾil* 100 (Ms. $68B_{7-10}$). The doctrine that the prayer without recitation of the Quran is valid is expressed in traditions from ʿAlī and from ʿUmar. Against it is directed the sweeping maxim from the Prophet: "No prayer is valid without recitation". See Schacht, *The Origins* 154–155.

3 Crone – Zimmermann (eds.), *The Epistle of Sālim Ibn Dhakwān* 144 (Arabic), 145 (English trans.).

is accused of having shunned the *sunna* of God's Messenger and followed a way other than that of his guidance.[4]

ʿAbd Allāh ibn Ibāḍ, the alleged founder of the Ibāḍī movement, who is credited with two letters addressed to the Umayyad caliph ʿAbd al-Malik b. Marwān, also accused ʿUthmān of having betrayed the *sunna* of the Prophet by introducing innovations. Therefore, the Ibāḍīs did not recognize his authority and disputed the legitimacy of his caliphate.

In the early Ibāḍī sources respecting the "*sunna*" means mainly following a well-attested "precedent", as Sālim Ibn Dhakwān states:

> After consulting with the Muslims, he [Abū Bakr] appointed ʿUmar b. al-Khaṭṭāb (to succeed him) as caliph. ʿUmar acted in accordance with the Book of God, followed the *sunna* of God's Messenger, and adopted the *sunna* of Abū Bakr. But he was also confronted with cases which were not covered by Quranic pronouncements or prior *sunna*, whether (received) from the Messenger of God, may God's blessing and peace be upon him, or instituted by Abū Bakr. [...] For many other problems, too, ʿUmar b. al-Khaṭṭāb instituted precedents (*sanna sunan*) as they arose after consulting with the Muslim; and it is the duty of every Muslim to endorse them and follow them in practice.[5]

Abū ʿUbayda, who succeeds Jābir b. Zayd to the leadership of the Ibāḍī Basran community, follows his precursor's method for the formulation of legal judgements. He maintains that the decision in any legal case should be based in the first instance on the Quran and, if there is no ruling to be derived from the Quran, recourse should be made to the *sunna* of companions. As a theologian and lawyer, Abū ʿUbayda was a fervent supporter of the role of tradition and vehemently opposed the use of *raʾy* (personal reasoning). However, if the subjective, personal view may be contested, he recognizes the value of the jurists' prudent systematic reasoning and assumed that *ijmāʿ* (consensus) is binding if based on it (*raʾy al-jamāʿa baʿda ijtihādihim*):

> In deciding they apply their prudent systematic reasoning (*wa-ʾjtahidū raʾyahum fīhi*), based on what God has ordered concerning the distribution [of the tithes] among those who he has ordered shall receive them.[6]

---

4 Crone – Zimmermann (eds.), *The Epistle of Sālim Ibn Dhakwān* 78, 80, 82, 84 (Arabic); 79, 81, 83, 85 (English trans.). See also index 375.

5 Crone – Zimmermann (eds.), *The Epistle of Sālim Ibn Dhakwān* 76 (Arabic), 77 (English trans.).

6 Abū ʿUbayda, *Risāla* 4, 17, 24.

In the age of al-Rabīʿ, Abū ʿUbayda's successor, the first divided opinions on the hermeneutics of the sources can be seen among the Ibāḍī jurists. ʿAbd Allāh b. ʿAbd al-ʿAzīz, his companion Abū ʾl-Muʾarrij and others argued with al-Rabīʿ about a freer use of rational criteria (*raʾy* and *qiyās*) and personal reasoning.[7] Although the community was dismayed by this circumstance, ʿAbd Allāh b. ʿAbd al-ʿAzīz's legal responses were accepted, as the Ibāḍī historian al-Wisyānī writes:

> The doctrine (*qawl*) of al-Rabīʿ is more balanced and wiser, but Ibn ʿAbd al-ʿAzīz's doctrine has been accepted by most of the people.[8]

4.3 The *Sunna* in the Omani Sources

After the 9th century, Ibāḍī-Omani sources of law entered a new stage of development: works dating from this period contain records of debates and arguments of individual authors concerning questions of *uṣūl al-fiqh*. A large portion of these works debates how the accepted sources of the law might be interpreted; discussion focuses on three broad areas of investigation: authority, authenticity and interpretation. These works contain descriptions of how God's law has come to be known and will continue to be discovered by the Muslim community's expert jurists in the future. Among the earliest surviving works on these issues there is the *Kitāb al-Raṣf*, a compendium of *kalām* theology from an Ibāḍī point of view, composed between 260/874 and 270/884 by Abū ʾl-Mundhir Bashīr b. Muḥammad b. Maḥbūb (d. 290/908), a prominent Omani scholar and the grandson of Abū Sufyān Maḥbūb b. Ruḥayl, leader of the Basran community before Ibāḍīs moved to Oman.

The author recognizes three sources of Law: the Quran, the *sunna* (not just the Prophet's) and the tradition of the Ibāḍī community (*āthār al-muslimīn*). In the chapter on the *sunna*, he examines the degree and the extent of obligation arising from the practice of the Prophet and the community: the acceptance of the *sunna* is mandatory (*farḍ*) upon every believer and there is no need to find confirmation in the Quran before following the *sunna*, as it is authoritative independent of the Holy Book. The latter is considered superior

---

7 Ibn Sallām, *Kitāb Ibn Sallām* 114; al-Shammākhī, *Siyar* (1884) 104, 119–121; van Ess, *Theologie und Gesellschaft* ii, 208–209; idem, *Untersuchungen* 39, 41. The quarrel concerned theological questions as well, see Cuperly, *Introduction* 27 n. 63, 315.

8 Al-Wisyānī, *Kitāb al-Siyar* 69.

in status, but the *sunna* outnumbers it in sheer quantity. Moreover, the *sunna* explains, integrates and can even abrogate the Quran.[9]

Nothing in the Abū 'l-Mundhir's work, nor indeed in other 9th century sources, implies that *sunna* was confined to the Prophet. The *al-Jāmiʿ* by the highly respected Omani jurist Ibn Jaʿfar (Abū Jābir Muḥammad) al-Azkawī (3rd/9th century), which is considered a major work of *fiqh*, quotes traditions from the Prophet along with traditions from the Companions as well as from early Ibāḍī Basran authorities and from Omani jurists.[10]

The 4th/10th century marked a new phase in the development of Ibāḍī law with works of *uṣūl* and *furūʿ*, in which the doctrine of the sect's authorities was expressed on the basis of a plan that reflected the structure and themes discussed in the treatises of the Sunni school. The development achieved by Ibāḍī jurisprudence is clearly visible in the work of Muḥammad b. Saʿīd al-Kudamī (who lived between the end of the 4th/10th and the beginning of the 5th/11th centuries) entitled *al-Muʿtabar*, which was a critical edition of the *al-Jāmiʿ* by Ibn Jaʿfar. There, order is given to the discussion of the problems of the sources' hermeneutics (*uṣūl al-fiqh*) and the *ʿibādāt* (acts of worship) provided in Ibn Jaʿfar's work. According to al-Kudamī, the *sunna*'s main function (as well as that of the community's consensus, *ijmāʿ*) is interpreting God's Book. Judges and jurists have to rely on these three sources (Quran, *sunna* and *ijmāʿ*) in issuing their judgements or legal opinions.[11]

Along with al-Kudamī's treatise, the *Kitāb al-jāmiʿ* by ʿAbd Allāh b. Muḥammad b. Baraka al-Bahlawī (second half of the 4th/10th century) became a fundamental reference point for Ibāḍī jurisprudence.

Ibn Baraka, born in the village of Bahlā in Oman, studied under the *imām* Saʿd b. ʿAbd Allāh b. Maḥbūb who was killed in 328/939–940. He was a prolific writer, though only few of his works have survived, and he played a significant part in political life of Oman. Among his juridical works worthy of mention is the *Kitāb al-jāmiʿ*, dealing with the principle of law and a commentary (*sharḥ*) of the *Jāmiʿ* by Ibn Jaʿfar.[12]

In his *Kitāb al-jāmiʿ* Ibn Baraka made a notable contribution to the Ibāḍī *fiqh*, affirming the centrality of the prophetic traditions, which constitute the fundamentals (*qawāʿid*) of both jurisprudence and hermeneutics (*uṣūl al-fiqh*, which he calls *uṣūl al-dīn al-sharaʿiyya*). He was familiar with the Sunni sources, which he studied to affirm the superiority of the Ibāḍī school against

9 Al-Salimi – Madelung (eds.), *Early Ibāḍī Literature. Bāb al-sunna* 19–22.
10 Ibn Jaʿfar, *al-Jāmiʿ* i, 48, 49, 56; iii, 599.
11 Al-Kudamī, *Kitāb al-Istiqāma* iii, 6–7.
12 Lewicki, Ibn Baraka, EI2.

the "*mukhālifūn*", opponents, and introduced into Ibadism some elements of the Sunni *ḥadīth* classification. Dealing with the *isnād*, traditions (*akhbār*) are arranged into *muttaṣil* (traditions with an unbroken *isnād* traced back to the Prophet), *mawqūf* (traditions going back only to a companion), *maqṭūʿ* (traditions going back to a successor), *matn* (when companions do not appear into the *isnād*) and *ṣaḥīfa* (traditions with a family *isnād*). With reference to the test, the traditions could deal with a matter in specific or general terms (*khāṣṣ wa ʾl-ʿāmm*), could be contradictory (*mutāʿāriḍa*), could abrogate each other (*khabar al-nasīkh wa ʾl-mansūkh*), or could complement each other (*khabar al-zāʾid ʿalā ʾl-nāqis*).[13]

Ibāḍīs find no problem with the traditions of other doctrines as long as their chains of transmission are trustworthy and there is no other reason not to accept them. Ibn Baraka said, "we do not deny the traditions of others as long as they are not corrupt".[14]

The ongoing process of "hadithification" in the Ibāḍī *madhhab* is evident in the works by the Omani encyclopaedists at the end of the 5th/11th and the beginning of the 6th/12th century, in particular the *Kitāb al-ḍiyāʾ* by Salma b. Muslim al-ʿAwtabī (end 5th/11th century–early 6th/12th century), the *Bayān al-sharʿ* by Muḥammad b. Ibrāhīm al-Kindī (d. 508/1115) and the *Muṣannaf* by Abū Bakr Aḥmad b. Mūsā al-Kindī (d. 557/1162). By the mid-12th century Muḥammad b. Ibrāhīm al-Kindī collected the *siyar*, epistles on different matters of theology and jurisprudence written by the early Ibāḍī authorities, which played a crucial political and pedagogical role within the community. They constitute an instrument of legitimization of Ibāḍī political and religious ideology and a guarantee of the collective cohesion.[15]

As J. Wilkinson argues, the opening discussion of *uṣūl al-fiqh* by al-ʿAwtabī in the third book of his *Kitāb al-Ḍiyāʾ* shows how far Ibāḍīs had become aligned with the Sunni/Shāfiʿī criterion that *sunna* primarily means "the tradition of the Prophet", but rather than using the Sunni criterion of *ḥadīth* transmission they rely on their own line of transmission (*isnād*) based on the heritage (*āthār*) of the school. For al-ʿAwtabī, the reliability of a tradition lies in a teacher–pupil line, a chain of leading scholars transmitting and elaborating the doctrine over generations, reaching back from the predecessors of his Rustāq school[16] –

13 Ibn Baraka, *Kitāb al-jāmiʿ*i, *bāb al-awl fī ʾl-akhbār* 14–15; on *ḥadīth* classification see *bāb fī ʾl-akhbār al-murawiyya ʿan al-nabī* 16–21.

14 Quoted in Ibn Ḥammū Kurrūm, *Ishāmāt al-madrasa al-Ibāḍiyya* 13–15.

15 Dridi, La communauté ibadite entre Orient et Occident musulmans (iiie/ixe–viie/xiiie siècle) 353–355.

16 The Omani jurists split between the so-called Rustāq and Nizwā parties after that the first imamate collapsed in a civil war because of the controversial deposing of the *imām*

al-Bisiyānī (middle of the 5th/11th century) and his teacher Ibn Baraka – to al-Rabīʿ, Jābir b. Zayd, Ibn ʿAbbās and other companions, whose authority was recognized by the Ibāḍī community, and thence the Prophet. Along with traditions with a purely Ibāḍī line of transmission, al-ʿAwtabī' – as other contemporary authors – picked up traditions from the Sunni collections, very rarely with an *isnād* and certainly with no critique of authenticity. This "communal" *sunna* was absorbed into the Ibāḍī *madhhab* but only to emphasize certain desirable behaviour (*faḍīla*), never for determining dogma; for that Ibāḍī authors alone were valid.[17]

The monumental work *Muṣannaf* by Abū Bakr Aḥmad b. Mūsā al-Kindī (d. 557/1162), which – along with the *Bayān al-sharʿ* by his teacher Muḥammad b. Ibrāhīm al-Kindī – is a manifestation of the encyclopaedic process in the Ibāḍī school, does not reflect any significant changes into the development of the principles of hermeneutics. The *sunna* going back to the Prophet is a root of law second only to the Quran. Every prophetic tradition must be respected unless it was abrogated by another/a successive tradition. He says:

> The righteous conduct in the faith is called *sunna* because it is the way (*ṭarīq*), the example (*mithāl*), the life (*sīra*), the purpose (*wajh*), the sign (*ʿalāma*), the trace (*rasm*) from the Prophets (may God bless them). Through it, they lead their followers and bring the people to their faith. The Prophet (PBUH) said: Whoever leaves my *sunna* will be cursed; that means that every man who leaves my way, my conduct of life, whatever I put as example to my community or as sign for the faith, and whatever I approved, he will be cursed.[18]

The cogency of the *sunna* is based on the Quran, which is its "companion" (*zawj*). The *sunna* can explain, integrate and even abrogate the Quran. Some subjects related to law and ritual are mentioned so concisely in the Quran that interpretation must be distilled from data proliferated in the *ḥadīth*; moreover, previously related verses may be considered to have been abrogated by Prophetic traditions expressing a different ruling that came down at a later

---

al-Ṣalt b. Mālik al-Kharūṣī at the end of the 3rd/9th century. The different viewpoints over the deposing of al-Ṣalt not only had enormous consequences for the political and social life of the Ibāḍī movement in Oman, but also influenced its legal development over centuries, as the jurists split into three parties, the pro-deposing, the anti and the neutralist. The former disappeared early on, the second transformed into the Rustāq party and the last into the Nizwā party. See Wilkinson, Bio-bibliographical Background to the Crisis Period 137–164.

17 Wilkinson, *Ibâḍism* 413–414, 419–420.

18 Al-Kindī, *Muṣannaf* i, first part 18.

date, as is the case of the verses concerning inheritance from unbelievers and legacy in favour of parents or relatives, which have been abrogated by the Prophetic traditions prohibiting any hereditary relationship between Muslims and unbelievers, and limiting the legacy to one third of the estate.[19]

The prophetic *sunna* is related through those jurists of the Nizwā party who preceded him, thus demonstrating that the moderate Nizwā views were preferred over the extremist ones of the Rustāq school. In particular he quotes the famous Abū Saʿīd Muḥammad b. Saʿīd al-Kudamī al-Salūtī, pupil of Abū ʿAbdallāh Muḥammad b. Raw b. ʿArabī. The line of transmission is traced back through Maḥbūb b. al-Ruḥayl, a "bearer of knowledge" (*ʿilm*) from Basra, al-Rabīʿ, Abū ʿUbayda, Ḍumām, Abū Ḥurr, Ibn Ḥusayn who died during the ʿAbd Allāh b. Yaḥyā (Ṭālib al-Ḥaqq)'s uprising (*istashada ʿinda*), Jābir until the Prophet's companions, particularly Ibn ʿAbbās and ʿĀʾisha.[20]

4.4 The *Musnad al-Rabīʿ b. Ḥabīb*

4.4.1 The "Hadithification" Process in the Maghribi Sources

In North Africa, after a period of stasis following the political collapse of the movement with the fall of the Rustumid imamate to the Fatimid army in 909, there was a reflowering of jurisprudence, akin to that found in Oman. Though we already find, in the legal work by ʿAmrūs b. al-Fatḥ (d. 283/896),[21] a tentative classification of the legal sources with the statement that *ʿilm* has three basic components (Quran, *sunna* and *raʾy*), it was at this crucial juncture of the history of North African Ibadism that the process of *ḥadīth* formation took off in a significant way.

This process was characterized (as in the Omani sources) by the assimilation of Sunni material into the community's *āthār*, partly as a result of being exposed to the regional influences of the Maliki school, which was dominant in the Maghrib. Nevertheless, up to the time of al-Barrādī (8th/14th century), Ibāḍī scholars still discouraged the reference to Sunni collections of *ḥadīth*: in his treatise *al-Ḥaqāʾiq*, al-Barrādī advises students as far as possible not to read them.

In the work by the famous scholar Abū Yaʿqūb Yūsuf Ibn Khalfūn al-Mazzātī (6th/12th century), Sunni jurists (namely Mālik, Shāfiʿī, Abū Ḥanīfa) and

---

19 Al-Kindī, *Muṣannaf* i, first part 18–21.
20 Al-Kindī, *Muṣannaf* i, first part 140–143.
21 Wilkinson, Ibāḍī *Ḥadīth* 255.

Prophet's companions (particularly Ibn ʿAbbās, ʿIkrima, ʿĀʾisha) are quoted along with early Basran authorities (Jābir, Abū ʿUbayda, Ḍumām b. al-Sāʾib, al-Rabīʿ, Abdallāh b. ʿAbd al-ʿAzīz). In his epistle addressed to the Ibāḍīs of Jabal Nafūsa and related to issues concerning marriage, concubinage, repudiation and adultery, Prophetic traditions are quoted with a simplified/shorted *isnād*: ʿan ʿIkrima –ʿan Ibn ʿAbbās – ʿan *al-nabī* or directly with the formula "*qāla al-nabī*" or "*jāʾa ilā al-nabī*". The author draws from both the Ibāḍī tradition (*āthār aṣḥābinā*) – in particular he quotes the *Aqwāl Qatāda*, the *Jawābāt Jābir b. Zayd*, the *Āthār al-Rabīʿ/Riwāyāt Abī Ṣufra* – and Sunni collections, namely those by al-Bukhārī, Muslim and Mālik.[22]

The Maghribi Ibāḍī scholars narrated traditions from those companions and successors they regarded as good Muslims, thus carefully selecting the authorities on which they established their jurisprudence. According to Abū Zakarīyāʾ al-Jannāwunī (first half of the 6th/12th century), the Law derives from Quran, *sunna* and *raʾy* (personal reasoning), which became assimilated into *ijmāʿ* (consensus). Prophetic traditions are accepted insofar as they do not contrast with the Quran, in which case they must be rejected or submitted to a process of interpretation (*taʾwīl*).[23]

The 6th/12th century scholar Abū Yaʿqūb Yūsuf al-Warjlānī (d. 570/1174) pioneered the "hadithification" process in the Maghrib.[24] It was mainly due to him that Ibāḍī juridical heritage was no longer a collection of raw materials of quotations going back to the Prophet and/or his companions and of reports by Ibāḍī authorities but rather developed into a consistent juridical *corpus* within the framework of the Islamic tradition of the *uṣūl al-fiqh*. He was a well-qualified Muslim jurist and mastered Islamic jurisprudence. In his works *al-ʿAdl wa ʾl-inṣāf* and *al-Dalīl wa ʾl-burhān* he mentions certain Sunni collections of *ḥadīth* which he had probably known during his stay in Cordoba thanks to his Sunni teachers. Al-Warjlānī experienced both the intellectual life of the Ibāḍī community and that of the communities he visited during his many travels and was able to contextualize Ibadism within the broader development of the Islamic schools of law.[25]

In Cordoba he also learnt the Sunni rules concerning *ḥadīth* classification, which he quotes in his work along with those handed down to him from

22 Ibn Khalfūn, *Ajwibat* 13–20, 38, 54.

23 Cuperly, *Introduction* 57–58, 113, 168–169; Rubinacci, La professione di fede di al-Ǧannāwunī 553–595.

24 Darjinī included him in the 14th *ṭabaqa*. Darjinī, *Ṭabaqāt* ii. 491. For a biography of al-Warjlānī see also the editor's preface to his *Kitāb al-asmāʾ* 15–21.

25 Ech-Cheikh, Ignored Pages of the History of Ibāḍī Theology in North Africa during the Middle Ages 108.

Ibāḍī authorities of earlier times. According to these rules, after the *isnād* came into existence, the transmitters' veracity needed to be carefully investigated. Honesty, accuracy and expertise were qualities set against mendacity. Moreover, al-Warjlānī states that all the people involved in the process of collecting the prophetic traditions – the writer, the man who dictates and the two men who inspect the dictation – must be pious individuals who have not committed grave sins, nor are prone to committing minor sin often, therefore deserving the *walāya* (association) of the community.[26]

In his *al-Dalīl wa 'l-burhān*, al-Warjlānī provides a conventional view of the external opponents of Ibadism (*ahl al-khilāfa*) and the points of divergence with them, confirming the attitude of representing Ibadism as the only "true" Islam (ii, part iii 67–75). On the other hand, he gives a more nuanced approach to the questions of *ikhtilāf*, where the opinions diverge, which he considers a sign of divine blessing. He relies on the famous prophetic tradition which states that diversity of opinion is, in itself, not considered to be negative but rather it is a concession (*raḥma*) on the part of God (i, part i 6–9; ii, part iii 67–76). He also refers to a legal maxim attributed to the Prophet "every qualified interpreter is correct" (*kullu mujtahid muṣīb*), which gave rise to a fervent debate among the Sunni jurists (ii, part iii 48). These maxims, along with the saying that every interpreter will be rewarded no matter if his opinion is correct or not, stress that legal reasoning (*ijtihād*) undertaken in good faith is ethically valid (i, part ii 74). Thus, al-Warjlānī's discourse paves the way to a broader acceptance of legal diversity both within the Ibāḍī school and with the Sunni jurists whose doctrine at his time started to be taken into consideration. This commitment to pluralism applies to matters related to the *furūʿ al-fiqh*, the rules governing ritual and social activities, only; as far as the principles of dogma are concerned, there must be unity (i, part ii 75–78).

As Ennami proves, Ibāḍīs strongly oppose *taqlīd*, i.e. the reliance on the teaching of a master, and consider it a duty of those who attain the required standard of knowledge to use their individual judgement (*ijtihād*). Among the earliest Ibāḍī works concerning the rules of *ijtihād* is the *Kitāb al-Tuḥaf* by the Maghribi scholar Abū Rabīʿ Sulaymān b. Yakhlaf al-Mazātī (d. 471/1078), whose opinions are often quoted in al-Warjlānī's works.[27]

According to al-Warjlānī, the qualified interpreter (*mujtahid*) – the one who masters Arabic and has a full competence in both *uṣūl* and *furūʿ* – is allowed to exercise his autonomous reasoning (*raʾy*), according to his intellectual

26 Ennami, *Studies* (online edition) 88.

27 Ennami, A Description of New Ibāḍī Manuscript 72–73; idem, *Studies* (online edition) 88.

capacities (*ʿaql*) and within the framework of the revealed law (*sharʿ*), in those matters which are not dealt with in the Quran or *sunna*, or by previous authorities He calls this process *ijtihād al-raʾy* which, once confirmed by the *consensus* of the community (*ijmāʿ*), gives rise to binding rules. The *ijtihād* extends the law originating from the revealed texts to the new cases that arise, while the *ijmāʿ* identifies the correct solutions that have been attained through *ijtihād* and are present in the community. It is not a creative process; it is rather a declaratory one. *Ijtihād* manifests the truth and maintains the continuity of the legal system, while *ijmāʿ* merely transmits this truth to a wider public and fixes it beyond the reach of dispute.[28]

Al-Warjlānī conceives *ijtihād al-raʾy* almost as a form of *qiyās* (analogy), the latter means, at its most basic level, positing a link between two apparently disconnected items, comparing a new case-law to those laws that are explicitly stated in the texts. The *mujtahid* examines the ruling and then tries to determine the *ratio legis* (*ʿilla*) that reveals the logic that grounds that ruling. The fundamental element in this process of *qiyās* is determining divine *ʿilla* behind the legal rule. Both extrapolating the *ʿilla* and expressing a legal opinion (*raʾy*) through the exercise of *ijtihād* are an accurate reflection of the divine intention in the framework of the revealed sources.[29]

The extent to which believers are bound to accept and follow new rulings derived from *qiyās* and *ijtihād al-raʾy* is defined by *ijmāʿ*, which ensures a balance between the *mujtahid*'s freedom to formulate novel legal injunctions and the power of the scholars' community in deciding which ruling achieves a normative status for all succeeding generations. To encourage a jurist to engage in *taqlīd* is to promote a view of Islamic law as more static, restricting *taqlīd*, by contrast, affords the *mujtahid* greater freedom in formulating legal injunctions and suggests that Islamic law may develop in different ways depending on the context in which it is applied.

Ibadism never adheres to the principle of the closure of the "door of individual judgement" and maintains that in case of differing opinions resulting from personal judgement, only one opinion can be right. People are allowed to adopt other opinions if they believe them to be right, even though, in fact, they are not. According to Ennami, this principle was opposed by two Ibāḍī scholars who founded groups of their own: Naffāth b. Naṣr, founder of al-Naffāthiyya, and Aḥmad b. Ḥussayn, founder of al-Ḥusainiyya. They maintained that only

28 Zysow, *The Economy of Certainty* 117.

29 Al-Warjlānī, *al-Dalīl wa ʾl-burhān* i, part ii 121–127.

the right opinion was to be followed, and those who followed by other opinions were sinners.[30]

Al-Warjlānī regards as normal the disagreement of opinions concerning cases of positive law and holds it lawful for everyone to keep to his own opinion regardless of whether it is the correct opinion or not. This freedom does not bring to any anarchy within the jurisprudence, since any legal opinion does not become a source on par with the legal texts, unless when the contemporaneous community agreed to its validity by consensus. In that case, the legal opinion changes its status from considered opinion to cogent ruling.[31]

Both *ijtihād* and *ijmāʿ* – as al-Warjlānī points out – originated from the Quran (see Q. 4:83) and are set forth by prophetic traditions in more forthright terms, as for example by the saying stating "God will not unite my people in error (*ḍalāla*)".

The discussion on *ijmāʿ* in al-Warjlānī's works centres mainly on the consensus of the community, on the method of reaching it, and also on the cases in which a doctrine is supported by a single prominent jurist.[32] He underlines that only legal scholars enter into the consensus, and discusses belief, piety and intellectual capacities of the scholars whose opinions count for *ijmāʿ*. The infallibility of the community is a divine grace, but what does happen when divergent opinions rise? In these cases, he states, the community must rely upon the teachings of its leading scholars. The doctrine of consensus ensures that the integrity of revealed law will remain unimpaired throughout the ages, while the *ijtihād* guarantees its capacity to adapt to changing circumstances.

The jurist is not completely autonomous as his authority stems entirely from the authority of God. What the jurist declares is authoritative only if its validly derived from the textual sources and is therefore an acceptable expression of the law of God. The jurist's authority is dependent upon the methodology he employs; nonetheless, he can be fallible. The factuality of error is implicit in the *ikhtilāf*, the disagreements among the jurists. When the jurists disagree on a particular rule, they cannot all be right. In this case, the *ijmāʿ* of the school authorities, whose opinions are generally agreed upon, guarantees the stability of the law. Al-Warjlānī places a great amount of confidence in the knowledge of the leading Ibāḍī jurists and regards their opinion as being generally reliable. The presence of these leading jurists makes Ibadism comparable to the Sunni schools of law.

---

30 Ennami, *Studies* (online edition) 89.

31 Al-Warjlānī, *al-Dalīl wa 'l-burhān* i, part ii 73–86. To *ikhtilāf* and related question is also devoted almost all part iii of vol. ii.

32 Al-Warjlānī, *al-Dalīl wa 'l-burhān* i, part ii 73 (*inna al-ḥaqq fī wāḥid*).

4.4.2 The *Musnad al-Rabīʿ b. Ḥabīb*: a Critical Assessment

In the first half of the 6th/12th century, Abū Yaʿqūb Yūsuf al-Warjlānī completed his arrangement (*tartīb*) of a collection of *ḥadīth* attributed to al-Rabīʿ b. Ḥabīb, in which traditions of the Prophet and the companions are handed down through the *imām*s of the school, known as *Musnad al-Rabīʿ b. Ḥabīb* or *al-Jāmiʿ al-ṣaḥīḥ*. The original version of the book, attributed to the third *imām* of the Ibāḍī community in Basra, al-Rabīʿ b. Ḥabīb, has not survived.

The *Musnad al-Rabīʿ b. Ḥabīb* is the most important Ibāḍī collection of *ḥadīth*, in the technical sense of the term. For the Ibāḍī *madhhab* it fulfils two important functions: that of providing an independent Ibāḍī collection of *ḥadīth* without having to refer to other schools; and that of affirming the pupil-*imām* transmission line from the founder of the *madhhab* Jābir b. Zayd, via his successor Abū ʿUbayda, via the successor of the latter, al-Rabīʿ.

The work by al-Warjlānī is divided into four books. The first two contain 742 traditions on legal and religious matters, arranged in the same manner as the Sunni collections of *ḥadīth*. The material is almost the same as that reported by Sunnis: most of the traditions transmitted by al-Rabīʿ are reported in Sunni collections by other Sunni authorities with the same wording, or with slight differences. The *isnād* of the first two parts is as follows: al-Rabīʿ b. Ḥabīb – Abū ʿUbayda – Jābir b. Zayd – a companion – Prophet. The companions are mainly: Ibn ʿAbbās, Abū Hurayra, Abū Saʿīd al-Khudrī, Anas b. Mālik, ʿĀʾisha.

Parts three (comprising *ḥadīth* 743–882) and four (comprising *ḥadīth* 883–1005) of the *tartīb* are more heterogeneous.[33] Part three collects *munqāṭiʿ* (lit. "broken") traditions from al-Rabīʿ and Jābir, in which the Prophet's or his companions' sayings are reported with a chain disconnected at one or more points. It is politically interesting, including traditions on the Ibāḍī attitude towards the caliphates of ʿUthmān and ʿAlī (see chaps. 9–10), the *taqiyya* (dissimulation of the belief, no. 794–795), the attitude towards sinners and unbelievers (*mushrikūn*, no. 791–792), and the question of *qadar* and predestination (no. 769–811). As is well known, a dispute concerning faith, free will and predestination arose during the imamate of Abū ʿUbayda and culminated in the expulsion of Ḥamza al-Kūfī and ʿAṭiyya, who supported the Qadarī Jaylān al-Dimashqī, from the Ibāḍī Basran community. The anti-Qadarī predestinarian stand of Abū ʿUbayda has prevailed among the Ibāḍīs ever since.[34]

The last section of part three contains traditions on allegoric interpretation of the seemingly anthropomorphic references in the Quran. For the Ibāḍīs, as

33 Wilkinson, Ibāḍī *Ḥadīth* 232.
34 Al-Darjīnī, *Ṭabaqāt* ii, 233; al-Shammākhī, *Siyar* (1884) 84–85.

for the Muʿtazilī, any similarity between God and His creation is impossible. They reject the naïve anthropomorphism of the traditionalist schools where Quranic terms, such those referring to the representation of God (7:54, 10:3, 13:2) and the beatific vision of God, seem to be understood literally.[35]

In the *Musnad* God's throne as well as His hand are symbol of His power (the hand represents also the reward and guidance; cf. chaps 22–25, 28, 32), the eye of God is His science (chap. 30), the divine light ("God is the light of heaven and earth", Cor. 24:35), symbolizes the justice of God in the universe. The verse "And all things perish except His face" (Cor. 28:88) means that nothing will remain other than God (chap. 29).

In short, part three offers an in-depth insight into some controversial matters pertaining to religion and dogma which were debated in the Ibāḍī community in the generations of Abū ʿUbayda and his successor al-Rabīʿ.

Part four is a sort of appendix of traditions from Ibāḍī authorities post al-Rabīʿ. It collects traditions (no. 883–901) deriving from the last *imām* of the Basran community, Abū Sufyān Maḥbūb b. al-Ruḥayl (second half of the 2nd century), traditions (no. 902–922) from the third Rustumid *imām* al-Aflaḥ b. ʿAbd al-Wahhāb (r. *c.*823–871), who took them from books by Ibāḍī scholars (*kutub aṣḥābinā*), which were probably preserved in his father's library, the celebrated *al-Maktaba al-Maʿṣūma*. In particular, he quotes an epistle (*siyar*) by Abū Yazīd al-Khawārizmī, which had been handed down/passed to him by Abū Ghānim al-Khurāsānī, the author of the *Mudawwana*, during his travels to Tahert, the capital of the Rustumid imamate.[36]

The vast majority of the traditions collected in the chapter are transmitted on the authority of Abū Ghānim, from Abū Yazīd or Ḥātim b. Manṣūr al-Khurāsānī.[37] Abū Ghānim relies also on Ibāḍī scholars from Egypt, whom he met during his travels to Tahert (see tradition no. 910), and on Iraqi authorities such as, for instance, al-Ḥasan al-Baṣrī (no. 904 and 917) and Muḥammad

35 On the question of anthropomorphism, see al-Shammākhī, *Siyar* (1884) 104; Cuperly, *Introduction* 27, 169–170, 188 ff., 315.

36 The work by Abū Yazīd has not survived. According to Wilkinson it was included into the *Kitāb Abī Sufyān* (Ibāḍī *Ḥadīth* 251). Abū Yazīd was sent by Abū ʿUbayda to convert the people of Khurāsān along with a team of missionaries (*ḥamalat al-ʿilm*), which included also Hāshim b. ʿAbd Allāh al-Khurāsānī. In Khurāsān, Abū Yazīd met Abū Ghānim and passed him his book. Abū Yazīd's fame spread throughout the Maghrib: Ibn Sallām (3rd/9th century) counts him among the jurists of recognized competence on matters of penal law (*dimāʾ*) in the East, along with ʿAbd al-Raḥmān b. Rustum (160/777–168/784) in the Maghrib. Ibn Sallām, *Kitāb Ibn Sallām* 114; al-Darjīnī, *Ṭabaqāt* ii, 258; al-Shammākhī (1884), *Siyar* 95.

37 He was among Abū ʿUbayda's pupils and teacher of Abū Ghānim. Ibn Khalfūn, *Ajwibat* 111; Rebstock, *Die Ibāḍiten im Magrib* 179, 181; van Ess, *Theologie und Gesellschaft* ii, 601.

b. Ḥasan (no. 908 and 909), who might be identified as al-Shaybānī.[38] The last traditions of part four are *maqāṭī*ʿ on matter of faith and doctrine related by Jābir b. Zayd.[39]

The presence in the last part of the *Musnad* of traditions by al-Aflaḥ b. ʿAbd al-Wahhāb is significative. Ibāḍī sources celebrate the first Rustumid imāms as symbols of the Ibāḍī golden age, in the same vein as they celebrate the time of the Ibāḍī founding fathers in Basra. In particular, the figures of al-Aflaḥ, his father ʿAbd al-Wahhāb (784–823) and his son Abū ʾl-Yaqẓān Muḥammad (872–894) emerge as political leaders as well as jurists and theologians, embodying the Ibāḍī ethos of the righteous *imāms*, who were elected thanks to their personal virtues of political leadership, religious knowledge, devotion and justice. Not only did the Tahert imamate flourish under their guidance, but the sources describe them also as learned men credited with fundamental books. ʿAbd al-Wahhāb allegedly authored an epistle on the creation of the Quran, and Abū ʾl-Yaqẓān a book called *Kitāb masāʾil Nafūsa*. To al-Aflaḥ b. ʿAbd al-Wahhāb are attributed several works, including *qaṣāʾid* and *rasāʾil*, among which there is a collection of unpublished *Jawābāt*, which – if proved authentic – can rank among the earliest North African juridical sources. He is also credited with a didactical short poem, titled *Qaṣīda fī faḍl al-ʿilm waʾl-mutaʿallim*, celebrating the *ʿilm* (religious knowledge) and the quest for it, which reflects a vision of authority dating at least from the 11th century.[40]

The Ibāḍī historical sources underline the centrality of the Rustumid imamate in the relationship between the Eastern and Western communities, in particular the reign of al-Aflaḥ experienced a broader process of knowledge transmission from the East to the West with Abū Ghānim and other prominent figures of Eastern Ibadism travelling to Tahert. From the 11th century onwards, al-Aflaḥ emerged in the sources – in particular in those in the basin of al-Warjlānī – as transmitter of traditions coming from Jābir, al-Rabīʿ, Abū Sufyān and other early Ibāḍī authorities. According to Cyrille Aillet and Mohamed Hassen, the role attributed to al-Aflaḥ, as author and transmitter, reflects the motive of the Rustumid dynasty as "*bayt al-ʿilm*", prevailing in the Ibāḍī-Wahbī heresiographical works, which converted the first Rustumid *imāms* into heroes of the orthodoxy, fighting against the schisms, such as those

38 van Ess, Untersuchungen 35.

39 *Maqāṭīʿ* are traditions in which the authority for the transmission between the Successor (*tābiʿī*) and the Prophet is not mentioned.

40 Aillet and Hassen, The Legal *Responsa* Attributed to Aflaḥ b. ʿAbd al-Wahhāb (208–58/823–72) 137–146.

of the Nukkār and the Wāṣiliyya (the Muʿtazilis), that had weakened Western Ibadism.[41]

To conclude, the legal and theological material included in the *Musnad* probably belongs to a different historical sequence, at least from the 9th century to the 11th century. Ibāḍī scholarship regards the *Musnad* as the most trustworthy book of *ḥadīth*, comparable as far as the accuracy of content and the line of transmissions are concerned to the books of al-Bukhārī and Muslim.[42] The *Musnad* inspired several works, including a commentary titled *Ḥāshīyat al-Tartīb* by Abū ʿAbd Allāh Muḥammad ibn ʿUmar b. Abī Sitta, an abridgement of this work (*mukhtaṣar*) by ʿAbd al-ʿAzīz al-Thaminī, and the fundamental commentaries by the reformers Nūr al-Dīn al-Sālimī (d. 1914) and Muḥammad Aṭfayyish (d. 1914), which I will deal with in the last chapter of this book.

Recently Sāmī b. ʿUmar b. Yaḥyātanī edited a *Kitāb al-asmāʾ*, a collection of short biographies of the authorities quoted in the *Musnad*, attributed to al-Warjlānī himself. The work, called also *Risāla fī tarājim rijāl al-Musnad*, was considered long lost, though fragments were preserved in the library of Beni Isguen (Algeria). The discovery of a complete manuscript, dating to 1097 AH, in the library Abū Sitta on Jerba Island can shed new light on the process through which the *Musnad* came into existence.

The *Musnad al-Rabīʿ b. Ḥabīb* drew the attention of eminent scholars such as L. Massignon, J. van Ess, M. Talbi, M. Cook and J.C. Wilkinson, who questioned its authenticity.[43] In fact, inconsistencies in the texts and in the *isnād*s give rise to the doubt that al-Warjlānī collected material from different stages of development of Ibāḍī law.[44] I agree with Wilkinson's theory postulating that the *Musnad* was the fruit of the process of "rationalisation", which Ibāḍī law underwent with the aim of safeguarding the school from outside influences and placing it on the same level as its opponents. The *Musnad* had the important function of furnishing the Ibāḍī school with a collection of independent *ḥadīth*s, which resemble in their transmission lines and contents the classical Sunni collections, which the scholars of the sect could return to. However, it reflects a later stage of development with regards to the doctrine which the first Ibāḍīs had discussed in Basra, preserved in the sources, such as the *Aqwāl Qatāda*, the *Āthār* and the *Futyā al-Rabīʿ*.

41 Ibidem.

42 Ibn Ḥammū Kurrūm, *Ishāmāt al-madrasa al-Ibāḍiyya* 21–26.

43 Massignon, Islamisme et religions de l'Arabie 410; van Ess, Untersuchungen 36–38; idem, *Theologie und Gesellschaft* ii, 134; Talbi, *Études d'histoire ifriqiyenne* 36; Cook, *Early Muslim Dogma*, 56; Wilkinson, Ibāḍi *Ḥadīth* 231ff.

44 Francesca, La fabbricazione degli *isnād* nella scuola ibāḍita 55–56.

As Wilkinson points out, neither the Omani sources[45] nor the Maghribi ones throw light on where al-Warjlānī got his material from. In his catalogue of Ibāḍī books, al-Barrādī simply quotes a book titled *Ḥadīth al-Rabīʿ* along with the arrangement of al-Warjlānī, testifying that an original version of the latter existed. Al-Darjīnī mentions the *Musnad* in the biography of al-Rabīʿ, but he provides no details about it.

Some polemical issues, such as the rebuttals of the Qadariyya, the interpretations of ambiguous Quranic verses, and the question of Quran creation, may have given rise, as early as the Rustumid imamate, to a collection of valuable *ḥadīth*s "à la Sunni" – as Wilkinson calls them[46] – which could be used in debate with opponents. Moreover, it was in reaction to foreign influence following the political collapse of Ibadism in Oman and the Maghrib that the Ibāḍī movement developed into a *madhhab* with a literary *corpus* of laws, which came to terms with the Sunni rules of the branches and the fundamentals of law. Al-Warjlānī played a decisive role in the development of Ibāḍī school. Through his works, he facilitated the assimilation into the Ibāḍī juridical heritage of the methodological criteria of the *uṣūl al-fiqh*, which he had learned mainly in al-Andalus, and made the contents of earlier Ibāḍī works accessible to a large number of jurists. His main achievement in the development of an Ibāḍī *ḥadīth* theory was the introduction of the standardized pupil–teacher line of transmission according to the imamate lineage of the early Ibāḍīs. It is noteworthy to underline that this happened at a time when the imamate institutions had long since disappeared in the Maghrib to give rise to the more secret organization of *ḥalqa*.[47]

As Gaiser proves, legitimacy is of paramount importance for the Ibāḍī institution of authority, which was profoundly shaped by the movement's formative experience in Basra. Ibāḍīs preserve a reference to a conceptual past as a means of strengthening their claim to legitimacy. They view themselves as the guardians of the authentic form of Islam, based upon the belief in an unbroken line of transmission reaching back to the original sources of authority. Despite the differences between Maghribi and Omani Ibāḍīs, the formative period in Basra provided them with a core conceptual vocabulary and practice of the authority, mainly embodied in the guidance of the righteous first leaders.[48]

---

45 A recent comparison between the *Musnad* and the *Kitāb al-Jāmiʿ* by Ibn Baraka fails to offer a convincing response in order to solve the problem of the source/s of the traditions preserved in the *Musnad*. Bū Larwāḥ, *Musnad al-imām al-Rabīʿ ibn Ḥabīb wa-kitāb al-Jāmiʿ li-Ibn Baraka*.

46 Wilkinson, Ibāḍī *Ḥadīth* 257.

47 Wilkinson, Ibāḍi *Ḥadīth* 235–239, 255–257.

48 Gaiser, *Muslim, Scholars, Soldiers* 11–12.

In both *al-ʿAdl wa ʾl-ʿinsāf* and *al-Dalīl wa ʾl-burhān*, al-Warjlānī deals with the question of imamate. He clearly attests the role of the early Ibāḍī Basran leaders as *imāms*, and he builds up Jābir b. Zayd as leader of the movement and ultimate authority in legal matters.[49] He developed the narrative of an unbroken chain of transmitters of knowledge reaching back directly to the Prophet through the early Basran *imāms*. He was not the only one: the Omani jurists Abū Muʾthir, al-Qalhātī and al-Kindī also identified the early Basran scholars as *imāms*, tracing through them the line of the Ibāḍī tradition back to the Prophet.[50]

The *Musnad* mirrored the concept of authority al-Warjlānī developed in his works.[51] This concept is intimately tied to the core of the Ibāḍī sectarian identity based on egalitarian conceptions rejecting any succession to the Prophet based on pure dynastic ties, and on the principle of proper politico-religious leadership stemming from faith and personal capacities alone. Several traditions in the *Musnad* refuse the Qurayshi claims to authority in favour of piety as the final legitimating criterion of leadership: the Qurayshis will remain leaders of the community "as long as they refrain from reproachable deeds".[52] The *Musnad* also warns against the temptations of kinship (*mulk*) with the familiar connotation that the Umayyads have usurped legitimate leadership of the Muslim community while transforming it into a kinship. The exclusive claim of the Quraysh to rule is outdated by the condition of moral probity expected of the *imām*. So long as the leader is pious he can be anyone, even "an Ethiopian slave with a mutilated nose" as another famous tradition claims.[53]

In the *Musnad*, al-Warjlānī's conception of authority is embedded into the standardized *isnāds*, which testify an unbroken line of transmission of knowledge through the first Ibāḍī *imāms*, whose authorship is widely accepted. Despite the religious-political importance of such assertion, the chains of transmitters of the *Musnad al-Rabīʿ* do not stand to any close examination, mainly due to the fact that in the early Ibāḍī works rarely we can find an ascendancy which goes back to the Prophet. In the *Āthār* and *Futyā al-Rabīʿ* (comprising together 539 traditions), only a scant number of traditions record

---

49 *"huwwa imām fī maqām al-jamāʿa wa innama yurāʿī al-shāhid fī aḥkām allātī tajri bayna al-nāss", al-Dalil wa ʾl-burhan* ii, part iii, p. 200. The sentence is partially quoted in Gaiser, *Muslim, Scholars, Soldiers* 76.

50 Gaiser, *Muslim, Scholars, Soldiers* 76–77.

51 *al-Dalīl wa ʾl-burhān* ii, part iii, 67ff.

52 Al-Rabīʿ b. Ḥabīb, *Musnad* 18, no 45, 200 no 818.

53 Al-Rabīʿ b. Ḥabīb, *Musnad* 18–19 nos. 44–49; 211, nos. 817–820; Gaiser, *Muslim, Scholars, Soldiers* 42.

the Prophet's opinion and in an elementary manner: "*al-Rabīʿ ʿan Ḍumām anna an-Nabiya suʾila ʿan* …", or "*yuqālu inna Rasūla Allāh* …".[54]

The concept of *sunna* identified with *sunnat al-nabī* is conspicuously absent from the early Ibāḍī legal works. In short, the *isnād* "al-Rabīʿ – Abū ʿUbayda – Jābir" does not emerge in the early Ibāḍī legal works, nor does the "raising" of the reports to the level of prophetic sayings. Although the concept of *sunnat al-nabī* occasionally appears in these sources, in the vast majority of cases the Companions' and Successors' behaviour was taken as normative as the Prophet's behaviour. As I have shown in the previous chapters, the transmission lines incorporated in the early Ibāḍī legal works are more nuanced than the standardized "*imām*s line", including several early Ibāḍī authorities whose contribution in the formation of Ibāḍī law disappears in the *Musnad*.

The strenuous moves to identify a body of religious-legal norms as originating from the early Ibāḍī *imām*s line (Jābir – Abū Ubayda – al-Rabīʿ) was momentous for the formation of a truly sectarian Ibadism. Nonetheless the traditions collected in part one and two of the *Musnad* reveal some inconsistencies in their structure as well as in their contents when compared with the traditions of the early Ibāḍī sources based mainly on real-life legal cases or expressed on a *fatwā* base, with a question by a layman and an answer given by the jurist. The first inconsistency emerges from the form: the standardized expression of the legal rules, sometimes formulated as legal maxims, is far from the case-law of the ancient texts. Three examples seem significant for attributing the traditions preserved in the *Musnad* at a stage of legal development later than the generation of Jābir b. Zayd. They concern the problem of wiping footwear instead of performing the ablution, the prohibition of the bequest in favour of legitimate heirs and the question of hereditary vocation between the patron and freed slave.

1. The doctrine of *masḥ ʿalā ʾl-khuffayn* means that the believer can perform the dry ablution (*tayammum*) wiping over their shoes instead of performing the ablution when there is not enough water or under further special circumstances. Traditions permitting the *masḥ ʿalā ʾl-khuffayn* going back to the Prophet are a seminal matter in the Sunni legal literature as they are often mentioned as proof that *sunna* can abrogate the Quran.[55] In the *Musnad* the *masḥ ʿalā ʾl-khuffayn* is firmly rejected (see *ḥadīth* nos. 121–125). The most imperative saying against the practice goes back to ʿĀʾisha through al-Rabīʿ – Abū ʿUbayda and Jābir, stating that the favourite wife of the Prophet would have preferred to cut her foot with a knife rather than to wipe over her shoes

54 See *infra* pp. 23–24 and footnote 1.
55 Rumee, *Narratives of Islamic Theory* 108.

(no. 125). Nonetheless, traditions related in the *Āthār* and the *Futyā al-Rabīʿ* prove that the question of the legitimacy of the *masḥ ʿalā ʾl-khuffayn* was still debated among the Ibāḍīs by the middle of the 2nd–8th century. Indeed, Jābir answered affirmatively the question by Tamīm b. Khuwayṣ whether it was permissible to wipe over the shoes when it was too cold to take the shoes off because of snow.[56] In a further tradition it is debated whether the tradition on the *masḥ ʿalā ʾl-khuffayn* could abrogate the verse prescribing the ablution in Quran 5:6.[57]

2. With regard to the bequest verse and the inheritance verse, the *Musnad* is unambiguous, recording the *ḥadīth* of the Prophet "so make no bequest to inheritors" (nos. 667 and 676). According to the prevailing doctrine the *ḥadīth* abrogated the bequest verses completely (Q. 2:180, 240), and they could never be put into practice because the verses "on heredity" (Q. 4:11–12) and the *ḥadīth* nullified their application. In constrast to what is stated in the *Musnad*, early Ibāḍī law preserves a tradition of Jābir related from ʿAmr b. Harim which allows the creation of a bequest for relatives (*aqāriba*) without specifying that the legitimate heirs (*ahl al-farāʾiḍ*) are excluded.[58] In the generation of Abū ʿUbayda, while abiding that the inheritance verse was meant to nullify all bequests to parents and relatives, thereby abrogating the bequest verse, ʿAbd Allāh b. ʿAbd al-ʿAzīz still allowed the bequest to relatives even if he considered it inappropriate (*makrūh*).[59]

3. In the *Musnad* patronage is viewed as a type of kinship tie (*nasab*) with all the legal consequences for the freedman and former master (or client and patron) included in hereditary ties. This is synthetized in the legal maxim: "The patronage is like a kinship tie" (no. 666).[60] On the contrary, as I have already said, the early Ibāḍī sources preserve traditions from Jābir attesting the lack of a hereditary tie between the slave-owner and the freed slave when the latter had no legitimate heirs.[61]

---

56 Al-Kharusi (ed.), *Āthār* 66, no. 301 (Ms. 19_9). The saying is quoted in Ibn Khalfūn, *Ajwibat* 80 and al-Kindī, *Muṣannaf* iv, 89. Abū Nūḥ relates that ʿĀtīqa bint Abī Ṣufra, sister of Yazīd b. al-Muhallab asked Jābir a similar question and got the same answer. Al-Darjīnī *Ṭabaqāt* ii, 225; al-Shammākhī, *Siyar* (1884) 88–89.

57 Ibn Khalīfa (ed.), *Futyā* 135–137 (Ms. 40_{14}). See also Abū Ghānim, *Mudawwana* i, 24. See *infra* pp. 66–67.

58 Al-Salimi (ed.), *Aqwāl* 444 (Ms. 123_{12}).

59 Abū Ghānim, *Mudawwana* ii, 209.

60 See also *ḥadīth* no. 675.

61 See *infra* p. 70.

4.5 The Process of "Rationalization" of the Ibāḍī School: From the School Heritage to the *Sunna* of the Prophet

The concept of *sunna* underwent different stages culminating in its terminological meaning as the exemplary behaviour of the Prophet. This development defines religion, with its all fields, such as belief, law, ethics, as a phenomenon that was perfectly embodied in the practice of the Prophet and his companions, who emerged as representatives of the true Islam. Therefore, the succeeding generations should imitate these early Muslims by respecting the sound traditions going back to them regarding what they believed and how they practised all aspects of religion. The narrowing down of the concept of *sunna*, comprising the exemplary behaviour of the Prophet and his companions, to the behaviour of the Prophet only started toward the end of the 1st/7th and beginning of the 2nd/8th century. This process ended in an increasing number of collections, which emerged as a true reflection of the Prophet's legacy. The "hadithification" of the *sunna* – meaning the idea that written *ḥadīth* were the best vehicle of knowledge transmission – also defined the relationship between the Quran and the *sunna*, with the majority of the jurists supporting the view that the *sunna* rules over the Quran. In fact, it has the major role of specifying and defining in detail the rules that the Quran gives in succinct or general terms. Notwithstanding the resistance by the *ahl al-raʾy* supporting their own view of the *sunna* and of the role of the jurists' speculation (*raʾy*) in interpreting the sources, the stance of the *ahl al-ḥadīth* prevailed. They pointed out the centrality of the Quran and the *ḥadīth*-based *sunna* and constrained the use of *raʾy* to those cases in which the two major sources of law do not offer an explicit solution.[62]

This process that has been highlighted for the Sunni schools can be attested for the Ibāḍī school as well. Early Ibāḍī tradition collections – as well as the early Sunni works – abound with reports traced back to companions and successors, and although the concept of "*sunnat al-nabī*" occasionally emerges in the earliest sources, in the vast majority of cases we find merely *sunna* referring to both the "living tradition" of the school and the traditions related from the Prophet's closest followers. Ibāḍīs considered the early period of the first two *al-Rashidūn* Caliphs as being the ideal age for the Muslim community, and they tried to trace back to the example set by the Prophet, his two successors and the upright companions.

62 Juynboll, *Muslim Tradition* 30–33; Duderija, Evolution in the Concept of Sunnah 393–437; idem, *Introduction*, in A. Duderija (ed.), *The Sunna and its Status in Islamic Law* 3–4.

When the community was still settled in Basra, the first Ibāḍī authorities were in close contact with Sunni scholars, exchanging advice and opinions with them, thus contributing to the general development of Islamic law. When the community left Basra and settled in Oman, Ḥaḍramawt and the Maghrib, there was no rivalry between the main centres of Ibadism even if they developed *isnād* of their own where local authorities were mentioned. There were transmitters who, having learnt the *ʿilm* in one centre, moved to another centre and disseminated the learned material there (the so-called "bearers of knowledge", *ḥamalat al-ʿilm*), so the bulk of traditions going back to the early Ibāḍī Basran authorities became the "common property" of the whole Ibāḍī community.

The 3rd/9th century scholar Abū ʾl-Mundhir Bashīr b. Muḥammad b. Maḥbūb, is considered the first theoretician of the *sunnat al-nabī*, which he regarded as pre-eminent over the *sunna* ascribed to other persons. He, more than any other scholar before him, was determined on granting the *sunna* of the Prophet a position as the guiding principle second in importance only to the Quran. Nonetheless, during the 3rd century, and still at the beginning of the 4th century, Ibāḍī jurisprudence does not show any development concerning the method of referring to statements made by the Prophet, the Companions or the Ibāḍī authorities. Evidence of that can be found through an investigation into the most important legal works of this period: the *Tafsīr* by the Maghribi Hūd b. Muḥakkam al-Hawwārī (first half of the 3rd century), the *Tafsīr* of the verses dealing with legal matters written by the Omani Abū ʾl-Ḥawārī (second half of the 3rd century) and the *Kitāb al-Jāmiʿ* written in the same period by the leading Omani *ʿālim*, Muḥammad b. Jaʿfar.

The later Ibāḍī sources concentrated on *isnād* criticism. The *isnād*, if found to be sound, was thought to guarantee the authenticity of the text (*maṭn*) it supported. This scrutiny of *isnād* resulted in an increasingly sophisticated criticism, which developed into a regular scholarly discipline constituting one of the branches of the science of tradition (*ʿilm al-ḥadīth*). The recording of traditions with an Ibāḍī *isnād* reached its zenith with the compilation of the *Musnad al-Rabīʿ*. This work gained so much authority in the eyes of Ibāḍī scholars that it came to be considered the most accurate collection of traditions, thus overshadowing the contributions of early collections, such as the *Aqwāl Qatāda*, the *Āthār* and the *Futyā al-Rabīʿ*, which preserved the ancient teachings of the school.

Most arguments presented by the Ibāḍī authors dealing with the position of the *sunnat al-nabī* as second root of law after the Quran are the same as those given in Sunni treatises on this subject. The substance of this argument is that since, in many verses of the Quran, God has ordered the men to obey

His Messenger (16:44), this implies that everything preached by the Messenger should be taken as truth. The *sunna* is indispensable as the guiding principle in all human activities, if the Quran does not provide the decisive answers. All traditions judged sound after rigorous scrutiny must be put into practice by the whole community; whosoever does not respect them is considered an infidel.

According to Wilkinson, we can take the period between the end of the 4th and the beginning of the 5th century as the starting point for the process of "normalisation" of Ibāḍī jurisprudence, meaning converting the primitive form of Ibadism into a model *madhhab* based on norms which had been evolving in the Sunni schools.[63] In Oman this process coincided with a resurgence of the imamate after the collapse of the first imamate. In the Maghrib, where the institution of the imamate had long since disappeared to give rise to the more secret organisation of the *ḥalqa*, the process of normalisation emerged probably in reaction to foreign influence.

But in this attempt to make itself a "respectable" school, Ibadism lost its genuine tradition and, at the same time, diminished the contribution of the old authorities, such as Ḍumām, Abū Nūḥ and others, in the foundation of the school. This spuriousness becomes evident as we begin to study later sources such as the *Musnad al-Rabīʿ b. Ḥabīb*.

The origins of a specifically Ibāḍī collection of *ḥadīth* and the attendant emergence of a body of religious-legal norms are clearly of major significance in the evolution of a truly sectarian Ibadism. As I have argued, the first major impulse towards identifying a coherent and comprehensive set of Ibāḍī religious-legal traditions distinct from those of the majority of Muslims occurred during the time of al-Warjlānī. This development came as corollary to a development of Ibāḍī law, which started approximately a century earlier.

The corpus of doctrine developed starting from the revealed sources and the "living tradition/practice" and was further augmented by the application of personal opinion (*raʾy*) of individual scholars on the basic material. At the same time, the concept underlying the theory of law was rationalized and came to be expressed as the tradition or *sunna* of the school, defined through the consensus (*ijmāʿ*) of those acknowledged to be the school's leading representatives. The *mujtahids* were the principal elements participating in *ijmāʿ* and held a monopoly of exegetical technique. The concept of *ijmāʿ* was used to overtly assert the authority of the community over the law development process. According to the Ibāḍīs, the major function of the *ijmāʿ* is to unite the divergent opinions on a problem progressively and to ascertain the truth of *qiyās*. The *ijmāʿ* renders this judgement irrevocable and it acquires a validity

63 Wilkinson, Ibāḍī *Ḥadīth* 253–259.

tantamount to that of the Quran and *sunna*. Nonetheless, Ibāḍīs recognize the right of later generations of *mujtahid*s to challenge or reinterpret the law. This freedom of interpretation was balanced by *ijmāʿ* as well as by the unquestioned authority of ancestors, which functioned as a source of law, a source which was infallible.

Ijmāʿ assured the emergence of a substantiated corpus of legal material from which it was unusual for the adherent of the Ibāḍī school to depart. Although a canonical collection of Ibāḍī *ḥadīth*s appeared at a relatively late date, the initial coalescence and dissemination of the Ibāḍī corpus of traditions (*āthār*) began approximately the same time as those of the Sunnīs.

Though the process of Ibāḍī "hadithification" was not to reach maturity until later than the Sunni, and whatever dating is finally adopted, the emergence of a *corpus* of Ibāḍī *ḥadīth*s had a momentous effect on the future course of Ibadism and was clearly fundamental to the crystallization of the various strands of Ibadism into a *madhhab*.

As mentioned above, al-Rabīʿ was the first to give impulse to the systematic collection of *ḥadīth* and all other *āthār* within the Ibāḍī school; nonetheless his own role in transmitting traditions should not be overstated. It is true that we have a *Musnad* devoted to all the traditions in whose transmission he has supposedly been instrumental, but an opinion as to whether these traditions, or at least part of them, can be considered authentic is – as is always the case in these matters – difficult to form. The *Musnad* was the fruit of the process of "rationalization" which Ibāḍī law had undergone with the aim of safeguarding the school from outside influences and placing it on the same level as the other schools of law. In the Maghrib it was partially a reaction to the ongoing malikization in the central part of the region, which marginalized Ibadism, as well as other minorities considered as heretical.

The malikization of the central Maghrib was long and complex. It started already with Saḥnūn b. Saʿīd al-Tannūkhī (d. 240/854), who was appointed chief *qāḍī* in Ifrīqiya in 232/849, and continued thanks to two prominent Malikī figures, Abū ʾl-Ḥasan al-Qābisī (d. 403/1012) and Ibn Abī Zayd al-Qayrawānī (d. 386/996). As result of this process, there was first a ban on the teaching of Ibāḍī doctrine, and then a ban on intermarriage. Moreover, the construction of new Ibāḍī mosques was forbidden and the demolition of existing mosques was ordered in the areas gained by Malikism. Though the regression of Ibadism in the Maghrib had no direct connection with the spread of Malikism, and was rather essentially the result of internal struggles within the Ibāḍī communities and of the Fatimid military intervention, the malikization played a significant role in the disappearance of Ibadism from certain regions of the Maghrib. The Hilālī immigration accelerated the decline of Ibadism. It provoked a new spatial and social configuration marked by the abandonment of Ibadism in favour of Sunni Sufism and the integration the Hilālī tribes into the Sunni-Maliki fold.[64]

It was at this crucial juncture in the history of Ibadism that al-Warjlānī lived. He played a major role in the "rationalization" process of the Ibāḍī school, developing protocols of transmission that strove to protect the integrity of the transmitted material. His juridical position was essential to his *Tartīb*'s future renown. Such renown was based above all on the consensus of the community, which regarded as good all that al-Warjlānī put in the *Musnad*. The *Musnad* reflects not only the increasing eclipse of Companions' authority by Prophet's *ḥadīth*, but also establishes the authoritative legacy of the early Ibāḍī Basran leaders as well as those of the first Rustumid imāms by extolling the authenticity of their traditions, as reflecting a "golden age" of the Ibāḍī history. By adopting this view of *ḥadīth* transmission al-Warjlānī moved away from the perception characteristic of the regional legal schools with the "*sunna*" embedded in the local practice and gave precedence to a body of legal rulings based on generally accepted principles, including some widely known traditions. He went deeper by striving to systematize the methodological basis of the law as a whole and by declaring the consensus of the community a gatekeeper of normativity. Through the *Musnad* he affirmed the canonization of the Quran and Prophetic *sunna* as primary sources of law and the consequent transformation of the discourse of Ibāḍī law, which was tantamount in preserving both integrity and identity of the Ibāḍī school.

The period between the 11th and the 16th centuries saw the crystallization of the Ibāḍī *madhhab*. This included a clear-cut definition of the community's historical, juridical and theological boundaries but at same time the adoption of some standard features of the Sunni schools in term of legal reasoning, *ḥadīth* transmission and historical narrative. This process, called "madhhabization" by John Wilkinson, saw the composition of fundamental works of jurisprudence, prosopography, *ḥadīth* compilation and theology. Ibāḍīs emerged as an identifiable *madhab* among others, in part thanks to the increasing interaction between Ibāḍīs and non-Ibāḍīs. Though Eastern and Western Ibāḍī communities preserved their own textual traditions, the stages of the "rationalization" process overlap both in Oman and the Maghrib.[65]

---

64 Amara, L'ibadisme et la malikisation du Maghreb central 340–344.

65 Wilkinson, Ibāḍī *Ḥadīth*, in part. 252–259; Wilkinson, *Ibâḍism* 413–437.

CHAPTER 5

Law and Knowledge: the Development of *Uṣūl al-Fiqh* in Ibāḍī Jurisprudence

5.1 Introduction

In this chapter I will assess the weight and impact of the authoritative tradition within Ibadism by analyzing the construction process of a coherent theory of *uṣūl al-fiqh*. The Ibāḍī legal system anchored in the authority of the jurists as a restricted category of learned men. Religious knowledge (*ʿilm*) and mastery of scholarly skills necessary for attaining an understanding of the law defined their leading role within the community. Some elements are relevant to this point. In particular, the fact that "the doors of *ijtihād*" were never sealed among the Ibāḍīs. The high-ranking jurists might exercise independent interpretation (*ijtihād*) of the sources and question the opinions of earlier jurists. The parallel act of *taqlīd* entailed, on the contrary, a decision to live in accordance with this system of authority by following a *mujtahid*'s doctrine rather than by going directly to the scriptural texts for guidance. The role of *ijtihād* was only restricted by the consensus aiming at maintaining a recognizable balance between the *madhhab*'s legal tradition and the authority of the *mujtahid*s. As *taqlīd*, *ijmāʿ* undermines the inevitable indeterminacy in law that resulted from independent interpretation of sources by individuals. Within the Ibāḍī school, the primary impetus of consensus was the search for recognizable repositories of authority. It had the function of declaring statements to be correct or incorrect within the conventions of the school.

The aspiration toward certainty, already evident in the doctrine of consensus, found another and more immediate outlet in the infallibility of the community, represented by its leading *ʿulamāʾ*, in deciding who was interpreting and applying the principles of the Ibāḍī dogma in the right way, and thus deserving the community's association/friendship. The doctrine of *walāya* and *barāʾa* (association and dissociation) ensured that the integrity of Ibāḍī law and theology remained unimpaired throughout the ages despite the rivalries and conflicts which threatened the community. The jurists, who held the monopoly on the exegetical technique and were the key elements participating in *ijmāʿ*, defended their primacy in expressing *walāya* and *barāʾa* as a criterion of normativity. This approach allowed them to occupy a powerful position from which to critique state policies, societal customs and to establish

 | HTTPS://DOI.ORG/10.1163/9789004765764-007

orthodoxy and orthopraxy. The instrumental use of the *walāya/barā'a* dynamic to define belonging and to establish a set of power relations emerged clearly in the conflict, ignited by the deposition of Omani *imām* al-Ṣalt b. Mālik in 886, between the Rustāq school rejecting the deposition, and the neutralists, the Nizwā school.

The deposition of the *imām* al-Ṣalt ibn Mālik was a major turning point in the history of Oman, providing the Ibāḍī scholars with the impetus to reflect on a detailed theory of the imamate and on their own role in relation to (and in competition with) political power.

5.2 *ʿIlm*/Knowledge in Islam

The concept of knowledge is one of the key concepts throughout the history of Islam, deeply informing/permeating almost all aspects of Muslim intellectual life, the value of knowledge was never questioned within the theological and juridical discourse. Faith depended on the acquisition of knowledge (*maʿrifa*) of its fundamental elements, without possessing or needing a deeper insight into them. In this vein, *maʿrifa* was the acknowledgement of God's existence, and nothing more. In contrast, *ʿilm* functioned culturally as an expression of faith, and the two (ilm and faith) mutually reinforced each other's prestige as supreme values in the life of a Muslim. In jurisprudence, *ʿilm* opened the way to *ijtihād*, meaning jurists' capacity for understanding God's will as expressed in the Quran and *sunna*, with reasonable probability (*ẓann*).[1]

According to F. Rosenthal, the discourse on knowledge dominated intellectual life in Medieval Islam, providing Islamic civilization with its distinctive shape and complexion. The semantic depth of the term *ʿilm*, and the wide incidence of its use, emerged in a vast range of juridical and theological sources, with books, prefaces and introductory chapters on the merits of knowledge becoming a well-established practice.[2]

The *ḥadīth* collections paved the way for the development of the concept of *ʿilm*. The *Muwaṭṭaʾ* by Mālik (d. 795) contains a chapter on "the search for knowledge" along with other moral prescriptions. In his generation, *ʿilm* had not yet achieved its full meaning in religious thought and scholarly methodology. Almost two generations later, al-Shāfiʿī (d. 820) wrote a treatise on "The sum of knowledge" (*Jimāʿ al-ʿilm*) setting the role of *ʿilm* in the establishment of legal principles. Al-Shāfiʿī's treatise is the earliest genuine example of

1 Kevin, *Authority, Conflict, and the Transmission of Diversity* 152.
2 Rosenthal, *Knowledge Triumphant* 93.

a methodological discussion of knowledge. He exalted the religious merit of knowledge and study over independent judgement (*ra'y, ijtihād, kalām, qiyās*), which he also included in the discussion on the methodological problems involved in the transmission of knowledge.

After al-Shāfiʿī many other Sunni jurists devoted books or chapters to the search for knowledge. Al-Dārimī (d. 865) was the first author of a *ḥadīth* collection to dedicate a large part of his introduction to various aspects of *ʿilm* as illustrated by the statements of the Prophet and other Muslim authorities. In the *Ṣaḥīḥ* by al-Bukhārī (d. 870) we find a chapter on knowledge focused on what is connected with knowledge and on the need for knowledge. He quotes a tradition of the Prophet attesting that the disappearance of knowledge and scholars will herald the end of the world. The brief chapter on *ʿilm* in the *Ṣaḥīḥ* by Muslim (d. 875) gathered together some Prophetic traditions on the role of knowledge in the proper interpretation of the sources of law, Quran and *sunna*. Chapters on *ʿilm* are also spread over the *Miṣbāḥ al-sharīʿa wa miftāḥ al-ḥaqīqa* (Lantern to the *sharīʿa* path and the key to reality) attributed to Jaʿfar al-Ṣādiq (d. 765) but probably written much later. They deal with the search for knowledge being a duty, and with particular aspects of knowledge, such as certain knowledge (*yaqīn*) and wisdom (*ḥikma*). The custom of an initial chapter on knowledge reached its apex in the *Iḥyāʾ* by al-Ghazālī (d. 1111). He opened this book discussing several aspects of knowledge, including the relationships between knowledge and faith, the methodology of scholarship and knowledge transmission and some questions connected with the adjudication of religious and moral values.[3]

The establishment of the kind and degree of knowledge a scholar should achieve was crucial to defining the role of jurists in shaping and embodying the normative tradition. Jurists, who were linked to each other through an uninterrupted teacher–pupil chain, participated in a cumulative process of knowledge construction around a communal religious and legal patrimony. They saw themselves, and were seen by the community, as the guardians of the legal tradition. Their role in the canonization and interpretation of the sacred law was fundamental. In particular, the scientific hermeneutic system they developed subjected the *ḥadīth*s to strict principles of classification and interpretation, thus dismissing the role of other actors (caliphs, governors and judges) in the lawmaking process. According to A. El Shamsy, this process of canonization entailed both the emergence of a fixed textual paradigm and the consolidation of the class of jurists as the ultimate interpreters of sacred texts.[4] Patricia

3 Rosenthal, *Knowledge Triumphant* 70–95.

4 El Shamsy, *The Canonization of Islamic Law* 4, 86, 176.

Crone and Martin Hinds suggest that the shift in religious authority from the caliphs to the community of scholars saw the emergence of Prophetic *sunna* as the only source of normative practice, superseding any extra-Prophetic authority, including the caliph's. Hence, the aegis of the Prophet offered a concrete alternative to caliphal practice, and the scholars claimed their role as the only qualified experts to interpret rules concerning doctrine, ritual and law.[5]

An important point here is to understand how we can define the concept of authority within the context of Islamic religious traditions. In their introduction to *Speaking for Islam: Religious Authorities in Muslim Societies*, Gudrun Krämer and Sabine Schmidtke point out how the distinction between authority and power became blurred in pre-modern Islam due to the varieties of forms and discourses through which religious authority was articulated. Though the failure of *miḥna* – inaugurated by the caliph al-Maʾmūn (r. 813–833) – allegedly confirmed the authority of the scholars in defining and defending the Islamic law, Sunni caliphs and rulers continued to exert religious authority to a certain extent. They intervened in dogmatic issues and enjoyed significant power in organizing the administration of justice and the juridical sphere. The nature, scope and locus of religious authority are difficult to define. A key way in which religious authority was articulated involved the ability to set or lay down a canon of authoritative texts and a legitimate method of interpretation. This process culminated in the exclusion of alternate methodologies of interpretation, which came to be classified as deviant and heretical in light of the emerging norms.[6]

The class of *ʿulamāʾ* claimed their role as "heirs of the Prophet" and the subsequent right to interpret the foundational texts of the Islamic tradition, the Quran and the *sunna*. They also defined the level of knowledge required and the requisite training as relevant criteria to access the elaborate process of canon building. Legal discourses of the 10th and 11th centuries reflect a growing awareness of consensus (and violation of consensus) as a conceptual framework through which "orthodoxy" and "heresy" came to be defined.[7]

The development of Ibadism as movement in general and a school of law in particular was mainly in the hands of the *ʿulamāʾ* and *fuqahāʾ*. They were deeply connected with local political factions. In fact, their activities were not

5 Crone and Hinds, *God's Caliph* in part. chap. 5.
6 Krämer and Schmidtke, *Speaking for Islam* 1–14.
7 Skreslet Hernandez, *The Legal Thought of Jalāl al-Dīn al-Suyūṭī* 9–10. The relevance of religious authority to the development of Islamic law has attracted the attention of several authors, as for example: Abou El Fadl, *And God Knows the Soldiers* and idem, *Speaking in God's Name*; Johansen, *Contingency in a Sacred Law*; Hallaq, *Authority, Continuity and Change*.

limited to a legal discourse, power struggles of different kinds and the promulgation of theological belief were also part of their agenda. In his history of Ibadism in Oman, A. Ubaydli underlines that the triad of *ʿulamāʾ*, *imāms* and tribal chiefs worked in near equilibrium, with the *ʿulamāʾ* acting as the supreme point of reference.[8]

In this chapter, I will try to assess the weight and impact of the authoritative tradition within Ibadism and to analyze the process of canon building involved. This process strongly favoured the scholarly class (*ʿulamāʾ*) in general and the jurists (*fuqahāʾ*) in particular as a subcategory of the *ʿulamāʾ*. Some elements are relevant to this point. In particular the definition of background training and field of activities of the scholars, their place and image in their respective community; the way knowledge related to personal conduct; how the interpretive tradition built up over generations and played a key role in relating the canonical texts to changing circumstances.

5.3 *Ṭalab al-ʿilm, Ijtihād, Taqlīd* and *Ijmāʿ*: the Emerging Role of the *ʿulamāʾ* in Ibadism

Far from being cut off from their Sunni counterparts, Ibāḍī jurists developed their own *madhhab* and legal framework in conjunction with (and in response to) parallel development in the Sunni centres of learning. The legal theory provided an overreaching discourse through which Ibāḍī religious elites came to understand their role in society and justify their ruling to the masses. The process of canonization of Ibāḍī law consisted in transferring the locus of religious authority from the lived practice of the community (*āthār*) to a written canon of sacred sources consisting of the Quran and the body of prophetic traditions.[9] The maturity of Ibāḍī law was the result of the way scholars articulated doctrines and rulings covering all aspects of believers' rituals and social life. The process of interpreting the sacred sources coalesced into a repertory of hermeneutic techniques theorizing the relationship to the revelation and the community's heritage. Ibāḍī hermeneutic (*uṣūl al-fiqh* or *uṣūl al-dīn*) focused not only on the sources of the divine law and their interconnections but also on the nature of language, interpretation and communication. On the other side, literature on positive law (*furūʿ al-fiqh*) established the parameters underpinning Ibāḍī identity and regulating communal life in the here and now.

8 Ubaydli, *Early Islamic Oman and Early Ibāḍism in the Arabic Sources* 140–147.

9 Wilkinson, *Ibâḍism* 414–417; Gaiser, *Ballaghanā ʿan an-Nabī* 11.

As Abdulrahman al-Salimi argued, the 9th to 10th century was marked by the appearance in the Omani-Ibāḍī literature of *Jāmiʿ*, compendia, in which both matters of *furūʿ* and *uṣūl* were discussed. They included the *Jāmiʿ Abī Qaḥṭān* by Abū Qaḥṭān Khālid b. Qaḥṭān, the *Jāmiʿ Ibn Jaʿfar* by Muḥammad b. Jaʿfar, the *Jāmiʿ Abī ʾl-Ḥawārī* by Abū ʾl-Ḥawārī Muḥammad b. al-Ḥawārī, the *Jāmiʿ al-Faḍl b. al-Ḥawārī* and the *Jāmiʿ* by Ibn Baraka. The latter, in particular, made a major contribution to the *uṣūl al-fiqh* in early Ibāḍī jurisprudence, by reviewing earlier Ibāḍī works – especially the *Jāmiʿ* by Ibn Jaʿfar – according to the methodology of the sciences of the principles of Islamic law. He insisted that the fundamentals of the law (*uṣūl al-fiqh*) must be studied together with the branches of law (*furūʿ al-fiqh*) and he himself made important contributions to contemporary legal practice. As result of this effort, he clarified formal contradictions, corrected errors, inconsistencies and ambiguities that previously could not be easily explained. Ibn Baraka played a decisive role in the development of the Ibāḍī school, facilitating the assimilation of the principles of *uṣūl al-fiqh* within Ibāḍī law. He provided a classification of the sources of law (Quran, *sunna*, *ijmāʿ*, *qiyās*) and set out some hermeneutical criteria, such as the *istiṣḥāb* (presumption of continuity), the *istiḥsān* (juristic preference) and the *maṣāliḥ mursala* (considerations of public interest). He also adopted the *ʿurf* (custom) and the principle of the legal precedents (*sharʿ man qablanā*, "the way of those before us") as additional sources of law.[10]

Approximately between the 11th and 16th centuries, the Ibāḍī legal production is enriched with two further literary *genres*: the *mukhtaṣar*s (epitomes) and the encyclopaedic works. In the *mukhtaṣar*s, the authors employed a range of literary techniques, including abridgement and short quotation of other works in order to epitomize the ongoing legal debate as well the doctrine of the school.[11] Omani Ibadism witnessed the rise of influential *mukhtaṣar* works, such as the *Mukhtaṣar al-khiṣāl* by Abū Isḥāq Ibrāhīm Ibn Qays al-Ḥaḍramī, the last Ibāḍī *imām* of Ḥaḍramawt (r. *c*.443–475/1052–1083), and the *Mukhtaṣar* by Abū ʾl-Ḥasan ʿAlī b. Muḥammad al-Bisiyānī, pupil of Ibn Baraka (5th/11th century). Within Maghribi Ibadism, the *Ajwiba* by Ibn Khalfūn al-Mazzātī (6th/12th century), the *Kitāb al-Īḍāḥ* by Abū Sākin ʿĀmir al-Shammākhī (d. 792/1389),[12] and later the *Kitāb al-Nīl* by ʿAbd al-ʿAzīz al-Muṣʿābī (born *c*.1130/1717), which is based on the *Kitāb al-Īḍāḥ* stand out amongst the works

10 Al-Salimi, Early Islamic Theological Influence in Jurisprudence 55–71.

11 On the rise of epitomes (*mukhtaṣars*) as a genre, see the fundamental work by Fadel, The Social Logic of *Taqlīd* 193–233.

12 A commentary of the *Kitāb al-Īḍāḥ* written by Muḥammad Abū Sitta al-Qaṣbī (d. 1088/1677) is published on the margin of the 1886 lithography.

designed to summarize the doctrine of the school. The text was very popular and framed some important commentaries, including the 19th century commentary by Muḥammad Aṭfayyish, which I address in the last chapter of this book.

The *Ajwibat* by Ibn Khalfūn introduces a fundamental novelty in Ibāḍī legal methodology, by affirming the principle that Ibāḍī jurists should be familiar with Sunni law and jurisprudence. Though Ibn Khalfūn quotes Sunni authors mainly in order to demonstrate the genuineness of Ibāḍī rules, his approach is an open recognition of the validity of Sunni law. This approach to the Sunni sources can also be found in the *Bayān al-sharʿ* by Muḥammad b. Ibrāhīm al-Kindī (d. 508/1115). It was later adopted by the two main works on Ibāḍī dogma and law in the Maghrib, namely the *Qawāʿid al-Islām* by al-Jayṭālī (d. 750/1349–1350) and the the *Kitāb al-Īḍāḥ* by al-Shammākhī.

The encyclopaedic works take the form of commentaries or commentary-like works that consist primarily of substantial quotations and replication of earlier texts adding evidence, and eventually some criticism and correction. They show the authors' ability to distil the ideas of past scholars into a format that was adaptable to the new legal environment, with the ambition to cover the entire breadth of the school's doctrine. This genre flourished particularly in Oman with the *Kitāb al-ḍiyāʾ* by Salma b. Muslim al-ʿAwtabī (end 5th/11th century, early 6th/12th century), the *Bayān al-sharʿ* by Muḥammad b. Ibrāhīm al-Kindī and the *Muṣannaf* by Abū Bakr Aḥmad b. Mūsā al-Kindī (d. 557/1162).

An examination of these works reveals that they organize, digest, complement and criticize the former legal production by elaborating and recapitulating the arguments presented in the earlier works in a fragmented manner. While the evolution of abridgements and encyclopaedic legal texts marks a radical departure of the Ibāḍī school from its beginnings in Basra, they nonetheless contribute to constructing and preserving a cherished memory of the epitomes whose actions were considered worthy of emulation. Both genres played an important sociological function in institutionalizing the rule of law reducing legal indeterminacy. This canonization process enabled the preservation of Ibāḍī legal patrimony, and it prompted a metadiscourse on questions of interpretation and consistency. Moreover, this critical engagement creates a hierarchy of authority and personal and intellectual connections among scholars.

Students and scholars travelled widely and met together in different centres of the "Ibāḍī archipelago", in both the Western and in the Eastern communities, creating a complex network of relationships and exchanges. Trade and pilgrimage routes facilitated travel and provided opportunities for these interactions. A formalized system of education emerged along with a large body of texts. As P. Love proves, among the North African Ibāḍīs the literary genre of biographical texts (*ṭabaqāt*) or prosopographies (*siyar*) recorded the intergenerational connections among scholars and acted as a suitable forum for the discursive negotiation of rank and authority. *Ṭabaqāt* and *siyar* collected biographies and anecdotes from exemplary Ibāḍī figures and scholars starting from the idealized origins of the movement up to the author's own time. Therefore, they created a collective memory and constructed the Ibāḍī tradition by marking the roles of scholars over several generations.[13]

Excavating *ṭabaqāt* and *siyar* obliquely shed light on Islamic law and on transmission of knowledge across time and space, and it allows us to understand the links among scholars and places.

Reflecting on the origins and development of *ṭabaqāt* as a form of biographical literature distinct from annalistic history, Michael Cooperson suggests that the genre arose out of a compelling interest on the part of pre-modern scholars in compiling lists and genealogies of people with similar attributes and eventually organizing them into distinct professional groupings (*ṭāʾifa*, pl. *ṭawāʾif*). Scholars' biographies serve to reinforce the authority of the group with respect to rival groups and to strengthen its symbolic heirship to the Prophet. Jurists benefitted from the *ṭabaqāt* genre to fulfil a number of pragmatic aims, including legitimizing the authority of the *madhhab*, preserving knowledge, defending the "orthodoxy" of the doctrine and practice of the group, and incorporating scholars of different times and generations into the same community.[14]

According to Paul Love, for the Maghribi Ibāḍīs of the mid-period (11th–16th century), books complemented the webs of personal relationships connecting students and teachers. The main biographical works he focuses on prove that the scholars and their connections represented the glue holding the community together.[15] Evidence of the growing importance of books as methods for the transmission of knowledge and the increasingly defined role of the scholars come from the 14th century *Kitāb al-Jawāhir* by al-Barrādī. Al-Barrādī wrote his book in a time of great turbulence for the Maghribi Ibāḍī communities, which had already lost their strongholds in Ifriqiyya and had to cope with the growing expansion of both Sunnism and Sufism. As an addendum to

13 Love, *Ibadi Muslims of North Africa* 2.

14 Cooperson, *Classical Arabic Biography* 1–23.

15 Love (*Ibadi Muslims of North Africa*) focuses mainly on the following biographical sources: *Kitāb al-sīra wa-akhbār al-aʾimma* by Abū Zakarīyā al-Warjlānī (late 10th and early 11th centuries); *Siyar al-Wisyānī* (late 11th to early 12th century); *Kitāb ṭabaqāt al-mashāʾikh bi-ʾl-Maghrib* by al-Darjīnī (d. mid-13th century); *Kitāb al-siyar* by Abū ʾl-ʿAbbās al-Shammākhī (d. 1522).

his book, al-Barrādī put an impressive list of works (fifty-nine titles, including thirty-six from the Maghrib and twenty-three from the east) mainly on law, theology and doctrine written by Ibāḍī authors. This *corpus* of written Ibāḍī texts testifies to the scholars' effort to collect and preserve the communities' legal, theological and doctrinal heritage and indicates once again the importance of knowledge and of knowledge transmission for the Ibāḍī scholars.[16]

In the same vein, almost all Omani-Ibāḍī legal sources, starting with Ibn Jaʿfar's *al-Jāmiʿ*, devote a long chapter to the topic of the *ṭalab al-ʿilm*, the quest for knowledge.[17] Though Ibāḍīs share the attitude towards the importance of the search for knowledge with the Sunnis, it acquires among them a unique flavour in conjunction with scholars' projects to renew and reinterpret the tradition to meet the various needs of their specific circumstances.

Ibāḍī religious elites relied on the status achieved through the acquisition of a high degree of knowledge when articulating Islamic positions, doctrines and rulings. Thus, knowledge could colour the way in which they would apply the law and understand their role in society, while legal theory could provide them with an overarching narrative through which to justify their rulings to the masses.

Al-Kudamī uses the legitimacy of the tradition as a starting point for his chapter on the *ṭalab al-ʿilm*. He begins with a report saying:

> It has come to us (*ballaghanā*) that all acts of devotion, the *jihād* on the way of God, enjoining the right and forbidding the wrong (*al-amr bi-ʾl-maʿrūf wa-ʾl-nahy ʿani ʾl-munkar*) are but a spit (*tifla*) in the sea compared to the quest for knowledge. The *ʿulamāʾ* are the heirs of the prophets, the salt of faith. It is said: Remembering (*ḥafaẓa*) a tradition is better than six years of practice of faith (*ʿibādāt*).[18]

In the chapter, he further elaborates on the issue of the *ṭalab al-ʿilm*, dealing with the importance of this obligation and detailing how to accomplish it in conjunction with Quran and Prophetic *sunna*. The *ʿulamāʾ* base their judgements on these sources and on the practice of the righteous Ibāḍī leaders (*āthār aʾimmat al-ʿadl*). The use of intellect does not stand in opposition to reliance on tradition. In fact, faith and knowledge reinforce mutually: knowledge leads the scholar to a better understanding of the texts of Quranic verses and prophetic *ḥadīth*, and only scholars who master these sources of law may issue legal opinions. On the other hand, the cornerstone of knowledge is the

16 Love, *Ibadi Muslims of North Africa* 110–115.
17 Ibn Jaʿfar, *al-Jāmiʿ* i, 45–63. See also: al-Bisiyānī, *Mukhtaṣar* (1977) 7–12.
18 Al-Kudamī, *al-Muʿtabar* i, 22.

recognition of *tawḥīd*, the oneness of God and of the absolute dependence of the creature on the Creator. Thus, the obligation for the quest for knowledge defines a central expression of the scholar's personal ethos and orthopraxis.[19]

Al-Kudamī's remarks enrich the treatment of the topic and yield the interpretation that pursuing knowledge means mastering the sources of law, namely Quran, *sunna*, consensus (*ijmāʿ* of those who are truthful in the *umma* of Muḥammad, *ijmāʿ al-muḥiqqīn min ummat Muḥammad*) and rational methods (*ḥujjat al-ʿaql*). *Sunna*, *ijmāʿ* and *raʾy* (a scholar's legal opinion) provide the correct interpretation of the Quran. The authority (*thubūt*) of the *sunna* is confirmed by the Quran itself, when it states: "And whatever the Messenger has given you – take; and whatever he has forbidden you – refrain from" (Q. 59:7). The authority of the consensus comes from Q. 3:110, "You are the best nation produced [as an example] for mankind. You enjoy what is right and forbid what is wrong and believe in God". The validity of consensus can also be inferred from the famous Prophetic tradition, stating: "My community will never agree on an error". Finally, the authority of the rational methods can be deducted from Q. 59:2 ("So take warning, O people of vision (*abṣār*)"); Q. 4:82 ("Then do they not reflect upon the Quran"); Q. 7:184–185 ("Then do they not give thought? ... Do they not look into the realm of heavens?").

Al-Kudamī's high regard for the texts of the Quran and the *ḥadīth* does not diminish but, on the contrary, enhances the value of scholars' rational capacities applied to hermeneutics. The authority of scholars' legal opinion (*raʾy*) is based on Q. 4:83,[20] and on the *sunna* where the Prophet says: "What Muslims find right (*ḥasan*) is right with God, and what Muslims find ugly (*qabīḥ*), is ugly with God".

The jurist's personal opinion can help in interpreting the Quran but cannot contradict it. Moreover, only the scholars (*ʿālim* and *muftī*) who reach a high level of knowledge (*maʿrifa*) and mastery of knowledge (*ḥifẓ*) may issue personal opinions (*raʾy*, *fatwā*). Jurists of lower rank are bound to explicit rules and their power of issuing personal opinions and interpreting the sources is limited to marginal matters. Al-Kudamī is adamant about restricting the power of the lower rank jurist (*ḥākim*) to the application of pre-existing rules, amongst which he may choose the one he finds most appropriate. In other words, he calls him to engage in *taqlīd* (i.e. the unquestioning acceptance of the legal decisions of earlier authoritative scholars), meaning that he must respond to

---

19 Al-Kudamī, *al-Muʿtabar* i, 13–38.

20 "And whatever comes to them, information about public security or fear, they spread it around. But if they had referred it back to the Messenger or to those of authority among them, then the ones who can draw correct conclusions from it would have known about it".

changes and unforeseen exigencies only by referring to precedents within the body of the school doctrine, from which he may construct his conclusion. In case of *ikhtilāf* (divergence of opinions) or in novel cases, he must refer to the established authorities, the "people of knowledge" (*ahl al-ʿilm*), whose consensus (*ijmāʿ*) is capable of validating his opinion and defining its acceptability within the community at large. Hence, the consensus guarantees both change and continuity in the school legal tradition, on one hand by supporting new conclusions and assimilating them in the legal system and on the other by perpetuating the school doctrine.[21]

Abū Bakr al-Kindī argues that the scholars of each generation (*ahl al-zamān min al-muslimīn*) have the right to define the consensus, thus stressing the fact that "the door of *ijtihād*" was never sealed among the Ibāḍīs. In fact, high-ranking jurists may exercise independent interpretation (*ijtihād*) of the sources, and question the opinions of earlier jurists if the school's prevailing rules could not be applied to the case at hand.[22]

The paradigm of the "closing of the gate of *ijtihād*" has been put to rest within the scholarship; though it reemerges to some extent in the dichotomy of rupture/continuity, which identifies dramatic moments of change in Islamic history rather than an unfolding process involving disagreement, dialogue, hybridity, creativity and negotiation.[23] Muslim jurists' manner of proceeding in hermeneutics provides us with useful insights into the social context in which they operated as well as into their understanding of long-term developments by aggregating scholarly findings about individual thinkers and texts.

The question of the relationship between *ijtihād* and *taqlīd* gave rise to a heated debate within academia in the last decade of 20th century. On one hand, authors like Coulson and Schacht asserted that Islamic law starts performing *taqlīd* in the 4th/10th century, while, on the other hand, Hallaq and Makdisi maintained that Muslim jurists never stopped exercising independent interpretation, or that it met its end only in a relatively late period. In particular, Wael Hallaq persuasively disputed the view that the right of independent interpretation had been withdrawn for future generations of Muslim jurists, arguing that it did not appear as an issue within the Islamic jurisprudence prior of the 7th/13th century.[24]

---

21 Al-Kudamī, *al-Muʿtabar* i, 14–17.

22 Al-Kindī, *Muṣannaf* i, 1st part, 36–68, see in part. 48.

23 Siddiqui, *Locating the Sharīʿa* 4–5.

24 Coulson, *A History of Islamic Law* 80; Schacht, *An Introduction to Islamic Law* 70–71; Makdisi, *The Rise of Colleges* 285, 290–291; Hallaq, Was the Gate of Ijtihād Closed? 3–41; idem, On the Origins of the Controversy 129–141.

Beyond dismissing the misconception that the gate of *ijtihād* was permanently closed in the 4th/10th century, scholars have demonstrated that *taqlīd* played an important role in the development of the *madhhab* and the adjudication of legal issues. Mohammad Fadel, for example, challenges the dominant approach that privileges *ijtihād* over *taqlīd* on the assumption that the former is an intellectually superior mode of legal reasoning. By analyzing the role of *taqlīd* as discussed by post-6th/12th century jurists of the Maliki school, he concludes that *taqlīd* resulted from the desire to have uniform rules rather than as a result of intellectual stagnation. The purpose of *taqlīd* was to limit the discretionary power of the jurists at the bottom of the legal hierarchy, who had to accept the decisions of the early authorities. *Taqlīd* never extended to all jurists and the high ranking jurists retained the right to revise old doctrines or to create new ones in the absence of established rules.[25]

Sherman Jackson offers an alternative to the leading views on this crux by treating the *fatāwā* by the jurist Shihāb al-Dīn al-Qarāfī (1228–1285) as a reflection of the manner and direction in which the Islamic legal tradition tended to develop subsequent to the so-called settling down of the four schools of law. He proves that, while clearly reflecting a commitment to *taqlīd*, al-Qarāfī's work renders problematic the description of blind acceptance of precedents to the institution. The tendency to recognize a higher status to *ijtihād* over *taqlīd*, as a liberal and progressive way of operating versus a conservative one, is misleading. It was through *taqlīd* that the *madhhab*s were able to sustain themselves and perpetuate school doctrine. Moreover, *taqlīd* and *ijtihād* did not represent exclusive moments in the history of Islamic law, but rather competing approaches that we can encounter simultaneously. *Ijtihād* dominated the formative period, and *taqlīd* gained momentum from about the 6th/11th century onwards, but these were, again, only dominant tendencies, and in fact some post-formative figures as Ibn ʿAbd al-Salām, Ibn Taymiyya, al-Suyūṭī and al-Shaukānī could both practise and advocate *ijtihād* well after the 6th/12th century.[26]

As far as Ibāḍī school is concerned, *taqlīd* marks the apex in legal thinking as it requires the scholars to build their arguments from pre-existing recognized methodologies, in this sense it paves the way for later *mujtahids* to actually change the doctrine of the school. The Ibāḍī school is adamant in affirming that each generations has one or more *mujtahid*/s who is/are allowed to solve issues that are not explicitly covered by Quran, *sunna* and tradition of

25 Fadel, The Social Logic of *Taqlīd* 193–233.

26 Jackson, *Taqlīd*, Legal Scaffolding and the Scope of Legal Injunctions 165–192; idem, Kramer versus Kramer in a Tenth/Sixteenth Century Egyptian Court 27–51.

the school (*āthār*) by employing individual reasoning. The Quran itself (e.g. 88:17; 7:184–185) praises the value of rationality (*iʿtibār*) as a way towards the search of Truth (*fī ṭalab al-ḥaqq*). Moreover, the *mujtahid* may not refuse to proffer a new interpretation of the scriptural references to solve new legal cases, nor may he rely on another *mujtahid* (*taqlīd al-mujtahid*). He exercises independent interpretation of the rulings (*aḥkām*) of the *sharīʿa* carrying out his efforts through rational methods.[27] Jumayyil b. Khamīs al-Saʿdī (d. 1278 AH, 1861–1862 CE), author of the monumental compendium of Ibāḍī law titled *Qamūs al-sharīʿa*, quotes a prophetic *ḥadīth* stating that the *ʿulamāʾ* became bound to operate under the regime of *ijtihād*, whose value and effectiveness is attested when it is backed with the required degree of authority through the consensus (*ijmāʿ*). He distinguishes between *ijmāʿ* expressed by the highest legal authorities on matters of substantive law (*furūʿ al-fiqh*) that provides an objective basis upon which legal decisions and legal rulings could operate, and the general agreement (*ittifāq*) on the principles of faith on which no one is allowed to perform *ijtihād*.[28]

From this viewpoint, the individualistic and solipsistic exercise of *ijtihād* is circumscribed by the consensus aiming at maintaining a recognizable balance between the *madhhab*'s legal tradition and the authority of the *mujtahids*. As *taqlīd*, *ijmāʿ* undermines the inevitable indeterminacy in law that resulted from independent interpretation of sources by individuals. Within the Ibāḍī school, the primary impetus of consensus was the search for recognizable repositories of authority. It had the function of declaring statements to be correct or incorrect within the conventions of the school; this way was not possible under the system of *ijtihād*.

The *ijmāʿ* balanced the *mujtahid*'s individualistic power, in fact *ijtihād* by itself was not able to create new rules unless it generated consensus among the jurists in that generation. Al-Kindī understands such consensus as a sign of God's blessing.[29] The first jurists to have the right to express consensus were the Prophet's companions (*ijmāʿ al-muhtadīn*, the consensus of the well-guided), after them the *ahl al-raʾy* of each generation of Ibāḍī scholars may exercise the consensus, representing the third pillar/fundamental (*aṣl*) of the *uṣūl al-fiqh*, after Quran and *sunna*. Consensus is a legal "proof" (*ḥujja*), along with the sacred sources and the rational methods of hermeneutics (*ḥujjat al-ʿaql*).

27 al-Saʿdī, *Qāmūs al-sharīʿa* i, 221–225; Ibn Khalfūn, *Ajwibat Ibn Khalfūn* 98–102; al-Warjlānī, *al-Dalīl wa ʾl-burhān* 2nd part, 74ff (*ijtihād al-ray*ʾ); Harmūsh, *al-Qawāʿid al-fiqhīya al-ibāḍiyya* vi, 430.

28 Al-Saʿdī, *Qāmūs al-sharīʿa* i, 243, 264–265.

29 Al-Kindī *Muṣannaf* i, 1st part, 48–51.

The famous *ḥadīth* supporting the authority of consensus, i.e. "my community will never agree upon an error", contributes within the Ibāḍī hermeneutics to strengthening the prestige of those mastering the school tradition (*ʿilm al-āthār*), the sacralized past of the Ibāḍī community.[30]

Through the delineation of sacralized past as fount of normativity, both religious and legal, the Ibāḍī scholars came to occupy a powerful position from which to establish orthodoxies and orthopraxies. They embodied the collective and accumulated lineage of the community and guaranteed the veracity of the *sunna/āthār* that they established. As Adam Gaiser argued, this notion of a communal pedigree finds its reflection in how Ibāḍīs presented their community as the most upright and accurate, and the sole remnant of the true Muslim community, thus proving the soundness of Islam in the Ibāḍī way.[31]

The consensus of the jurists in each generation was justified in terms of its connection to paradigms set by the founding jurists and their followers, which emerged as a normative sacralized past. Legal discourses of the 10th and 11th century Ibāḍī sources reflect a growing awareness of consensus (and violation of consensus) as a conceptual framework through which "orthodoxy" could be defined. The chief function of *ijmāʿ* was to confirm the results of legal procedure, analogy, interpretation and the acceptance of traditions that are not in themselves certain. *Ijmāʿ* represents within the Ibāḍī school a shift from individual interpretation to group interpretation. Placing an upward limit on the legal indeterminacy of free access to the sources, it turned a probable interpretation into an authoritative and incontrovertible rule of the school. On the other hand, the power of *mujtahid*s to exercise *ijtihād* enabled Ibāḍī law to evolve even after the genre of epitomes and commentary-like works came to dominate the school's writing.

5.4 *Qiyās* and Juridical Speculation

The science of *uṣūl al-fiqh* fulfils two main functions within the Ibāḍī school: on one hand it provides the parameters for setting a hierarchy of the sources and explaining the genesis of the law, on the other it serves the intellectual elite to set out their conception of authority and teaching. Quran, *sunna* and *ijmāʿ* are manifestations of revelation and thus foundation of *ʿilm*, but still they are not comprehensive enough to encompass all the legal cases that may arise in everyday life, and therefore Muslim jurists developed modes of analogical

30 Al-Saʿdī, *Qāmūs al-sharīʿa* i, 221–226; Ibn Khalfūn, *Ajwibat* 97.

31 Gaiser, *Ballaghanā ʿan an-Nabī* 443–444.

reasoning that, when applied to the text of revelation, allowed for finding solutions to novel legal cases through comparison with injunctions established by texts.[32]

Ibāḍī jurists subject these tools to a hierarchy that clearly prioritizes the Quran and the prophetic *sunna*, and they are adamant in restricting the application of rational methods – mainly *qiyās* and *istiḥsān*, which they understand as a form of *qiyās* – to the realm of jurisprudence in matters that had practical ramifications for personal and societal laws (*muʿāmalāt*). They did not admit *qiyās* to manipulate or establish axioms in speculative theology (*kalām*) and in any matters pertaining to God or His attributes.[33]

Writing at the outset of the classical era, and using earlier texts as his foundation, Abū Bakr al-Kindī, the author of the *Muṣannaf*, one of the most comprehensive Ibāḍī legal texts, incorporates a wide range of interpretive strategies and procedures. He offers a narrow interpretation *qiyās*, as it can only be used for deriving jurisprudence in specific circumstances and for extending existing rules to new cases.[34] His elaboration of hermeneutic techniques confirms the traditional methods of relating the principles of *uṣūl* to positive law (*furūʿ*). He understands the *uṣūl* as a way to follow divine guidance connecting positive law in an intelligible and reproducible way to the revealed sources. Within this framework, he elaborates on the analogical reasoning stating that the analogy process has four components, namely primary situation (*aṣl*), secondary situation (*farʿ*), cause (*ʿilla*) and ruling (*ḥukm*). The causative factor (*ʿilla*) is at the heart of the analogy process. It links the two situations, allowing that by analogy the ruling in the first situation applies to the second.

Ibāḍī jurists turned to *qiyās* when they were confronted with new problems for which no explicit rule could be found in revelation or in the body of prophetic traditions. They took the rule derived from the original case and applied it to the new one; therefore, it was crucial to understand the context and to evaluate whether the *ratio legis* in both the original and new case was analogous. Once the *ʿilla* is determined it is easy to arrive at the legal rule of the parallel case, since it stems from the rule of original case, from which the legal cause is inferred. The *ʿilla* could be identified by carefully analyzing the revealed texts (Quran and *sunna*), it could be based on consensus (*ijmāʿ*) or could be inferred through rational methods, namely juridical preference (*istiḥsān*) and resemblance (*shabah*).

---

32 For the development of *uṣūl al-fiqh* among the Sunnis and the Shiʿites, see for example Weiss, *Studies in Islamic Legal Theory*.

33 Al-Kindī, *Muṣannaf* i, 1st part, 67; see also al-Saʿdī, *Qāmūs al-sharīʿa* i, 283.

34 Al-Kindī, *Muṣannaf* i, 1st part, 52–67. On the application of *qiyās* and other rational methods in Ibāḍī law, see also al-Saʿdī, *Qāmūs al-sharīʿa* i, 283–306, 327–337.

Determining the divine *ʿilla* behind a legal injunction is a fundamental element, but also the most controversial one, of the process of *qiyās*. It implies an accurate reflection of the divine intention behind the legal injunction in the text in order to understand its rationale and pose a link between two apparently disconnected cases.[35] For instance, in the case of the prohibition of the wine, Abū Bakr al-Kindī argues that the *ʿilla* lies in the characteristic of the wine to give intoxication, therefore any other juice that does not have this characteristic is allowed. However, not all Ibāḍī jurists agree. According to some, as the ban on wine is laid down in the Quran, it extends to its derivatives. In fact, vinegar – although it does not give intoxication – is prohibited, even if drunk to attenuate the taste of salt.[36]

A further case discussed in the Ibāḍī sources to substantiate the difficulty of depicting the *ratio legis* is the prohibition of usury (*ribā*). As is well known, the famous *ḥadīth* of the Prophet extends the prohibition to all exchanges of gold, silver, wheat, barley, dates and salt, demanding not only the immediate delivery of the two lots being exchanged, but also absolute equality in quantity if the two lots belonged to the same kind. Starting from this tradition, Muslim jurists tried to depict what the effective cause (*ʿilla*) of the prohibition could have been, in order to extend the legal rule to parallel cases by *qiyās*. Drawing analogy from this original case (*aṣl*) meant understanding what the common quality among the commodities mentioned in the *ḥadīth* was. However, as the rationale of the legal rule was not obvious, the jurists held different views on the criteria for the legal causation. The jurists' search for the most proper quality among the qualities of the original case necessitated that they should be well versed in the main objectives of the *sharīʿa*. The Maghribi-Ibāḍī jurist al-Shammākhī offers a systematic defence of hermeneutic method the Ibāḍī school used, comparing it with that used by the other schools of law:

> According to some [jurists], the non-simultaneous exchange of everything that can be eaten or hoarded is not allowed. This is the opinion by Mālik and his companions, they rely on the fact that the four species (wheat, barley, dates, salt) mentioned in the Prophetic *ḥadīth* on usury (*ribā*), suggest that the Prophet intended to indicate their use. Indeed they are foodstuffs. The same applies to hoarding. The meaning of the prohibition of usury is that people should not cheat each other and that they should safeguard the property of others. Thus concerns the basic things of subsistence, namely foodstuffs. […]

35 On this question, see also al-Saʿdī, *Qāmūs al-sharīʿa* i, 287.
36 Al-Kindī, *Muṣannaf* i, 1st part, 52; al-Saʿdī, *Qāmūs al-sharīʿa* i, 290–291.

According to others, the *ratio legis* (*ʿilla*) of the prohibition of usury concerns land products. This is the opinion by al-Shāfiʿī and some of our companions, they rely on the fact that it is handed down that the Prophet forbade the sale of foodstuffs in exchange for foodstuffs in different amount (*bayʿ al-ṭaʿām bi-ʾl-ṭaʿām*) [...].

According to others, the *ratio legis* of the prohibition of *ribā* relates to measurement and weight, so it is not allowed to exchange with a timelapse goods that are measured for goods that are measured and goods that are weighed for goods that are weighed. They rely on the fact that the Prophet mentioned in the tradition about usury only things that can be measured or weighed, so the *ratio legis* [of the prohibition of usury] concerns weight and measurement. This is the opinion by Abū Ḥanīfa and some of our companions. However, Abū Ḥanīfa contradicts his thesis by permitting the exchange of one fruit for two, one *fals*[37] for two and one grain for two, although these things belong to those that are measured or weighed.

According to our tradition (*wa fī ʾl-āthār*), the evidence against Mālik and Abū Ḥanīfa, on which our companions agree, lies in the fact that they allowed the exchange of iron, lead and bronze for gold and silver in double quantities (*bi-aḍʿāf*), either at the same time or with a delay. Mālik's argument contradicts itself as he believes that the *ratio legis* of the prohibition of usury concerns things that can be hoarded and eaten, which cannot be exchanged for each other in double quantities. Abū Ḥanīfa's argument contradicts itself on this issue as he allows the exchange of things that can be hoarded for similar items in double quantities. There is no evidence against al-Shāfiʿī as he believes that the *ratio legis* of the prohibition of usury concerns food, while the mentioned things are not food. However, God knows better.

Others say that wheat and barley prove that [the prohibition of usury] concerns foods of the grass family and the like; dates prove that [the prohibition of usury] concerns fruits and sweet things that can be mixed with honey, such as grapes, apples, plums, pistachios, bananas, walnuts, almonds and all autumn fruits; salt proves that [the prohibition of usury] concerns spices with which food is flavoured. All the foods that belong to these categories cannot be exchanged for others of the same kind, except contextually. But God knows better.

Others say that all foods that can be mixed with honey, such as dates, raisins, figs and the like, form a single category, so it is not permissible to exchange them with each other with a delay. Likewise, oily substances, such as oil, butter, animal fat and the like; meat; spices, such as pepper, cardamom, cumin and the

37 *Fals* pl. *fulūs* (from the Latin world *follis*) was the copper coin.

> like; beverages, such as milk, water, *nabīdh*[38] and the like, form a single category. [...] According to them, it would not be lawful to exchange the goods we have mentioned for others of the same category with a delay. According to others, the goods we have mentioned belong to different categories, so that it is permissible to exchange them with a delay. The latter opinion seems to me to be the fairest.[39]

According to the Ibāḍī school, in cases where the jurist deduces a cause that invalidates the primary situation (*aṣl*), his deductive effort would yield the reverse of the original ruling (*ḥukm*). This would mean that he has failed to arrive at the effective cause, and that his conclusion is invalid. The establishment of the inferential cause (*ʿilla mustanbaṭa*) ensures the establishment of the legal rule; and if the cause is incorrectly established, then the legal rule will invalid.

Moreover, the Ibāḍī jurists make clear that an injunction resulting from *qiyās* does not itself become a source on par with the texts, unless it is validated by the consensus of the contemporaneous community. In that case, *qiyās* changed its status as a source of law from weighed opinion to consensus.[40]

The establishment of the inferential cause is further discussed in the *Qāmūs al-sharīʿa*, where the author reviews earlier Ibāḍī jurisprudence, making the contents of earlier legal works accessible to a large number of jurists and facilitating the assimilation of the methodological criteria of the science of the *uṣūl al-fiqh*.[41] Locating the *ʿilla* in controversial analogical processes requires resorting to other methodologies, such as resemblance (*shabah*) and juristic preference (*istiḥsān*), which developed out of *qiyās al-ʿilla* and expanded the abilities of jurists to rationalize previous practice and to find new solutions that responded to the changing needs of the community.

The *qiyās al-shabah* is based on pinpointing specific relevant parallels between the root-case and the branch-case, which should make the process of transferring the relevant juridical ruling plausible. Conclusions obtained by *qiyās al-shabah* change depending on where the correlational inferences are located. For example, a slave may be considered a responsible adult (*mukallaf*) or a good (*māl*) like any other commodity (*sulʿa*). In the first case, his *diya* (compensation paid to the heirs of a victim) will be one half of that due for a

38 *Nabīdh* was a traditional drink made from raisins or dates steeped in water.

39 Al-Shammākhī, *Kitāb al-īḍāḥ* iii, 15–18. The case of *ribā* is mentioned also in al-Kindī, *Muṣannaf* i, 1st part, 66 and in al-Saʿdī, *Qāmūs al-sharīʿa* i, 286, 328.

40 Al-Kindī, *Muṣannaf* i, 1st part, 65–66.

41 Al-Saʿdī, *Qāmūs al-sharīʿa* i, 327–337.

free man. On the other hand, if he is considered a good, the *diya* will depend on his value (*qīma*), whatever it is.[42]

The application of *qiyās al-istiḥsān* is a considerable source of controversy among Ibāḍī jurists. It takes into account practical social considerations, such as the principle of public interest, the necessity, the convenience or the ease, in the effort to find legal solutions for a new case. One of the examples adduced in the *Qāmūs al-sharīʿa* for the application of *qiyās al-istiḥsān* concerns the compensation due for the *dhimmī*. In this case the primary situation (*aṣl*) is represented by Quran 4:92.

> It is not for a believer to kill any believer, except by mistake. Whoever kills a believer by mistake, then, a believing slave has to be freed, and the blood money must be paid to his family, unless they waive it charitably. If the victim belongs to a people hostile to you and is a believer, then, a believing slave has to be freed. If the victim belongs to a people between whom and you there is treaty, then, blood money is to be paid to his family, and a believing slave to be freed.

Starting from this verse, the jurists decide, in accordance with the principle of *istiḥsān*, that the *diya* due for a *dhimmī* is one half of that due for a free Muslim man, and the *diya* due for a *dhimmiyya* is one third of that due for a free Muslim woman.[43]

The plausibility of a conclusion attained by relying on necessity or convenience (*qiyās al-istiḥsān*), or obtained by resemblances based on sharing properties (*qiyās al-shabah*), has a lower degree of epistemic plausibility than conclusions inferred by the deployment of *qiyās al-ʿilla*.

Reasoning by analogy and consensus became sources of law that were as authoritative as the Quran and *sunna*, nonetheless rational methods (*qiyās* and *raʾy*) follow the Quran and *sunna* in the hierarchy of the sources. In the *Qāmūs al-sharīʿa* this argument is eloquently summarized in some examples that ostensibly deal with the superiority of tradition and *ijmāʿ* over the inferences that would be obtained by analogical reasoning. The first case is the one of the punishment for *zinā* (meaning both fornication and adultery). The Quran makes it clear that those found guilty of *zinā*, regardless of their marital status, will be liable to receive a punishment of one hundred lashes, whilst slaves, married or unmarried, should receive fifty lashes (Q. 24:2). However, the complexities surrounding the issue of punishment for adultery gave rise to a heated debate in early Islamic juristic circles, which crystallized into a number

42 Al-Saʿdī, *Qāmūs al-sharīʿa* i, 332.
43 Al-Saʿdī, *Qāmūs al-sharīʿa* i, 337.

of traditions conveying a growing strictness towards married adulterers who were punished by stoning. Such traditions were substantiated by the consensus of the jurists, who agreed that the Quranic verses applied to non-married people only.[44]

The second example of hierarchical relationship between *ijmāʿ* and reasoning is the triple divorce. The Quran (2:229–230) states that a man may divorce his wives three times, taking her back after the first two, the triple divorce, pronounced on successive occasions or at same time, made divorce both irrevocable and absolute. However, this rule applies to free women only, whereas the slave girls can only be divorced twice on the basis of the consensus of the jurists.[45]

As a further example of the higher degree of *ijmāʿ* – and therefore of the power of jurists as a cohesive group – the *Qāmūs al-sharīʿa* deals with the punishment for drinking wine. Drinking wine (*khamar*) is forbidden in Q. 5:90. The penalty, however, is based on the prophetic tradition reporting that Muhammad prescribed forty lashes but ʿUmar increased the punishment to eighty lashes:

> Once a man who had drunk wine was brought before the Prophet. He then inflicted about forty strokes with two palm-leaf stalks on him. Abū Bakr did the same. But when ʿUmar came to power he consulted the people and then ʿAbd al-Raḥmān b. ʿAwf said: The lightest of all fixed penalties is eighty [strokes]. Thereupon ʿUmar decreed this.

Thus, the author of the *Qāmūs al-sharīʿa* concludes that the Ibāḍī jurists follow the example of ʿUmar, as his decision was supported by the consensus of the community.[46]

The legal theory that the Ibāḍī jurists constructed laid the basis for the understanding of the respective roles of *ḥadīth* and communal consensus in jurisprudence and contributed to their systematizing approach to jurisprudence characterized by a concern with certainty. The preoccupation with producing a coherent result gave rise to a theory of interpretation that does not exclude the possibility of differences of opinion but prioritizes consensus,

44 Al-Saʿdī, *Qāmūs al-sharīʿa* i, 299–300. On the punishment for adultery in early Islam, see Francesca, Flogging, Banning, Lapidation.

45 Al-Saʿdī, *Qāmūs al-sharīʿa* i, 299; Lucas, Divorce, *Ḥadīth*-Scholar Style.

46 Al-Saʿdī, *Qāmūs al-sharīʿa* i, 300–301. The *ḥadīth* (ʿAsqalānī, *Bulūgh*, no. 1061) is quoted in Peters, *Crime and Punishment in Islamic Law* 64. The Shafiʿites follow the example of the Prophet and make drinking alcohol punishable with forty lashes. The other schools follow the example of ʿUmar, who increased the punishment to eighty lashes.

which represents a truthful and certain interpretation of the sacred sources and a key element in ascertaining the truth of *qiyās*. Consensus embodies the legal memory of the community; it asserts the authority of the community in making and changing law. Therefore, its normative force surpasses that of other juristic tools such as analogy and rationalist methods as vouchsafed by the legal debate outlined in this section.[47]

5.5 Jurists and Politics: the Rustāq and Nizwā Party in Oman

Mastering the law was also an instrument of power. Not only did Ibāḍī jurists claim fully legitimate representation of the sacred law, since they were rooted in the teachings of the early authorities who had settled in Basra, in their knowledge of the religion and their legal reasoning, but they were also embedded in a network of power dynamics with state and tribal organizations. Jurists articulated in their *fatāwā* and oftentimes in their treatises the political and social problems they were trying to solve or with which they were attempting to come to terms. There were a number of developments that laid the basis for the growth of the jurists into a prominent and politically patronized social group within the Ibāḍī-Omani community.

In 272/886, following the deposition of the *imām* al-Ṣalt b. Mālik (r. 237/851–272/886), Oman entered an unstable and difficult period that led to the fall of the imamate. The al-Ṣalt affair resulted, on one hand, from the scholars' desire to gain full control of the imamate and, on the other, from the tribal rivalries that fuelled violent conflicts in Oman. Al-Ṣalt was deposed by a group of *ʿulamāʾ* under the leadership of the judge Mūsā b. Mūsā, a member of the Banū Sāma family, which was part of the main Yaḥmad tribal confederation, the same that had supported the election of al-Ṣalt. Al-Ṣalt retired to his tribal homeland where he lived peacefully with his son until his death three years later. Mūsā installed Rāshid b. al-Naḍr/Naẓr al-Fajḥī; the latter was in turn deposed in 277/890, and replaced, again by Mūsā, with ʿAzzān b. Tamīm al-Kharūṣī, who was killed by the invading caliphate force in 280/893. The circumstances of the deposition (or maybe of the resignation) of al-Ṣalt are unclear. It was true that al-Ṣalt, who had been ruling for thirty-five years, was losing control and making wrong and senile decisions, but the question of whether he was a just *imām* or not remained unsettled. Was his misconduct demonstrated, and therefore was rebellion, *khurūj*, against him permitted, or

47 For a comparison with the Sunnī view, see Abd Rahim, The Concept of *Ijmāʿ* in Islamic Law 91–103.

not? The point was: what position should the community take? The adversary party did not confront him with his wrong behaviour nor give him the chance of public repentance (*tawba*). Moreover, Mūsā not only deposed a properly elected *imām*, but he chose a new leader who was elected by a part of the *ʿulamāʾ* only, so he did not enjoy general consensus.[48]

The outbreak of a civil war (273–280/886–893) ended the first imamate, one of the most important and influential periods of the history of Oman. Building on an epistle by Abū Qaḥṭān (Khālid b. Qaḥṭān, second half of the 3rd/9th century–beginning of the 10th century), Ubaydli suggests that the stability and independence that the country experienced during the imamate created relative affluence, which reflected in the attitude of the population and especially the younger generation. The influence of the strict Ibāḍī principles fell away, giving way to a more pragmatic standard of living: "Young men and people grew up in the state. They showed off piety without being really God-fearing. They pretended to be religious, while they concealed their worldliness. They took over worldly interests under the cover of religion".[49] If we take the comment by Abū Qaḥṭān seriously, we can imagine how much such a change displeased the *ʿulamāʾ* as it did not fit into their religiosity and their preconceived ideas about a righteous society.

The reconstruction of the tragic events of the deposition and of the ensuing civil war is not an easy task and it is made doubly difficult by the fragmentary nature of the material available, most of which stems from the anti-Mūsā faction (the so-called Rustāq party) considering the overthrowing illegal. However, the downfall of the imamate and the civil war shocked many *ʿulamāʾ* who revised their previous position on the legitimacy of the *imām* al-Ṣalt's ousting. They moved to follow the Kharūṣī family and other leaders of the Yaḥmad tribe, who finally succeeded in uniting Oman under the leadership of al-Khalīl b. Shādhān al-Kharūṣī (1016–1029), a grandson of the *imām* al-Ṣalt.

---

48 Wilkinson, *The Imamate Tradition of Oman* 10; idem, *Ibâḍism* 322–323. The issue of the legitimacy and eventually obligation of fighting against an unjust imām is discussed in the last part of *Kitāb al-Muḥāraba* by Abū ʾl-Mundhir Bashīr b. Muḥammad b. Maḥūb (d. *c.*290/908), the grandson of Abū Sufyān Maḥbūb b. Ruḥayl, written in the last years of al-Ṣalt's imamate. The *Sīra* by Abū ʾl-Mundhir also deals with al-Ṣalt's deposition condemning the revolt, which caused a split in the Ibāḍī community. Al-Salimi and Madelung (eds.), *Early Ibāḍī Literature* 47–60; 61–75. See also *Sīra li-baʿḍa fuqahāʾ al-muslimīn ilā ʾl-imām al-Ṣalt b. Mālik*, in Kāshif (ed.), *al-Siyar wa ʾl-jawābāt* i, 181–228. The epistle, written probably long before his deposition, discusses the question of just revolt.

49 *Sīra tunsab ilā Abī Qaḥṭān Khālid b. Qaḥṭān*, in Kāshif (ed.), *al-Siyar wa ʾl-jawābāt* i, 81–147, see 124; quoted in Ubaydli, *Early Islamic Oman* 132–133. On the *Sīra* see Radivilov, Rereading Omani Siyar: Khālid b. Qaḥṭān 83–92. See also Ziaka, The Roots of the Uṣūl al-Fiqh in the Ibāḍī Madhhab 94.

About the middle of the 11th century, his successor, Rāshid b. Saʿīd al-Yaḥmadī succeeded in defeating the last strongholds of Buwayhids, supporters of the Abbasids, gaining control over the coasts of Oman. This second imamate did not recreate the peaceful environment of the first one: the Rustāq school issued an edict in 443/1052 against the supporters of Mūsā b. Mūsā, declaring them renegades, thus nullifying all hopes of creating a new unity.[50]

The deposition of the *imām* al-Ṣalt turned out to be an event that divided Oman for centuries and had a dramatic impact on the development of the Ibāḍī school. It prompted a split of the jurists into three parties: the pro-Mūsā party approving the deposition (which disappeared early on); the anti-Mūsā (the Rustāq party) rejecting the deposition; and the neutralists (the Nizwā party).[51] The terms Nizwā and Rustāq parties began being used by the first half of the 10th century. It was at this juncture that the Ibāḍī jurists developed a set of principles of creed, such as the doctrine of *walāya* and *barāʾa* (association/dissociation) to boost their political and organizational goals. They differentiated between just and unjust ruler and between rulers and tyrants. Although the *ʿulamāʾ* gave wide powers to the *imām*, they made it clear that the *imām* could only practice his powers as long as he consulted them and observed Ibāḍī principles. Moreover, the election of the *imām* was ultimately in the hands of the *ʿulamāʾ* and the tribal chiefs.[52]

5.5.1 The *Walāya* and *Barāʾa* Doctrine

By designating themselves authoritative exponents of a salvific knowledge, the jurists of Rustāq and Nizwā schools were attempting to detribalize the imamate and maintain it at its proper capital. The doctrine of *walāya* and *barāʾa* provided them with a dogmatic and legal framework to articulate their discourse. The *walāya* served as a prerequisite of faith, affirming bonds of devotion with the community's designated leaders and solidarity with community members who carried out the precepts of religion in a satisfactory manner. The obvious corollary of *walāya* was dissociation from those viewed as opponents. When the Ibāḍī community was divided into two rival camps, each of them convinced of being in the right, the majority would form a body whose report was of certain reliability. Consequently, the doctrine of *walāya* and *barāʾa* could be used to eliminate rival ideas from contention. If the errors were significant enough, the rivals were expelled from the Ibāḍī community, which

50 Wilkinson, Bio-bibliographical Background 137–139; Wilkinson, *Ibâḍism* 321–360.
51 Wilkinson, Bio-bibliographical Background 148–149.
52 Ubaydli, *Early Islamic Oman* 146.

declared *barāʾa* – a sort of excommunication – against them. The aspiration toward certainty, already evident in the doctrine of consensus, found another and more immediate outlet in infallibility of the community, represented by its leading *ʿulamāʾ*, in deciding who was interpreting and applying the principles of the Ibāḍī dogma in the right way, thus deserving the community's association/friendship. The doctrine of *walāya* and *barāʾa* ensured that the integrity of Ibāḍī law and theology remained unimpaired throughout the ages, despite the rivalries and conflicts which threatened the community. It is the expression of a profound theological insight. The jurists, who held the monopoly on the exegetical technique and were the key elements participating in *ijmāʿ*, defended their primacy in expressing *walāya* and *barāʾa* as a criterion of normativity. This approach allowed them to occupy a powerful position from which to critique state policies, societal customs and to establish orthodoxies and orthopraxies.

As already argued above, through the delineation of a certain sacralized past as the sole fount of normativity, religious authority shifted to the jurists whose expertise allowed them to access and recapture this past. The theory of *walāya* and *barāʾa* was in continuity with their role as the main interpreters of the law, and it provided them with an interpretive tool/instrument whose parameters were set by the paradigm of being a righteous follower of Ibāḍī law and dogma.

Throughout the history of Ibadism, religious authority assumed a number of forms and functions: the capability of defining a 'canon' of authoritative texts and the legitimate methods of hermeneutics, the right to classify the correct belief and practice and the power to marginalize and punish deviance, heresy and apostasy.[53] The ability of religious authority to shape and influence the views and the conduct of the community members was symbolized among the Ibāḍīs by the *walāya/barāʾa* doctrine.[54] The *walāya/barāʾa* system determined the Ibāḍī attitude towards non-Ibāḍīs as well as membership and leadership of the community. The latter stemmed from personal excellence, and the confidence which the community placed in its *imām* constituted his authority.

The Ibāḍīs saw the imamate as a compulsory religious duty directly related to the obligation of "commanding what is right and forbidding what is wrong", which guarantees the maintenance of order and justice on earth according to

---

53 For a general overview, see Krämer and Schmidtke (eds.), *Speaking for Islam*, Introduction 1–14.

54 The doctrine of association and dissociation among the Ibāḍīs is discussed in Ennami, *Studies* (online edition) 162–196. See also Hoffman, *The Essentials of Ibāḍī Islam* 156–211, and idem, Ibāḍī Scholars on Association and Dissociation from the 10th to the 21st century 185–193; Francesca, Self-defining through Faith 29–41. The Ibāḍī attitude towards major and minor sins is discussed in Ibn Idrīsū, *Al-fikr al-ʿaqadī ʿinda al-Ibāḍīyya* 394–455.

divine law. They required obedience towards the righteous *imām* while, conversely, allowing people to revolt against a tyrannical and unjust leader.[55] Ibāḍī sources provide us with excellent examples to study the complex relationship between knowledge, conduct and charisma in defining leadership. The nature, scope and locus of religious authority were discussed with regard to knowledge (*ʿilm*), personal conduct, piety and charisma. The Ibāḍīs were deeply concerned with defining and defending correct belief and practice, and with preventing apostasy and heresy. In Ibāḍī thought, religious and political authority is firmly grounded in the acquisition and possession of *ʿilm*; that is, knowledge in the broadest sense, and particularly religious knowledge based primarily on the Quran and *sunna*. Knowledge, as part of the constellation of essential traits possessed by the morally excellent individual, has particular resonance in the discourse on the construction of the theory of imamate. In fact, knowledge, along with piety, was a requirement for the optimal leader, i.e. the *imām al-ẓuhūr* appointed under ideal conditions of stability following the defeat of all enemies. Knowledge and piety were also prerequisites for the leader who assumed a (limited) authority over the community when its survival was jeopardized and the faithful were forced to live under the rule of their opponents practising dissimulation (*taqiyya*). Under this condition (*kitmān*), the obligation to appoint an *imām* could be waived and the scholars wielded the leadership of the community.[56] The Ibāḍī scholars represented the community's elite, the guardians of the law, those who could dissolve or sanction an election (*ahl al-ḥall wa ʾl-ʿaqd*) and therefore were entrusted with the responsibility of protecting and defending the people against unjust *imāms*. This concern with knowledgeable leaders and the claim to a line of *ʿilm* formation and transmission bolstered the *ʿulamāʾ*'s role within the community and represented the core of their authority. In fact, as Wilkinson points out, "the development of the theory of imamate was parallel with the development of a formal legal and theological school".[57]

---

55 See, for example, Muḥammad b. Maḥbūb, the son of Abū Sufyān Maḥbūb b. al-Ruḥayl, in a letter to the Maghribī Ibāḍīs in Kāshif (ed.), *al-Siyar wa ʾl-jawābāt* ii, 242–245.

56 On the rules concerning the leadership of the *ʿulamāʾ* see for example al-Bisiyānī, *al-Jāmiʿ* iv, 194.

57 Wilkinson, *The Imamate Tradition of Oman* 10, 187–198; Gaiser, *Muslim, Scholars, Soldiers* 140–141. As Adam Gaiser has argued, the construction of a proper politico-religious authority among the Ibāḍīs was closely linked to the question of Ibāḍī sectarian identity. The medieval Ibāḍī vision of the imamate was built upon several layers of historical precedents going back to the early Kharijite era, the Medinan caliphate, the Quran, the Prophetic model of leadership and even the pre-Islamic era. These models, conveyed to Ibadism via the early Basran community – which constituted the celebrated Ibāḍī

Discussion regarding the imamate occurred within an overall context of fervent debate in Ibāḍī circles, which addressed the question of legitimation and the body of religious-legal norms based on the authority of the early *imāms*. The doctrine of *walāya* and *barāʾa* provided such debate with a conceptual framework that was bound up with problems concerning the soundness of doctrine, the reliability of sources and early schisms. It took the form of a structuralized doctrine and formal dogma, according to which individuals, schools and rival groups were classified and eventually rejected.

Since the beginning, Ibāḍīs followed the *walāya/barāʾa* doctrine as a religious and social obligation; nonetheless, it had several political implications, in particular in defining the Ibāḍī attitude towards the first *fitna*. Therefore, the *walāya/barāʾa* system not only decided membership in the community, but also defined the Ibāḍī attitude towards Sunnis and Shiʿites.

The Ibāḍīs recognized the authority of the Prophet and his first two successors, Abū Bakr and ʿUmar; they also acknowledged the first six years of the caliphate of ʿUthmān and the rule of ʿAlī until he accepted arbitration. The Umayyad caliphs were considered illegitimate and as such were regarded as tyrants who deserved *barāʾa*.

Among the Companions who deserved *barāʾa* were Ṭalḥa b. ʿUbaydallāh and Zubayr b. al-ʿAwwām, who broke the pledge of allegiance and fought against the legal Caliph, ʿAlī. ʿĀʾisha, though she took part in the strife and was present at the Battle of the Camel, was exempted from *barāʾa* as she repented from her sins. The Caliph ʿAlī was also treated with *barāʾa* for accepting the arbitration of men in a matter that has been already decided by the Quran. Muʿāwiya and ʿAmr b. al-ʿĀṣ were treated with *barāʾa* for their rebellion against ʿAlī, the legal Caliph.

According to the general rule, true believers must declare *barāʾa* from the tyrants and their followers and they must not take any of them as *walī*. Any country governed by tyrants and unjust rulers must be declared a land of tyranny and injustice. Tyrants are those who rule the people by force and do not comply with the rules of *sharīʿa*. They live in luxury, drink wine and wear silk. The Ibāḍī sources indicate Ziyād b. Abī Sufyān and al-Ḥajjāj b. Yūsuf as examples of tyrants.[58]

The doctrine of *walāya*, *barāʾa* and *wuqūf* was already set forth in detail by ʿAbd Allāh b. Yazīd al-Fazārī (2nd/8th century), the famous Kufan Ibāḍī

'Golden Age' – were systematized and expanded by the Ibāḍī religious literature over the centuries.

58 Ennami, *Studies* 187–188 (online edition); Crone-Zimmermann, *The Epistle of Sālim b. Dhakwān* 40–145, see in particular 106 ff., 114 ff., 122–131, 140ff.

mutakallim, in his responses to questions of the Maghribi Ibāḍiyya concerning the Nukkār schism and the status of ʿAbd al-Wahhāb and of all later Rustumid *imāms* of Tahert. Al-Fazārī argued that after the schism of the Muslim community over the Caliphate of ʿUthmān, the status of many Muslims became uncertain and *wuqūf* was obligatory until the soundness of their faith and creed was properly tested and ascertained. The doctrine of *wuqūf* allowed giving the benefit of doubt to the great majority of Muslims who might in fact be righteous believers rather than hypocrites.[59]

A serious threat to the Ibāḍī rigorous position was represented by the early Murji'ite doctrine, which propounded the dogma of suspended judgement over the fate of sinners in the afterlife and over the first *fitna*. That was wholly contrary to the Ibāḍī view on ʿUthmān and ʿAlī and their rejection of the Umayyad dynasty. Sālim b. Dhakwān disagreed with the Murji'ites about the fact that they suspended their judgement on the first schism (*fitna*) for not having experienced it as it happened before their time. He argues that the Murji'ites do not rely on fundamental Islamic principles but rather on their own criteria and therefore are themselves guilty of unbelief (*kufr*).[60]

The discussion on Murji'ism was crucial among Ibāḍīs and some Murji'ite ideas penetrated into the movement and were propagated by Hārūn b. al-Yamān (3rd/9th century), causing a serious split in the Mashriqī Ibāḍī community. Hārūn propounded a very tolerant attitude to *walāya* and *barāʾa*, according *kufr* status only to those committing sins deserving *ḥadd* punishment in this world and hell in the next. He recognized a "middle way" (the *manzila bayn al-manzilatayn*) for people committing sins that his predecessors, such as Abū Ayyūb, had considered to be major. Furthermore, Hārūn tied faith to individual piety (*taqwā*) rather than to strict interpretations of religious observances.

Hārūn's doctrine is recorded in his correspondence with the *imām* Muhannā b. Jayfar (r. 226–237/841–852) and in the fierce confutation by Abū Sufyān Maḥbūb b. al-Ruḥayl in his letters to the Omanis and Hadramis.[61] Abū Sufyān's letters are ferociously outspoken in their polemic against Hārūn: it is clear that the fundamental issue was to take a clear stance over the status of the sinner, which was challenged by the Muʿtazilī and Murji'ite concepts of doubt (*shākk*) and suspended judgement (*wuqūf*). Abū Sufyān confuted Hārūn's division of

---

59 Al-Fazārī, *Kitāb al-Futyā*, in al-Salimi and Madelung (eds.), *Early Ibāḍī Theology* 147–152.

60 Crone-Zimmermann, *The Epistle of Sālim b. Dhakwān* 114–117; al-Salimi, *On the Reception of Early Ibadi Theology* 63–65 (Arabic text).

61 Kāshif (ed.), *al-Siyar wa 'l-jawābāt* i, 273–304 (*Sīrat Maḥbūb b. al-Ruḥayl ilā ahl Ḥaḍramawt fī amr Hārūn b. Yamān*); i, 305–321 (*Sīrat Maḥbūb b. al-Ruḥayl ilā ahl ʿUmān fī amr Hārūn b. Yamān*); i, 323–336 (*Risālat Hārūn b. al-Yamān ilā 'l-imām Muhannā b. al-Jayfar*).

sins into major sins and minor sins and rejected his idea of suspending judgement over persons whom the earlier generations had accorded *walāya* or *barā'a*. The main focus of dispute was that Hārūn was propagating a real heresy in borrowing from Murji'ism and its notion of *shakk*, Muʿtazilism with its *manzila bayn al-manzilatayn* and the doctrine that what is good comes from God and what is bad from man, and Qadarism with the debate on free will.[62] The Maghribi-Ibāḍī author Tibghūrīn b. ʿĪsā al-Malshūṭī (lived in the last half of the 5th/11th century) considers alliance and dissociation as one of the fundamentals (*aṣl*) of the *uṣūl al-dīn* and asserts their compulsory on the basis of the Quran and *sunna*, in opposition to the ideas of both Murji'a and Ḥashwiyya.[63]

Some of these doctrines represented a serious challenge to the *daʿwa* and to the Ibāḍī attitude towards the Umayyad caliphate. Indeed, the doctrine of association and dissociation attacked the very basis of Caliphal authority as represented by Umayyad orthodoxy; it undermines the privileged position occupied by the Arabs, and the position of the Umayyads who relied on Arab support.

From the overall tone of the early Ibāḍī sources, it is clear that the *walāya/barā'a* principle reflects specific political and historical conjunctions. Not only does it define the community's attitude to other Muslims, but the internal schisms are connected to this question.[64]

The religious and political unity of the Ibāḍīs was broken at a fairly early date by a number of schisms. Following the *walāya/barā'a* principle throughout Ibāḍī history, a number of adherents broke away from the community and formed their own groups. In Eastern as well as in Western Ibāḍī sources, the link between *walāya/barā'a* and political power remains prominent. Religious duties are associated with political activism, rebellion against unjust rule and the exercise of the legitimate imām's authority. The Ibāḍīs developed a concept of a community founded on the moral obligations of piety and rectitude, where the leadership was based on religious knowledge (*ʿilm*), consultation and consensus within the community.[65]

The system of *walāya* and *barā'a* helped in securing the growth of the Ibāḍī movement in the right direction. One of the basic rules for the new member who converted to Ibadism was to declare *barā'a* from the opponents of the Ibāḍī movement and to declare *walāya* from the upright members of the Ibāḍī

62 Wilkinson, *The Imamate Tradition of Oman*164–165, idem, *Ibâḍism* 231–235.

63 Al-Malshūṭī, *Kitāb uṣūl al-dīn* 73–76.

64 See, for example, Muḥammad b. Maḥbūb, the son of Abū Sufyān Maḥbūb b. al-Ruḥayl, in a letter to the Maghribī Ibāḍīs, Kāshif (ed.), *al-Siyar wa 'l-jawābāt* ii, 242–245.

65 Savage, Survival through Alliance 15–16.

communities. Furthermore, the repentant sinner had no right to *walāya* unless he/she made amends for the sins committed and submitted to a penalty. This is what we can infer from the following opinion expressed by al-Rabīʿ b. Ḥabīb, collected in the *Futyā al-Rabīʿ b. Ḥabīb*:

> I asked al-Rabīʿ about someone of our people (*min qawminā*)[66] who was impious (*fāsiq*): he neglected prayer, refused to pay alms (*zakāt*), swore repeatedly without making atonement (*kaffārat al-yamīn*), neglected fasting during *ramaḍān*, practised usury, sold wine and took its price and stole the property of others. Afterwards he repented and recognized Islam, what should he do as amends for what he had done when he was impious and did not recognize Islam? He replied: I asked Ḍumām about this, and he told me: If he converts (*idhā aslama*),[67] he must return the stolen goods to the person robbed and the usury to the one from whom he took it; he must also return the price of the wine, recite the neglected prayers, give the outstanding *zakāt* and perform all the precepts (*farāʾiḍ Allāh*) that he neglected. In case he repents, he must perform all these duties as well as he must perform fasting. I went to Abū ʿUbayda and I told him that Ḍumām believed that if one of our people converts to Islam and repents, he must perform the prayers he has neglected, give the *zakāt* [which he has neglected], make atonement for the oaths if he has been perjured and return to the rightful owners what he has stolen or taken by deception. Abū ʿUbayda replied: Ḍumām is right.
>
> I told to al-Rabīʿ: So if he sold the wine and took usury or sold at usury pocketing the price, and then repents, should he return [the money]?
>
> He replied: Certainly!
>
> I said: Why?
>
> He replied: Because he is among those who acknowledge [Islam] (*min ahl al-iqrār*) and admit the prohibition of these things and the obligation of others. These are not mandatory for the infidels (*mushrikūn*) if they repent, since they do not recognize their prohibition. ʿAbd Allāh was also of this opinion.
>
> I said: So, if a man kills another man unjustly (*ẓulman*), his repentance is not accepted until he voluntarily submits to the punishment of retaliation.
>
> He replied: Certainly![68]

66 Meaning a non-Ibāḍī Muslim.
67 Meaning converted to Ibadism.
68 Ibn Khalīfa (ed.), *Futyā* 115–116 (Ms. 35_{28}–36_{12}).

5.5.2 The *Walāya* and *Barā'a* Doctrine in the Works of the Rustāq and Nizwā Schools

Though the *walāya/barā'a* doctrine had already been discussed in the early Ibāḍī sources, it assumed particular relevance during the crisis of the imamate in Oman. In fact, this topic is discussed at length in the *fiqh* works written in this period, with each party claiming to be in the right and trying to outlaw the rivals. Ibn Ja'far, al-Bisiyānī, al-Kudamī and Muḥammad b. Ibrāhīm al-Kindī – to quote just the most relevant authors – include long chapters or books on *walāya/barā'a* in their works.[69]

As Wilkinson demonstrated, the Rustāq-Nizwā polemic is a label for a dogma dispute over the nature of the imamate. In such a polemic, the use of the *walāya/barā'a* doctrine was crucial to defining arguments supporting their own views and to marginalizing political as well as religious adversaries. It endorsed the community (represented by the *'ulamā'*) with the power to choose, monitor and potentially depose the *imām*.[70]

The debate on *walāya/barā'a* came into being as consequence of the theological and political confrontation; it was not only a result of legal stances taken by the authors, but rather a result of power struggles that were central components of the jurists' agenda. They were not only groups of scholars who shared a legal outlook but local political factions as well.

According to the Omani sources, *walāya* was obligatory towards the faithful in general; those who are praised in the Quran; the righteous *imāms*; and the individuals who carry out the precepts of religion in a satisfactory manner. It was matched by active dissociation (*barā'a*) against: infidels in general; those blamed by the Quran; and the unjust imāms. Within the Ibāḍī community, *barā'a* took place against a person who committed a major sin or persisted in committing a minor sin. Supporting a *bid'a* – meaning a heretical doctrine or even a belief or a practice for which there was no precedent in the community's tradition – entailed also the pronouncement of *barā'a* against the culprit. Major sins (*kabā'ir*) are those incurring severe punishment on earth and deserving chastisement in hell for the perpetrators in the afterlife, such as stealing, committing adultery, drinking wine, eating pork or practising usury.[71] Sin implies the misbelief (*kufr*) of its perpetrator and banishment from Ibāḍī

69 Ibn Ja'far, *al-Jāmi'* i, 147–253; al-Bisiyānī, *al-Jāmi'* iv, 184–208; al-Kudamī, *Kitāb al-istiqāma*, vols. 1 and 2 are almost dedicated to *walāya/barā'a*, as well as the 3rd volume of *Bayān al-Shar'* by Muḥammad b. Ibrāhīm al-Kindī.

70 Wilkinson, *The Imamate Tradition of Oman* 166–168; Ib., *Ibâḍism* 336–343.

71 Ibn Ja'far, *al-Jāmi'* i, 148–151; al-Bisiyānī, *al-Jāmi'* iv, 184–188; al-Kindī, *al-Takhṣīṣ* 121–126.

community as long as he remains dissident (*mukhālif*) and does not repent. The community should declare *barā'a* against him, but no one had the right to kill him or to expropriate his wealth. Suspending judgement (*wuqūf*) over the behaviour of a sinner was not admitted as long as it is ascertained through the testimony of at least two people of integrity, except in the case where someone committed a major sin without knowing it, for example if he ate pork but was unaware what it was.[72]

The pronouncement of the *barā'a* required one of the following conditions: the confession of the offender (*iqrār*); the eyewitness testimony of two persons of integrity (*'udūl* – the validity of the testimony by a single witness is controversial, while the testimony by a reliable woman or by a slave was accepted); common knowledge, the reputation (*shuhra*) of someone for being a sinner. Significantly, al-Kudamī excludes recourse to *taqlīd* (imitation) for pronouncing *barā'a*, except for what expressly is stated by the Quran or the tradition of the Prophet. Conversely, the *walāya* relied on the statement of at least two experts and well-informed people (*ahl al-khibra*) as well as on prevailing opinion (*shuhra*) in non-contentious cases.[73]

The system of *walāya/barā'a* strengthened the feeling of being members of a close community, so it influenced Ibāḍī jurisprudence in many respects. As regards *walāya*, the legal discussion brings out a number of facts: the polytheist – man or woman – (*mushrik/a*) who converted to Islam brought his/her children to Islam and they were entitled to *walāya* like their father/mother. In general, a woman in status of *walāya* could transmit her status to her children. Some scholars opposed this view arguing that the father only could convey the *walāya* status to his children. On the question of *'adāla* (the quality of religious probity and moral integrity which a witness must possess for his testimony to be admissible), only the testimony of the Ibāḍī deserving *walāya* was admissible in all cases. With regard to *zakāt*, the unjust leader/tyrant was not entitled to collect taxes, and only the Ibāḍī poor deserving *walāya* could receive the community's charity. In the matter of performing *ḥajj* on behalf of another person, the Ibāḍī should not perform *ḥajj* for another person unless he was of *ahl al-walāya*.[74]

---

72 The issue of sin begins to be discussed among the Ibāḍis at the beginning of the 3rd/9th century. Early sources equate sin with misbelief (*kufr*). Al Salimi, Themes of the Ibāḍī/Omani *Siyar* 483–484.

73 Al-Kudamī, *Kitāb al-istiqāma* i, 236–238; al-Kindī, *al-Takhṣīṣ* 134–138.

74 Al-Bisiyānī, *al-Jāmi'* iv, 199. On the legal implications of *walāya/barā'a* status s. also Ennami, *Studies* (online edition) 173–178.

Walāya and *barā'a* were dynamic principles changing over generations; they were defined not only according to the tradition of the ancestors but also following given political and social circumstances.

On the political level, they provided the leading *'ulamā'* with a powerful tool for regulating membership of the community, and for deciding under which conditions a political leader was a just *imām*, or was unjust and as such could be deposed. The *'ulamā'* were an active political organization in Omani history, attempting to influence the constitution of the imamate. After the first generation of missionaries trained in Basra, as soon as the imamate become established, the *'ulamā'* developed their own local centres, sometimes they helped to integrate the state with tribal leaders, sometimes they were themselves tribal leaders and therefore could influence the overall structure of the imamate.[75]

In his "Bio-bibliographical Background to the Crisis Period in the Ibāḍī Imāmate of Oman", Wilkinson provides with a valuable reconstruction of the literary production of the Pro-Mūsā party and of the Rustāq and Nizwā schools, linked to this period of major crisis. The celebrated *'ālim* Ibn Ja'far, author of the *Jāmi'*, considered a major *fiqh* work, was a leading figure supporting the deposition of the *imām* al-Ṣalt. He came from Izkī, the homeland of the Mūsā family, and had problems with al-Ṣalt, who had removed Ibn Ja'far from his role in charge of Sohar (Ṣuḥar) two months after appointing him. The appointment had obvious advantages: not only was a post as governor a major responsibility, it also entailed the chance for personal enrichment and patronage, as Sohar was one of the main centres of Omani overseas commerce.[76] The chapter on *walāya* and *barā'a* of the *Jāmi'* is almost totally devoted to clarifying the rules concerning the status of the believer and the circumstances in which he deserves association or dissociation.

Proto-Rustāq ideas first appeared in the works by Abū 'l-Mu'thīr (al-Ṣalt b. Khamīs al-Kharūṣī, second half of the 3rd/9th century), whose politically active career involved him in several controversial issues and gave his view considerable authority. He is credited with two treatises relating to the dispute: *al-Aḥdāth wa 'l-ṣifāt*, written during the Rāshid b. al-Naḍr's imamate (886–890), and *Kitāb al-bayān wa 'l-burhān* dealing with the Nizwā views. Abū 'l-Mu'thīr probably influenced his pupil, Abū 'l-Ḥawārī, author of the famous *Tafsīr*,

75 Wilkinson, *Ibâḍism* 220–21; Al Salimi, Themes of the Ibāḍī/Omani *Siyar* 487–503.

76 Wilkinson, *Ibâḍism* 322.

who wrote a lengthy epistle addressed to the Ibāḍīs of Ḥaḍramawt, where he excommunicated (*barā'a*) the two *imāms* appointed by Mūsā b. Mūsā.[77]

Among the first generation of members of the Rustāq party there was also Abū Qaḥṭān, whose epistle condemned al-Ṣalt's deposition. He admitted that the *imām* had become senile, however there was no evidence that he had lost his faculties. From the general tone of his epistle, it is clear that the real cause of the conflict lay in the tribal tensions that marked out the imamate of al-Ṣalt.[78]

The full doctrinarian development of the Rustāq party viewpoint came two generations later, with the works by Ibn Baraka and his pupil al-Bisiyānī, who were both adamant in condemning the deposition. In his *Kitāb al-Muwāzana*, Ibn Baraka discusses all-important issues on the question of the deposing of the *imām* al-Ṣalt b. Mālik, in an almost objective way, although he was unable to completely hide some radicalism inherent in his party.[79] In another work, the *Sīrat al-shaykh Abī Muḥammad 'Abd Allāh b. Muḥammad b. Baraka*, he elaborates on the distinction between *ṭarīq al-'aql* and *ṭarīq al-sam'* (the way of the intellect and the way of the 'hearing'/tradition) blaming his opponents for basing their views on human reasoning, like the Mu'tazilites, while the revealed law was the only path to deal with specific areas – in particular eschatology – in which reason has its limitations and can inform us only whether a thing is conceivable but not how it is or will be. Within this theological speculation, he asserts his position on *barā'a* by rejecting the moderate position of the Nizwā school, and in particular that of its main exponent, al-Kudamī.[80]

Ibn Baraka's pupil al-Bisyānī connects the doctrine of association and dissociation with the principle of "commanding what is right and forbidding what is wrong" (*al-amr bi-'l-ma'rūf wa 'l nahy 'an al-munkar*) since affiliation is owed to those who are obedient to God's commands, and dissociation is due to anyone who openly commits acts of disobedience to God.[81] He writes:

> It is the duty of the Muslim to give the *walāya* to the friends of God and to love them, and to distance himself from the enemies of God and to practise the *barā'a* towards them. Whoever loves one who believes in God is as though he loves God Himself. This is the noblest of acts of faith and the highest degree of the soul.[82]

---

77 Kāshif (ed.), *al-Siyar wa 'l-jawābāt* i, 337–365 (*Sīra Abū 'l-Ḥawārī Muḥammad b. al-Ḥawārī al-'Umānī ilā ahl Ḥaḍramawt*); Wilkinson, *Ibâḍism* 337.

78 Kāshif (ed.), *al-Siyar wa 'l-jawābāt* i, 81–147 (*Sīra tunsab ilā Abī Qaḥṭān Khālid b. Qaḥṭān*).

79 Al-Salimi, *The Omani* Siyar *as a Literary Genre* 28–29; al-Sālimī, Min maṣādir al-ta'rīkh wa 'l-thaqāfa 79–94.

80 Wilkinson, Bio-bibliographical Background 150–151; Wilkinson, *Ibâḍism* 340.

81 Al-Bisyānī, *al-Jāmi'* iv, 184–193. See also Cook, *Commanding Right and Forbidding Wrong* 393–426.

82 Al-Bisyānī, *al-Jāmi'* iv, 185.

In particular, the rightful *imām* (*imām al-ʿadl*) deserves obedience and *walāya*. In Ibn Baraka' and al-Bisiyānī's views, al-Ṣalt's affair was clear, he was a legitimate *imām*, his misconduct was not demonstrated, so a revolt against him was not permitted, nor dissociation from him. Their polemic was mainly directed against the Nizwā party which developed a moderate attitude towards al-Ṣalt b. Mālik and suspended judgement (*wuqūf*), arguing that the opinions of the scholars on the affair were so different that it was almost impossible for succeeding generations to know the real truth.

On the Nizwā side, Abū Saʿīd Muḥammad b. Saʿīd al-Kudamī had a prominent role in mitigating the harshness of the Rustāq–Nizwā dispute, which had a nefarious effect on the history of the imamate in Oman.[83] The first volume of his *Kitāb al-istiqāma* is entirely devoted to defining the rule of the *walāya* and *barāʾa* in connection with the *imām* al-Ṣalt's deposition. The event signalled the beginning of an unprecedented split in the Ibāḍī community, creating disagreement (*ikhtilāf*) over who deserved *walāya* and who deserved *barāʾa*, and posing for the first time the question of who could be considered part of "the people of righteousness" (*Ahl al-istiqāma*, i.e. the Ibāḍīs):

> We never knew that at the time of Maḥbūb b. al-Raḥīl and Wāʾil b. Ayyūb up to the time of Muḥammad b. Maḥbūb and ʿAzzān b. al-Ṣaqr [d. 268/882] there had been disagreement over the faith of the Muslims. It was the faith of the "people of righteousness" (*Ahl al-istiqāma*) within the *umma* of Muḥammad, the seal of the Prophets.[84]

Al-Kudamī set a tone of reconciliation between the opposing parties. His moderate approach to the issue of imamate paved the way for overcoming the rancour generated by al-Ṣalt's deposition, thus allowing the survival of the institution of the imamate in Oman. According to Wilkinson, it is on the basis of the Nizwā party's flexibility and moderation that the Ibāḍī theorists could develop the kind of imamate rulers which emerged in the 18th century, and further permitted the institution to survive until the middle of the 20th century.[85]

Al-Kudamī's views also influenced the authors of the moderate Rustāq party, who themselves began to react to the extremist doctrines their predecessor had articulated. It is worth quoting, in particular, al-Kindī authors, who flourished between the end of the 11th century and the middle of the

---

83 Al-Kudamī, *Kitāb al-istiqāma*; idem, *al-Muʿtabar*; see also Al-Kudamī's collections of *Jawābāt*, titled *al-Jāmiʿ al-mufīd min jawābāt Abī Saʿīd*, and a book collecting his decisions, titled *al-Jāmiʿ al-mufīd min aḥkām Abī Saʿīd*.

84 Al-Kudamī, *Kitāb al-istiqāma* i, 226.

85 Wilkinson, Bio-bibliographical Background 156.

12th century: Muḥammad b. Ibrāhīm, author of the famous seventy-volume *Bayān al-sharʿ*, Muḥammad b. Mūsā who wrote the fifty-one-volume *Kifāya* and Abū Bakr Aḥmad b. ʿAbdallāh who wrote the forty-one-volume *Muṣannaf*. The latter also authored a long epistle titled *al-Takhṣīṣ fī ʾl-walāya wa ʾl-barāʾa* where he carefully elaborated the doctrine of association and dissociation.

With the restoration of the imamate and the expulsion of foreigners from the coast by the middle of the 11th century, Oman seemed to enter a new age of peace. But this was illusory. A new period of turbulence came, mainly due to the divisions between the *ʿulamāʾ* and the tribal element of the Rustāq party. The final clash took place in 579/1183, when Muḥammad b. Mālik from Rustāq, with a force of his Yaḥmad tribesmen, defeated the *ʿulamāʾ* under their Nizwan *imām*, Mūsā b. Jābir, the grandson of Najjād b. Mūsā. Thus vanished the last vestiges of the second imamate. It began what Wilkinson calls the Ibāḍī "dark age", which he says: "must be viewed as a gestation period which eventually produced a new order in Oman".[86]

Ibāḍī-Omani scholars during the period under investigation succeeded in consolidating their identity as men of distinct piety and knowledge. They integrated their practice as jurists into their distinctive training, encouraging a broad basis of public recognition for their unique integrative agenda. Presenting themselves as the ultimate heirs to the religious-spiritual authority embedded into the first Ibāḍī *imāms* in Basra, Omani scholars enjoyed a great degree of public veneration, being the most outspoken and undisputed representatives of the Ibāḍī tradition in times that witnessed the crisis of the imamate. They cultivated sophisticated interpersonal relationships, and their social agenda took place around dynamics of power and authority. Internal power struggles among certain scholars, which echoed in their compendia, seemed to be one of the inevitable outcomes of this sophisticated social fabric.

86 Wilkinson, Bio-bibliographical Background 159.

CHAPTER 6

Ibāḍī Law and Society in the Pre-modern and Modern Maghreb

6.1 Introduction

A turning point in the history of North African Ibadism was the fall of the Rustumid imamate following the Fatimid victory in 909, which paved the way to new forms of political organization. The Ibāḍī communities renounced the idea of imamate and survived in hiding (*kitmān*), led by councils of elders. This implied a dramatic switch to a political organization based on the power of a collective body instead of a centralized and hierarchal structure.

As mentioned earlier, within Maghribi Ibadism the authority exercised by elders and tribal chiefs prevented the rise of permanent or tyrannical rulers, allowing Ibāḍī communities to move beyond the unstable imamates of their earlier history. In this decentralized setting, jurists played a crucial role: they upheld social stability and safeguarded Ibāḍī scholarly traditions at a time when North African Ibāḍīs were increasingly interacting with the Maliki school. The Ibāḍīs reacted to the threat of disappearing or being assimilated by the institutionalization of the *ḥalqat al-ʿazzāba* (the circle of the elders), which went hand-in hand with a process of systematization and rationalization of the theological, juridical and historical knowledge. The collection of biographies by al-Wisyānī (d. second half of the 5th/11th century), Abū Zakariyyāʾ al-Warjlānī (d. after 504/1110–1) and Abū ʾl-ʿAbbās al-Darjīnī (d. 670/1271–1272) were intended to gather the collective memory of the Ibāḍī heritage.

A "clericalization" of the class of *ʿulamāʾ*, as well as a division of the society between clerics and laity came to the fore in pre-modern Maghribi Ibāḍī communities, deeply affecting intellectual and social life. As I will argue in this chapter, understanding the development of Ibāḍī law and jurisprudence goes hand in hand with an analysis of the social role and political agenda of the intellectual elite, as represented by *fuqahāʾ* and *ʿulamāʾ*.

The doctrine of the chains (*silsilāt*) of transmitters of knowledge, who, having learnt the *ʿilm* in Basra, moved to Oman and North Africa, created the narrative of a web connecting the main centres of Ibadism. It also gave rise to a bulk of traditions going back to the early Ibāḍī Basran authorities, which became the common heritage of the whole Ibāḍī community.

 | HTTPS://DOI.ORG/10.1163/9789004765764-008

A chronological analysis of Ibāḍī legal sources goes beyond the scope of this chapter, as well as of the entire book. For this reason, I have chosen to focus on the historical periods and the related sources that I consider most relevant for depicting the main turning points in the history of Ibadism. The focus of this chapter spans from the 11th to the 19th century, but concentrates mainly on sources from the 11th to 12th century. This period saw the emergence of collective works called *Dīwān al-ʿazzāba, Dīwān al-mashāʾikh, Kitāb al-ashyākh* or simply *al-Dīwān*, which claim to gather the Ibāḍī legal doctrine established up to that point. It was also in this period that the Ibāḍī *madhhab* consolidated epistemically as a formal doctrinal school and the jurists established themselves as a socially relevant class. In particular from the 11th century onwards, Ibāḍī religious authorities embarked on a wide-ranging process of systematization of law and dogma. The great doctrinal and legal synthesis elaborated by Abū Zakariyyāʾ al-Jannāwunī and Abū Yaʿqūb al-Warjlānī in the 11th and 12th centuries, and by Abū Sākin ʿĀmir al-Shammākhī and Abū Ṭāhir al-Jayṭālī in the 14th century are the main results of such efforts. Thanks to this systematization process, the Maghribi Ibāḍīs were able to confront their Sunni counterparts and to preserve their identity. Later the *Kitāb al-Nīl* by ʿAbd al-ʿAzīz al-Muṣʿābī (born *c.*1130/1717), which is based on the *Kitāb al-Īḍāḥ* by Abū Sākin ʿĀmir al-Shammākhī, stands out amongst the works designed to summarize the doctrine of the school.

On the other hand, the growing involvement of the *ʿazzāba* in the management of the town along with the *jamāʿat al-ʿawāmm* (the assembly of laymen) gave rise to the production of legal texts governing the life of the town, called agreements/conventions (*ittifāqāt*), based on both Ibāḍī law and Berber customary law. For this study I used 21 *ittifāqāt*, the oldest one dated 807/1405, the most recent dated 1346/1928 (the famous decision on the prohibition on women leaving Mzab), but we can assume that the documented period is illustrative of earlier periods as well.

By analyzing the *ittifāqāt*, one gets closer to understanding the praxis of Ibāḍī law in the daily lives than through simply reading the classical scriptures. Legal practice, like religious practice, was embedded in cultural practice. Mzabi Ibāḍī legal practice – as well those of other Berber groups such as the Kabyles – was, to some extent at least, culturally hybrid. Indeed, customary law (*ʿurf*) and local tradition (*ʿāda*) were legal determinants alongside the classical sources of the law, especially when the legal manuals failed to provide answers or when the local law prevailed.

An example of this hybridization process was the emergence of banishment as punishment for the most serious offences (theft, adultery, rape). The Mzabi jurists envisaged banishment as a bodily punishment as well as a psychological sanction, involving the offender being excluded from all public matters and considered socially unacceptable until he atoned for his sin and showed public repentance.

This judicial function, which the *ʿazzāba* perceived as a direct feature of the duties of "enjoining what is right and forbidding what is evil", became, in conjunction with the *walāya* and *barāʾa* principle, a powerful tool in their hands. In fact, the use of *walāya* and *barāʾa* by the *ʿazzāba* culminated in the effort to discipline society through an increasingly vigorous and intrusive imposition of coercive rules of behaviour and the inculcation of a standard of obedience among subjects. Ostracism and banishment, in particular, were powerful methods to instil the *ʿazzāba*'s strict ethos into the society.

6.2 The Scholars as Learned Elites and Regional Notables: the Twilight of the Imamate Era in the Maghrib

In the previous chapter we have seen how the deposition of the *imām* al-Ṣalt ibn Mālik in 886 was a major turning point in the history of Oman, providing Ibāḍī scholars with the impetus to reflect on a detailed theory of imamate and on their own role in relation to (and in competition with) political power. An analogous turning point in North Africa was the fall of the Rustumid imamate following the Fatimid victory in 909. After this tragic event, Ibāḍī communities survived in a number of areas within the Maghrib, creating what Cyrille Aillet calls the "Ibāḍī archipelago", consisting of isolated – but at the same time interconnected – communities.[1] The increasing spread of the Maliki Sunnism forced the Ibāḍīs to abandon areas such as the Jarīd and the Zāb and to take refuge in the remote oases of the Algerian Mzab, on the island of Jerba (Tunisia) and in Jabal Nafūsa (Libya), where they managed to survive in hiding (*kitmān*), led by a council (*ḥalqa*, literally circle) of elders (*ʿazzāba*).[2] Between 1012 and 1350, Ibāḍīs built five fortified towns in the Mzab valley, which formed the so-called Ibāḍī pentapolis: Ghardāya/Ghardaïa, Mālika/Melika, Bū Nūra/Bou

1 Aillet, Cressier, Gilotte (eds.), *Sedrata* 85; Aillet, *L'archipel ibadite* in part. chap. 7, 259–326; Gouja, *Essai d'une lecture patrimoniale d'une source théologique ibāḍite* 16–17.

2 The noun *ʿazzāba*, pl. of *ʿazzābī*, derives from the verb *ʿazaba* and the noun *ʿuzub* or *ʿazaba*, meaning "take distance" and designating – in this context – the act of devoting oneself to a cause and giving oneself to the service of the community. The *ʿazzāba* constituted a sort of "clergy" for the Ibāḍī communities; they gathered in a council (*ḥalqa*) lead by a sheikh, a pious man known for his knowledge and wisdom. See: Prevost, *Ibadites*; idem, Genèse et développement de la ḥalqa 118; Gouja, *Essai d'une lecture patrimoniale d'une source théologique ibāḍite* 56; Jaabiri, *L'organisation des Azzabas* 53–55.

Noura, Banī Yasqan/Beni Isguen and al-ʿAṭf/El Atteuf. With the settlements of Qarāra/Guerrara and Baryān/Bérianne in the 17th century, the confederation of Mzab was completed. In this remote region, Ibāḍīs managed to secure a virtual independence and preserve their way of life and their religious and cultural heritage.

The fall of the imamate, which degenerated into a situation of political chaos and of legal and institutional fracture, led the Ibāḍīs to reconsider the very nature of power and state organization. They reacted to the institutional vacuum by creating a new form of political and social organization that ensured both continuity and evolution in the doctrine and safeguarded the communities' cohesion under the leadership of the *ʿulamāʾ*. The constitution in the first half of the 5th/11th century of the *ḥalqa* of the *ʿazzāba* (a religious council) by Abū ʿAbd Allāh Muḥammad Ibn Bakr al-Fursuṭṭāʾī (d. 440/1048–49) was in response to an urgent need of the communities to provide themselves with an institutional structure and a space of knowledge production. This tendency to institutionalize the transmission of knowledge had strong political implications as it turned the *ḥalqa* into a powerful decision-making body.[3] The switch to a political organization based on the power of a collegiate/collective body instead of a centralized and hierarchized structure implied a definitive renunciation of the imamate.

In this environment, marked by the absence of a unified state or dominant political authority, jurists assumed a central and indispensable role. Their involvement was crucial both for preserving social cohesion and for ensuring the continuity and internal coherence of Ibāḍī scholarly transmission. Ibāḍī learning practices emphasized different specializations and the existence of a pyramid shaped socio-educational order in which the criteria of respectability and status ranged from mere command of literacy at the base to full erudition at the pinnacle, with the fully fledged jurists, who were highly honoured and supervised the main body of scholars, which comprised mosque functionaries and scribes down to students.

This shift was imposed as the only way for the survival of the Ibāḍī communities in the Maghrib within the framework of an oasis economy based on limited resources in an environment that was both fragmented and interconnected. However, the era of *kitmān* was, therefore, not synonymous with withdrawal or isolation. On the contrary, an intense scholarly interaction along with large-scale commercial networks ensured continuity in the relationships between North Africa and Oman. As is well known, Malikism came

3 Dridi, La communauté ibadite entre Orient et Occident musulmans 361–362; Cuperly, *Introduction* 37.

to predominate in North and West Africa following the Almoravid movement (1040–1147) originating in the missionary activity of Maliki scholars from Ifriqiyya who spread the Maliki orthopraxy in the region. The targets of the initial thrust of the Almoravid expansion were local unorthodox communities such as the Sufri Kharijis of Sijilmāsa. The conversion of the Ghanaian capital Kumbe Saleh in 1076 marked the shift from the Ibāḍī school – which for centuries had dominated the trans-Saharan trade route passing through Tahert – to the Maliki school. The spread of Maliki/Sunni Sufism in the Maghrib also had lasting influence in North and West African religiosity.

The rise of Maliki Islam over Ibadism was largely a peaceful process that proceeded very slowly, and entire areas, such as Jerba and Jabal Nafūsa, remained practically autonomous for a long time, notwithstanding the triumph of the Sunni orthodoxy in the Maghrib.[4] Alongside the malikization process of the region, the unity of North African Ibadism was shattered by a series of internal disputes, the most serious of which was the Nukkār schism against the Wahabite majority that threatened the very stability of the Tahert imamate. The Nukkār, under the leadership of Abū Yazīd, mounted a widescale anti-Fatimid rebellion culminating in a major revolt in 943, which was curbed by Abū Yazīd's defeat and subsequent death in 947. After this ineffective act of resistance, the loss of ground of Ibadism accelerated. This was also due to the arrival of the Hilalian tribes in the 11th century, leading to the formation of a new socio-religious map in the region. Though the historical sources do not provide clear evidence to establish when and for what reason the Ibāḍī communities of the Zāb region either converted to Malikism or migrated, as a result of these multiple pressures, the region, previously an Ibāḍī stronghold, became Maliki in the 12th and 13th centuries. The Ibāḍī tribes that didn't migrate or convert to Sunnism suffered marginalization as political and religious opponents of the Almohads and of the Banū Ghāniya, the Almoravid Sanhāja Berber dynasty and as a Berber-speaking minority in a region which had become increasingly an Arabic-speaking territory. Faced with political, religious and linguistic marginalization, the Ibāḍīs relocated to one of the settlements in the Algerian desert, the Fezzan region and Jerba Island.[5]

As I have already discussed in the previous chapters, the collection of biographies by al-Wisyānī, Abū Zakariyyā' al-Warjlānī and Abū 'l-'Abbās al-Darjīnī gathered the collective memory of the Ibāḍī heritage. In the same vein,

4 Aillet, L'ibâḍisme, une minorité au cœur de l'islam 13–36; Lydon, *On Trans-Saharan Trails*, 70–71.

5 Amara, Entre le massif de l'Aurès et les oasis 115–135; Love, *Ibadi Muslims of North Africa*, 84; Prevost, *L'aventure ibāḍite dans le Sud tunisien* 307–318.

legal-theological knowledge was collected in numerous *fiqh* works and in treatises on questions of creed and dogma (*ʿaqīda*).

From the 11th century onward, Ibāḍī religious authorities undertook an extensive effort to systematize legal and doctrinal thought. The major doctrinal and juridical syntheses produced by Abū Zakariyyāʾ al-Jannāwunī and Abū Yaʿqūb al-Warjlānī in the 11th and 12th centuries, and later by Abū Ṭāhir al-Jayṭālī in the 14th century, stand as the principal outcomes of this undertaking. This process of systematization enabled Maghribi Ibāḍīs to engage more effectively with their Sunni counterparts and to safeguard the distinctiveness of their communal identity.[6]

6.2.1 The Organization of the Circle of Elders (*ḥalqat al-ʿazzāba*)

The organization of circles of scholars and students has ancient roots within Ibadism. These circles already existed under the leadership of Abū ʿUbayda in Basra for the training of the missionaries, as well as during the Rustumid imamate with the main purpose of bringing together scholars from the various Maghribi Ibāḍī communities. The foundation of the system of circles of *ʿazzāba* is attributed to the scholar Abū ʿAbd Allāh Muḥammad b. Bakr who reached the Wādī Rīgh on Jerba Island in 409/1018–1019 and settled there with his seven disciples in a cave called Majmāj.[7] This semi-legendary figure was born towards the end of the 4th/10th century in al-Fursuṭṭāʾ in Jabal Nafūsa and died in Jerba in 440/1048–1049. The Maghribi-Ibāḍī historian Abū

6 Aillet, *L'archipel ibadite* 397.

7 Prevost, Maǧmāǧ et les sept savants 35–58; Jaabiri, *L'organisation des Azzabas* 126 ff. The seven scholars of the cave (*ʿulamāʾ al-ghār*) were Abū ʿImrān Mūsā ibn Zakariyyā al-Mazātī al-Damrī, Jābir b. Sadarmān (Sadrahām, according to Jaabiri, *L'organisation des Azzabas* 127), Kabāb b. Maṣlaḥ (Muṣliḥ, according to Jaabiri, *L'organisation des Azzabas* 127) al-Mazātī, Abū Mujbir Tūzīn al-Mazātī, Abū ʿAmr al-Namīlī al-Zuwāghī, Abū Yaḥyā Zakariyyā ibn Jarnāz al-Nafūsī and Abū Muḥammad ʿAbdallāh b. Mānūḥ al-Limāʾī (Lammāʾī according to Jaabiri, *L'organisation des Azzabas* 127) al-Hawārī. The Ibāḍī myth of the seven scholars of the cave is a clear reference to the legend of the seven sleepers of Ephesus that is recounted in Quran 18, eponymously called the "Sura of the Cave" (*Sūrat al-kahf*). The cult of caves was widespread in North Africa among the Berber before Islamization and was later integrated into the Islamic tradition. The Ibāḍīs, in particular, venerated the caves and considered them the ideal place for scholarly meetings as they favour concentration and intellectual activity. The same foundation of Ghardaïa, the main city of the Mzab, is linked to a cave. In fact the town takes its name from Ghār Daïa, the cave of Daïa, a legendary woman who took refuge there. So it is not surprising that the creation of the *ḥalqa*, which intended to preserve the Ibāḍī tradition, took place in a cave.

Zakariyyā' al-Warjlānī devotes an entire chapter of his chronicle to this figure and to the foundation of the *ḥalqa*.[8] In the same vein, later Maghribi-Ibāḍī historians, namely al-Wisyānī, al-Darjīnī and al-Shammākhī, report numerous anecdotes on the legendary life and works of Abū ʿAbd Allāh Muḥammad b. Bakr.[9] According to these sources, he was the custodian of both the Jarīd tradition, through his teacher Abū Nūḥ Saʿīd b. Zanghīl, and of Jabal Nafūsa tradition, through Faṣīl b. Abī Miswar, who was his teacher in Jerba. In turn, he passed on this knowledge to Abū 'l-Rabīʿa Sulaymān b. Yakhlaf al-Mazātī, who himself passed it on to Abū Zakariyyā', author of the *Kitāb siyar al-a 'imma*.

Faṣīl b. Abī Miswar was the son of the celebrated Abū Miswar Yasja, who was born in Jabal Nafūsa and moved by the end of the 9th or beginning of the 10th century to Jerba, where he founded the Great Mosque and ushered in a period of stability and intellectual activity. As Paul Love argues, the leadership of Abū Miswar in Jerba marks the transition from the era of the Tahert imamate to the later period in which local sites such as Jerba became centres of Ibāḍī learning. Abū Miswar's connection with Abū ʿAbd Allāh Muḥammad b. Bakr, who is credited with the foundation of the new political and religious organization of the *ḥalqa*, provides with a narrative of both continuity and rupture with the glorious Ibāḍī past. His son Faṣīl in turn represents the link between Jerba and the central regions of North Africa. He sent his two sons and his nephew in search of Abū ʿAbd Allāh Muḥammad b. Bakr, whom the sources present as a champion of Ibāḍī Islam, and convinced him to found a series of *ḥalqa*s throughout the Ibāḍī archipelago. According to this narrative, Abū ʿAbd Allāh provided the connections between Jerba and the other Ibāḍī communities scattered in North Africa, as well as an ideal link with the "golden age" of the Rustumid past. But the creation of this network could not be ephemeral if it was to ensure the survival of Ibāḍī heritage. On the contrary it had to grow thanks to new cohorts of scholars trained by the elder generation. In addition, it required devising a new method of preserving and transmitting knowledge, which gave the scholars a crucial role within the communities.[10]

The process of reproduction of Ibāḍī identity through the person-to-person transmission of knowledge ensured certain continuities and permitted

8 Al-Warjlānī, *Kitāb siyar al-a'imma* (ed. 1985) 247–248, 252. V. Prevost considers trustworthy the account by Abū Zakariyyā'. Prevost, Genèse et développement de la *ḥalqa* 116.

9 For a biography of Abū ʿAbd Allāh Muḥammad b. Bakr see Jaabiri, *L'organisation des Azzabas* 29–51; Prevost, Genèse et développement de la *ḥalqa* 109–124; Meouak, Les communautés ibadites du nord du Sahara au Moyen Âge 262–265; Gouja, *Essai d'une lecture patrimoniale d'une source théologique ibāḍite* 59–60; Cherifi, La Ḥalqa des *ʿazzāba* 39–68.

10 Love, *Ibadi Muslims of North Africa* 43–44.

obvious adaptations over time in dialogue with changing circumstances. Ibāḍī scholars responded to social developments through the formation of dispositions, resulting in what was perceived as coherent articulations of an adapted cultural inheritance. The transmission of learning also deepened relations between teachers and students by articulating the transformative potential of knowledge in new ways. Scholars were the custodians of every aspect of society and state which was governed by the religious law. They were widely revered as pious ascetics, as responsive to popular needs, as sources of political stability and as repositories of spiritual power. Pedagogical techniques among these scholars centred on person-to-person knowledge transmission from master to pupil. The intellectual dynamism of the Ibāḍī scholarly tradition produced scholarly communities that laid down the heritage of both the Basran community and the Tahert imamate, but also made significant adaptations to fit present circumstances. The factors of erudition and piety made it possible for the members of the *ḥalqa*s to adopt a posture of superiority vis-à-vis other accomplished scholars. The same factor added a strong element of stability to the various layers that linked the scholars to the society at large. Implicitly recognized criteria of prerogative and procedure governed the entire social and economic life of the Ibāḍī communities. The *ḥalqa*s of *ʿazzāba* formed important, though subtle, links in a complex of relationships, which made it possible for the communities within the Ibāḍī archipelago to achieve a certain sense of order and unity without the need for an imamate. Ibāḍī scholars reacted to the challenge of a fragmented distribution of political power by building a normative order based on sacred law in dialogue with local custom. They broadened their institutional functions to become the organizers and supervisors of the local population, as happened in other Saharan pre-modern societies that experienced the absence of a centralized state authority.[11]

In the Ibāḍī historical literature, the figures of Abū ʿAbd Allāh Muḥammad b. Bakr and of the seven scholars of the Majmāj cave acquire a characteristic messianic trait containing the true explosive force of their mission, which took place in conspiratorial conditions. Their mission began first of all in a cave at the fringes of the Islamic world and continued in the remote oasis of Algerian Mzab, which was inaccessible to the power of any central state, or simply beyond its control. According to Ibāḍī sources, in the Majmāj cave Abū ʿAbd Allāh Muḥammad b. Bakr and his disciples led the basis of the *ḥalqa*s system, approving a rule (*sīra*) regulating the organization of the communitarian

11 Warscheid, *Droit musulman et société au Sahara prémoderne* 155–158.

life that bound together the members, and writing a mysterious twelve volume Ibāḍī juridical encyclopaedia called *Dīwān al-ʿazzāba*.[12]

Originally, the *ḥalqa*s were religious brotherhoods, resembling in some ways the Sufi *ṭarīqa*s, whose members were distinguished by the tonsure of the hair, a special white wool dress – symbolizing their simple style of life implying a withdrawal from daily life – and their celibacy. At the head of the *ḥalqa* there was the *Shaykh al-ʿazzāba* assisted by a council (*majlis*) of four members. Further prominent figures within the community were the *imām*, who guided the Friday prayer; the *muʾadhdhin*, who recited the call to prayer; the *waqf* assistants, who were responsible for the mosque's properties; the teachers, who were responsible for the education and the supervision of the students; and four or five members who were responsible for the burial ceremonies and the distribution of the inheritances.[13]

In the first half of the 12th century, the *ḥalqa* emerged from its isolation to meet in the great mosque. The *ʿazzāba* progressively abandoned some original rules of their community life, such as celibacy, and became involved in the management of the town along with the *jamāʿat al-ʿawāmm* (the assembly of laymen), a secular body somewhat similar to a town council gathering together the representatives of the principle notable families. The *ḥalqa* and the *jamāʿa* elaborated legal texts governing the life of the town, called agreements/ conventions (*ittifāqāt*), based on both Ibāḍī law and Berber customary law.[14]

The creation of numerous *ḥalqa*s throughout the Ibāḍī archipelago strengthened the involvement of the Ibāḍī scholars in urban socio-economic life. They controlled the market prices, supervised the slaughterhouses and the auction sales, issued judgements against misdemeanours and crimes and proclaimed excommunication (*barāʾa*) for certain offences. By taking charge of all religious, social and political matters, the *ḥalqa* actually replaced the state.[15]

The system of the *ḥalqa* of the *ʿazzāba* disappeared in Jerba in the 19th century, whereas it has survives in Mzab – though profoundly modified – until today. From the 1870s the hold of the conservative *ʿazzāba* over their coreligionists in Algiers gradually weakened due to the combined effect of the annexation of Mzab to French Algeria and the activity of the reformist party.

12 Prevost, Genèse et développement de la *ḥalqa* 117, Aillet, *L'archipel ibadite* 368–369. The rule of *ḥalqa* was copied by al-Darjīnī under the title *siyar al-ḥalqa* and later by al-Barrādī under the title *sīrat al-ḥalqa*. See Aillet, *L'archipel ibadite* 376 n. 34. The *sīrat al-ḥalqa* reported by al-Barrādī has been translated by Rubinacci, Un antico documento di vita cenobitica musulmana 37–78.

13 Gouja, *Essai d'une lecture patrimoniale d'une source théologique ibāḍite* 62.

14 Prevost, *Les Ibadites* 156–157.

15 Prevost, Genèse et développement de la *ḥalqa* 122.

Once Mzab became part of French Algeria, the *ʿazzāba* no longer formed part of the official political leadership of towns and the Ibāḍīs had to abide by the French law and recognize its superiority over their traditional system. From the beginning of the 20th century the modern world slowly penetrated Mzab, weakening the authority of the conservative *ʿazzāba*, who were no long able to dictate their will to the population. Meanwhile, a new generation of Ibāḍī scholars pursuing the reformist trend and calling for relaxation of some strict Mzabi rules of behaviour came to the fore. They were championed by *shaykh* Ibrāhīm b.ʿUmar Bayyūḍ (1899–1981) of Qarāra (El Guerrara), himself a member of the *ʿazzāba*, whose energetic reformist activity secured the scholars a position of considerable moral influence among their coreligionists.[16]

6.3 The *Siyar* and the *Dīwān al-ʿazzāba*

The narrative that the first rule of the *ḥalqa* was written by Abū ʿAbd Allāh Muḥammad b. Bakr between his arrival in the Wādī Rīgh in 409/1018–1019 and his death thirty years later is questionable, since the first written evidence of the document dates to two centuries later, to the *Ṭabaqāt* by al-Darjīnī (13th century), which was echoed by the *Kitāb al-Jawāhir* by al-Barrādī in the 14th century. As Cyrille Aillet argues, the rules of the *ḥalqa*s form a *corpus* of works resulting from the evolution of the institution in the various regions of the Ibāḍī archipelago, the Rīgh, Warjlān and Mzab. In this region, for example, Abū ʾl-Qāsim b. Yaḥyā al-Ghardāwī (d. 1102–1690) compiled the *Siyar ahl Ghardāya* or *Siyar ʿAzzābat Ghardāya*, which was first translated by A. de Calassanti-Motylinski under the title “*règle traditionelle des gens de Ghardaïa*”.[17] The oldest extant rule of the *ḥalqa* is attributed to Abū ʿAmmār ʿAbd al-Kāfī al-Tanāwūtī al-Warjlānī (d. before 570/1174), a pre-eminent Ibāḍī scholar and theologian who was born in the village of Tanāwūt, in the oasis of Warjla, where he studied with Abū Zakariyyāʾ Yaḥyā b. Abī Zakariyyāʾ (d. 571/1175–1176) and Abū Sulaymān Ayyūb b. Ismāʿīl al-Yazmātī al-Mazātī (d. 550/1155). He also studied in Tunis under Sunni authorities. The *Siyar al-ḥalqa*, the rules of the circle, were reported by one of his disciples and they are indebted more to Ghardāya scholarly tradition than to the original rule attributed to Abū ʿAbd

16 Jomier, *Islam, réforme et colonisation* chap. 8, in part. 320; Hoexter, Effects of the Transition from the Turkish to French Regime in Algiers 121–137.

17 Aillet, *L'archipel ibadite* 369; Motylinski, *Notes historiques sur le Mzab* 24–28.

Allāh Muḥammad b. Bakr.[18] The *siyar* are a concise twelve-page document describing the duties incumbent on the members of the circle, who form a small group of chosen people distancing themselves from any worldly business and striving for knowledge and justice. They engaged in scholarly activity and teaching, as well as exercising the *ḥisba* function supervising market transactions and mosque maintenance. This involvement in the town's governance, along with the use of *barā'a* (excommunication), implying the banishment of the culprit from the community, was the hallmark of the *ḥalqa* institution, differentiating it from the Sufi orders with which it nonetheless shared many features. It is worth mentioning that the *ḥalqa* system flourished in parallel with the Sufi orders in Sunnism, while – at the same time – mysticism entered into Ibadism: the *Qanāṭir al-khayrāt* (*The bridges of good deeds*) by the North African Ibāḍī scholar Ismāʿīl b. Mūsā al-Jayṭālī (d. 737/1336–1337) echoed al-Ghazālī's project to re-found religious knowledge.[19]

Ultimately the *ḥalqa* filled the vacuum left by the fall of the imamate, exercising the same power in matters of law and justice as the just ruler (*al-ṣulṭān al-ʿādil*). On the contrary, the Sufi groups were embedded into a state system, though they developed their own forms of organization and structures independent of the state. They came to represent Islam socially and doctrinally and, in turn, received state support by way of the construction of *madrasa*s and Sufi lodges, the payment of salaries and other endowments.

According to the *Siyar* of Abū ʿAmmār, the organization of the *ḥalqa* was structured in three levels: the *shaykh* and his four lieutenants formed the first two, while members and students formed the third and last one. The *shaykh*, along with his lieutenants, constituted a council, a "pole" (*quṭb*), governing all matters of the circle. Internal consensus was grounded in the criteria that the *shaykh* and his first disciples dictated in the early phase of the *ḥalqa*. They aimed at creating a homogeneous group and it appears that, to a remarkable extent, they were successful. The accomplished master was the one who had

18 For a description of the *Siyar* by Abū ʿAmmār, see Aillet, *L'archipel ibadite* 372–376. Abū ʿAmmār is also credited with the *Kitāb al-Mūjiz* (*Mūjaz*) *fī taḥsīl al-su'āl wa takhlīṣ al-ḍalāl* (or *talkhīṣ al-maqāl*), a large manual of Ibāḍī theology and polemics, with a commentary of the anonymous *Kitāb al-Jahālāt*, a brief collection of questions and answers used by the Ibāḍī missionaries for their propaganda, and with th *Kitāb al-farā'iḍ*, dealing with law of inheritance. His *Kitāb al-Istiqāma* has been lost. Abū Yaʿqūb Yūsuf al-Warjlānī incorporates in his *Kitāb al-dalīl li-ahl al-ʿuqūl* an epistle addressed to Abū ʿAmmār by a certain ʿAbd al-Wahhāb b. Muḥammad b. Ghālib b. Numayr al-Anṣārī on the question of *al-waʿd wa 'l-waʿīd*, "the Promise and the Threat". On Abū ʿAmmār and his work, see Hoffman, Abū ʿAmmār ʿAbd al-Kāfī b. Abī Yaʿqūb; Ansari, H. and N. Husayn, The Concise Book of Doctrines 140–147.

19 Aillet, *L'archipel ibadite* 384.

internalized the Quran, the *sunna* and Ibāḍī law and theology. Moreover, he should have been a disciple of someone who can trace his spiritual lineage to the *ḥamalat al-ʿilm*, the "bearers of knowledge", the missionaries sent to North Africa by the second Basran *imām* Abū ʿUbayda. Therefore, the *shaykh* was part of a *silsila* (a chain) that reached back through the time to the earliest Basran Ibāḍī heritage. By becoming part of a *silsila*, an Ibāḍī scholar acquired the authority necessary to transmit sacred knowledge and a particular spiritual ethos.

The process of establishing the high *ʿazzāba* ethos within the *ḥalqa* was undertaken by means of different procedures and strategies regulating the boundaries of the communal life. The *shaykh* and the council repressed all forms of behaviour that did not conform to the ideal high ethos. They enjoyed a great deal of authority over their companions. Members had to obey the *shaykh* in whatever he commanded. He could rebuke them in the event the latter showed certain codes of behaviour that did not correspond with the codes that the master themselves had introduced and tried to impose. The members who committed minor sins (*ṣaghīra*) were banned from the community from one month to two years, while those who committed major sins (*kabīra*) were sentenced to a perennial banishment and could be readmitted only if they repented and the community accepted such repentance.

The rule attributed to Abū ʿAbd Allāh Muḥammad b. Bakr is longer and more nuanced than the one by Abū ʿAmmār ʿAbd al-Kāfī.[20] Once again it urges the member to exercise caution in association with others, to keep their seclusion and remain committed to the principle of ordering good and prohibiting evil. Having meals together, being committed to mutual aid and financial backing are examples of the ideal of social-communal collaboration.

> Among the good manners (*ādāb*) and the norms of conduct (*aḥwāl*) of the people of the way (*ṭarīq*) there are those of not being arrogant towards the humble nor humble before the arrogant; of not frequenting common people and keeping company with them, except in case of necessity one cannot escape from, or if these people seek the company of "those who know well and practise well" in order to improve their own faith.
>
> The old man is more excusable than the young man if he associates with the common people, since he is able to guide them along the right path, while the young man can be led astray. The *ʿazzābī* who was forbidden to frequent common people and does not abstain, is expelled.

20 Aillet, *L'archipel ibadite* 376–383.

> It must be known that the rebuke (*mu'akhadha*) for minor mistakes (*'atharāt*) and the punishment of the guilt (*ilzām al-dhanb*) of committing major sins (*khaṭāyā*) depend on who commits them. The culprits are in fact divided into classes: the deeds of the pious elder (*mubtahil*) are well interpreted, and if he commits a serious fault, he is rebuked with affectionate words and kind allusion (*ishāra*). If one who is inferior to him behaves in obstinate (*rāsikh al-qadam*) and conceited (*shāmiq al-qadar*) manner, the *shaykh* punishes him for both major (*kabīra*) and minor (*ṣaghīra*) faults. Even his minor sins are considered serious. If, on the other hand, he is not so [e.g. obstinate and conceited], his minor sins will be forgiven and his good deeds will be multiplied. He will be treated with affable manners instead of with brusque manners; for how often is rebuke done with kindness better than the brusque rebuke, and I have often seen *shaykh*s compare these two manners to water and milk.
>
> The *shaykh* of the *ḥalqa* must examine the condition (*aḥwāl*) of the students and seek for the one who is affluent (*mūsir*) those who will provide him with food for a fee; for the one who is in precarious conditions (*muqattir*) the *shaykh* will seek those who will provide him with service and food for free.[21]

In the rule by Abū 'Abd Allāh Muḥammad b. Bakr, the frugal ethos and the exhortation about a mystical path fit well within a didactic programme intended for an audience of young students and for the society at large. The bond between teachers and disciples was hierarchical and formal but also intensely personal. The primary focus of the educational system was the study of the Quran, *ḥadīth* and *fiqh*, subjects that the *'azzāba* mastered very well. The training of the students was carefully organized on three levels: the first was intended for the memorization of the Quran, the second one was devoted to the learning of religious sciences (*'ulūm*), while the third level was for students with physical or mental disabilities (*'ājizūn*) who were provided with special training. Inspectors (*'arīf* pl. *'urafā'*) watched over the entire teaching system, checking that the students arrived on time and met the planned class schedule, and allowing no distraction during classes nor delay in the submission of assignments. Half-hearted, distracted, inattentive students suffered more or less severe corporal punishments, or expulsion from the school in the most serious circumstances. The most important inspectors were those in charge of Quran teaching, followed by the inspectors in charge of Quran recitation, school hours, common meals and bedtime.

21 Quoted in Rubinacci, Un antico documento di vita cenobitica musulmana 77–78.

> The inspectors of the Quran. On each of them depends a group of Quran students equipped with blackboards; he dictates to them, corrects the blackboards and requires the students to learn them by heart. The group depending on each Quran teacher (*ḥāfiẓ*) comprises a maximum of ten people and a minimum of two; the number is at discretion, but that is the most widespread and common rule. However, if necessary and in case of lack of teachers, there is no limit: the disciples may be more or fewer.
>
> In the late morning (*ḍuhā*), when students are ready to write, a representative (*naqīb*) of each group of disciples calls on his companions, gathers them together and summons the *ʿarīf*. When the latter arrives, the one on his right asks him for permission to recite by heart what he wrote on the previous day; then one after the other they recite proceeding to the right. When all have recited, they ask the *ʿarīf* for permission to write under dictation; and he dictates to them.
>
> When one stops during the recitation, he is forgiven five mistakes if he is a beginner (*mubtadi*); if he is an advanced student (*fawqahu*) he is forgiven three mistakes, if it is the first time he is writing; the following time, one mistake. For anyone who makes more mistakes, the punishment will be at the discretion of the *ʿarīf*: the most common rule is that the young student is put in a corner and whipped, while the elder one is banned severely (*al-khiṭṭa wa ʾl-ṭard*).[22]

The rule of Abū ʿAbd Allāh Muḥammad b. Bakr clearly demonstrates that the *ʿazzāba* established themselves as a highly learned intellectual elite in charge of the education and of the legal and religious organization of the society. Their effort to instilling into generations of pupils their strict ethos went hand in hand with the systematization process of the Ibāḍī law and established the basis of their power within the Maghribi Ibāḍī communities. A "clericalization" of the class of *ʿulamāʾ*, as well as a division of the society between clerics and laity (*ʿawāmm*) came to the fore, deeply affecting Ibāḍī intellectual and social life in pre-modern time.[23]

Along with the rule of the circle, Abū ʿAbd Allāh Muḥammad b. Bakr and his companions were also credited with a juridical encyclopaedia titled *Dīwān al-ʿAzzāba*. The work was penned between 409/1018–1019, when Abū ʿAbd Allāh Muḥammad b. Bakr studied under Abū ʿImrān Mūsā ibn Zakariyyāʾ, who is considered the creator/architect of this collective work, and 431/1039–1040, when Abū ʿAmr al-Numaylī, who was also one of the seven scholars of the cave

22 Quoted in Rubinacci, Un antico documento di vita cenobitica musulmana 69–70.

23 Aillet, *L'archipel ibadite* 384–385.

and an alleged author of the *Dīwān*, died.[24] The *Dīwān al-ʿAzzāba* consisted of 12 parts devoted, respectively, to purity (*ṭahāra*), prayer (*ṣalāt*), fasting (*ṣawm*), pilgrimage (*ḥajj*), alms (*zakāt*), rulings (*aḥkām*), wills (*waṣāyā*), liabilities (*ḍamāmāt*), lease (*ijāra*), sales (*buyūʿ*), pledge (*rahn*), compensation and retaliation (*diya* and *qiṣāṣ*).[25]

Al-Darjīnī provides many details about a book also titled *Kitāb al-ʿazzāba* in the biography of Ismāʿīl ibn Yadīr, classified in the tenth *ṭabaqa* (450–500/1058–1107). He reports that the *ʿazzāba* gathered to write a work in twenty-five parts, dealing with the doctrine and intended to facilitate its memorization by beginners. He quotes the four authors of the parts on prayer, marriage, menstruation and wills, as well as further additional authors who contributed to the book.[26] According to Cyrille Aillet this compilation was penned between 462/1070 and 471/1078 in Wadī Rīgh (Jerba) by authors coming from Jarīd, Jabal Nafūsa and Warjla. It appears to be distinct from the "original" *Dīwān* as well as from another *Dīwān* quoted by al-Barrādī as *Kitāb al-ashyākh*, consisting of three large parts or six small ones, which – according to Jaabiri – was composed in Warjla in 468/1068–1069.[27]

The existence of several collective works called *Dīwān al-ʿazzāba*, *Dīwān al-mashāʾikh*, *Kitāb al-ashyākh* or simply *al-Dīwān*, is confusing. Moreover, none of them has survived in its entirety but fragments attributed to an original work called *Dīwān* are scattered in the Ibāḍī libraries in the Mzab and on Jerba Island, still waiting for a comprehensive study.[28]

The narrative of Ibāḍī scholars engaged with the collection of legal rules for the sake of memorization as well as for application in life and society is coherent with the *ʿazzāba*'s purpose of providing society with a stable system of law. It was also in this period that the Ibāḍī *madhhab* consolidated as a formal doctrinal school epistemically and the jurists established themselves as a class socially relevant. Their role in regulating scholarship implied preserving the Ibāḍī intellectual and legal production, meaning the plurality of

24 Prevost, Mağmāğ et les sept savants 42. Prevost dating is fully resonant with Jaabiri, *L'organisation des Azzabas* 199–203 and Aillet, *L'archipel ibadite* 398–400.

25 Gouja, *Essai d'une lecture patrimoniale d'une source théologique ibāḍite* 84–86.

26 Al-Darjīnī, *Ṭabaqāt* ii, 280; Prevost, Mağmāğ et les sept savants 44–45; Aillet, *L'archipel ibadite* 398.

27 Aillet, *L'archipel ibadite* 399–400; Jaabiri, *L'organisation des Azzabas* 200–201.

28 The parts of purity and on fasting were published in Cairo in 1315/1897–1898 and in 1915. The part on purity has been recently analyzed by Gouja, *Essai d'une lecture patrimoniale d'une source théologique ibâdite*. Jaabiri (*L'organisation des Azzabas* 201–203) provides some information on two manuscripts of the *Dīwān* quoted by al-Barrādī preserved in the library of the shaykh Sālim b. Yaʿqūb and of the sheikh al-Bārūnī in Jerba.

juristic opinions formulated over generations and deemed worthy of memory. Through writing, the memory of the legal heritage was preserved. This preservation and conservation occurred not only through the mere act of transmission but also through constant engagement in keeping alive the memory of past juristic efforts. The opinions produced by qualified jurists served as precedent *in potential* and thus were deemed worthy of being preserved and remembered. The *Dīwān* in its functional and rhetorical dimension takes care of both preserving and transmitting the heritage left by earlier generations. Its principal values and its mechanisms for continuity, change and application in society were developed and settled by creating a code to which jurists, judges or *muftī*s could turn in order to learn the legal rule to be applied in a given case or issue. Moreover, as didactic tool it acquired a pedagogical and transmissive dimension.

6.4 The *Walāya* and *Barā'a* Dynamic among the *ʿazzāba*

Investigations into the functions of scholars in Mzab confronts us with some problematic aspects of their activities. The difficulty arises mainly from the fact that they controlled a rather limited number of public posts, and yet they were custodians over every aspect of society and enjoyed an acknowledged ascendancy over the entire civilian population of the town. The judicial functions of the judge *per se* were also shared in varying degrees by the general body of the *ʿazzāba*. They were in charge of settling legal disputes arising within the community by appointing a judge from among them, or among the students of the *ḥalqa*. If this judge was not able to set the litigation, then it was up to the whole council of the *ʿazzāba* to examine the case and solve it.[29]

This judicial function, which the *ʿazzāba* perceived as a direct feature of the duties of "enjoining what is right and forbidding what is evil", became, in conjunction with the *walāya* and *barā'a* principle, a powerful tool in their hands. In fact, the use of *walāya* and *barā'a* by the *ʿazzāba* culminated in the effort to discipline society through an increasingly vigorous and intrusive imposition of coercive rules of behaviour and the inculcation of standard of obedience among subjects. Unable to rely solely upon coercion, the council of the *ʿazzāba* resorted to ostracism to rid the community of particularly troublesome

29 See the rules of the *ʿazzāba* from Ghārdāya, quoted by Jaabiri, himself an *ʿazzābī* with a profound knowledge of the Ibāḍī history, *L'organisation des Azzabas* 71. For a comparison with the role of the scholars in other Maghribi pre-modern societies, see Saad *Social History of Timbuktu* 94–108.

offenders, using a public ritual that accompanied the boundaries of inclusion (*walāya*) and exclusion (*barā'a*) within the community. Abū ʿAbd Allāh Muḥammad b. Bakr considered the role of *barā'a* crucial in order to give to the organization a spiritual and practical power over the community. Abū Rabīʿa Sulaymān b. Yakhlaf al-Mazātī (d. 471/1078–1079), another founding father of the *ḥalqa* system, devoted a chapter of his book *Tuḥfa fī 'l-uṣūl* to *walāya* and *barā'a*, which he considered fundamental principles of faith mandatory for all the believers.[30] *Barā'a* applied also to the members of the *ḥalqa*: Abū ʿAmmār ʿAbd al-Kāfī said that the *ʿazzābī* who committed a major sin should be excommunicated immediately.[31]

The *walāya* and *barā'a* practices offer a fascinating glimpse into the religious and ideological currents that sparked and sustained early modern disciplinary efforts. The spiritual and social reform led by the *ʿazzāba*, centred on paternal authority and on the rigorous maintenance of morality in order to create a rightful community of stable patriarchal households. This broad-based effort to reorder society in the aftermath of the fall of the imamate was based upon a conception of a society as imagined in terms of a strict division between good believers and offenders. Consequently, excluding outsiders from the community was crucial for both the expression of communal norms and the experience of cohesion. The analysis of *barā'a* also clarifies the role of law enforcement, particularly the public application of punishment in Maghribi medieval society. *Barā'a* was pronounced against any adult who didn't obey the orders of God and committed unlawful acts. The evidence against the alleged offender was gathered through self-confession, the eyewitness testimony of two reliable and trustworthy witnesses (two free male Ibāḍīs, or one man and two women), or through the publicity or notoriety that he had committed a major sin.

The declaration of the excommunication was carried in public after that the *ʿazzāba* reached their verdict in an in-camera session, and included a profusion of formulaic, ritualized elements including the public reading of an account of the convict's heinous offences and the call to a public repentance. The sources are adamant on this point: excommunication could not be pronounced unless the culprit was called to repent; only for the accusation of adultery, excommunication was pronounced immediately before the call to repentance. In the case of minor sins, and if the offenders admitted their guilt and declared their repentance, the *shaykh al-ʿazzāba* accepted this declaration and waived the right to pronounce excommunication. In the other cases, the

30 Jaabiri, *L'organisation des Azzabas* 79, 83.
31 Quoted in Jaabiri, *L'organisation des Azzabas* 84.

shaykh pronounced the excommunication in the mosque after the Friday collective prayer.

The purgation of the offenders who had failed to conform to the communal norms consisted in the banishment and/or severe forms of ostracism whose symbolic meaning was to punish and purge deviants. Being ostracized meant to be devaluated emotionally and socially, and to be kept apart from others physically. All community members – including the offender's family members – were required to break off all relations with the culprit: no one could speak to him, invite him to a gathering or a celebration, give him his daughter in marriage, or do any business with him. His donation could not be accepted, and if he died the *ʿazzāba* did not take care of the ritual ablutions before the burial and no one was allowed to attend his funeral. Hence, ostracism was a painful event that not only threatened the self-esteem and the need for belonging of the culprit, but it represented a very serious threat to survival. Those who were ostracized were more vulnerable to predation and missed the benefits of social interaction and group living such as shared assistance. Ostracism also represented a serious threat to reproductive fitness and marriage rights.

As in many other medieval urban societies, the Ibāḍī towns of the Maghribi interior sanctioned morally unacceptable behaviours. Their specific legal character as entities juridically separate from their surroundings meant that anyone who would not conform to the town community's legal and moral codes could be ousted. Moreover, if the culprit took refuge in another town, the *ʿazzāba* informed their counterparts, who in turn announced excommunication against him.

A town provided access to legal protection. Being cast out meant that this protection was gone and that exiles were left in relative insecurity and lawlessness. When exiled individuals were forced to leave their communities, removing them from the environment in which they had been causing trouble, from their home, families and social networks, they might be forced into a life on the road potentially causing even more problems. In their turn, original communities lost productive members, nonetheless banishment continued to be a popular punishment into the early modern period.

On the other hand, banishment was also easily reversible and in general left honour intact. As a result, exiles could reintegrate relatively easily if they were willing to undergo the ritualized mechanism of public repentance and redemption. In fact, the *ʿazzāba* showed mercy to those who were willing to mend their ways and granted them full pardon. The culprit was allowed to return to the fold after having professed a public repentance. He should present himself in all humility before the *ʿazzāba* after the collective Friday prayer and confess the act he committed, announcing his repentance. Thus, the community had the opportunity to acknowledge his repentance and to realize that the *ʿazzāba* did not condemn him wrongly. The repentant should mention his first name, his father's first name and the name of his tribe or family; he should confess the act for which he was excommunicated, and he should repeat three times aloud "I repent before God and before the Muslims".

After the culprit's public confession, the *ʿazzāba* met to deliberate and decide whether to accept the repentance. They based their decision on two points: the nature of the sin (major or minor) and the time taken by the culprit to announce his repentance. In case of a minor sin and if the culprit has announced his repentance quickly, they accept it immediately. In case of a major sin, and if the culprit was too arrogant to repent immediately, the *ʿazzāba* let him repeat his repentance several times publicly in the mosque before accepting it and announcing that he deserved again the community's solidarity (*walāya*).[32]

In the state of *kitmān* (secrecy) the application of *ḥadd* punishment was suspended (except for adultery). In this setting, ostracism and other punishments sentenced by the *ʿazzāba* were elaborate performances intended to display communal norms as well as power relations. The *ʿazzāba* relied upon the rituals that accompanied public expulsion to define and demonstrate their authorities, to regulate inclusion and exclusion and to provide good discipline and order.

Given the function of ostracism and banishment in the display of power, and their importance in reordering society and policing inclusion and exclusion within the Ibāḍī communities, it is not surprising that they had a prominent role in furthering the *ʿazzāba*'s attempts to construct a rightful community. Thus, ostracism and expulsion served to make clear the limit of acceptable behaviour and to relegate undesirables from the ordered urban community. Banishment and ostracism provided a striking illustration of the *ʿazzāba* social control efforts, and demonstrated that these efforts were not aimed exclusively at inculcating and enforcing Ibāḍī morality, but also at consolidating political authority.

However, social control did not represent the imposition of norms dictated from above. On the contrary, the *ʿazzāba*'s traditional agenda was advanced through the cooperation of large segments of the populace. The action of the *ʿazzāba* was informed by the norms and expectations of their subjects, just as official coercion bounded the action of these very subjects. The whole mechanism of excommunication and redemption elucidates the extent to which early authorities relied on the cooperation of their subjects in disciplinary

32 Jaabiri, *L'organisation des Azzabas* 84–89.

initiatives. It provides ample evidence of such negotiation in social control initiatives, showing how communities turned to customary authorities and traditional norms to provide order and security and actively supported official disciplinary efforts.

6.5 Law and Custom: the *Ittifāqāt*

The council of elders played an essential role as decision-making and legislative authority with a great influence over the daily commercial and legal affairs of the city, though this did not transform the scholars into a legislative body per se. They shared this function with the *jamāʿa*, which was a corporate high body drawn from the most influential members of the local tribes. The cooperation between the secular and religious sides represented a phenomenon of collective leadership. It embodied a dynamic balance within the town's life that was from time to time maintained with difficulty but was in itself crucial in the organization of the Mzabi towns. As in other fragmentary and acephalous societies in pre-modern western Africa, tribal leaders and the religious establishment became groups whose basic interests, economically and politically, merged with those of the community itself.[33] General features of such fragmentary societies were diffusion of power and maintenance of order by local authorities rather than by a central government. Nonetheless, they were not culturally independent but were embedded in the wider civilization of Ibāḍī Islam with which they shared religion, concepts and symbols. For the Mzabi-Ibāḍīs, the religious tradition operated within the concept of a community of believers that transcended the parochial identities of tribe, ethnic group and local community. This Ibāḍī heritage also contained the possibility of sanctioning the legitimation of power through the Quran, through consensus, and through transmission of knowledge from teachers to pupils, which ensured authority, leadership and succession. In great measure the Ibāḍī *ʿulamāʾ* provided the cornerstone for the town legal system over and above the invaluable visible role they fulfilled in the local sociopolitical structure. The *ʿulamāʾ* anchored the local society in the wider system of Ibāḍī Islam and, though they shared the political role with secular and feud-prone tribal chieftains, they represented the ultimate and most valuable expression of the Ibāḍī tradition and guaranteed the tribesmen's incorporation in it. To facilitate legal practice, the *ḥalqat al-ʿazzāba* and the *jamāʿa* began to list in written

33 Saad, *Social History of Timbuktu* 126–167; Warsheid, *Droit musulman et société au Sahara prémoderne* 5–9.

catalogues specific legal precedents and the degree of punishment involved. Their decisions/judgements (called *ittifāqāt*), concerning legal matters ranging from penal law to family and property law, represent a wide-ranging juridical corpus of invaluable importance which has been only partially explored.[34]

The balance of power between the *ḥalqat al-ʿazzāba* and the *jamāʿa* changed dramatically after the French occupation of Algeria, when the *jamāʿa* became the official organ for the city administration. From September 11th 1895, the members of the *jamāʿa* were elected every three years and were one or two per tribal group. They were chaired by the *qāʾid* who also represented his tribal group. But the clergy did not completely lose its influence, as proved by the fact that on March 28th 1928 they were able to issue the famous resolution barring women from leaving Mzab, on pain of excommunication, which had the clear intention of maintaining control over the community and preventing external influences:

> We strictly forbid all Mozabites to take their wives, daughters or any other Mozabite female family member with whom marriage would be considered illegal (*maḥram*), to any town unless it is one of the seven towns mentioned above.[35] We set this [ban] as an absolute defence, as a well-built and cemented wall, as a strong barrier. Whoever transgresses it, violates God's limits (*ḥudūd Allāh*), incurs the allegation of turpitude and deserves curse and shame in this life and in the afterlife.
>
> O company of our brothers! We do not claim to abolish the laws of the Republic. We have neither the right nor the power to oppose them. [Taking women out of Mzab] is, moreover, something that the Government neither forbids nor orders to be done; we are aware of that, but we warn you and remind you of what is not permitted to Muslims. The consequence of [taking women out of Mzab] would be our certain loss, for it can only damage our religion and reputation, destroy our belief, ruin our country and create opposition to our will.

34 For translation and comment of the *ittifāqāt* see Motylinski in the journal *Le Mobacher*, June 9th, 16th and 23rd 1883 (see Robin, *Le Mzab* for comments on the *kanouns/ittifāqāt* translated by Motylinski); Morand, *Les Kanouns du M'zab*; Milliot, *Recueil de délibérations des djemaa du M'zab*; and more recently Baamara, *Ittifāqiyāt al-ʿazzāba* (The rules of the *ʿazzāba*) 30–33; Cherifi, *Le M'zab* 341–393; Cherifi, La Ḥalqa des *ʿazzāba* 56; Chikh, La délibération des Azzaba de Beni-Isguen 165–186. See also Masqueray, *Chronique d'Abou Zakaria*. On Masqueray: Ould-Braham, Émile Masqueray au Mzab 5–35.

35 E.g. Ghardāya/Ghardaïa, Mālika/Melika, Bū Nūra/Bou Noura, Banī Yasqan/Beni Isguen, al-ʿAṭf/ El Atteuf, Qarāra/Guerrara and Baryān/Bérianne.

> It is a heretical innovation in our customs. The Prophet, peace be upon him, said: "Cursed be the one who does not follow the example of the Muslims, even if it is only to tie the strap of his sandals".
>
> What we say is the recommendation of God Himself.[36]

However, despite this strict prohibition, those who wanted to take their wives to the Tell (the Algerian coast) sought permission from the *Bureau des Affaires Indigénes*, which had no reason to refuse, ignoring the excommunication of the *ʿazzāba*.[37]

Through their joint decisions the *ḥalqat al-ʿazzāba* and the *jamāʿa* delved into the more controversial aspects of the law including those pertaining inheritance, maintenance and property, which are often open to different interpretations. Scholars used their knowledge emanating from the Quran, other sources of Islamic law, analogy (*qiyās*), consensus (*ijmāʿ*), legal doctrine and customary law to issue rulings and supply legal assistance. Consensus stood out as a crucial source, as argued in an *ittifāq* dating to 1830:

> The *ʿulamāʾ* of the seven towns, convened in assembly at ʿAmmī Saʿīd,[38] agreed on the points that would help them to issue non-contradictory decisions. The purpose of their meetings is to accommodate their differences as well as their disputes. For, among the sources of law, there is the unanimous agreement among scholars over a period of time. Consensus (*ijmāʿ*) is a peremptory argument. No one is allowed to regard it as futile. The transgression is a sin. The Prophet, peace be upon him, said: "Everything of which the Muslims approve is good in the sight of God, and everything of which the Muslims disapprove is bad in the sight of God".[39]

The consensus referred to in this decision concerns two cases that were judged differently in the previous legislation. The first concerns the maintenance of the daughter. The father is required to support her until the age of 12, whereas previously he was required to do so until marriage. The second case concerns the inheritance of the freedman (*mawlā*, manumitted slave) who dies leaving

36 Milliot, *Recueil* no 21, 218–219 (Arabic text and French translation). On the female condition in Mzab, see Goichon, *La Vie Féminine au Mzab*; Jomier, Muslim Notables, French Colonial Officials, and the Washers of the Dead.

37 Milliot, *Recueil* 229. The ban preventing women from leaving the Mzab continued to be enforced until the early 1950s, see Jomier, Muslim Notables, French Colonial Officials, and the Washers of the Dead 15–18.

38 The ʿAmmī Saʿīd mosque and cemetery are located north Ghardaïa, between Ghardaïa and Melika.

39 Milliot, *Recueil* no 15, 210–213.

no heirs. As mentioned in the previous chapters, Ibāḍī *fiqh* does not recognize (as the other law schools do) the master's right to inherit in this case. Conversely, in this decision the *ʿulamāʾ*, through their unanimous consensus, agreed that the property of the freedman who has no heirs goes to the master or to his male heirs, excluding any female heir. In fact, women can inherit only from their own freedmen.

An examination of the *ittifāqāt* offers a far more direct insight into the practical application of Ibāḍī law in everyday life than a reading of the classical texts alone. As with religious practice, legal practice was deeply embedded in local cultural norms. Customary law (*ʿurf*) and local tradition (*ʿāda*) functioned as authoritative legal references alongside the classical sources, particularly in cases where legal manuals offered no clear guidance or where local norms held precedence. In order to approach the problems posed by the study of customary law in Muslim society, we must take into account the porosity of Islamic law on one side and the pervasiveness of the local culture in Islamic jurisprudence on the other. Though from the formal standpoint Islamic legal methodology did not recognize custom as a source of law, in day-to-day practical reality a compromise was maintained between theory and practice. Elements of customary law managed to infiltrate into legal practice in this way, especially in tribal societies but in urban and non-tribal contexts as well. The legal infrastructures created institutions that not only constrained activities but also shaped the incentives to modify them. In this regard, for example, the study of legal practice helps to determine the extent to which legal doctrine is applied in daily life and to observe the operation of courts and the behaviour of *qāḍī*s and legal experts. Likewise, research on the implementation of the law depicts those aspects of legal doctrine which tend to be circumvented because they run counter to the requirements of social and economic reality.[40]

Being part of the divine revelation, Islamic law was perceived as having a legitimacy superior to tribal law. Nonetheless, traditional Muslim societies never excluded the practice of local forms of law distinct from Islamic law. Customary law might simply complement Islamic law, but also partially conflict with it. The two legal systems might not overlap in content; they might also be in blatant contradiction.[41]

As L. Rosen argued, custom did not stand apart but was indissolubly linked to the *sharīʿa* to the point that local practice and universalizing principles merged in popular conceptualizations as well as in the perception of legal officials.

40 Serrano, Legal practice in an Andalusī-Maghribī Source from the Twelfth Century CE 187–234.

41 Layish, *Sharīʿa and Custom in Libyan Tribal Society*; Dostal and Kraus (eds.), *Shattering Tradition*.

Law and custom blurred in practice and customary principle and procedures were regarded as Islamically legitimated categories for all local practices that were not in contradiction with the *sharīʿa*. Thus, local practices which were not strictly forbidden could be included within the ambit of Islamic law in ways that contributed to the capacity of the legal system to respond to changing circumstances.[42]

The range of affairs covered by customary law was probably widest in tribal groups with a high degree of political autonomy, though – given its ideological superiority – Islamic law's validity was not challenged in the name of tribal law. The *ittifāqāt* collections provide rich information about legal procedures among the Mzabi Ibāḍī communities, as they crosscut numerous domains of social life. They compelled individuals to obey the sacred law, and they provided sanctions for those acts which deviate from its norms. This presupposed that the members of the communities should know and agree to the social norms from which their rules were derived. The dynamic tension which characterized the relationships between the *ʿazzāba* and the laymen, was mirrored in the conceptual universe of their legal production, with the *ittifāqāt* existing at the meeting point of custom and religion. Laymen could thus interpret many of their local practices and assumptions as truly Islamic, while scholars, sharing in the same conceptual order, could incorporate and utilize the local practice in the application of the *sharīʿa*.

As for the types of cases that were included in the *ittifāqāt* collections, they are mostly about aspects of daily life: property, family law, inheritance disputes, family disputes connected to maintenance and repudiation. Penal law and punishments for crimes such as adultery, rape and theft also appear frequently. In this chapter, I rely on the work by Morand (*Les Kanouns du M'zab*, 1903) and, in particular, on the work by Milliot (*Recueil de délibérations des djemaa du M'zab*, 1930), which provide us with valuable examples of *ittifāqāt* dealing with different legal matters. Indeed, the *ittifāqāt* represent a strand of research that has only been partially explored and which has the potential to offer significant improvements in the understanding of Ibāḍī legal history.

Milliot provides the Arabic text and French translation of 21 *ittifāqāt*, the oldest dated 807/1405, and the most recent dated 1346/1928 (the famous decision on the prohibition for the women to leave Mzab), but we can assume that the documented period is illustrative of earlier periods as well.

As far as the topics are concerned, seven *ittifāqāt* deal with family law, in particular with maintenance of minor children and repudiated women (no. 1 and 2); wife's disobedience (*nushūz*, no. 5); marriage concluded without the

42 Rosen, Law and Custom 194–208.

presence of a guardian (*walī*) and secret marriage (no. 6); rules for the bridal party (no. 9) and waiting period (*ʿidda*) of the woman repudiated by an absent husband (no. 16). Three *ittifāqāt* tackle inheritance law, more specifically: bequests (no. 6); the woman whose pregnancy occurs after having been repudiated who has no right to her husband's inheritance (no. 16);[43] minors' property rights (no. 19). Nine *ittifāqāt* concern penal law, e.g. adultery (no. 3), rape (no. 3 and 4), the death penalty for a woman who bore a child out of wedlock (no. 6), fines (no. 8),[44] theft (no. 10 and 11), banishment (no. 12), injuries (no. 13), flogging (no. 20). Commercial law casuistry appears in five *ittifāqāt*: the right of withdrawal; hidden defects guarantee in the sale of animals resulting from redhibitory vices; pre-emptive right (no. 5); the use of the new coin minted in Algiers (no. 14, dated 1242/1827); acquisitive prescription (usucaption, Latin "*usucapio*"); presence of an *ʿālim* (scholar) at the signing of a contract of sale (no. 16); prohibition of making a loan to a minor or a woman without the presence of the guardian (no. 18). Moreover, decision no. 17 deals with the sale of stolen or usurped property. This is significant as it represents one of the few cases in which the classical Ibāḍī *fiqh* is quoted without relevant changes. It states/reads as follows:

> It should be remembered that if one whose property has been stolen or usurped finds it in the hands of someone else, who purchased it, he can take it back and the buyer has a right of recourse against the seller to reclaim the price paid.
>
> If the buyer bought the goods at the markets, the owner can take it back by paying the price to the buyer and has a right of recourse against the seller to reclaim it.[45]

The way of presenting the legal cases is not always the same: some *ittifāqāt* merely list the resolutions of the *ʿazzāba* and laymen, providing a short summary of the cases discussed, like decision no. 8, dated 1052/1643, which

43 Islamic law allows the concept of the sleeping foetus (*al-rāqid*) according to Q 46:15, which sets the maximum length of time between conception and weaning of the child at 30 months. Law schools accepted pregnancies longer than nine months, and considered legitimate the child borne from a prolonged pregnancy after the dissolution of the marriage by husband's death or divorce. The Malikis permitted pregnancies up to seven years.

44 Within the Sunni schools of law, the Malikis unanimously allow fining as *taʿzīr* punishment; among the Hanafi school only Abū Yūsuf regarded it as lawful as a deposit guaranteeing the offenders future proper behaviour, not as a confiscation of private property by the state. However, in spite of any legal concern, fining was a common form of punishment. Peters, *Crime and Punishment in Islamic Law* 33.

45 Milliot, *Recueil* 214.

provides a list of offences and the corresponding fines. On the contrary, other *ittifāqāt* resemble sentences pronounced by a judge, going into the details of the cases, as in a brilliantly crafted *ittifāq* (no. 6 dated 975/1568) discussing the nullity of the marriage contract stipulated without the presence of the *walī* and of secret marriage. Secret marriage – according to the decision – was a widespread practice, perhaps a way to legalize prostitution or extramarital relationships, against which scholars reacted vehemently in order to restore the superiority of *sharīʿa* over local practice. Moreover, in the same decision, the scholars prohibit the *muftī*s from issuing *fatwā*s declaring the nullity of expiatory testamentary bequests, in order to increase the share allocated to voluntary bequests in favour of the relatives of the deceased, in contradiction of the rules of Ibāḍī law (the famous jurist Abū Sākin al-Shammākhī is quoted). This *ittifāq* sheds light on a relevant facet of legal practice in Mzab, testifying that the two systems coexisted side by side, not always in a perfectly harmonious manner. The scholars' attempt to stand in defence of the purity of Ibāḍī law and of a frugal standard of living is testified also in decision no. 9 dated 1108/1697. In this decision, the *ʿazzāba* react against the Berber custom concerning the bridal party, issuing a number of prohibitions – under the penalty of excommunication for the offenders – intended to reduce luxury and expenses, including the practice of carrying the bride on a canopy, the use of tobacco or perfumes during the bridal party, the recruitment of more than one servant for the groom's and bride's households.

Some *ittifāqāt* refer to actual disputes that occurred within the Mzabi community, such as no. 7, dated 1052/1643, which provides a solution to the affair of the Benī (Banū) Mthahar. The Benī Mthahar occupied the upper part of the town of Bou Noura and the Oulād (Awlād) ʿAbd Allāh the lower part. The latter plundered the upper part, forcing the Benī Mthahar to take refuge in Melika. Here, they allied from time to time with one of the two tribes in the town, the Oulād Khalīfa and the Oulād Brāhīm, causing disruption to the fragile power balance within the town. Issuing a Solomonic judgement (which unfortunately they were not able to enforce), the *ʿazzāba* decided that the Benī Mthahar would form an autonomous tribe in Melika, subject to the same rules as the other two with regard to taxes and military service.[46]

The *ittifāqāt* dealing with penal law are significant as they introduce penalties (fines and banishment), which are not dealt with in Ibāḍī law. Imprisonment appears only as an ancillary penalty/supplementary measure, despite the fact that the *ʿazzāba* inclined towards this more canonical punishment.[47]

46 On the Benī Mthahar affaire see Masqueray, *Formation des cités* 61, 250–251, 257.

47 Milliot, *Recueil* 225; Masqueray, *Chronique d'Abou Zakaria* 29, note 1; idem, *Formation des cités* 35, 45. Pre-classical and classical Islamic law (8th–13th centuries) imposes

Ittifāq no. 12, dated 1197/1782, mentions punitive detention in a case of theft committed by a slave: he shall be confined in the mosque until the master sells him. If the culprit is a free man, the punishment is banishment, and it is up to his clan (*ʿashīra*) to expel him from the town. If this does not happen then he will be imprisoned in the mosque until his departure.[48]

The available evidence in the collection of *ittifāqāt* indicates that major offences (theft, rape, adultery) were punished with banishment from the community (*hijrān al-muslimīn*):

> This banishment, which is called banishment from the Muslim community (*hijrān al-muslimīn*), is enacted against the one who pursued an immoral or sinful behaviour (*faʿala al-munkar*), it is not of the same nature as the banishment (*nafy*) that the town or the *ʿashīra* pronounces against one of its members […] nor it is the banishment of one of the clergy (*ahl al-masjid*), *khuṭṭāb* or *ʿulamāʾ* […] The banishment of the thief, the prostitute, or the one who pursued an immoral or sinful behaviour depends on a decision of all the *qaṣr* (clergy and laity assembled).[49]

Indeed, a note at the end of the decision states that the assembly was attended by a large number of the inhabitants of Mzab (free Berbers, slaves and Arabs) and the representatives of all the towns, who were informed of the decision taken. This decision provides that the thief was punished with two years banishment to the coast (Tunis or Algiers) combined with the obligation to prove, with the testimony of two witnesses, that they have seen the sea (*yarā al-baḥr*).

The application of the penal law in Mzab posed a series of problems connected on the one hand with the prohibition – according to the Ibāḍī doctrine – on enforcing *ḥadd* penalties until a legitimate *imām* was elected, and on the other hand with the difficulties of ensuring the implementation of the *ʿazzāba*'s court judgements. There are several explanations for the

imprisonment (*ḥabs*) as a form of pretrial custody, pending the investigation of the crime, as well as a means of coercion to force debtors to fulfil their obligation. Imprisonment appears also as *taʿzīr* punishment, mostly in conjunction with corporal punishment, when *ḥudūd* punishments could not be enforced. For example, according to the Malikis and the Shiʿites, in case of murder, if the victim's family renounced to the vengeance, the murderer should be whipped 100 times and imprisoned for a year. The Hanafite school admits imprisonment also as a punishment for theft after two previous sentences of amputation. In principle prisoners must support themselves. However, if they do not have sufficient means, the state must feed and clothe them. Schneider, Imprisonment in Pre-Classical and Classical Islamic Law 157–173; Peters, *Crime and Punishment in Islamic Law* 34–35.

48 Milliot, *Recueil* 204–206.

49 Milliot, *Recueil* no 12, 205.

reluctance of the jurists to implement *ḥadd* penalties during the state of concealment (*kitmān*). Ibāḍī jurists regard it as a consequence of the fact that *ḥadd* penalties are the claims of God, which only a legitimate *imām* could fulfil. Moreover, generally speaking, Islamic law meant *ḥudūd* as rhetorical devices: the severity of the punishments (stoning to death, amputation) served in the first place as a warning to the community by emphasizing the seriousness of the violation of property rights and of the rules governing legitimate sexual relations. That's why *ḥadd* crimes in Mzabi towns were usually punished through discretionary penalties (*taʿzīr*), among which banishment was intended to dissuade the perpetrator from committing the crime again and to reorder society through purgation as well as regulation.

Banishment, a sanction involving the physical removal of undesirables in order to cleanse the town of miscreants, is among the most basic punishments and has been prevalent in societies throughout the world since ancient times. It was common especially in cases of sexual misconduct or other behaviour considered to have been immoral, with the aim of regulating and remaking society. Banishment occurs in Q. 5:33 apropos of banditry, and in Prophetic *ḥadīth*s in connection with unlawful intercourses. The schools of law interpreted banishment as imprisonment until the culprits show repentance. Only the Malikites regard it as actual deportation, but they apply it only to male bandits. As to illicit sex committed by a person who is not a *muḥsan*, banishment for a year is a complementary punishment according to all Sunni schools except the Hanafites.[50]

The Mzabi jurists envisaged banishment as a bodily punishment as well as a psychological sanction, involving the offender being excluded from all public matters and considered socially unacceptable until he atoned for his sin and showed public repentance. Upon the resolution of the joint assembly of clergy and laymen, the offender was expelled from the community and had to leave the territory of Mzab, going so far as to reach the coastline. Hence, the main rationale of banishment was protecting society by incapacitating the offender from repeating the offence and demonstrating publicly his inadequacy to be a member of the community.[51]

Retribution and deterrence played a role in the selection of the appropriate punishment. It was more severe if the accused was a repeat offender or if an example needed to be set. For example, if a slave committed robbery, he should be sold, but if he was considered to be a member of the Mzabi community (i.e.

50 Peters, *Crime and Punishment in Islamic Law* 34.

51 See *ittifāqāt* no 10, 11, 12, 13. For the occurrence of banishment in other Arab tribal societies see Dostal, Tribal Custom Law 132.

if he was born in the master's house or was a Mozabite Arab), the penalty for him was exile to the coast for four years, with the obligation to see the sea. In the event of a second offence, the banishment was forever and he could no longer return to Mzab.[52] In the case of theft, the personal situation of the offender (being a free man or a slave) was crucial in determining the type and severity of the penalty, for it was assumed that a slave needed more severe punishments in order to be disciplined than a free man. The meting out of chastisement, therefore, was individualized and people were not treated equally: status as well as aggravating or mitigating circumstances played an important role.

In cases of illicit sexual intercourse (no. 3, dated 811/1409), the claim of having been raped was considered a mitigating circumstance for the woman. The rapist was punished with 80 lashes, two years' banishment and a fee of 200 reals, while she should observe a waiting period (*ʿidda*) of three months and offer alms as expiation (*kaffāra*). After that the husband could resume conjugal relations. If the rape resulted in a pregnancy, the child was attributed to the rapist, and the woman was repudiated. On the contrary, if it was established that the woman in some way consented to the intercourse, she should return the dowry to her husband and be repudiated, but no further penalty would be imposed.

If a man raped an unmarried woman, he was liable to her guardian (*walī*) for the proper bride price (*mahr al-mithl*),[53] for having enjoyed her sexual services, and was obliged to marry the woman (even if she was a slave girl) after that she observed a waiting period of one month. If the man refused to marry the woman he had deflowered, he was punished with four years banishment (with the obligation to prove that he had seen the sea) and a fine of 100 reals. If he fled, he could return to Mzab only after four years, and in the meantime the woman's maintenance was the responsibility of his family. This ruling is significant because it apparently contradicts the Ibāḍī principle of rejecting the marriage of fornicators. It proves that, on this topic, the *ʿazzāba* took a more moderate position, closer to Sunni law.

The death penalty for illicit sex appears only in the case of the woman who bore a child outside of marriage (no. 6).

---

52 Milliot, *Recueil* no 10–11, 201–203.

53 *Mahr al-mithl* meant the average bride price that a woman of the same age and social status would receive upon marriage in that region. According to the Islamic law this was the rule in case of rape of an unmarried/virgin woman. Peters, *Crime and Punishment in Islamic Law* 54.

Illegitimate sexual relations posed a serious threat to patriarchal authority and the texts of the *ittifāqāt* demonstrate how the *ʿazzaba* dealt with the subject, determining the appropriate punishment and probably ensuring implementation of their judgement. Their decisions were based on a pragmatic approach to the relevant facets of legal practice, with elements of local and customary law often prevailing on Ibāḍī law.

The examination of 21 *ittifāqāt* cannot provide a comprehensive and representative picture of the application of the law in pre-modern Ibāḍī Mzab. Nonetheless, they expand our knowledge on the elusive principles surrounding the relationships between doctrine and practice, especially in the application of penal law.

The *ittifāqāt* shed light on the way the legal scholars worked on the basis of the established rules of Islamic jurisprudence as they always argue from and justify their opinions within the same system of Islamic legal discussion that we find in the Ibāḍī *fiqh* works. At the same time, they make an effort to use custom and local practice to make their decisions fit the social reality of the Mzabi region. In Islamic legal scholarship, the rules of *fiqh* are universal, but their application can – or must, under some circumstances – be adapted to local conditions. This adaptation of custom to Islamic law, or even more, adaptation of Islamic law to social reality, was the core function of the *ittifāqāt*.

Ittifāqāt embodied the criteria of status and the prerogative, which made for close identification between scholars and society in pre-modern Mzab. The factor of autonomy of the region was an import part of this phenomenon, along with the accessibility of learned status to at least the leading sector of society. The parochial and religious aspects of Ibāḍī learning were also important, especially as they created pedagogical links, which surpassed familial and interfamilial affiliations and gave the learned hierarchy a strong and wide base in the social structure of Mzabi towns. In fact, they linked the hierarchy to a number of urban institutions and provided scholars with access to avenues of influence and control which were open to them at level of law and adaptation of law through jurisprudence. This had influence not only on the organization of the towns but also upon conception of legitimacy as it helped legitimize an autonomous parochial-style leadership.

The most important criterion, which influenced the status of the scholars, was their own ideological emphasis on their distinctiveness from the rest of population. Moral rectitude and piety, to the point of blamelessness, formed a significant part of the status of the body of scholars, as did their ability to settle disputes justly. The command of learning was the fulcrum around which the whole idea of legitimacy and power revolved.

CHAPTER 7

The Legal Implications of the Ibāḍī Reform Movement: Muḥammad Aṭfayyish and Nūr al-Dīn al-Sālimī

7.1 Introduction

The 18th and 19th centuries saw a shift in the development of Ibāḍī law with the Ibāḍī reform movement, which anticipated and partially paralleled the better known *nahḍa*, "renaissance", in the Sunni intellectual milieu. Leading Ibāḍī intellectuals began to advocate for significant legal reform and for a rapprochement with Sunnism in the name of the common fight against colonial power. One of the eventual outcomes was a pragmatic eclecticism that entailed various forms of cross-fertilization and exchange among the different schools of law. Two personalities stood out in this context: the Mzabi Muḥammad Aṭfayyish (1820–1914) and the Omani Nūr al-Dīn al-Sālimī (1869–1914). They both make it clear that mastering the Ibāḍī heritage meant knowing its various aspects but also recognizing its relativity and historicity. Therefore, these authors referred to the search for an Ibāḍī identity in modernity, which could blossom only where there were no bans on innovation and rethinking. *Ikhtilāf* (difference of opinion) was a source of intellectual wealth that ought to be utilized for the benefit of the whole community, and *tarjīḥ*, or preponderance, provided the epistemic and methodological starting point for choosing the epistemologically soundest or weightiest opinion among different views on a single matter. *Ijtihād* and *talfīq* (the derivation of rules from various schools of law) were fundamental means to reform Islamic law. Aṭfayyish and al-Sālimī argued passionately in favour of *ijtihād* to respond to the intellectual and practical problems of the modern age and of *tajdīd* (renewal) in the interpretation of legal texts. Although couched in scholarly terms, this paradigm sanctioned the pursuit of political goals under the aegis of religion.

A central point in al-Sālimī's reform discourse was the restoration of the imamate in Oman, the theoretical framework of which is based on his theories about religious authority and the role of the *ʿulamāʾ* within society. The key mission of the *ʿulamāʾ* was to strengthen the state and ground it in the *sharīʿa* within a process of reform. Therefore, the debate about the role of *ijtihād* and *taqlīd* assumes a new dimension in which its meta-legal and political aspects are accentuated.

 | HTTPS://DOI.ORG/10.1163/9789004765764-009

The efforts by the Ibāḍī reform movement to renew the Islamic law – along with the efforts of many other activists in the Muslim world – were almost contemporary with the process of progressive abandonment of the *sharīʿa* with the adoption of codes modelled on those of Europe in many Muslim countries. In a vast realm of civil, criminal, commercial and constitutional law, secular codes replaced religious law at an unprecedented speed, with the significant exception of the law of personal status, which still today remains the last stronghold of the *sharīʿa*.

Ibāḍī reformers tried to resist the replacement of the *sharīʿa*, arguing that importing European institutions and laws to the Arab countries would create a system that could not harmonize with their juridical environment and, because nobody understood these imported laws, nobody would respect or obey them. According to Aṭfayyish, in order to be effective, laws must have some relationship with the standards and circumstances of the country to which they apply, otherwise they will not fulfil the essential function of law, which is to direct human actions and mould human habits. European imported laws did not fulfil such conditions. Both Aṭfayyish and al-Sālimī made no attempt to reconcile Islam with Western civilization: their reform was essentially fundamentalist, seeking a return to a pure Islam and the elimination of all innovation. Only in this way could the Muslim countries be protected from the moral as well as the physical assault of the European powers.

7.2 The Islamic Renewal Movement

The late 18th to early 19th century Islamic revival movement was the first major Islamic response to the European challenge to the world of Islam. It faced a wide range of questions which have dominated the Arab and Muslim intellectual arena ever since. Although widely connected and sharing a common ground in the call for the revival of Islam, the Arab-Islamic reform movement reflected the complexity and diversity of its members. Its legacy enabled the reformists of the late 19th and early 20th century to develop their revolutionary ideas on *ijtihād* (independent reasoning), reason, free will and a return to the original texts. Thanks to these reformists, the Muslim world experienced a genuine awakening through an intellectual and literary renaissance (*nahḍa*), and through actions towards social reform and political development which supported a growing spirit of nationalism.[1]

1 Nafi, *The Rise and Decline of the Arab-Islamic Reform Movement* 4, 31; Haj, *Reconfiguring Islamic Tradition: Reform* 77. See also Hourani, *Arabic Thought in the Liberal Age*.

The initial impulse for this movement originated from the teaching and influence of Jamāl al-Dīn al-Afghānī (1838/39–1897), the founding father of Pan-Islamism who spent the years 1871–1879 in Egypt. Here modernism took the form of a definite movement during the last quarter of the 19th century under the leadership of Muḥammad ʿAbduh, who was among the many young Egyptians profoundly influenced by the ideas of al-Afghānī. The reform movement in Egypt constituted an attempt to free Islam from the chains of an overly rigid orthodoxy and accomplish reforms, which would help it to fit into modernity. It was mainly a religious reform movement, in contrast with the Pan-Islamic movement launched by al-Afghānī, which was a cultural movement aimed at an adjustment of Islam to the condition of modern civilization. Nonetheless, both movements assumed that Islam was a world religion, suitable for all people, all times and all cultural conditions.[2]

The reformist vision of the Islamic renewal was built around three founding principles: *tawḥīd*, reason and *ijtihād*. The call to *tawḥīd*, i.e. to the essence of Islamic belief, was the cutting edge of the reform movement, by which the scholars sought to free "true" Islamic belief from the popular and Sufi manifestations. The Islamic reform movement thereby assumed a dual function: reaffirming the role of religion in the development of the Islamic community and supporting the ideas of free will and independence of mind. Out of this emphasis on the original spirit of Islam and the role of reason, the reformists advocated *ijtihād* as a means of restoration and a driver of progress. It was imperative for all Muslims, and particularly for the *ʿulamāʾ*, since it was perceived as the most powerful instrument for reinterpreting Islam, keeping pace with Europe and endorsing the idea of progress. Through *ijtihād* and reason, the reformists attempted to reconstruct Islamic intellectualism and sanction the introduction of Western ideas, values and sociopolitical systems.

The Arab-Islamic reformists sought to define the reasons for the crisis that weakened the Muslim world and prescribe its remedies. They advocated a new system of education, based on a dynamic understanding of Islam, along with a systematic legal renewal whereby Islamic law would be made relevant to the Muslim world. The European legal system, which was progressively introduced to Muslim countries, was believed to be unworthy of respect and obedience as it did not address the needs of Muslim people.

The major problems of the reform movement were its eclectic nature and its ambitious mission to reconcile Islamic tradition and European modernity, thus overlooking the sharp contradictions separating them. Only during the inter-war period did the reformists begin to change the ways in which their

2 Adams, *Islam and Modernism in Egypt* B-B2.

aims were expressed. On the one hand, Europe confronted the Muslim world with the ugly face of colonialism, thereby engendering strong doubts about the validity of the reformists' early assumptions. On the other, it was the eclectic nature of the reform movement, which turned it into a rising tide of radical Arab and Islamic expressions during the inter-war period.[3]

As is well known, *ijtihād* has played an important role in the development of Islamic law from its very beginning until the present day. In the first three centuries of Islam, scholars enjoyed great freedom in the formation of legal opinions. Gradually, as a result of the crystallization of legal doctrines and principles and the formation of the schools of law, such freedom was more and more restricted by the requirement to adhere to the teachings supported by the schools of law. Gradually, independent jurists (*mujtahidūn*) disappeared and were replaced by jurists who were, to a greater or lesser extent, imitators (*muqallidūn*) of the leaders and masters of their school. The shift from the creative period to the era of precedent (*taqlīd*) was gradual and the gate of *ijtihād* was closed under the assumption that the task of interpreting the sources had been achieved and that *fiqh* did not need any fundamental alterations or adjustments. The closure, however, was never complete and many Muslim jurists continued to engage in limited *ijtihād*. Wael Hallaq argued that the conclusion that the gate of *ijtihād* was not closed entails a reevaluation of what has thus far been considered to be the legal history of Islam. He demonstrated that the classical theory of the closing of the gate of *ijtihād* did not appear during the first five centuries of Islam and it only began to emerge by the 6th/12th century. This is entirely consistent with the fact that the practical and theoretical importance of *ijtihād* had not declined throughout Islamic history and developments in positive law, legal theory and the judiciary have indeed always taken place in order to adapt Islamic law to changing circumstances and new issues.[4]

During the reform movement, Muslim scholars maintained either that the gate of *ijtihād* had never closed or that it should be reopened, as it was absolutely necessary to reassert the leading role of Islam and *sharīʿa* in the organization and regulation of Muslim countries in order to help them to emerge from stagnation. They assumed that Islam endorses modern liberal Western values and recognizes man's independence of judgement.

Although the immutable rules of the *sharīʿa*, as represented by the Quran and *sunna*, are not questioned, reformist scholars thought that Islamic law and

---

3 Basheer, *The Rise and Decline of the Arab-Islamic Reform Movement* 45–47, 77.

4 Hallaq, Was the Gate of *Ijtihād* closed? 33–34; idem, Was al-Shāfiʿī the Master Architect of Islamic Jurisprudence? 600–601.

jurisprudence should be renewed and new ideas and rules should be accepted and incorporated. The renovation of religion and renovation of the foundation of jurisprudence were the pillars of the reform movement. The real problem was defining the limits and criteria for the change into the Islamic law. Scholars underlined the intrinsic ability of the Islamic sources of law, in particular Quran and *sunna*, to provide jurisprudence with the necessary tools to effect the desired changes.

However, in attributing a general spirit of permissiveness and adaptability to Islam, the modernist writers overlooked the substantial renunciation of independence in judgement that is implicit in depending on revealed sources for authorization to flexibility. They tended to undermine the epistemological view of the Quran: as long as it is regarded as God's Word, every change must be harmonized with it.[5]

7.3 The Geography of the Ibāḍī *Nahḍa*: the Maghrib, Oman and Zanzibar

Starting from the late 18th century, Ibāḍī scholarship had experienced a revival, in both Oman and the Maghrib, which Wilkinson calls "the modern Ibāḍī renaissance".[6] By the late 19th century, a significant development took place within the Ibāḍī revivalist movement: from a religious and literary renaissance, the movement shifted to a political engagement seeking to find common ground with other Muslims in the shared battle against colonial and imperial power.[7] This was the emergence of a 'neo-Ibadism' – a term coined by Wilkinson – which was characterized by a self-conscious renewal of Ibāḍī Islam and by a wide area of agreement with Sunni Islam.[8]

7.3.1 The Maghrib

The founding father of the Mzabi renaissance (*nahḍa*), was Abū Zakariyyā' Yaḥyā b. Ṣāliḥ al-Afḍalī (1714–1788), whose most important student was 'Abd al-'Azīz al-Thamīnī al-Muṣ'abī (1718–1808), a contemporary of the Omani reformer Abū Nabhān al-Kharūṣī (1734–1822).[9] He wrote the monumental

5 Omar, *Reasoning in Islamic Law* 103; Kerr, *Islamic Reform* 209–211.
6 Wilkinson, Ibāḍī *Ḥadīth* 232.
7 Ghazal, *Islamic Reform and Arab Nationalism* 20.
8 Wilkinson, *The Imamate Tradition in Oman* 243–245.
9 Biography in Mercier, *Etudes sur le waqf abadhite* 25–31; Rubinacci, La purità rituale 7.

Kitāb al-Nīl wa shifāʾ al-ʿalīl, a compendium of Ibāḍī *fiqh* which Wilkinson calls the 'Mozabite Bible' of the Ibāḍī renaissance.[10] The book compares Ibāḍī jurisprudence with the Sunni sources, thus presenting the Ibāḍī *madhhab* as one of the Islamic schools of law.[11] Al-Muṣʿabī was alarmed by the pervasive moral laxity and decadence ailing the Ibāḍī communities. They were not just experiencing moral degeneracy but were also suffering from cultural and material stagnation, which made them vulnerable. To revitalize the socially stagnant Ibāḍī communities, in which innovation (*bidʿa*) and polytheism (*shirk*) had become deeply rooted, he invoked the practice of *ijtihād*, and he invited his co-believers back to the values of the Quran. This was the first step towards a religious reform aimed at purifying Islam and bringing it back to its original form. The return to the authoritative texts required a particular form of reasoning through which existing interpretations of the texts were challenged and a new understanding put forward. According to al-Muṣʿabī, this involved a deep understanding of the Ibāḍī as well as the Sunni authoritative corpus, in order to evaluate whether contemporary norms and beliefs fell within the institutional and conceptual boundaries authorized by the Quran and the *sunna*.[12]

He spent a good deal of his life and fortune in collecting books from Jerba, Tunisia and Oman. Thanks to his monumental library, the Mzabi Ibāḍīs were exposed to intellectual developments from outside their community.[13] Several students benefitted from his heritage. Among them was Ibrahīm b. Yūsuf Aṭfayyish, who was in turn the teacher of his younger brother Muḥammad Aṭfayyish (or Aṭṭafayyish/ Iṭfayyish/ Aṭfayyash) (1820–1914) – referred to as *Quṭb al-aʾimma* (Pole of the *imāms*) – the most celebrated scholar of the Ibāḍī renaissance in Mzab. Muḥammad Aṭfayyish was a strong supporter of Muḥammad ʿAbduh; he looked for a rapprochement with Sunni Islam as he thought that internal divisions were one of the causes of Muslim decadence, but, at the same time, he advocated Ibadism as the most authentic expression of Islam.[14]

His legacy was built around his celebrated scholarship and religious piety but was also entrenched in his "patriotic" thinking, which shaped his resistance to the French occupation of Mzab. He firmly opposed the treaty signed between the French and the Mzabis in 1853 and was placed under arrest when

---

10 Wilkinson, Ibāḍī *Ḥadīth* 232.

11 Ghazal, *Islamic Reform and Arab Nationalism* 42.

12 *Kitāb al-Nīl wa shifāʾ al-ʿalīl*, in Aṭfayyish, *Sharḥ kitāb al-Nīl* xvii, 483.

13 Ghazal, *Islamic Reform and Arab Nationalism* 41.

14 Ouinten, *Ārāʾ al-shaykh Muḥammad b. Yūsuf Aṭfayyish al-ʿaqdiyya* 84–87. For Aṭfayyish's biography and works, see Ourghi, *Die Reformbewegung in der neuzeitlichen Ibāḍīya* 106–126.

the French occupied Mzab. In protest, he quit his position as a judge and called on Muslims to resist the colonizers, not only by boycotting them but also by fighting against them. Indeed, for him the resistance against the growing European imperialism required both instruments of power and solidarity among Muslims.[15] Developing within the context of European colonialism, Aṭfayyish's religious and legal project was simultaneously embedded in the Islamic discursive tradition. He wrote many books presenting and comparing the opinions of Sunni, Shiʿite and Zahirite schools, selecting the most appropriate. He evaluated, judged and appropriated certain views without demonstrating any fanatical adherence to the Ibāḍī doctrine. Starting from Quran 13:11,[16] he called Muslims to unity because he thought that the ossification and sectarian fanaticism of Islamic schools led to division among Muslims, thereby weakening the community and paving the way for the European powers:

> The existing discord among Muslims caused the people of unbelief to rule over them. If Muslims come back to the fundamentals of our schools, if they ask themselves what the reasons for their disagreement are, and overcome them and unite, then the polytheists will be defeated.[17]

This very idea of a revival of Islam shaped Aṭfayyish's ambivalence toward modernity: modernization should help Muslims free themselves from ignorance and construct a modern community, yet this must be recognizably different from Western customs. He firmly rejected any attempt to reconcile Ibadism with Western mores and civilization. He opposed the use of alcohol and tobacco, the adoption of a Western dress code, and the opening of modern schools on the European model, whether established by foreign missions or by the government. In particular, he openly opposed the establishment of religious schools by the Pères Blancs in 1884 in Ghardāya. He admitted that the Islamic religious schools suffered from stagnation and slavish imitation,

---

15 On the ambiguous attitude of Aṭfayyish towards French occupation, see Jomier, *Islam, réforme et colonisation* 67–70.

16 "[…] Indeed, Allah will not change the condition of a people until they change what is in themselves. And when Allah intends for a people ill, there is no repelling it. And there is not for them besides Him any patron". In his Quran commentary he also quotes Q. 8:46: "And obey Allah and His Messenger, and do not dispute and [thus] lose courage and [then] your strength would depart; and be patient. Indeed, Allah is with the patient". Aṭfayyish, *Taysīr al-tafsīr* v, 338f. Quoted in Ourghi, *Die Reformbewegung in der neuzeitlichen Ibāḍīya* 337.

17 Aṭfayyish, *Taysīr al-tafsīr* v, 338. Quoted in Ourghi, *Die Reformbewegung in der neuzeitlichen Ibāḍīya* 336.

the characteristic ills of traditional Islam, but nonetheless the mission schools, whether consciously or not, were tools of the colonial power. They brought their pupils near the religion of the teachers and could let them turn into Christians.[18]

Aṭfayyish's trips to the Ḥijāz introduced him to other scholars and, in particular, to the Sunni reformer Muḥammad ʿAbduh, with whom he corresponded and who held him in great esteem. During his visit to Tunisia, ʿAbduh instructed the people of Zaytuna University to refer to Aṭfayyish in legal matters, thus proving the reputation the latter had gained among the Sunni reformers.[19]

Aṭfayyish's works, as well as those by other Ibāḍī reformers, revealed a tone of reconciliation. In his *Izālat al-iʿtirāḍ ʿan muḥiqqī al-ibāḍī*,[20] a summary of Ibāḍī doctrine and belief, he reduced the points of conflict between Ibāḍīs and Sunnis to four: 1. The belief that God cannot be seen in the Afterlife; 2. That His attributes are not separated from his essence; 3. That faith is not separate from one's deeds; 4. And that the Quran is created and is not eternal.[21] Moreover, in his *ʿaqīda* (summary of faith) entitled *Kitāb al-jāmiʿ al-ṣaghīr*, Aṭfayyish argues that every Ibāḍī should understand, and develop a deep knowledge of the beliefs of the other Muslim groups (*milal*).[22]

Like the Sunni Salafi scholars, Aṭfayyish insisted on a return to the Quran and the *sunna* as the basis for all Islamic teachings and strongly supported the ideals of Pan-Islamism, though while claiming a distinct Ibāḍī identity and insisting on disseminating Ibāḍī principles. He stressed the revivification of Quranic duties, the eradication of the 'heretical' practices of Berber origin and the improvement of public morals and educational reforms. His works were first published in Zanzibar by the printing press established by Sultan Bargash b. Saʿīd, who intensely promoted Ibāḍī scholarship, and later in Cairo by the printing press established by al-Bārūnī, called al-Maṭbaʿa al-Salafiyya/al-Bārūniyya.[23]

From the late 1860s to the 1880s, the Ibāḍī revival movement in North Africa started radicalizing due to the increasing European colonial power and it took a turn towards actual reform under the influence of two personalities: Sulaymān

18 Ourghi, *Die Reformbewegung in der neuzeitlichen Ibāḍīya* 340–344.

19 Ghazal, *Islamic Reform and Arab Nationalism* 44.

20 52–54.

21 Ghazal *Islamic Reform and Arab Nationalism* 44–45; Ghazal, Seeking Common Ground 122–123.

22 i, 78ff.

23 Hoffman, *The Essentials of Ibāḍī Islam* 26; idem, The Ibadis 242–245; Ghazal, *Islamic Reform and Arab Nationalism* 41–49.

al-Bārūnī and the nephew of Aṭfayyish, Abū Isḥāq Ibrahīm Aṭfayyish, who embraced reformist and Pan-Islamic ideology. The latter moved from Mzab to Tunisia in 1917 to study at al-Zaytūna and to serve as a supervisor to the Mzabi students attending al-Zaytūna and al-Khaldūniyya. At that time Tunis represented the centre of the Mzabi intellectual diaspora and a hub for the network of anticolonial activism in North Africa. In 1923, the French expelled Ibrahīm Aṭfayyish from Algeria due to his support for the Tunisian al-Dustūr party and his anti-French activities. He moved to Cairo, where he died in 1965. His anticolonialism and search for a rapprochement with Sunni Islam, delineated through his definition of the relationship between Kharijism and Ibadism. Distancing the Ibāḍīs from the Khārijīs created a new framework for an understanding with the Sunni reformists, and broadened the spectrum of possible interconnections, overlap and coalescence between Sunnism and Ibadism within area of shared nationalist ideals.[24]

Ibrahīm Aṭfayyish's arguments resonate in the *Mukhtaṣar tarīkh al-ibāḍiyya* by al-Bārūnī, a compendium of Ibāḍī history starting from the origins in Basra, written to rebut those who considered Ibāḍīs to be among the Khārijīs. Al-Bārūnī was a prominent figure of the late 19th to early 20th century Ibāḍī reform movement. He combined his Berber-Tripolitanian background and Ibāḍī faith with Pan-Ottoman and later Pan-Arabist feelings. For him, religious identity became "nationally" salient and served to conceptualize and give sense to anticolonial ideals, forging large-scale political solidarity with the Muslim reform movement. He was born in Jabal Nafūsa and studied in Tunis, Mzab and Cairo before joining the 1908 Young Turk Revolution and being appointed a member of the Ottoman parliament. Later he was dispatched in Tripolitania to organize the resistance against the Italian invaders. Banished from North Africa and suspected of having sought an understanding with the Italians for the creation of a Berber-Ibāḍī independent state in Tripolitania, he left activism and entered into a phase of political quiescence. He spent the last part of his life in between Oman and Iraq, and he died in 1940 during a trip to Bombay in the company of the Omani ruler Sultan Saʿīd b. Taymūr. In 1906 al-Bārūnī established a publishing press in Cairo named after him – al-Bārūniyya – which served as platform for expanding the ideas of the Ibāḍī reform movement. Several Ibāḍī books were printed at al-Bārūniyya along with a newspaper titled *al-Asad al-Islāmī*, which survived for only two years and was distinguished by its pan-Islamic attitude.[25]

---

24 Ghazal, Politics and Polemics 274–275.

25 Ghazal, Tensions of Nationalism 54; idem, An Ottoman Pasha and the End of Empire 40–58; Peterson, Arab Nationalism and the Idealist Politician 124–139.

Al-Bārūnī put great emphasis on a Muslim unity and the urgent need for such unity was a recurrent argument in his writings:

> Do you agree that one of the main reasons behind the division among Muslims is the numerous *madhāhib* and their disparities?
>
> If you do not agree, what is the main reason behind their division?
>
> If you do agree, is it possible to unite [the *madhāhib*] and eliminate the differences since we are in a critical need of unity at all levels?
>
> If it is impossible to unite the *madhāhib*, why is it so and how can we solve the problem?
>
> If it is possible to unite the *madhāhib*, what is the easiest way to achieve this unity, in what country should we attempt it first, and approximately how much money do we need?
>
> How do we organize it? And how do you judge the person seeking to achieve this? Is he a reformer or a corrupt [Muslim]?[26]

Ibāḍī reformists believed that only through unity would Muslims liberate themselves from colonialism and forge a network of scholars and reformists spanning from North Africa and Egypt to the Middle East and East Africa.

7.3.2 Oman

In Oman the *nahḍa* started with Abū Nabhān Jā'id b. Khamīs al-Kharūṣī (1734–1822), the celebrated Abū 'l-Nahḍa, and continued with his son Nāṣir (1778–1847) who moved to Zanzibar with Sultan Sayyid Saʿīd. There he published on different matters spanning from dogma to jurisprudence, medicine and astronomy. Among the Nāṣir's students was Saʿīd b. Khalfān al-Khalīlī (1811–1871), a mystic and a poet who mastered also theology and law. Through his work, he championed the idea of the establishment of a righteous imamate in Oman and supported the movement that overthrew Sālim b. Thuwaynī in 1868 and installed ʿAzzān b. Qays al-Bū Saʿīdī as *imām*.[27]

The famous jurist Jumayyil ibn Khamīs al-Saʿdī was also among Nāṣir's pupils. He composed the monumental compendium of Ibāḍī *fiqh* titled *Qāmūs al-sharīʿa* between approximately 1840 and 1863. It was the first work published

26 Quoted in Ghazal, An Ottoman Pasha and the End of Empire 48. The excerpt is from a letter addressed to the representatives of the Islamic groups titled "Islamic unity".

27 Ghazal, *Islamic Reform and Arab Nationalism* 21; Hoffman, *The Essentials of Ibāḍī Islam* 25.

by Sayyid Barghash's printing press in Zanzibar in 1880. Volumes 1–21 out of a total of 90 volumes have been published in Oman to date.[28]

The work is an encyclopaedic commentary on the *Bayān al-sharʿ* by al-Kindī (Muḥammad b. Ibrāhīm, d. 508/1115); it also collects the legal opinions of other Ibāḍī as well as Sunni scholars, referred to as *ahl al-qibla*. Among the contemporary Omani scholars, he quotes in particular his master Nāṣir and the latter's father Abū Nabhān Jāʾid b. Khamīs al-Kharūṣī. The main objective of the *Qāmūs al-sharīʿa* is to sum up the Ibāḍī-Omani juridical and theological tradition up to the 19th century and to put it in the framework of a common Muslim heritage. In the preface (*Muqaddima* i, 7–9) the author advocates the use of personal reasoning and the 'search for knowledge' (*ṭalab al-ʿilm*) as means for renewal.

In 19th and 20th century Oman the great *ʿulamāʾ* had enormous social authority and political influence. They were the last prominent representatives of a long-lived teaching tradition in which learned piety emanated from classic individual study as well as from interaction between teachers and pupils. It was a complex process, in which religious and political authority was interwoven with teaching networks, familial kinship and tribal dynamics.[29]

Among the leading figures of the late 19th and early 20th century Omani *ʿulamāʾ* was Nūr al-Dīn ʿAbd Allāh bin Ḥumayd al-Sālimī (1869–1914), who played a crucial role in recent Omani history, and is today considered a source of national pride. His writings disseminated his ideas far and wide, cultivating a following for his views in Oman as well as among the educated Ibāḍīs in the Maghrib and Zanzibar. The key role of his writings in spreading the revivalist interpretation of Ibāḍī Islam placed his arguments at the centre of Ibāḍī intellectual and political debate. In intellectual and ideological terms, he propagated the idea of the necessity of a 'reign of virtue' – an Islamic order – where power was related to the ideal of the past and to the reality of the Ibāḍī reform movement.

Al-Sālimī's life spanned over a period of only 45 years: he was born in Ḥawqayn (near Rustāq) and, despite being blind since the age of 12, he distinguished himself as a prominent and prolific scholar (he wrote at least 22 books) mastering poetry, literature and history, as well as the sciences of *fiqh* and *ḥadīth*. He died in 1914 after falling from his donkey on the way to al-Ḥamrāʾ

28 The date 1256/1840 is quoted in the introduction by the editor (p. 10). According to Hoffman (*The Essentials of Ibāḍī Islam* 25) and Wilkinson (*The Imamate Tradition of Oman*, 353, note 7) Jumayyil ibn Khamīs al-Saʿdī started writing his book in 1260/1844. See also Ghazal, The Other 'Andalus' 57 note 26.

29 Wilkinson, *The Imamate Tradition of Oman* 256.

where he was going to visit his former teacher Mājid bin Khamīs al-ʿAbrī. He was buried in Tanūf.

His historical works (particularly the *Tuḥfa al-aʿyān*) are crucial for reconstructing Ibāḍī history, while his contribution to the field of jurisprudence was influential for several generations after his death. He inherited the "knowledge" from the great tradition of the 19th century Ibāḍī *ʿulamāʾ* of the Rustāq area. His teachers were Mājid b. Khamīs al-ʿAbrī (*c.*1837–1927) and Ṣāliḥ b. ʿAlī al-Ḥārithī (1834/5–1896), who was connected to Abū Nabhān Jāʾid b. Khamīs al-Kharūṣī through his teacher Saʿīd b. Khalfān al-Khalīlī and the latter's teacher Nāṣir b. Abī Nabhān.[30] This chain of learned teachers linked al-Sālimī to some of the leading figures of the ʿAzzān b. Qays imamate (1868–1871), and to the famous Abū Nabhān, who was a direct descendant of the just *imām* al-Khalīl b. Shadhān, the first *imām* of the second imamate, and grandson of the *imām* al-Ṣalt b. Mālik whose deposing in 272/886 signalled the fall of the first imamate.[31] Al-Sālimī himself was in turn the teacher of two *imām*s-to-be, Muḥammad b. ʿAbd Allāh al-Khalīli and Sālim b. Rashīd al-Kharūṣī, and of a number of leading *ʿulamāʾ* in both Oman and Zanzibar.[32]

Al-Sālimī saw the *sharīʿa* as a holistic system and the imamate as the preeminent political organization in Ibadism. The question of Ibāḍī tradition is central in his thought. He invokes a sense of authority in which tradition was synonymous with order, sacredness and equilibrium. In his view, political leadership had to be in accordance with the goals and objectives of the *sharīʿa*. He thus advocated for reform that aimed to utilize to the fullest possible extent the legacy of pre-modern Ibāḍī thought. In his numerous writings, he unequivocally expressed his view that recent Islamic revivalist thought had increased Muslim awareness of the need for the faithful to renew links with their heritage, and find their own solutions to their problems by returning to the Islamic law. He interpreted 'traditionalism' as a form of Islamic resurgence and juxtaposed the present state of decline and peripherality of the Muslim world to the past when Islam was confident in itself and expanded beyond its original territory.[33] Like his Maghribi coreligionists, Aṭfayyish and al-Bārūnī, with whom he had close contact, al-Sālimī strongly opposed colonialism on the grounds of its fostering religious alienation and cultural dependency. His deep commitment to the restoration of Ibāḍī authentic tradition reflects the

---

30 Wilkinson, Bio-Bibliographical Background 141–144.

31 Wilkinson, *The Imamate Tradition of Oman* 231.

32 Wilkinson, *The Imamate Tradition of Oman* 253–256.

33 Al-Sālimī, *Jawābāt* i, 565–578; idem, *Sharḥ al-Jāmiʿ al-Ṣaḥīḥ* i, 99–116; idem, *Tuḥfa* 192.

deep anxiety and identity crisis permeating late 19th century Muslim societies confronting colonialism and Western power.

However, al-Sālimī's Ibadism ought to be interpreted not simply as a rejection of foreign values and ideas, but rather as an attempt to give a new distinctively Ibāḍī meaning to the literary sources and to society as a whole by reformulating a redemptive Ibāḍī dogma. As both Amal Ghazal and Valerie Hoffman have demonstrated, the Omani *nahḍa* became a militant movement with active involvement from the religious authorities in opposition to colonization and unjust rulers, accused of being dependent on British power.[34]

The Ibāḍī resurgence was the product of adverse circumstances, such as colonial rule and Western domination, which eventually offered new openings and resulted in new opportunities for the *ʿulamāʾ*. Like the Maghribi scholar Aṭfayyish, al-Sālimī favoured the introduction of rationalism to the study of Ibāḍī law and legal sources. The notion of depending on the previously charted path was rejected by the Ibāḍī *ʿulamāʾ*, along with the very idea that it might be illegitimate to take a critical view of their forebears.

Al-Sālimī argued passionately for the need to continuously undertake *ijtihād* to respond to the intellectual and practical problems of the modern age in such a way as to enable one to take full account of Islam while addressing the needs of the time.[35] He remained strongly committed to the established doctrines and the authoritative texts of Ibadism, but he nonetheless used the paradigm of *tajdīd* (renewal) in the interpretation of these texts. Although couched in scholarly terms, this paradigm sanctioned the pursuit of political goals under the aegis of religion. Al-Sālimī defended the need for *tajdīd* by asserting that Muslim communities had lost touch with the original impulse and premise of Islam, which had been diluted to the point of being sometimes lost due to *taqlīd* (i.e. the unquestioning acceptance of previous legal decisions), colonialism and secularism. He considered *tajdīd* to be responsive to the situation of backwardness prevailing in Muslim countries.

This is evident in al-Sālimī's writings. Obscurantism, wrong practices and *taqlīd* had so dominated Islam that a large percentage of the faith was defective and incorrect. The need to renew (*tajdīd*) and reform (*iṣlāḥ*) in order to reinstate true Islam was, therefore, self-evident. Although not divorced from traditional Ibadism, al-Sālimī was an innovator and a supporter of *ijtihād* as a mechanism for legal reforms to break free of the idea that the *sharīʿa* as it stood was immutable and could not be tampered with.

---

34 Ghazal, *Islamic Reform and Arab Nationalism* 21–23; Hoffman 2012: 23–26.

35 Al-Sālimī, *Jawābāt* i, 264, 289, 296.

The Ibāḍī reform movement was closely linked to pan-Ibadism and to a rapprochement with Sunni Islam.[36] The Ibāḍī reformers looked for a rapprochement (or a "desectarization" of Ibadism, according to Hoffman)[37] with Sunni Islam and agreed with the Salafi notion that internal divisions were one of the causes of the Muslim weakness that had allowed Europeans to dominate the Muslim world. They emphasized Ibāḍī Islam's commonalities with Sunni Islam. The works by Nūr al-Dīn al-Sālimī in Oman and Muḥammad Aṭfayyish in Mzab made it clear that the Ibāḍīs and Sunnis shared the same doctrinal heritage. Looking for an Ibāḍī identity in modernity meant mastering Ibāḍī tradition but also recognizing its relativity and historicity as well as rethinking and innovating Ibāḍī doctrines and principles. In his works, al-Sālimī advocated strongly for the practice of *ijtihād* and *talfīq* (the derivation of rules from various schools of law) as a means to reform Islamic law. *Ikhtilāf* (difference of opinion) represents the methodological terrain in which the jurists were trained to deal with conflicts in textual evidence and in the methods of legal reasoning by weighing up conflicting or incongruent opinions in order to eliminate the weakest ones.[38] *Tarjīḥ* can be adopted only in matters concerning the *muʿāmalāt*, i.e. the acts involving interaction and exchange among people such as sales, marriage, repudiation and so on. The *ʿibādāt*, the acts of ritual worship, such as praying or fasting, are not susceptible to innovations and therefore cannot be subject to any juridical speculation, including *tarjīḥ*.[39]

As al-Sālimī argued in his correspondence with al-Bārūnī, reconciliation within the Islamic schools of law was paramount, as the existence of a variety of diverging schools and opinions was the leading cause of weakening the Muslim community.[40] He explains the growing dominance of Western/Christian powers over Muslims as God's punishment for abandoning the obligation to "command the good and forbid the evil" (*al ʿamr bi-ʾl maʿrūf wa ʾl-nahy ʿan al-munkar*), meaning the enforcement of both a good law and of a correctly constituted Islamic government. He says: "Our Prophet – peace of God be upon him – narrates that if you omit ʿ*al-amr wa ʾl-nahī*, the unbelievers (*kuffār*) will prevail upon you, and this is a worldly punishment and a foreordained supremacy".[41]

36 Ghazal, *Islamic Reform and Arab Nationalism* 20.
37 Hoffman, Historical Memory and Imagined Communities 193–194.
38 Al-Sālimī, *Jawābāt* i, 302–304, 327–328.
39 Al-Sālimī, *Jawābāt* vi, 396–397.
40 Ghazal, *Islamic Reform and Arab Nationalism* 33–34.
41 Al-Sālimī, *Jawābāt* vi, 216.

Al-Sālimī's writings played a pivotal role in disseminating the revivalist interpretation of Ibadism and in articulating his political programme effectively. They spread his ideas outside of Oman, particularly in Zanzibar and North Africa, cultivating a following for his views, especially among the educated, and placing his arguments at the centre of the intellectual and political debate over Ibāḍī reform. He remained strongly committed to the authoritative texts of the Ibāḍī school. In his *Lumʿa*, a general propaganda work written for the Maghribi Ibāḍīs in 1905, he provides a complete, although uncoordinated, list of books written by some of the most important early *ʿulamāʾ* which is crucial in reconstructing the Ibāḍī-Omani bibliographical sources.[42] The reference to an 'ideal past' is common in al-Sālimī's historical writings. He points out the antiquity and the characteristic features of the Ibāḍī school, while at the same time calling for unity among the Ibāḍīs and for a rapprochement to the Sunnis. In the *Lumʿa*, he claims the antiquity and originality of the Ibāḍī *madhhab*, which was named after Ibn Ibāḍ and was founded by Jābir b. Zayd who lived before Mālik b. Anas and the other Sunni jurists who are referred to as founders of the Sunni schools of law. Therefore, the Ibāḍī *madhhab* is the oldest and, in his opinion, the most relevant among the Muslim schools.[43] He connects Ibadism to the ascetism of the early Ibāḍī leader Abū Ḥamza, whose uprising in the Arabian Peninsula against the Umayyad caliphate circa 747–748 succeeded in establishing a short-lived Ibāḍī imamate. According to al-Sālimī, his famous sermon delivered from the Prophet's pulpit in Medina was appreciated also by Mālik b. Anas.[44] In the same vein, al-Bārūnī, who quotes in his *Mukhtaṣar tarīkh al-ibāḍiyya*, Abū Ḥamza's sermon which stigmatizes the iniquitous behaviour of the Umayyad caliphs and describes the cohesiveness of proto-Ibadism under the leadership of ʿAbd Allāh b. Yaḥyā. It calls for unity thus: "O people of Medina, the people are of us and we are of them, excepting the idolaters and the polytheists, the unbelieving Christians and Jews and despotic *imāms*".[45]

The call to the truth and to the path of righteousness means for al-Sālimī a call for a leadership based on the ideas of personal merit, moral rectitude, piety and knowledge (*ʿilm*). This conception of authority is based on the model of the Prophet, on early Islamic caliphates and on the early Kharijites, and is

42 Al-Sālimī, *al-Lumʿa* 17–31. See also Wilkinson, Bio-Bibliographical Background 144.

43 Al-Sālimī, *Lumʿa* 5–8. Usually al-Sālimī refers to Ibadism as "*al-madhhab*"; in the *Lumʿa*, the label "Ibadism" is a reference to Ibn Ibāḍ in order to differentiate the Ibāḍīs from the other groups, which split from each other within the Muslim community. See also Ghazal, *Islamic Reform and Arab Nationalism* 32.

44 Al-Sālimī, *Lumʿa* 5.

45 Al-Bārūnī *Mukhtaṣar* 79.

fully implemented in the Ibāḍī institution of the *ẓuhūr imām*: the type of *imām* who represented the optimal leader, and who ruled under ideal conditions.[46]

7.3.3 Zanzibar

With the establishment of the Omani Āl Bū Saʿīdī dynasty in Zanzibar (1833–1964), the Ibāḍī *nahḍa* spread from Mzab and Oman to the East African coast. Sultan Saʿīd bin Sulṭān, who ruled Oman and Zanzibar from 1806 to 1856, kept Nāṣir b. Jāʾid b. Khamīs al-Kharūṣī close by his side along with other prominent Ibāḍī scholars, such as ʿAbd Allāh b. Mubārak b. ʿAbd Allāh al-Nizwī and Muḥammad b. ʿAlī al-Mandhirī. In Zanzibar the Ibāḍī *nahḍa* strengthened thanks to the Sultan's patronage of the Ibāḍī intellectuals and reformers and to the introduction of a printing press in the 1870s by Sultan Barghash (r. 1870–1888), which increased the circulation of Ibāḍī teachings. Among others, the works of Aṭfayyish were first published in Zanzibar. Coming back from a visit in England, Sultan Bargash imported a printing press that used both Roman and Arab typefaces. The al-Maṭbaʿa al-Sulṭaniyya (the Sultanate Press), the first Arabic press in East Africa, began its activities in 1879–1880, publishing the works of contemporary Ibāḍī authorities along with a number of canonical works considered as primary texts for Ibāḍī scholarship. In 1886, it published a classical compendium of Ibāḍī law, *al-Mukhtaṣar* by al-Bisiyānī. Between 1886–87 and 1890–91, the press published the *Kitāb ḥāshiyyat al-tartīb* by Abū Sitta, an authoritative Ibāḍī collection of *ḥadīth* based on *al-Jāmiʿ al-ṣaḥīḥ* by al-Warjlānī. The Sultanate Press continued its new publication projects under Sultan Bargash's successors, and in 1898 it published another basic text *Madārij al-Kamāl fī naẓm Mukhtaṣar al-Khiṣāl* by al-Sālimī, a rhymed summary of the *Mukhtaṣar al-Khiṣāl* by Abū Isḥāq, Ibrāhīm b. Qays al-Ḥaḍramī. The activities of al-Maṭbaʿa al-Sulṭaniyya in Zanzibar interweaved with those of the Bārūniyya in Cairo, which started printing in the same period, and with those of an almost unknown press in Tunis, which started publishing Ibāḍī works in the 1890s. These three presses were significant in making many Ibāḍī canonical works available in print for the first time, and in providing new material that encouraged further debate among scholars.[47]

The Āl Bū Saʿīdī sultans had both Ibāḍī and non-Ibāḍī advisers, they invited Sunni scholars to Zanzibar and appointed judges for each of the different

46 Al-Sālimī, *Sharḥ al-Jāmiʿ al-Ṣaḥīḥ* i, 99–106; idem, *Jawābāt* i, 570–573.

47 Sadgrove, From Wadi Mizab 184–211. Custers provides a list of books published by Ibāḍī printing presses during the *nahḍa*. See *Ibāḍī Publishing Activities* in part. 5–7, 23–24, 38–42, 56–57, 64–66, 84, 91.

Islamic legal schools, making no attempt to propagate Ibadism on the island and on the East African coast. Nonetheless, under their rule, there was an unprecedented spread of Ibāḍī literary traditions thanks to the financial support and publication services they offered to the Ibāḍī reformers. The Sunni reform movement, supporting the ideas of Abduh and Riḍā, also spread to Zanzibar in the late 19th century among the Egyptian community in diaspora, thanks to the Arabic press circulating in Zanzibar.[48]

Under the Āl Bū Saʿīdī dynasty Ibāḍīs came face to face with the cosmopolitan society in Zanzibar (comprising Shafiʿī scholars and merchants, Twelver Shiʿites, Ismaʿilis, Bohoras, Hindus and Christian missionaries), and drew upon its vibrant intellectual environment, which encouraged learning and attracted scholars from other parts of East Africa and from other countries bordering the Indian Ocean. The Ibāḍīs worked closely and cooperated with Sunni Muslims to such an extent that some scholars warned that the Shafiite doctrines could influence Ibadism. ʿAlī b. Muḥammad al-Mundhirī wrote a short treatise in 1899 and a *fatwā* in 1914 defending Ibāḍī Islam against the attacks by Shafiites.[49]

Zanzibar emerged as a new intellectual, commercial and political centre in East Africa thanks to the intensification of trade with North America, Great Britain and France and the intensification of agriculture exploitation of Zanzibar, Pemba and the coast. Sultan Saʿīd created what Heinz Gaube calls "System Saʿīd", an agricultural revolution in Zanzibar and Pemba based mainly on the cultivation of cloves.[50] This unique system – based mainly on slave labour – was challenged by the growing Western colonial interests in the region. The struggle for the throne after Sultan Saʿīd's death reinforced British power on the island and demonstrated that the West was too strong to allow any further development of the "Saʿīd's methods". The split of Zanzibar from Oman in 1861 had devastating consequences for both countries. In Oman the *nahḍa* radicalized in a militant movement aimed at restoring the imamate and at overthrowing the Āl Bū Saʿīdī dynasty, accusing it of having surrendered to the British imperialism.[51]

48 Ghazal, *Islamic Reform and Arab Nationalism* 37; Hoffman, The Articulation of Ibāḍī Identity 201–216.

49 Hoffman, Ibadi Muslim Scholars and the Confrontation with Sunnī Islam 96–99, 103–109.

50 Gaube, *The Ibadis in the Region of the Indian Ocean* 435–436.

51 Ghazal, *Islamic Reform and Arab Nationalism* 21; Jones and Ridout, *A History of Modern Oman*, 64–82.

7.4 Muḥammad Aṭfayyish's Contribution to Ibāḍī Law and Jurisprudence

Muḥammad Aṭfayyish was a very prolific author. He wrote over hundred works, some lost, but many available in print or still in manuscript in the Mzabi libraries. His modern ideals and inspirations can be seen from the great impact he made within the Ibāḍī scholarship in the field of *tafsīr*, Prophetic tradition, theology, law, grammar, philology and poetry. His importance in the context of the modern Ibadism and reform movement cannot be emphasized enough.

His main contribution in the field of law is his commentary (*Sharḥ*) on the *Kitāb al-Nīl wa shifāʾ al-ʿalīl* by ʿAbd al-ʿAzīz al-Thamīnī al-Muṣʿabī, which represents a cornerstone of contemporary Ibāḍī jurisprudence.[52] Aṭfayyish sent it to his young Omani contemporary al-Sālimī, whose books – especially his *Sharḥ* of the *Musnad al-Rabīʿ* – along with Aṭfayyish's works (in particular, the *Sharḥ kitāb al-Nīl* and the *Tartīb* of the *Mudawwana* by Abū Ghānim al-Khurāsānī) were part of the return to the sources which characterized the Ibāḍī *nahḍa* and allowed the Ibāḍīs to be integrated into the broader Islamic reform movement.[53]

The *Sharḥ* deals with the topics of the *Kitāb al-Nīl* in a comparative way, exposing along with the Ibāḍī teachings those of the Sunni and Shiʿite schools of law. Thanks to this multidisciplinary approach and the encyclopaedic knowledge of his author, the *Sharḥ* is regarded as a fundamental work for the study of Islamic law, comparable to the standard works of the Sunni juridical tradition, such as the works by Ibn Qudama, al-Kasānī and Ibn Ḥazm.[54]

Aṭfayyish first explains what all schools of law maintain about a certain topic, then he expresses his own opinion by saying *ʿindī* (according to me ...). Such opinion is based on both tradition and reasoning (*ʿalā dalīl al-naqlī wa ʾl-ʿaqlī*) and can also conform to that expressed by a non-Ibāḍī scholar. Before accepting a legal opinion (*raʾy*), he submits it to a careful critical review to verify its reliability, even if it is an opinion expressed by an Ibāḍī jurist. The non-Ibāḍī schools are referred to by their names (the Maliki, the Hanafi and so on)[55] or in general terms as *ahl al-khilāf* or *al-mukhālafūn*.[56] The use of this

---

52 The *Sharḥ kitāb al-Nīl* was first published in Cairo in 1342/1923 (see Brockelmann, Suppl. II, p. 892).

53 Wilkinson, *Ibâḍism* 435–436.

54 Kamāl al-Dīn, *Sharḥ Kitāb al-Nīl li-l-imām al-ʿalāma Muḥammad b. Yūsuf al-Aṭfayyish* i, 17–20.

55 See, for example, *Sharḥ* iii, 214–215.

56 *Sharḥ* xvii, 483.

word, meaning 'the dissidents', testifies that Aṭfayyish, despite his call to unity, retains the tenor of classical Ibāḍī sectarian concern.

Ibāḍī legal tradition is particularly emphasized when Ibāḍī law diverges from that developed by the Sunni schools, such as the case of *zakāt* on cattle which the Ibāḍīs treated as equal to the *zakāt* on camels, defining the *niṣāb* as five head.[57] A further example is the case of the two parties guilty of unlawful sexual intercourse. Ibāḍīs hold that such a relationship constitutes a permanent impediment to marriage between them.[58] In both these cases, Aṭfayyish discusses at length the opinion held by the Sunni schools and explains the reasons why the Ibāḍīs have a different view; usually this is due to the fact that the Ibāḍīs rely on their own traditions or authorities not accepted by the other schools.

As far as the case of the inheritance of the client (*mawlā*) who has no relatives is concerned, Aṭfayyish confirms that Ibāḍī law refutes the agnatization of the client for purpose of succession, and holds that his property is to be inherited by his people and not by his patron. Nonetheless, his long analysis of the legal maxim declaring that patronage is to be considered like a kinship (*inna al-walāʾ qarāba ka-qarābat al-nasab*), shows that he is almost sympathetic to the prevailing Sunni opinion asserting that the patron should inherit.[59]

In the case of usury, Ibāḍīs hold that there is no usury in the exchange of the same kind of precious metal (gold for gold, silver for silver) unless there is a time-lag in the transaction. This doctrine, formulated in the maxims "there is no usury except on loans" and "there is no usury when the payment is made on the spot", was ascribed to the Prophet and transmitted by the famous companion Ibn ʿAbbās. It is a serious infringement to the Sunni rules on usury to assert that the exchanges of gold for gold and silver for silver should fulfil both the conditions of simultaneity and of equality in the exchanged amount. Aṭfayyish considers Ibāḍī doctrine weak, therefore he accepts Shāfiʿī's reasoning, arguing that Ibn ʿAbbās had repented of his opinion in his later life. Moreover, the maxim "there is no usury except on loans" should refer to hand-to-hand exchange with an excess of different commodities, for example the exchange of gold with silver, of dates with wheat and likewise other articles with those of a different kind.[60] Interestingly, Aṭfayyish's reinterpretation of the rules concerning usury is almost contemporary to Muḥammad ʿAbduh's attempt to liberalize interest on postal saving accounts. Indeed, in a famous *fatwā* issued

57 *Sharḥ* iii, 213–217.
58 *Sharḥ* vi, 47–54.
59 *Sharḥ* xv, 516–529.
60 *Sharḥ* viii, 38–39.

in 1903, ʿAbduh argued for the legitimation of a 'dividend' of up to 2.5% to distinguish this from usurious interest on the basis of the social utilities of saving accounts instead of a strict interpretation of Islamic law.[61]

There is nothing in Aṭfayyish's approach to the law that reflects the modernist determination in reforming some aspects of Islamic law, such as slavery or polygamy, which were considered obsolete. Gender equality and the improvement of women's status was a major concern of several Sunni reformers trying to modernize Muslim society. Muḥammad ʿAbduh is one of the modernist exegetes who best reflects this tendency. He, along with his pupil Rashīd Riḍā, maintained that Islam permits polygamy only under strict conditions of justice among the wives, which is extremely difficult to satisfy. Thus, the practice of polygamy is highly discouraged and can exist only in exceptional cases. The practice of repudiation should also be restricted as it does not completely fit into the Quranic idea of justice between men and women.[62] On the contrary, according to Aṭfayyish, reforms entail the defence of Islamic morality as opposed to the value system of the colonial powers; therefore, he saw no need for any change in women's status and primarily called the Ibāḍī women back to their traditional roles as wives and mothers. His interpretation of the rules on marriages and repudiation is entirely conservative and reflects his general concern for a reassertion of the Ibāḍī tradition.[63]

7.4.1 *Ijtihād* and *Taqlīd*

As I have already argued, for the Ibāḍīs the gate of *ijtihād* has never been closed for qualified jurists. They firmly reject the idea of the closure of the gate of *ijtihād*, as they believe that such a decision would have led to a stagnation of law and doctrine. Moreover, disagreement on questions related to substantive law (*furūʿ al-fiqh*) was held to be lawful and each jurist could keep his own opinion regardless of whether it was the correct one or not.

The commentary to the work by al-Muṣʿabī gives Aṭfayyish the opportunity to expose his own conception of *ijtihād* and *taqlīd*.[64] He was unconventional in many respects and ready to re-examine issues that had long been settled in the Ibāḍī tradition. In the treatment of law, Aṭfayyish demands the right of independent investigation. His belief in the necessity of use of reason appears

61 Sedgwick, *Muhammad Abduh* 95–97.
62 Riḍā, *Tafsīr al-Manār* iv, 350.
63 See in particular *Sharḥ*, *bāb fī ḥaqq al-zawjayn* vi, 467–477 and *bāb fī ʿadl bayna al-nisāʾ* vi, 495–507.
64 See in particular *Sharḥ* xvii, 474–501.

frequently in all of his writings.[65] An inspirational figure for Aṭfayyish was the 15th century scholar Jalāl al-Dīn al-Suyūṭī (d. 1483) who, as Aṭfayyish did himself, claimed to have reached the degree of *mujtahid muṭlaq*, that is to say that he exercised *ijtihād* by following the method of one of the four founding imāms, in his case that of *imām* al-Shāfiʿī.[66]

According to Aṭfayyish, *ijtihād* is based on Quran 4:83[67] and it is understood as the pursuit of knowledge through the use of primary sources either in matters which have not been settled in Ibāḍī traditions (*āthār*), or in matters the scholars disagreed upon.[68] It is not a form of individual reasoning because it must always be based on the sources of law: the Quran, *sunna*, analogy and consensus. The *mujtahid* must know how to read between the lines of texts and answer new questions on matters, which the previous jurists have not yet dealt with.

According to Aṭfayyish, *ijtihād* is a peculiarity of the Muslim community. God (Q 10:94)[69] allows scholars (*ʿulamāʾ*) to practise *ijtihād* because in this way the Islamic teachings are constantly updated and renewed.[70] The abolition of *ijtihād* implies the abandonment of reason as a means of understanding. According to Aṭfayyish, progress (*taqaddum*) cannot take place without knowledge.[71] Like other Ibāḍī reformists, he strives to explain the importance of *ijtihād* for the development of Islamic teaching. His approach to the reform discourse is mainly characterized by an emphasis on returning to the sources. He quotes Q 22:78: "He has chosen you and has not placed upon you any difficulty in religion" and explains these verses as God's call and permission to *ijtihād* because it is intended to solve the people's problem.[72] The legal advice

65 Ourghi, *Die Reformbewegung in der neuzeitlichen Ibāḍīya* 243–257.

66 Ourghi, *Die Reformbewegung in der neuzeitlichen Ibāḍīya* 151.

67 "When there comes to them some matter touching (public) safety or fear, they make it known (among the people), if only they had referred it to the Messenger or to those charged with authority among them, the proper investigators would have understood it from them (directly)".

68 *Sharḥ* xvii, 43–44.

69 "So if you are in doubt, [O Muhammad], about that which We have revealed to you, then ask those who have been reading the Scripture before you. The truth has certainly come to you from your Lord, so never be among the doubters". See also 4:83 "And when there comes to them information about [public] security or fear, they spread it around. But if they had referred it back to the Messenger or to those of authority among them, then the ones who [can] draw correct conclusions from it would have known about it", quoted in *Sharḥ* xvii, 43.

70 *Sharḥ* xvii, 43–44, 50.

71 *Sharḥ* xvii, 54.

72 *Ibidem.*

obtained by the mental effort of scholars is accepted even if they are doubted. Indeed, a *mujtahid* can also be wrong, but even in this case God does not punish him. On the contrary, he is entitled to a reward for its mental effort, because only by conjecture in religious matters could one get soundly based knowledge.[73] Only the one who refuses to seek the truth is punished. The *mujtahid* is not infallible. God has granted him the ability to take decisions, even if they prove to be incorrect. According to Aṭfayyish, God alone knows the truth and men can access it only through prophecy. Since prophecy has been interrupted, those who are entitled to have to exercise *ijtihād* in order to get to the core of God's message. This is considered an act of worship.[74]

7.4.1.1 Who Is Entitled to Exercise *Ijtihād*?

The Ibāḍīs pay particular attention to defining the qualities that the *mujtahid* should possess (*shurūṭ al-ijtihād*).[75] Aṭfayyish makes a distinction between the *mujtahid muṭlaq* (universal *mujtahid*) and the restricted *mujtahid*, called *mujtahid al-madhhab*. The first is considered the highest authority and can call himself *muftī*. He has permission (*ijāza*) to issue novel legal judgements, which are not based on the opinion of another *mujtahid*, even if it is accurate. He can also devise the hermeneutical structure other jurists use to derive their judgements.[76] On the other hand, the *mujtahid al-madhhab* is only qualified to derive rulings according to the rules laid down by the *madhhab*'s founding-fathers. In particular, he must follow this teacher's steps, and he does not have the right to admit anything that his teacher refused and vice versa. Aṭfayyish does not address the question of whether there should be at all times a universal *mujtahid* or if it is possible to have in the meantime more than one. He admits that there may be in history (even in that of the Ibāḍī community) phases in which no *mujtahid muṭlaq* appears.[77]

As far as the question whether a *mujtahid muṭlaq* may follow the opinions of another *mujtahid*, Aṭfayyish answers in the affirmative: the companions of the Prophet also sometimes relied on the opinions of other companions.[78] However, he criticizes the *mujtahid* who refers to the opinions of another

73 *Sharḥ* xvii, 50.
74 *Sharḥ* xvii, 54.
75 Cuperly, *Introduction* 171.
76 *Sharḥ* xvii, 493–494.
77 *Sharḥ* xvii, 494.
78 *Taysīr al-tafsīr* ix, 322, quoted in Ourghi, *Die Reformbewegung in der neuzeitlichen Ibāḍīya* 252.

mujtahid without making any personal effort, because in doing so he neglects the search for knowledge, which is his duty. The *mujtahid* who is able to exercise *ijtihād* is required to do so. The universal *mujtahid* (*mujtahid muṭlaq*) must satisfy the following conditions:

1) He should master the Quran and the *sunna*.
2) He should know all the questions which have long been settled by consensus (*ijmāʿ*). Such knowledge is extremely important as the *mujtahid* should not issue an opinion that contravenes an established consensus unless he is convinced that such consensus was based on special circumstances which have changed or ceased to exist.
3) He should master Arabic; this includes an advanced knowledge of Arabic grammar, inflection, syntax and logic and eloquence of style and rhetoric.
4) Furthermore, he should take into consideration the *fiqh* works of other scholars (Ibāḍī as well non-Ibāḍī) as fundamental elements for the understanding of new legal cases and he should master the works of other law schools.[79]

The principle upon which the advocates of *taqlīd* based their claims was that of reverence for the early generations of Muslims who alone had the right to interpret Islam. Aṭfayyish on the contrary claimed equal participation of all generations in interpreting matters related to both religion and law. The pages of the Ibāḍī reformists abound with criticism of the principle of belief on authority. They argue that the age of precedent was a period in which Islamic law could not be developed, forcing Muslim nations to lose touch with the changing realities of the world. Iron rigidity – claims Aṭfayyish – has never been part of *sharīʿa*, as any rigid doctrine defies the open basis upon which it was built. Any generation has the right to exercise *ijtihād*, as juristic opinions are not valid if there is no compliance in the Muslim community, compliance being an essential part of a valid rule. Even rules which have already been settled and upon which there is a general agreement could be renewed if the conditions for their application have changed (*tajdīd al-taqlīd*).

Reference to Quranic verses supporting the free use of reason or denouncing those who oppose it is widely employed in order to circumscribe the practice of *taqlīd* and to restrict it to matters related to faith and dogma. Belief in God is reinforced by reasoning: in his *ʿaqīda* titled *Kitāb al-jāmiʿ al-ṣaghīr*, Aṭfayyish maintains that the *muqallid* (imitator) is weak in explaining the principles of profession of faith (*tawḥīd*) as a true understanding of the faith is not in *taqlīd*, meaning the adoption of opinions without providing any evidence, but in the

79 *Sharḥ* xvii, 44.

hermeneutical process of *taqyīd* (restriction, qualification), meaning the drawing of its significance out of a text through a process of reasoning.[80]

According to Aṭfayyish, the jurist can accept the *ijtihād* of a previous scholar when it is consistent with his own, and he calls this method of reasoning *taqyīd*, considering it something in between *taqlīd* and *ijtihād*. Even then, the scholar should not simply imitate in the field of law and religion and, although his reasoning is not comparable with that of the most qualified jurists, he is encouraged to reflect and to ask questions. The Quran has elevated reason to a place of first importance. Islam recognizes that man is able by his intellect to arrive at knowledge of God. Aṭfayyish attempts to give reason full authority in interpreting the revealed text. In reaffirming what he believed to be the fundamental attitude of Islam with regard to reason, he strongly opposed any acceptance of belief on authority of others without questioning or objecting.

Taqlīd is like a bridge connecting low-ranking jurists to the *mujtahid*. The latter cannot use *taqlīd* as he has the full competence (*ṣalāḥiyya kāmila*) for autonomous reasoning.[81]

In their judgement, both *mujtahid* and *mutaqallid* can adopt *tarjīḥ* (rule selectivity) as a principle for reforming Islamic law. They may select rules from all schools of law (either Ibāḍī or Sunni) in cases where there are several outcomes upon the same legal issue. *Tarjīḥ* can be considered a form of *istiḥsān*, since a choice is made between alternative interpretations in the interests of justice and in order to alleviate hardship for the believers. The concept of *tarjīḥ* in the Ibāḍī reform movement is also connected to that of reevaluation of diversity in Islamic law, since it calls for a rapprochement among the schools under the umbrella of the common faith in Islam.

According to Aṭfayyish, the disagreement among the scholars (*ikhtilāf al-ʿulamāʾ*) – both Ibāḍīs and Sunnis – should be taken as a sign of God's mercy (*raḥma*) and satisfaction (*rāḥa*), as it paves the way for the search for truth.[82] Nonetheless, this disagreement is possible only in the field of *furūʿ* (substantive law). On the contrary, on matters related to faith (*īmān*) or dogma (*tawḥīd*) there must be unity.[83] The principle that disagreement among scholars is a sign of divine mercy becomes in the reform discourse a call to unity, as his main implication is the duty for the Ibāḍī scholars to study and to teach the

80 *Kitāb al-jāmiʿ al-ṣaghīr* i, 20.
81 *Sharḥ* xvii, 476. See also Kamāl al-Dīn, *Sharḥ Kitāb al-Nīl* v, 272–276.
82 *Sharḥ* xvii, 53–54.
83 *Sharḥ* xvii, 57; see also *Kitāb al-jāmiʿ al-ṣaghīr* i, 80.

works of Sunni jurists, in particular in the fields where there are no special matters of divergence.[84]

Diversity is part of Muslim heritage. In the developing period, jurists derived diverse interpretations from the same sources. At the same time, diverse schools appeared, maximizing juridical discourse and enriching multiple understandings of the basic sources. Because Islam does not recognize the authority to select one of many juristic interpretations for any central institution, Islamic law developed in a free environment. No caliph or ruler in Islamic history was empowered to use his position to outlaw multiple *madhhab*s. Attempts to impose any ruler-sponsored *madhhab* failed. Starting from these considerations, Aṭfayyish underlines how Islamic law preserves some diversity of opinions while maintaining the supremacy of legal sources. In his reformist discourse, diverse interpretations are not offensive to the unity of Islam. On the contrary, according to a famous Prophetic tradition, such diversity is considered a divine blessing. Classical *fiqh* constitutes the shared treasure, the common law of Islam. Sharing this common heritage of Islamic law, each jurist is free to express his opinions. Diverse and even diametrically opposing opinions are consonant with Islam.

How should a jurist act when faced with conflicting judgements? In this case, according to Aṭfayyish, even an imitator (*muqallid*) has the right to limited autonomous reasoning and can choose among the diverse opinions of past authorities those that fit better. On the other hand, the *mujtahid* must not only issue legal advice and test it, it must also compare it with the viewpoints of other scholars. Therefore, "disagreement" turns into a fundamental dialogue among scholars, which helps to further knowledge.[85]

7.4.2 The Role of Human Reasoning and the Sources of Law

According to Aṭfayyish, legal provisions are conjectural and therefore can be empirically tested. Faith and knowledge go hand in hand as Islam is pre-eminently a religion of reason.[86] The man is not deprived of free will, nor must he surrender to predestination. The essence of man's responsibility for his deeds and choices is reason, which defines man's relationship to God. Therefore, reason and revelation cannot be contradictory; only improper and incorrect reasoning and interpretations must be rejected. The real Islam, he maintains, consists of certain beliefs about the greatest questions of human

84 *Sharḥ* xvii, 58.
85 *Sharḥ* xvii, 58ff.
86 Ourghi, *Die Reformbewegung in der neuzeitlichen Ibāḍīya* 203.

life, and certain general principles of human conduct. To enable us to reach these beliefs and embody them in our lives, both reason and revelation are essential. Doubts and knowledge play an important role in religion:

> Doubt (*shakk*) leads to weighing different incompatible opinions (*rujḥān*). Through this, man achieves knowledge, and through knowledge, he achieves certainty (*yaqīn*). He goes from doubt to conjecture (*ẓann*). But, this is necessary because man goes from conjecture to knowledge and from knowledge to certainty. Most of the legal provisions are conjectural. When conjecture is strong, it leads to knowledge. This is like a light that God throws into man's heart and thereby it opens the man's heart.[87]

Human reason is limited and there are certain things that we cannot know by our reason, for example divine essence, because our minds and language are not adequate to grasp the essence of God; certain attributes of God (His word, sight and hearing); the nature of the life to come, its judgement, its pleasures and pains. But, on the other hand, reason can teach us, first of all, that God exists, can tell us that there is a life to come, that our fate in it is connected with the good and evil of our acts, and that some things are good and others bad. By reason, moreover, we can understand the value of prophecy. Prophets are able to transmit to men a message concerning God and to teach them the principles of conduct and a right attitude to belief. These are things that can in principle be known by reason, but which most men do not in fact know, because their reason is imperfect or because mundane passions lead their minds astray. Therefore, God sends Prophets to help men to find the right path.

The textual sources of law coupled with a theory of legal hermeneutics allow Muslim jurists to draw on the content of the Quran and *sunna* and to devise practical legal rulings in specific circumstances. Extratextual sources of law, including juristic consensus and utility, aid the jurist in ruling in cases where the textual sources lack a clear answer to the questions at hand. A legal dialectic in which the jurist moves back and forth between principles of jurisprudence and substantive law is essential to the Islamic jurist's endeavour. It is in the adjustment of theory to fit practice and the reconsideration of practice in light of theory that a jurist carries out his task.

Aṭfayyish does not use the term *uṣūl al-fiqh*, but the term *uṣūl al-dīn*, which also includes the principles of faith.[88] His reformist approach to the

87 Aṭfayyish, *Shāmil al-aṣl wa ʾl-farʿ*, in Ourghi, *Die Reformbewegung in der neuzeitlichen Ibāḍīya* 201–202.

88 Ourghi, *Die Reformbewegung in der neuzeitlichen Ibāḍīya* 197.

hermeneutic consists in the fact that he calls for a return in regarding Quran as the first basis for the religious and juridical teaching of Islam. He calls for *tajdīd al-Qur'ān*, a revival of the Quran, meaning a new interpretation, which conforms to the condition of contemporary time.[89] *Ijtihād* is fundamental for a new interpretation of the Quran, as it is the way to understand the principles (*aḥkām*) of the *sharīʿa*, which are not clearly settled in the Quran, such as the way of performing prayer or the rule concerning the payment of *zakāt*. Jurisprudence (*fiqh*), Aṭfayyish maintains, is the knowledge of the principles (*aḥkām*) of the *sharīʿa* through the use of *ijtihād*.[90]

As far as the *sunna* is concerned, Aṭfayyish makes it clear that the Ibāḍīs shared the rules on the science of traditions with the other schools since they found no reason not to do. He regards highly the *Musnad*, which he holds as the most trustworthy book of Ibāḍī *ḥadīth*, comparable as far as the accuracy of content and the line of transmissions are concerned to the books of al-Bukhārī and Muslim.[91]

In his commentary to *Kitāb al-Nīl*, as well in further works, Aṭfayyish makes clear that he considers authentic only prophetic traditions transmitted through al-Rabīʿ – Abū ʿUbayda – Jābir – companion – Prophet.[92] As far as Sunni traditions are concerned, he considers authentic only those collected into the books of Bukhārī and Muslim.

Moreover, *sunna* is based on the Quran, according to the Prophet's tradition: "I allow and prohibit only what is in the Quran".[93] The authenticity of a tradition is tested not only according to the chain of the transmitters but also through a careful examination of the text. If this does not conform to the Quran, the tradition is considered weak.

Consensus (*ijmāʿ*) and analogy (*qiyās*) must also be based on the Quran and *sunna*.[94] Consensus can be based on traditions (*ijmāʿ naqlī*) but also on *ijtihād* (*ijmāʿ ijtihādī*). The *mujtahid* can confirm previous consensus but can also reject it when it does not conform anymore to community needs. In this way,

89 Aṭfayyish, *Sharḥ ʿaqīdat al-tawḥīd* 210. See also Ourghi, *Die Reformbewegung in der neuzeitlichen Ibāḍīya* 206–224.

90 *Sharḥ* i, 41–42.

91 Francesca, The Concept of Sunna in the Ibāḍī School 97–115.

92 *Jāmiʿ al-shaml* ii, 336, 346.

93 *Taysīr al-Tafsīr* iv, 91 cit. in Ourghi, *Die Reformbewegung in der neuzeitlichen Ibāḍīya* 227. On the concept of *sunna* according to Aṭfayyish, see Ourghi, *Die Reformbewegung in der neuzeitlichen Ibāḍīya* 224–233.

94 Concerning thus he agrees with al-Sālimī. See Ourghi, *Die Reformbewegung in der neuzeitlichen Ibāḍīya* 240.

consensus acquires new vitality and flexibility.[95] On the other hand, recourse to analogy is limited to the cases when no *mujtahid* can express his legal opinion.[96]

7.5 Nūr al-Dīn al-Sālimī and the Reform of Ibāḍī Law

Al-Sālimī was a very prolific writer. Despite his brief life, he left numerous publications spanning from history to law, jurisprudence, Quranic exegesis, dogma and the Arabic language. In the field of *uṣūl al-fiqh*, he wrote a rhymed work called *Shams al-uṣūl*, a commentary (*Ṭalʿat al-shams*) on this, and a polemical work on jurists exercising *ijtihād* without possessing the required conditions (*al-ḥujja al-wāḍiḥa*). In the field of *fiqh*, in addition to the numerous *fatwās* he delivered, he wrote a commentary of the *Musnad al-Rabīʿ b. Ḥabīb*, called *Sharḥ al-Jāmiʿ al-ṣaḥīḥ*, a rhymed commentary of the *Mukhtaṣar al-khiṣāl*, called *Madārij al-kamāl* and a commentary on this titled *Maʿārij al-āmal*, along with further minor works.

The principal source I use in the following analysis is the collection of *fatwās*, titled *Jawābāt al-Imām al-Sālimī*, which prove crucial for an understanding of al-Sālimī's contribution to the flourishing of reform ideas. He was a great expositor of the Ibāḍī creed and tradition and a major proponent of the idea that the renewal of Islam and Muslim societies could be accomplished mainly through a process of legal changes. In his reform agenda not only did he idealize the glorious Ibāḍī past, but he also reinterpreted and reformulated Ibāḍī ideals to respond to the political and social challenges of western powers. As is well known, his fundamental objective was the revival of the imamate in order to reclaim the genuine spirit of Ibāḍī tradition as practised within the early community.

In the six volume *Jawābāt*, al-Sālimī issued *fatwās* and judgements on matters of *ʿibadāt* (prayer, alms, fasting, pilgrimage and so on) and *muʿāmalāt* (marriage and divorce, sales, heritage and so on), reacting to questions posed by his pupil, Abū Zayd ʿAbd Allāh b. Muḥammad b. Razīq al-Riyāmī, in 1321/1903 before the latter returned to his home town of Azkā. Al-Riyāmī titled the collection "Solutions to Problems" (*Ḥall al-mushkilāt*), the present title is due to the editor, Abū Ghaddah ʿAbd al-Sattār, who published the work in Oman in 1996 (introduction 14).

---

95 Ourghi, *Die Reformbewegung in der neuzeitlichen Ibāḍīya* 233–238.

96 Ourghi, *Die Reformbewegung in der neuzeitlichen Ibāḍīya* 238–243.

One element of particular interest in the *Jawābāt* is the chapter on *uṣūl al-fiqh* where the topics of *ijtihād* and *taqlīd* and the role of the *ʿulamāʾ* are discussed. It is in this discussion, as we will see, that an underlying political theory, expressed through jurisprudence, emerges. Al-Sālimī consistently worked to issue *fatwās* based on the fundamental teaching of the Quran and *sunna* as well as on the main Ibāḍī sources, but he also accepted the legal precepts of the Sunni school of law, proving a dynamism of opinions and a genuine spirit of inclusivity and universality. He embraces the principles of *tajdīd* and *talfīq* as the basis of his reasoning, condemning *taqlīd* and upholding *ijtihād*, because – as he says in the introduction to the *Shams al-uṣūl* – "the knowledge of the law (*maʿrifat al-fiqh*) is based on the knowledge of the principle of jurisprudence (*maʿrifat uṣūl al-fiqh*)" (introduction 14). Consistent with this view, he even contradicts the opinions of his teacher Mājid b. Khamīs al-ʿAnbarī, for example regarding readings of the Quran during the funeral prayer (*ṣalāt al-mayyit*) and the option sale (*bayʿ al-khiyār*). In the first case, he maintains that the prayers due to the deceased cannot correspond with the time of the official prayers (introduction, 9; i, 511–512; v, 572). As far as the *bayʿ al-khiyār*, he disregards its use because he argues that in specific circumstances it can be an expedient (*ḥīla*) for taking advantage of the price thus covering the unlawful practice of usury (iv, 270, 297).

The main strength of the work by al-Sālimī comes from the avenues it opens rather than from the specific answers he provides. In answering the questions, he is confronted with several challenges, which he endeavours to address using both the tools of the Ibāḍī traditions and his autonomous reasoning. The way he proceeds and the seriousness of his work remain unmatched among his immediate contemporaries in Oman and his skills in mastering the *sharīʿa* allowed him to elaborate his own system of categorization.

Quoting the Maghribi jurist Sulaymān b. Yakhlaf al-Mazātī (d. 471/1078), al-Sālimī sets no limit to the use of the *ijtihād*: the *mujtahid* is allowed to apply his reasoning to legal matters that have not been clearly dealt with in the Quran, in the *sunna*, or in the Ibāḍī tradition (*āthār*), except questions pertaining the dogma and the principles of faith (vi, 345–346). As far as the Ibāḍī tradition is concerned, al-Sālimī considers topics appropriate for the *ijtihād* (*al-masʾala al-ijtihādiyya*) those whose ruling is debated among the Ibāḍī community, such as the case of the *ribā al-faḍl* versus the *ribā al-nasīʾa*. His *fatwā* on this subject provides us with interesting insights into his legal reasoning (vi, 334). He states that the prohibition of the *ribā al-faḍl*, which occurs in contracts of sale where there is an increase in terms of the exchanged amount, is general (*muṭlaq*), therefore it is referred also to the increase in the amount over a period of time (*ribā al-nasīʾa*). The opinion of the Ibāḍī scholars forbidding only the *ribā al-nasīʾa* – such as Abū Saʿīd al-Kudamī – proves to be weak. Moreover, already the Maghribi Abū Sākin al-Shammākhī (d. 792/1389), author of the *Kitāb al-īḍāḥ*, maintained that qualified jurists could apply their reasoning on the topic, thus proving that the Ibāḍī rules concerning usury were not regarded as definitive. The reasoning process, according to al-Sālimī, is affected by the nature of the text's evidence: the more definitive the text is, the less of a role is played by reasoning in the text's understanding.

In areas where the principles of the Ibāḍī faith are involved, the work of the *ijtihād* is restricted. This is the case of the distribution of the *zakāt* and the *kaffāra* (the donation due to be paid when the fast is broken) among the community's members only according to the principle of *walāya* and *barāʾa* (ii, 11, 249), and the permanent prohibition of marriage between the man and woman guilty of unlawful intercourses (ii, 566–567). According to al-Sālimī, they are considered sinners (*mufāsiq*) and the *ijtihād* cannot be used in cases where a judgement of *fisq* (immorality)[97] is issued, therefore *barāʾa* must be declared against them.

What endangers Muslim societies is the attempt to take for granted what should evolve and to change what should remain as it is. Al-Sālimī is a passionate supporter of a continuous undertaking of the *ijtihād*, which he conceived, as did his contemporary Aṭfayyish, as a return to the original Ibāḍī tradition. A central point in his writings is how to protect Ibāḍī identity from the social and cultural effect of colonialism on Muslim societies. He tends to set clear boundaries between Muslims and Christian Europeans, warning the Omanis to be vigilant against the pervasive effects of their cultural and political dominance on the Ibāḍī *madhhab* (v, 214–216). His reform discourse is dominated by an ideological rhetoric about Muslims versus Chistian Europeans, just rulers versus tyrants, separation versus unity and renewal versus imitation.[98]

In his historical works, al-Sālimī demonstrates that Ibadism was the first, and therefore the purest, *madhhab* of Islam. In the *Jawābāt* he reaffirms the specificity, independence and importance of Ibadism within the Muslim community, claiming its link to the righteous people of Nahrawān. In a *fatwā* dedicated to the Ibāḍī attitude towards ʿAlī and the early Kharijites, he discusses the events that led them to Nahrawān, the rationale behind opposing the arbitration and the obligation of *walāya* towards them and of *barāʾa* towards

97 *Fāsiq/mufāsiq* is the one who has committed a great sin as well as the one who perpetuates in committing minor sins. The qualification of *fisq* is the opposite of *ʿadl*. Only the *ʿādil*, the irreproachable Muslim, can act as witness or as a *walī*, the nearest relative who gives the bride in marriage.

98 Ghazal, *Islamic Reform and Arab Nationalism* 36.

ʿAlī, who unjustly massacred them (vi, 151–154). In a certain way, he begins a process of rationalization and systematization of Ibāḍī-Omani history, which proved to be crucial for the further development of the school.[99]

He is convinced that advancement in a society requires that people's political and social conduct must adhere to clear shared moral values. One of the most important means of protecting Ibadism from being corrupted is to follow the principles and beliefs the Ibāḍī community has agreed upon down the centuries, which provided them with the moral basis for their values, customs and traditions. He holds that, in order to apply the Islamic-Ibāḍī law in a way appropriate to the contemporary age, a source of authority is needed that will govern the application of the correct legal rulings. This source of authority can be envisaged in the *ʿulamāʾ*, the great scholars, whose primary mission is to employ the pure Ibāḍī doctrine as a framework for both thought and action in order to fight against the emergence of numerous deviations from the correct understanding of Ibāḍī teaching, which undermined knowledge and learning and weakened the Ibāḍī societies. In keeping with the images of the *ʿulamāʾ* as the "people of binding and loosing", "tying and untying", he strongly advocates their primacy as an authoritative source of guidance at a both religious and political level (vi, 541–542).

Al-Sālimī envisages an elitist division of the scholars into *muqallid*s and *mujtahid*s; only the latter, possessing the required conditions (*darajat al-ijtihād*), i.e. a full knowledge of the Quran, *sunna* and the opinions of previous authorities, can use his personal reasoning. As an adjunct to these qualifications, the Ibāḍī *mujtahid* should also be familiar with the Sunni jurisprudence and legal methods (vi, 276–277). The *mujtahid*'s assessments are binding according to the famous tradition "Every *mujtahid* is correct", because only God can judge the soundness of his rulings. He will be rewarded for his correct reasoning, but even if he proves to be wrong, he will receive the "reward of the *ijtihād*", meaning that the full expenditure of his effort in issuing the rulings deserves the divine blessing (vi, 282–283).

As soon as a person has obtained the capacity to perform *ijtihād*, he cannot abandon such a duty and turn to another for ruling, because he would renege his responsibilities towards God and the community. The community must recognize the role of the *mujtahid* and follow his judgements on any relevant matter.

Nonetheless, according to al-Sālimī, the opinion of a less qualified jurist can be binding even if it is contradicted by the opinion of a jurist with a better expertise, if a question of public interest is involved. Indeed, he integrates the

---

99 Coppola, Al-Sālimī and the Ibāḍī Theology 321.

principle of legal certainty into the law-finding process, asserting that in cases where an estate has been distributed (or partially distributed) among the heirs following the opinion of a jurist, which all the heirs have agreed upon, this opinion is binding, even if it proves to be less accurate compared to the opinion of a more learned jurist (vi, 380–381).

7.5.1 Reform and Activism: the Restoration of the Imamate in Oman

A central point in al-Sālimī's reform discourse is the restoration of the imamate in Oman, the theoretical framework for which is based on his theories about religious authority and the role of the *ʿulamāʾ* within the society. He argues that, when political thought is disconnected from Islamic principles, many Muslims begin thinking in a way that legitimates unlawful forms of power. The main mission of the *ʿulamāʾ* is to strengthen the state and ground it in the *sharīʿa* within a process of reform, which places legal, spiritual and political discourse in an analogous relationship to the *sharīʿa*. Once the *sharīʿa* is expanded to include the political and ethical dimension, it becomes possible to create a theoretical space in which an authoritative Islamic reasoning can take place on the basis of the genuine principle of the Ibāḍī tradition. Therefore, the debate about the role of *ijtihād* and *taqlīd* assumes a new dimension in which its meta-legal and political aspects are accentuated.

In Oman, the debate on the imamate and legitimate leadership forms part, according to Wilkinson, of the Omani nationalist discourse, seeking identity through the assertion of a religious ideology.[100] It goes back as early as the deposing of *imām* al-Ṣalt b. Mālik (r. 237/851–272/856) and the beginning of a civil war in the mid to late 9th century.

In political terms, the search for identity in al-Sālimī's work meant the rejection both of British colonialism and of Āl Bū Saʿīdī rulers due to their dependence to British power. Al-Sālimī played a key role in the restoration of the imamate in 1913 by mediating both inter- and intra-tribal affairs and converting the tribes to the idea of restoring the imamate.[101] Apparently, he made his decision on restoring the imamate in Oman during the pilgrimage to Mecca in 1906 after consulting the Maghribi Ibāḍīs, but only seven years later was he able to carry out his project to depose Sultan Fayṣal b. Turkī and declare the imamate. He succeeded in gaining the support of both the Ghāfirī and Hināwī confederations for the cause of the restoration of the imamate, thus overcoming the

---

100 Wilkinson, *The Imamate Tradition of Oman* 10.

101 His role in the restoration of the imamate has been reported by his son Muḥammad in his work *Nahḍa al-aʿyān bi-ḥurriyyat ʿUmān*.

natural tendency of Oman's tribal organization to work against national unity. Ḥimyār b. Nāṣir al-Nabhānī, *shaykh* of the Ghāfirī faction, in particular, played a crucial role in calling an assembly of notables in May 1913, which elected Sālim b. Rāshid al-Kharūṣī as *imām*. As the latter initially refused the appointment, al-Sālimī had no scruples about the end justifying the means. He threatened him with the death penalty, arguing that if a suitable candidate is elected as *imām* and he refuses to accept the appointment he must be killed, as by refusing the position of *imām* he is working against God's laws.[102]

Sālim b. Rāshid al-Kharūṣī's election was due to a combination of different factors: his personal character and religiosity, his Kharūṣī lineage which placed him in continuity with a line of prestigious medieval *imām*s, his relationship to al-Sālimī (he was his son-in-law) and the close relationship of his tribe, the Banū Kharūṣ with the tribe of Ḥimyār, the Banū Riyām.[103]

Within months of his election, Sālim b. Rāshid al-Kharūṣī raised an army, which succeeded in taking Nizwā on June 5, thus ensuring control for the imamate of the interior Omani regions. Fearing for the safety of Muscat and Matrah, the British government of India offered Indian Army troops to Sultan Fayṣal b. Turkī to defend his capital. The battle of Bayt al-Falaj in 1915 stopped the advance of the imamate forces on Muscat but it left the interior in the hands of the imamate, and this de facto division of the country, implicitly recognized by the Treaty of al-Sīb in 1920, continued until 1950.[104] The imamate, confined to the interior, was able to play its traditional game, containing dynastic and tribal ambitions whilst trying to maintain some sort of unified religious state. This cooling off period was followed by another outburst of violence. The end result was the unification of all of Oman. According to Amal Ghazal, the death of al-Sālimī in 1914 and the ratification of the Sīb agreement marked the end of any discourse about the restoration of the imamate within the Omani reform movement.[105]

In a long chapter of the *Jawābāt* devoted to the imamate (i, 540–555), al-Sālimī exposes his ideas about the restoration of legitimate power in Ibāḍī communities. He articulates a metaphysical view of power related to an ideal past but bound up also with the contemporary nationalist movement. The implication of his ethical stance is that obedience is given to a person insofar he represents/embodies rules that are regarded as binding. This view serves as

102 Al-Sālimī, *Jawābāt* i, 542. The episode of the denial of the appointment as *imām* is reported by Muḥammad b. Nūr al-Dīn al-Sālimī in his *Nahḍat al-aʿyān*, 162–163.

103 Peterson, The Revival of the Ibāḍī Imāmate in Oman 167.

104 Peterson, *Oman's Insurgencies*, 35–36.

105 Ghazal, *Islamic Reform and Arab Nationalism* 35–36.

an attractive doctrine in the struggle against enemies. The cause, and hence the solution, of the present decay of Muslim societies, which paved the road to Western supremacy, lay with the Ibāḍīs. The fall of Islam was not just the product of intellectual or institutional failures, or even of historical changes, it was more immediately the result of the fall of individual Muslims' obedience to God. The revival of faith at the individual level was the first step in revitalizing Ibāḍī social and political life. Intellectually, this proved to be the most complex dimension of his call. The only way to open up space for reform was to rejuvenate Ibāḍī Islam as a movement and to purify the Ibāḍī faith, explicating its ethos and putting its teachings into practice.

Al-Sālimī defines his effort in terms of the Islamic concept of *tajdīd*, which serves as the fulcrum of his synthesis, his struggle against stagnation in traditional Islam and his debate with the West.[106] He uses *tajdīd* as an historical paradigm to relate political exigencies to faith, mobilize Ibāḍīs and, above all, claim the authority to reinterpret and rationalize the Islamic faith. *Tajdīd* is a process, which begins at the individual level and encompasses the whole society, involving a qualitative change in the traditional worldview, moving it toward modernity. On the other hand, he chastises *taqlīd* insofar as it led to injustice and inefficiency making the *sharīʿa* ineffectual and undermining it as a normative basis of the political community.

Reiterating his stock argument in favour of reform, al-Sālimī asserted that Islam recognized no distinction between the spiritual and the mundane, between faith and politics. The revival of Ibadism hinged on its control of politics. The *sharīʿa* had to lay equal claim to the public and private lives of Muslims, and to do that it would have to be rationalized to strengthen its hold over Muslim social conduct and to reaffirm the fusion of Islam and politics. If there were no imamate, the whole reason for revelation would be called into question, for religious teachings were not sent by God to be ignored. Hence, not only does the true faith lead to political action, but also the very existence of religion is predicated on political goals. Al-Sālimī concludes that the imamate (and hence its restoration) is a religious obligation (*wājib*) and a duty (*farḍ*) according to the Quran, *sunna* and the consensus of the community (*ijmāʿ*).[107]

The convergence of Ibāḍī piety and religious values with political objectives found its embodiment in the doctrine of the obligation to accept the appointment as *imām* if there are no further candidates.[108] In a *fatwā*, reported in the *Jawābāt*, he argues as following:

106 Sālimī, *Jawābāt* i, 235ff.
107 On this point see also al-Sālimī, *Sharḥ al-Jāmiʿ al-Ṣaḥīḥ* i, 99–100.
108 Al-Sālimī, *Jawābāt* i, 574.

> The denial to take up the position as *imām* by the one who possesses the required conditions is a denial of the very essence of the imamate because the basis of its principles is that there must be an *imām*. ʿUmar b. al-Khaṭṭāb (May God bless him) ordered to behead the people of the *shurā* if they had not reached an agreement [about the investiture of the new caliph] within three days. Abū ʿUbayda (May the mercy of God be upon him) chose Abū ʾl-Khaṭṭāb al-Maʿāfirī [as *imām*] for the people of the Maghrib and he told them: "If he declines, kill him!" Thus, they might be encouraged in the knowledge (*ʿilm*), which God provided them in His perfect Light. However, the one who needs to be encouraged in the knowledge is like the one who hesitates, and one who causes harm (*ḍarar*), either material or spiritual, and it is lawful to kill him. Don't you think that the one who refuses [the knowledge] is like the one who pulls down the faith from its very foundations? He is an unpaired harm and an unpaired cause of corruption (*mafsada*). People of sound mind (*ʿaqil*) must defend themselves from such a corruption as soon as possible.[109]

Al-Sālimī stresses that carrying out the obligation of the imamate to the best of one's capacity is among the most meritorious of righteous deeds. In fact, the just *imām* (*al-imām al-ʿādil*) will be the first to enter Paradise, before the people whose only desire is to serve God and the faithful believer whose heart remains stuck in the mosque from the time he leaves to the time he comes back.[110]

He places a remarkable emphasis on justice (*ʿadl*) as the guiding virtue in law, ethics and most of all politics. Justice is epitome of religious piety, political virtue, moral rectitude and pursuit of knowledge, qualities that according to the Ibāḍī principle give the person right to the *walāya*, the agreement of the scholars.[111]

The scholars (*ʿulamāʾ*) are conceived as the carriers of the knowledge of the *sharīʿa* and examples of its teachings, they have superiority over the members of the community in their capacity for interpreting the *sharīʿa*, which is inclusive of just ruling policies. Thus, their authority over the *sharīʿa* provides them with all political authority in electing the *imām* because:

> They are the *imāms*' guidance, those who can loose and bind, the expert of the mundane affairs, and the deputies of the God's Prophets on earth. God ordered to the people to address them for every important matter. It is said: "Ask those

109 Al-Sālimī, *Jawābāt* i, 552.
110 Al-Sālimī, *Sharḥ al-Jāmiʿ al-Ṣaḥīḥ* i, 111.
111 Al-Sālimī, *Sharḥ al-Jāmiʿ al-Ṣaḥīḥ* i, 112.

> deeply embedded in knowledge (*ahl al-dhikr*)[112] if you don't know". [The Quran] says: "But if they had referred it back to the Messenger or to those of authority among them, then the ones who can draw correct conclusions from it would have known about it".[113] If you know that, you must recognize that only the agreement (*ʿaqd*) settled by the *ʿulamāʾ* is binding.[114]

Al-Sālimī stresses the importance of the correlation between the possession of knowledge and legitimate authority, which, according to Adam Gaiser, stretches back to the doctrines of the early *Muḥakkima*.[115]

In his *Jawābāt*, al-Sālimī identifies the trait of *ʿilm*, knowledge, as a fundamental requirement for the full *imām* and condition that identifies the best candidate to the position (i, 540). In case of necessity, when the hardship of the political situation prevailing in the country requires the presence of a leader to deal with, an *imām* with lesser degree of knowledge (*imām daʿīf*) can be appointed. However, his right to the people's obedience is conditional on his behaviour: if he behaves in an unlawful way the people have the right to rebel against him (i, 541).[116] When no optimal leader exists, the religious scholars (*ʿulamāʾ*) play the crucial role of advising and guiding the "weak" *imām*. Al-Sālimī's configuration of the imamate is consistent with the Omani-Ibāḍī medieval sources, which accommodate *imāms* with no knowledge trying to create a working institution of imamate, which embodied the authoritative role of the community, represented by the *ʿulamāʾ*, in relation to its leader.[117]

In the state of secrecy (*kitmān*), in which no *imām* exists, the leadership of the community is entrusted to the *ʿulamāʾ*, who lead and advise the community until the time when an *imām* can be properly elected. The duty of the *ʿulamāʾ* is to appoint the best man available, providing that, in the absence of the right man, they appoint the best man they can. Al-Sālimī shows a certain degree of political pragmatism maintaining that in politics one must make compromises to attain benefits. In fact, he affirms that all forms of recognized political authority (*sulṭān, imāra*) are preferable to anarchy (*fitna*),[118] and the rulers can lawfully exercise their authority, including levying taxes, as long as they act according to the principle of justice (*ʿadl*) (v, 7).

---

112 Reference to Quran 16:43 and 21:7: "So ask the people of the message if you do not know".
113 Quran 4:83.
114 Al-Sālimī, *Jawābāt* i, 541–542.
115 Gaiser, *Muslims, Scholars, Soldiers* 74.
116 On the question if obedience is due to the unjust *imām*, see also Al-Sālimī, *Sharḥ al-Jāmiʿ al-Ṣaḥīḥ* i, 108.
117 Gaiser, *Muslims, Scholars, Soldiers* 111–113.
118 Al-Sālimī, *Sharḥ al-Jāmiʿ al-Ṣaḥīḥ* i, 109.

Moreover, once, when asked about the obedience due by the people of Jaʿlān in Oman to their governor (*amīr*) Saʿīd b. Sālim, al-Sālimī answered that since they acknowledged (*bāyaʿū*) him as their leader, they have to follow him, according to the Quran (Q 5:1; 17:34) (i, 542).

The divine protection of the community is not a result of any infallible source of orthodoxy in a person, but in the entire community, actualized through a process of mutual correction, which according to the Ibāḍī principle is represented by the *walāya* and *barāʾa* dynamics. The *ʿulamāʾ* have the paramount responsibility to command good and forbid evil, thus protecting the community from error in a continuous historical process. Therefore, only with their investiture (*tawliyya*) the *imām* or the leader assumes full powers and deserves the approval (*walāya*) and the obedience (*ṭāʿa*) of the community (i, 550).

When we appreciate al-Sālimī's view of imamate and its relationship to community, we can see the political potential of this doctrine. His position over the years consolidated into a distinct notion that political power was the logical objective of faith. Faith turned into an active and dynamic process, and the struggle for salvation became manifest in a quest for a virtuous order.

The ethical and cultural basis of the Ibāḍī state makes the appointment of leaders an issue of great concern and puts it under the responsibility of the *ʿulamāʾ*, "the people of loosening and binding", who ensure the enforcement of virtuous leadership in place of existing mundane rulers (i, 566 ff.).

Al-Sālimī conceives the imamate in ahistorical terms as an ideal form of government because it creates the conditions most conducive to living according to Islam. The nature of the leadership is expected to confirm that it was based on the sovereignty of God.

7.5.2 Religious Authority and the Prophetic *Sunna*

Both Aṭfayyish and al-Sālimī wrote extensively on *ḥadīth*, making clear that they shared rules on the science of traditions with the other schools since they found no reason not to do. In particular, al-Sālimī wrote a celebrated commentary on the *Musnad al-Rabīʿ b. Ḥabīb*, called *Sharḥ al-Jāmiʿ al-Ṣaḥīḥ*, which contributed to disseminating the text further among the Omani and Maghribi Ibāḍī communities.

The 12th century arrangement of the *Musnad* by al-Rabīʿ, written by Abū Yaʿqūb al-Warjlānī, gained momentum within the works of the Ibāḍī reformists. It reinforces the role of the first three Ibāḍī Basran *imāms*, Jābir b. Zayd, Abū ʿUbayda and al-Rabīʿ, in transmitting the prophetic *sunna*, through lines which go back both to the Medinan tradition (Ibn ʿAbbās, ʿĀʾisha, Anas b. Mālik,

Abū Hurayra) and to the Iraqi tradition (Abdallāh Ibn Masʿūd). The *Musnad* highlights the position of the *sunnat al-nabī* as second root of law after the Quran, and as guiding principle in all human activities, whenever the Quran does not provide decisive answers. In his reformist discourse, al-Sālimī makes clear that the Prophetic *sunna*, as transmitted by the companions, surpasses all other traditions, both on the level of the contents and of the methods. Only its binding legal force can unite Muslims around a single point of view, since it preceded the emergence of the schools of law and the differences that arose over a wide range of topics.

In al-Sālimī's view the *Musnad* endorses the idea that Omani Ibadism is deeply connected with both the Medinan and Basran traditions, as expressed in the celebrated Omani saying that the egg of knowledge (*ʿilm*) was laid in Medina, it was hatched in Basra and then the "Bird of Knowledge" flew to Oman.[119] In the introduction, he underlines the Jābir connection with a large number of companions, in particular Ibn ʿAbbās, who was his teacher and close friend, and ʿĀʾisha, as well as his role in passing the "knowledge" to Abū ʿUbayda.[120] The latter is considered the most prominent jurist among the early Ibāḍī authorities in Basra; he was also an excellent political leader, ensuring the spread of Ibadism in the Maghrib through the "bearers of learning". Al-Sālimī suggests that Abū ʿUbayda met some companions, such as his teacher Jābir. He quotes, in particular, Jābir b. ʿAbdallāh, Anas b. Mālik, Abū Hurayra, Abū Saʿīd al-Khudrī and ʿĀʾisha.[121] Therefore, he considers the traditions from Abū ʿUbayda to a companion as *ḥadīth muttaṣil*, meaning traditions with a continuous chain of transmitters, in which each narrator has heard the tradition from his teacher. This high-ranking classification can be applied to the majority of the traditions collected in the *Musnad* since they present an uninterrupted chain of transmitters going back to the Prophet. Al-Sālimī considers authentic even the *ḥadīth mursal*, where the link between the narrator and the Prophet is omitted, insofar they are reported on the authority of a trustworthy transmitter, such as al-Rabīʿ. The latter plays a central role in al-Sālimī's reconstruction of the early development of the Ibāḍī school. He underlines his Omani origins (he was born in Oman and retired to Oman in the latter part of his life), and his role in spreading the knowledge from Basra to other regions of the Muslim world.[122] Al-Rabīʿ is the "common link" in the chains of transmitters who, trained at his school, contributed in propagating Ibadism in Oman (Maḥbūb

---

119 Al-Sālimī, *al-Lumʿa* 12. See also Almamari, *Oman and Ibadism* 48; Wilkinson, *Ibâḍism* 67.
120 Al-Sālimī, *Sharḥ* i, 1–9.
121 Al-Sālimī, *Sharḥ* i, 6. See also Ennami, *Studies* (online edition) 54.
122 Al-Sālimī, *Sharḥ* i, 4.

b. al-Ruḥayl), Ḥaḍramawt (Abū Ayyūb Wā'il b. Ayyūb), Khurāsān (Hāshim b. ʿAbdallāh al-Khurāsānī) and Iraq (al-Khamm b. Ghufayr).

Al-Sālimī affirmed the position of the *Musnad* as the most reliable collection of *ḥadīth* within the Ibāḍī school and compared it to the Sunni canonical collections. His main arguments supporting the centrality of the Ibāḍī "golden" past echo those he used in his historical works to propagate the myth of the ideal transmission of knowledge through the first three *imāms* of the school.[123] Using the lenses of an ideal past, he reaffirms his discourses on political reformism. His commentary on the *Musnad* thus acquires a political connotation linked to his ideas on the role of religious authorities in defining the political leadership.

Following the example of the charismatic members of the early community is the only way to return to a correct understanding of the revealed law. He strongly condemns deviation from the example of the early community. Commenting on the *ḥadīth* saying: "You must deny the one who acts in a way contrary to what we ordered", al-Sālimī argues that adhering to both justice and scriptural teachings is one of the pillars of Islam. Innovations, such as adopting Western dress codes or Western habits, violate this command and therefore cause disruption within the community.[124]

Invoking the authority of the first Basran *imāms*, al-Sālimī argues that only their traditions must be followed even when they contradict rules which have been previously accepted among the Ibāḍīs, such as those stating that the inheritance of the client who has no relatives must be distributed among his kin (*jins*). Indeed, the tradition "the patronate (*walā'*) is a tie like the kinship tie", reported in the *Musnad*, implies that the patronate detaches the client from his natal group giving him full membership of the patron's group. As consequence of this assimilation, the patron is supposed to inherit as an agnate of his client in the absence of any other certain heir. Al-Sālimī argues that *Musnad*'s tradition is confirmed by another tradition by Jābir – Ibn ʿAbbās – Prophet, reported by the Sunni al-Daraquṭnī, stating that when the client of the companion and uncle of the Prophet, Ḥamza ibn ʿAbd al-Muṭṭalib (*c.*570–625) died, the Prophet shared his estate between the client's daughter and Ḥamza's daughter, considering them as sisters. Abū Nūḥ Ṣāliḥ al-Dahhān was among the early Ibāḍī scholars to accept the doctrine of the agnatization of the client. Al-Sālimī acknowledges that the majority of Ibāḍīs disapprove of this doctrine. However, the tradition maintaining that the inheritance of the client who has no heirs must be distributed among his people is weak,

123 *Lumʿa* 5–8, 12–18.
124 *Sharḥ* i, 114–115.

and jurists have the right to exercise their *ijtihād* in order to restore the right prophetic *sunna*.[125]

7.6 Conclusion: the Rapprochement to the Sunnis

The 19th and early 20th century Ibāḍī revivalist scholars created a new network of authority, which relied on intellectual and genealogical connections as well as on the access to written textual sources circulating in the community thanks to the activities of the Ibāḍī printing presses. New practices were implemented; scholarship grew, giving impulse to the reform discourse based on the purification of Ibāḍī Islam from older or locally generated accretions and on a rapprochement to Sunni Islam. The locations of the Ibāḍī reform movement were no less relevant than the scholars. Ibāḍīs have always been actively travelling "in search of knowledge", but during this period the main centres of Ibadism were incorporated into a wider, globalized vision of Islam. They formed an Ibāḍī *ecumene* of scholars, intellectuals and reformers relying on the same texts and striving for the same ideals. Two personalities stood out in this context: the Mzabi Muḥammad Aṭfayyish and the Omani Nūr al-Dīn al-Sālimī. It may be stated without exaggeration that several trends in contemporary Ibāḍī thought can be traced back to the influence, direct or indirect, of these outstanding Islamic thinkers.

The commentary to the work by al-Muṣʿabī, gave Aṭfayyish the opportunity to expose his own conception of *ijtihād, taqlīd* and hermeneutics. In the treatment of law, Aṭfayyish undertook significant reform initiatives and demanded the right of independent investigation. He made no attempt to reconcile Islam with Western civilization: his reform project aimed at a return to a pure Islam and the elimination of all innovation. Only in this way would Muslim countries be protected from the moral as well as the physical assault of European power.

As Wilkinson states, Aṭfayyish developed the ideas of a neo-Ibadism, which was favourable to interaction with the other Muslim schools, and of a pan-Ibadism, which aimed at strengthening the relationships within the Ibāḍī communities and at developing a common ground for rejuvenating the movement.[126] His contributions in restoring religious principles of rationalism had a forceful brunt in founding contemporary Ibadism and projecting its cultural renaissance. The foundational aspect of his works can mainly be seen in his synthesis of Ibāḍī and Sunni principles, in his legal reform and in

125 *Sharḥ* iii, 418–419.

126 Wilkinson, *The Imamate Tradition of Oman* 243–245.

his defence of rational and religious liberty. His struggle, along with that of other Ibāḍī reformists, resulted in an unprecedented scale of rethinking and renewal in the school, which has represented a momentous contribution today in Ibāḍīs reclaiming their intellectual identity within the Muslim world.

In the same vein, al-Sālimī's discourse on Ibāḍī reform attested the central role played by the drive for identity and cultural authenticity. The problem with colonialism was essentially cultural. Its main evil laid in the propagation of moral and ethical models that ran contrary to the teachings of Islam. Undermining Islamic culture had in turn engendered the economic and political marginalization of Muslims. Al-Sālimī's significance does not lie in his scholarly contributions per se, but in creating an intellectual medium – in the form of a large number of texts – wherein he sets an example for independent religious thinking and activism. In many ways, in al-Sālimī's discourse, authority and plan of action were influenced by and drew upon the tradition of revival and reform in Ibadism. He viewed himself as part of this tradition. The legacy of Ibāḍī heritage in Basra was of immediate relevance to the articulation of al-Sālimī's programme. The backgrounds, ideas and modes of operation of the first Ibāḍī imāms showed such a clear resemblance to al-Sālimī's conception of ideal religious leadership that they were tapped into his reformist discourse.

Due to his ability to articulate his political programme effectively, al-Sālimī's writings disseminated his ideas far and wide within the Ibāḍī communities, placing his arguments at the centre of intellectual and political debate.

Both al-Sālimī in Oman and Aṭfayyish in the Mzab referred to the search for an Ibāḍī identity in modernity, which can blossom only in a rapprochement with Sunni Islam.

Conclusion

The objective of this volume is to provide its readers with more insight into Ibāḍī law and jurisprudence and to open the way to future inquiries on Islamic law beyond the parameters of a main Sunni tradition and Shiʿi and Ibāḍī subsidiary traditions. Recent decades in Islamic studies have seen an enlargement of sources and resources, including many valuable Ibāḍī texts that must be fully integrated into the field.

One of the main difficulties scholars must face in reconstructing the history of early Islamic schools of law is the very uneven survival of texts by ancient authorities. In the case of the Ibāḍī school an added difficulty is associated with the ignorance of its literary patrimony, which has been available to the scholarship only recently. The study of Ibāḍī legal thought presents a dual challenge: navigating through the – still partially unexplored – rich Ibāḍī legal heritage on one side, and tackling the vexed question of the authenticity of the ancient sources of Islamic law on the other. As I have argued in this book, not only do the early Ibāḍī sources reflect the legal debate underway during the first centuries of Islam, but they also provide us with valuable raw data that adds new dimensions to the whole history of medieval Islam. Though extreme caution should be exercised in analyzing early texts, their study proves essential for an understanding of the genesis of Islamic history and civilization. As I argued in the first three chapters of this book, Ibāḍīs were embedded into the intellectual milieu of Basra, which, along with Kufa, the other garrison city in Iraq, was the cradle of the formation process of Islamic law and theology. However, the early Ibāḍī sources challenge the assumption that the 8th century schools of law depended on geographically based collective doctrines, as in many cases they favour Hijazi authorities, due to Jābir's connections with Ibn ʿAbbās and other Meccan transmitters, in particular ʿIkrima and ʿAmr b. Dīnār. The notion of transformation of schools from regional to personal ones is problematic due to the scarcity of evidence substantiating the very existence of legal opinions that can be explicitly attributed to a collective regional doctrine. On the contrary, numerous circles of masters and pupils already existed at the beginning of the 8th century, constituting the core from which the personal schools developed into doctrinal ones. Early Ibāḍī juristic repertoire derives from an allegiance to individual authorities. Jābir received from Ibn ʿAbbās and other scholars operating in and outside Basra and Iraq, who had in turn received from the Successors and the Companions. They constitute the individual voices a consensus could be based on. We can label these jurists alternatively as "Basrans", "Kufans", "Meccans", "Medinans" but there

 | HTTPS://DOI.ORG/10.1163/9789004765764-010

is no indication that they culled their doctrine from a local anonymous legal practice that had a degree of geographically based uniformity.[1]

Early Ibadism possessed a vast corpus of opinions attributed to Jābir, its founding father, and to his immediate followers, relying on scriptural sources, mainly the Quran, and on traditions from other earlier authorities, but also on analogy and other rational methods taken from Basran Muʿtazilite circles. As is well known, Muʿtazilite rational theology had a greater impact on Ibāḍīs, as well as on Imani Shiʿites, than on the Sunni mainstream.[2] The struggle between relying on "tradition" or on rational criteria was very sharp in the generations of Abū ʿUbayda and al-Rabīʿ, and extended well beyond disagreement over juridical problems, to include also the polemic on Quran creation and free will.

In this work I have attempted to show that since the beginning the Ibāḍīs developed a cohesive legal system, which preserves its internal consistency even when the solutions given to the legal cases coincide (totally or partially) with those provided by other schools of law. Similarities between Ibāḍīs and Sunnis (and Shiʿites as well) were not simply copying, but a more complex process of crosscutting and mutual borrowing, which overlapped among all schools of law. I agree with Robert Gleave's arguments that the study of Islamic law has been methodologically impoverished by the assumption that non-Sunni legal systems mainly consist of borrowings from the wider Sunni milieu on one hand, and on the other that their internal dynamics are "exotic" at a point that they are not comparable to those of their Sunni counterparts. The result of such stereotypes is a lack of recognition of the great diversity which dominated the development of Islamic law.[3]

The analysis of the legal cases I presented in this book helps in appreciating the early stage of Islamic law not as a linear progress leading towards maturity, but rather as an unfolding process, a dynamic period of disagreement, dialogue, hybridity, creativity and negotiation. Studying early Islam also raises the question of the positioning of Islam with cognate legal cultures of the area, namely the Jewish and Christian legal cultures. A body of recent scholarship has attempted to stress the continuity between Late Antiquity and Islam. In particular, authors like Neuwirth, Sinai and Zelletin seek a more nuanced understanding of how to appreciate the Quran in its Jewish and Christian context, assuming that the myth of origins that identifies the beginning of Islam with the ministry of Muḥammad introduces a sharp dichotomy between the revelation and the pre-Islamic era; this dichotomy overlooks the notion

1 Hallaq, From Regional to Personal Schools of Law? 16.

2 Arjomand, *Sociology of Shiʿite Islam* 17–18.

3 Gleave, Sectarianism and Integration 14–15.

that Islam did not emerge in a vacuum. Lena Salaymeh points out that Late Antiquity persisted into the 8th and even 9th century and she suggests the definition of "Islamic Late Antiquity" to refer to the period from the beginning of Islamic history to the end of the 8th century.[4] The construction of a line of continuity between late antiquity and Islam can be a useful heuristic tool that would account for the conditions that made possible the emergence of Islam: what was to become Islamic civilization is related to late antique order in terms of continuity as one of its most successful crystallizations, but also in the direction of change as a religion of ecumenical vocation and ambition. Uncovering this dynamic past requires interdisciplinary approaches and conversations among scholars with different areas of expertise.

Like any other school, Ibadism evolved into intellectual circles in which scholars constructed an interpretative system that subjected legal tradition to hermeneutic principles; in so doing they turned themselves into a powerful class of jurists who derived their authority from their role as the expert interpreters of sacred texts.[5] From the end of the 10th century onwards, we can set the starting point for the process that John Wilkinson calls "normalisation" or "madhabization" of Ibāḍī jurisprudence, meaning converting the primitive form of Ibadism into a model *madhhab*, with a structure and a set of hermeneutical principles comparable to the Sunni schools. In Oman this process coincided with a resurgence of the imamate after the collapse of the first imamate. In the Maghrib, where the imamate institution was replaced by the organisation of the *ḥalqa* (circle), the process of normalisation emerged probably in reaction to foreign influence. Though Eastern and Western Ibāḍī communities preserved their own textual traditions, the stages of the "rationalization" process overlapped in Oman and the Maghrib resulting in a common development of law and jurisprudence.

One of the major outputs of this process was the emergence of a specifically Ibāḍī collection of *ḥadīth*, the *Musnad al-Rabīʿ b. Ḥabīb*, which, along with a corpus of religio-legal norms, gave rise to a truly sectarian Ibadism. As I have argued, the first major impulse towards identifying a coherent and comprehensive set of Ibāḍī religio-legal traditions distinct from those of the other schools of law occurred in the Maghrib during the time of al-Warjlānī (d. 1174). This development came as a corollary to the development of Ibāḍī law, which started approximately a century earlier.

The Ibāḍī legal corpus developed starting from the revealed sources and the "living tradition/practice" of the community (*āthār*) and was further boosted

4 Salaymeh, *The Beginnings of Islamic Law* 7.

5 El Shamsy, *The Canonization of Islamic Law* 86.

by the application of personal opinion (*ra'y*) of individual scholars on the basic material. At the same time, the concepts underlying the theory of law were rationalized and became part of the tradition of the school, defined through the consensus (*ijmāʿ*) of those acknowledged to be the school's leading representatives, who held a monopoly of exegetical technique. The concept of *ijmāʿ* was used to assert overtly the authority of the community over the law development process.

The period between the 11th and the 16th century saw the crystallization of the Ibāḍī *madhhab*. This included a clear-cut definition of the community's historical, juridical and theological boundaries but at same time the adoption of some standard features of the Sunni schools in terms of legal reasoning, *ḥadīth* transmission and historical narrative. This process saw the composition of fundamental works of jurisprudence, prosopography, *ḥadīth* compilation and theology. Ibāḍīs emerged as an identifiable "*madhhab*" among others, in part thanks to the increasing interaction between Ibāḍīs and non-Ibāḍīs.

The maturity of Ibāḍī law was the result of the way scholars articulated doctrines and rulings covering all aspects of believers' rituals and social life. Ibāḍī hermeneutic (*uṣūl al-fiqh* or *uṣūl al-dīn*) coalesced into a repertory of hermeneutic techniques focusing on the sources of the divine law and their interconnections but also on the nature of language, interpretation and communication. On the other side, literature on positive law (*furūʿ al-fiqh*) – in particular abridgements and encyclopaedic works – played an important sociological function in institutionalizing the rule of law reducing legal indeterminacy. This canonization process enabled the preservation of Ibāḍī legal patrimony, and it prompted a metadiscourse on questions of interpretation and consistency.

The Ibāḍī-Omani scholars during the period under investigation succeeded in consolidating their identity as men of distinct piety and knowledge. They integrated their practice as jurists into their distinctive training, encouraging a broad basis of public recognition for their unique integrative agenda. Presenting themselves as the ultimate heirs of the religious-spiritual authority embedded into the first Ibāḍī *imām*s in Basra, Omani scholars enjoyed a great degree of public veneration, being the most outspoken and undisputable representatives of the Ibāḍī tradition in times that witnessed the crisis of the imamate. They led sophisticated interpersonal relationships, and their social agenda took place around dynamics of power and authority. Internal power struggles among certain scholars, which echoed in their compendia, seemed to be one of the inevitable outcomes of this sophisticated social fabric.

The legal theory that the Ibāḍī jurists constructed laid the basis for the understanding of the respective roles of *ḥadīth* and communal consensus in jurisprudence and contributed to their systematizing approach to jurisprudence characterized by a concern with certainty. The preoccupation with producing a coherent result gave rise to a theory of interpretation that does not exclude the possibility of differences of opinion but prioritizes consensus, which represents a truthful and certain interpretation of the sacred sources and a key element to ascertain the truth of *qiyās*. Consensus embodied the legal memory of the community, it asserted the authority of the community in making and changing law and it counterbalanced the creative power of *ijtihād*.

As I already argued, "the gate of *ijtihād*" were never sealed among the Ibāḍīs. The high-ranking jurists might exercise independent interpretation of the sources and questioning the opinions of earlier jurists. The jurist who had the capacity of *mujtahid* might not refuse to proffer a new interpretation of the scriptural references to solve new legal cases nor might he rely on another *mujtahid* (*taqlīd al-mujtahid*).

In Ibadism the delineation of a sacralized past coexisted with the creative impulse of *ijtihād* and in both cases jurists emerged as the major authoritative body. Throughout the history of Ibadism, religious authority assumed a number of forms and functions: the capability of interpreting the sources, defining a canon of authoritative texts and the legitimate methods of hermeneutics, the right to classify the correct belief and practice. The corollary of the jurists' power to marginalize and punish deviance, misconduct and heresy, and to shape and influence the views and the conduct of the community members was symbolized by the *walāya/barā'a* doctrine. The *walāya/barā'a* system determined the Ibāḍī attitude towards non-Ibāḍīs as well as membership and leadership of the community. The key to this pivotal system, I argue, centred on jurists' paternal authority and on their rigorous maintenance of morality in order to create a rightful community of stable patriarchal households.

In the Maghrib this broad-based effort to reorder society in the aftermath of the fall of the imamate was based upon a conception of a society as imagined in terms of a strict division between good believers and offenders. Consequently, excluding offenders from the community was crucial for both the expression of communal norms and the experience of cohesion. The whole mechanism of excommunication and redemption shows how communities turned to customary authorities and traditional norms to provide order and security and actively supported official disciplinary efforts.

The intellectual dynamism of the Mzabi Ibāḍī scholarly tradition produced scholarly communities that laid down the heritage of both the Basran community and the Tahert imamate, but that also made significant adaptation to present circumstances. The *ittifāqāt* collections provide rich information about legal procedures among the Mzabi Ibāḍī communities, being at the meeting points of custom and religion.

They shed light on the way the legal scholars worked on the basis of the established rules of Islamic jurisprudence, but at same time they relied on custom and local practice to make their decisions fit the social reality of the Mzabi region. This adaptation of custom to Islamic law, or even more, adaptation of Islamic law to social reality, was the core function of the *ittifāqāt*. The autonomy of the region played an import part in this phenomenon, as did the accessibility of learned status to at least the leading sector of society. Ibāḍī learning created pedagogical links, which surpassed familial and interfamilial affiliations and gave the learned hierarchy a strong and wide base in Mzabi towns' social structure. In fact, they linked the religious hierarchy to a number of urban institutions and provided scholars with access to avenues of influence and control which were open to them at level of law and adaptation of law through jurisprudence. This had influence not only on the organization of the towns but also upon conception of legitimacy as it helped legitimize an autonomous parochial-style leadership.

Throughout the whole history of Ibadism, the quest for knowledge (*ṭalab al-ʿilm*) and the command of learning was the fulcrum around which the whole idea of legitimacy and power revolved. Ibadism enjoyed a long-lived teaching tradition in which learned piety emanated from classic individual study as well as from interaction between teachers and pupils. It was a complex process, in which religious and political authority was interwoven with teaching networks, familial kinship and tribal dynamics.

Knowledge led also the efforts of the Ibāḍī reformers towards the renaissance of the movement and the resistance against European/Western influence. The most prominent representatives of the Ibāḍī renaissance (*nahḍa*) in the 18th century, Abū Zakariyyāʾ Yaḥyā b. Ṣāliḥ al-Afḍalī, his student ʿAbd al-ʿAzīz al-Thamīnī al-Muṣʿabī in the Maghrib and Abū Nabhān al-Kharūṣī in Oman were learned men and prolific authors. They called for both a rapprochement with the Sunnis and internal reforms in order to revitalize the socially stagnant Ibāḍī communities. Al-Muṣʿabī invoked the practice of *ijtihād* to challenge existing interpretations of the texts and to put forward a new understanding of the sources, which involved a deep understanding of the Ibāḍī as well as the Sunni authoritative corpus.

The 19th and 20th century Ibāḍī reformers agreed with the Salafi notion that internal divisions were one of the causes of the Muslim weakness that had allowed Europeans to dominate the Muslim world and therefore they looked for a rapprochement with Sunni Islam that, according to Valerie Hoffman, turned into a "desectarization" of Ibadism.[6] The works by Nūr al-Dīn al-Sālimī

6 Hoffman, Historical Memory and Imagined Communities 193–194.

in Oman and Muḥammad Aṭfayyish in Mzab made it clear that Ibāḍīs and Sunnis shared the same doctrinal heritage. Looking for an Ibāḍī identity in modernity meant mastering Ibāḍī tradition but also recognizing its relativity and historicity as well as rethinking and innovating Ibāḍī doctrines and principles.

Aṭfayyish's reformist approach to the hermeneutic consisted in regarding the Quran as the first basis for the religious and juridical teaching of Islam. He called for *tajdīd al-Qur'ān*, a revival of the Quran, in which *ijtihād* was fundamental for a new Quran interpretation and a renewal of Ibāḍī law. The law – Aṭfayyish argued – should be deeply rooted in Muslim Ibāḍī legal tradition, otherwise it would not fulfil its essential function of directing human actions and moulding human habits. He strongly opposed the implementation of European institutions and laws in Mzab and made no attempt to reconcile Islam with Western civilization.

In the same vein, al-Sālimī's discourse on Ibāḍī reform attested to the central role played by the drive for identity and cultural authenticity. The problem with colonialism was essentially cultural. Its main evil laid in the propagation of moral and ethical models which ran contrary to the teachings of Islam. Undermining Islamic culture had engendered the economic and political marginalization of Muslims. With this in mind, al-Sālimī engaged in the restoration of the imamate tradition in Oman, his efforts entailed both a political and a reform discourse.

The main contribution of Ibāḍī reformers was the synthesis of Ibāḍī and Sunni principles and the defence of rational and religious autonomy. Their legal reform resulted in scholarly contributions and the creation of an intellectual medium – in the form of a large number of texts – wherein they set their rethinking and renewal of the school, which represents a momentous contribution today in Ibāḍī reclaiming their intellectual identity within the Muslim world.

The Ibāḍī reform movement was the last effort to implement Ibāḍī law and institutions. In the Maghrib, Ibāḍī tradition was sidelined by French colonization. In the East the Āl Bū Saʿīdī dynasty ruled over regions inhabited by Arabs, Indians, Baluchis, Africans and others. Their maritime empire was built through successful trading and a multicultural approach to politics and religion. All sultans had both Ibāḍī and non-Ibāḍī advisers. Sayyid Sulṭān, who ruled Oman and Zanzibar from 1806 to 1856, housed Ibāḍī as well Sunni scholars at his court and appointed judges from each of the legal schools present within his territory.

Epilogue

In this book I guided the reader through the history of Ibāḍī law and jurisprudence. But what remains today of this long tradition?

A rich literary patrimony, partially unexplored, is preserved in many public and private libraries spread across the Ibāḍī archipelago in North Africa, Oman and Zanzibar. The Omani Ministry of Heritage and Culture embarked on an ambitious project to catalogue and digitalize their rich manuscript collection along with publishing traditional and modern works on Ibadism. Ibāḍī presses in the Maghrib and in Europe (as for example Ibadica in Paris) stand out for their effort to disseminate knowledge on Ibadism, publishing in Arabic and in French.

The institution of the *ʿazzāba* is still alive in Mzab, though they lost almost all their power. In Oman Ibāḍī law resurfaces in some provisions of the Personal Status Law (PSL) codification, in particular family and inheritance law.[1] The 1997 Omani PSL reflects Sultan Qābūs's approach to modernity, which focused on the preservation of Omani traditional culture, while simultaneously emphasizing the necessity for national unity and social and economic development. This vision undermined any sectarian difference and stressed the tolerant and pragmatic Omani understanding of Islam. In line with this pattern, the 1997 PSL avoids any explicit allusion to Ibāḍī law, referring only to *sharīʿa* and to custom (*ʿurf*) in a number of articles. The PSL adopted almost entirely the "Muscat document", a model codified Muslim personal status law, which the GCC approved in December 1996. The Omani law makes few exceptions to the application of the provisions of the code, which indirectly allude to specific precedents of Ibāḍī law. Article 282 contains a clause guaranteeing non-Muslims the right to apply their own rules. Article 281 (regulation on divorce and inheritance) states that where the school (*madhhab*) of the husband has "stricter rules or particular procedures" concerning divorce, the judge must observe these conditions and procedures; and where the rules of the testator's school differ from the provisions of the code in regard to the inheritance of the daughter and grandfather, the judge must apply the dominant opinion of the testator's school unless all the heirs agree with the application of the

1 *Marsūm Sulṭānī* no. 32/97 publ. in *al-Jarīda al-Rasmiyya* no. 601 of 6.15.1997. PSL consists of five books and 282 articles covering marriage, divorce, legal capacity and guardianship, wills, inheritance and final provisions. On PSL in Oman, see Al-Azri, The 20th Century Islamic Legal Reform 58–73; idem, Change and Conflict 121–137; idem, One or Three? 277–296; idem, *Social and Gender Inequality in Oman*; Badry, A Matter of Limited Female Agency 225–239.

 | HTTPS://DOI.ORG/10.1163/9789004765764-011

provisions of the code. This clause refers to specific rules in Ibāḍī inheritance law that give preference to the paternal grandfather over brothers and sisters in the distribution of the estate.[2]

These clauses may result in a greater discretionary power of judges compared to state law because – as Lynn Welchman argues – the state consciously chooses to leave certain matters to be decided by the courts rather than take the political responsibility of setting them by legislation.[3] Though Ibāḍī praxis may emerge thanks to the judges discretion and recourse to custom, the Ibāḍī religious establishment disapproved of some elements of the PSL, namely the omission of any explicit reference to two well-known Ibāḍī features in family law, the prohibition of temporary marriage and the permanent impediment of marriage between couples who have fornicated, in order to avoid conflicts with those who do not accept these legal opinions.[4]

In today's Oman, distinctions among different religious affiliations are diluted in the idea of a common national belonging. Article 2 of Omani Basic Statute law (January 12, 2021, Royal Decree 6/2021) states that State's religion is Islam and Islamic *sharīʿa* is the basis for legislation, avoiding any specific reference to Ibadism, which represents the majority (*c.*53%) of the population. Moreover, article 21 states that "All citizens are equal before the law. They have equal public rights and duties, and there shall be no discrimination between them on grounds of sex, origin, colour, language, religion, sect, domicile, or social status".[5]

The construction of a modern state in Oman is mainly due to the modernizing process, which the late Sultan Qābūs (r. 1970–2020) initiated in the 1970s by promoting the idea of timeless Omani national identity based on history, heritage and symbolic references. This process of identity engineering created a feeling of belonging to a common "imagined community" through a selective reading of Omani history and a narrative of an oecumenic and tolerant Islam, which has become the hallmark of today's Oman.[6] In line with this discourse of a peculiar Omani Islam, the Ministry of Endowments and Religious Affairs since 1993 has supported the publication of a journal called *al-Tasāmuḥ* (Tolerance), replaced in 2003 by *al-Tafāhum* (Mutual Understanding), a quarterly Islamic intellectual publication whose vision is reinforcing "dialogue and

---

2 Badry, A Matter of Limited Female Agency 227.

3 Welchman, *Women and Muslim Family Laws in Arab States* 49.

4 Badry, A Matter of Limited Female Agency 227.

5 Royal Decree 6/2021 Promulgating the Basic Statute of the State – Decree, https://decree.om/2021/rd20210006/.

6 Valeri, *Oman: Politics and Society in the Qaboos State* 109–110, 116–117, 121.

providing a new approach to Islam through a moderate and innovative reading of all aspects of Islamic civilization".[7] Moreover, the Ministry sponsored interreligious dialogue centres, as Al Amana Centre for Muslim-Christian Understanding in Muscat, led by a Protestant pastor, which promotes dialogue and harmony among diverse faith communities.[8]

The College of *Sharīʿa* Sciences (*Kulliyat al-ʿulūm al-sharaʿiyya*), operating under the aegis of the Ministry of Endowments and Religious Affairs, teaches Ibadism within a broader training which offers classes on Islamic jurisprudence, law, theology and ethics viewed from a comparative perspective, including the teachings of all legal schools. The Ministry does not allow sectarian teaching in mosques or schools and discourages mention of sectarian differences in the standard Friday sermons, issued by the Committee for Friday Sermons. Nonetheless, Ibadism still maintains a symbolic and effective pre-eminence: since 1970 the authorities appointed as Minister of Religious Affairs, as *Muftī* of the Sultanate, as well as many leading *imāms* have been Ibāḍīs.[9]

The current Grand *Muftī* of the Sultanate, *shaykh* Aḥmad b. Aḥmad al-Khalīlī (b. 1942), the highest religious authority in Oman, appointed in 1975 by Sultan Qābūs, promotes the vision of Ibadism as a moderate and tolerant form of Islam, participates in pan-Islamic initiatives and dismisses the differences between Ibadism and Sunnism as irrelevant. Reading his *fatwā* collections, one notes his attempt to put Ibāḍī sources in conversation with Sunni ones. In giving his legal response on different topics ranging from religious practices (*ʿibādāt*) to interpersonal relations (*muʿāmalāt*), he relies on standard Ibāḍī sources, as the *Musnad al-Rabīʿ b. Ḥabīb*, but also explicitly mentions the Sunni *ḥadīth* collections. He makes some explicit references to Ibāḍī law (e.g. concerning the *zakāt* on cattle, which corresponds to that on camels regarding the minimum taxable amount and tax brackets), while in other cases he disregards specific rules of Ibāḍī law, aligning himself with the majority of Muslim schools, as is the case of the prohibition of *ribā al-faḍl*. Indeed, building on Sunni traditions, he states that *ribā al-faḍl* is forbidden, whereas almost all earlier Ibāḍī scholars did not consider *ribā al-faḍl* a prohibited transaction.[10]

The Grand *Muftī* al-Khalīlī is the head of the Omani *Iftāʾ* office, part of the Ministry of Endowments and Religious Affairs, whose most important objective is to preserve the Islamic identity of the society by issuing *fatwā*s to both

7 Al-Tafahom. https://tafahom.mara.gov.om/en/.
8 Al Amana Centre. https://alamanacentre.org/homepage/.
9 Hoffman, Ibāḍism: History, Doctrines, and Recent Scholarship 304.
10 al-Khalīlī, *Fatāwā* i, 270–271; 615–616; iii, 174–175.

individuals and state authorities and by supporting the government in running domestic policies. The *iftāʾ* office consists of three main offices: the Grand *Muftī*'s office, the Secretary General's Office and the Assistant Grand *Muftī*'s Office. Each office has different departments, including a *fatwā* department, a call centre established in 2015, a department of converts to Islam and a department of relationships and cultural interchange. There is also an office of scientific adviser to the Grand *Muftī*.[11]

According to Abdullah Ahmed al-Sulaimi, himself part of the *Iftāʾ* office' staff, under the current Grand *Muftī* the office played an effective role in maintaining the coherence and coexistence of the community with its different Islamic schools and ideologies, and it therefore gained the trust of not only Ibāḍī Muslims, but also of Sunni and Shiʿi Omanis as well as non-Omanis. He quotes some remarkable decisions by the *iftāʾ* office during the Sultan Qābūs era. The first was establishing the *jumʿa* prayer (Friday congregational prayer) in all cities of Oman. According to classical Ibāḍī jurisprudence the *jumʿa* prayer can be established only under the rule of a legitimate *imām*, elected by a group of highly qualified scholars. The previous and current Grand *Muftī*, however, disagreed with this condition and therefore issued a *fatwā* that allows establishing the *jumʿa* prayer in all Omani cities. Moreover, *shaykh* al-Khalīlī stated that the *jumʿa* prayer is *farḍ ʿayn*, namely compulsory for every believer, and not *farḍ kifāya*, namely a duty that can be performed by a small number of believers as Ibāḍī law states. The principal aim of the *Iftāʾ* office is to achieve unity of the Omani religious community: the office tried to avoid issues that may ignite conflict between Muslims and asserted in many occasions that every person "believing in Allāh and his messenger Muḥammad" should be considered Muslim. Nonetheless, the Office seeks to preserve the Ibāḍī identity within Omani religious diversity and to strengthen a positive perception of Ibadism in both the Islamic and non-Islamic world. In order to protect Ibadism's image, in 1987 *shaykh* al-Khalīlī countered publicly the Saudi *Muftī* Ibn Bāz's *fatwā* stating that Ibāḍīs are *kuffār* and therefore are not part of Islam.[12]

In contemporary Oman, preserving Ibāḍī heritage and identity means recognizing its relativity within the Islamic *umma* underlying the aspects of tolerance, interfaith dialogue and exchanges with the other Muslim school in the framework of an ecumenical Islam.

---

11 Al-Sulaimi, The *Iftāʾ* Office of Oman 247–261.

12 Al-Sulaimi, The *Iftāʾ* Office of Oman 251–256.

Bibliography

Ibāḏī Sources

Manuscripts

Aqwāl Qatāda, Ms. *al-Bārūniyya, Fiqh Ibāḍī* (no number), fol. 1–140.

Āthār al-Rabīʿ b. Ḥabīb, Ms. *al-Bārūniyya, Fiqh Ibāḍī* (no number), fol. 1–32.

Futyā al-Rabīʿ b. Ḥabīb, Ms. *al-Bārūniyya, Fiqh Ibāḍī* (no number), fol. 32–49.

Jawābāt Jābir b. Zayd, Ms. *al-Bārūniyya, Fiqh Ibāḍī* no. 1, fol. 64–91.

Kitāb al-Barbariyya, Ms. BINA, INALCO, Paris, https://bina.bulac.fr/search/results?fulltext_search=كتاب+البربرية.

Wisyānī [al-], Abū ʾl-Rabīʿ Sālim, *Kitāb al-siyar*, MS. Z. Smogorzewski, Cracow no. 00277, fol. 1–189. Ed. ʿUmar b. Luqmān Bū ʿAṣbāna, 3 vols., Muscat, Wizārat al-Turāth al-Qawmī wa ʾl-Thaqāfa 2009.

Printed Sources

Abū ʾl-Ḥawārī, Muḥammad b. al-Ḥawārī al-ʿUmānī, *al-Dirāya wa-kanz al-ghināya fī muntahā ʾl-ghāya wa-bulūgh al-kifāya fī tafsīr khamsimiʾat āya min tafsīr al-Qurʾān al-Karīm*, ed. Sālim b. Ḥumayd b. Sulaymān b. Ḥumayd al-Ḥārithī, Beirut 1394/1974.

Abū Ghānim, Bishr b. Ghānim al-Khurāsānī, *al-Mudawwana al-ṣughrā*, 2 vols., Muscat 1984.

Abū Ghānim, *al-Mudawwana al-kubrā*, 2 vols., Muscat 1984.

Abū Ghānim, *al-Mudawwana*, ed. I.b.M. al-ʿAsākir, Muscat 2006.

Abū Ghānim, *al-Mudawwana al-kubrā*, ed. M.b.S. Bājū, 3 vols., Muscat 2007.

Abū ʿUbayda, Muslim b. Abī Karīma al-Tamīmī, *Risālat Ibn Abī Karīma fī ʾl-zakāt*, ed. Sālim b. Muḥammad al-Ḥārithī, Muscat 1982.

Aṭfayyish, Muḥammad b. Yūsuf, *Shāmil al-aṣl wa ʾl-farʿ*, ed. Abū Isḥāq Ibrāhīm Aṭfayyish, 2 vols., Cairo 1348/1929–1930.

Aṭfayyish, *Izālat al-iʿtirāḍ ʿan muḥiqqī al-ibāḍī*, Muscat, Wizārat al-turāth al-qawmī wa ʾl-thaqāfa 1982.

Aṭfayyish, *Sharḥ ʿaqīdat al-tawḥīd*, Muscat, Wizārat al-turāth al-qawmī wa ʾl-thaqāfa 1403/1983.

Aṭfayyish, *Sharḥ Kitāb al-Nīl wa-shifāʾ al-ʿalīl*, 24 vols., Jedda, Maktabat al-Irshād 1985 (3rd edition).

Aṭfayyish, *Kitāb al-jāmiʿ al-ṣaghīr*, 3 vols., Muscat, Wizārat al-turāth al-qawmī wa ʾl-thaqāfa 1406/1986.

 | HTTPS://DOI.ORG/10.1163/9789004765764-012

Aṭfayyish, *Jāmiʿ al-shaml fī aḥādīth khātim al-rusul*, 2 vols., ed. ʿA. ʿAmīra, Muscat 1987.

Aṭfayyish, *Taysīr al-tafsīr*, 15 vols., Muscat, Wizārat al-Turāth al-Qawmī wa ʾl-Thaqāfa 1414/1994.

Bābāʿammī, Muḥammad ibn Mūsá et al., *Muʿjam aʿlām al-ibāḍiyya min al-qarn al-awwal al-hijrī ilá al-ʿaṣr al-ḥāḍir: qism al-Maghrib al-Islāmī. Dictionnaire des hommes illustres de l'Ibadisme, les hommes du Maghreb*, 2 vols., Beirut, Dār al-Gharb al-Islāmī 2000.

Barrādī (al-), Abū ʾl-Faḍl Abū ʾl-Qāsim b. Ibrāhīm, *Kitāb al-jawāhir al-muntaqatāt*, lit. Cairo 1302/1884–5.

Bārūnī [al-], S., *Mukhtaṣar tarīkh al-ibāḍiyya*, Dār al-istiqāma, Tunis 1358/1938.

Bisiyānī [al-], Abū ʾl-Ḥasan ʿAlī b. Muḥammad, *Mukhtaṣar*, Zanzibar 1304/1886. Ed. ʿAbd Allāh al-Khalīlī, Muscat, Wizārat al-Turāth al-Qawmī wa ʾl-Thaqāfa 1977.

Bisiyānī [al-], Abū ʾl-Ḥasan ʿAlī b. Muḥammad, *al-Jāmiʿ*, 4 vols., Muscat, Wizārat al-Turāth al-Qawmī wa ʾl-Thaqāfa 1984.

Crone, P. and Zimmermann, F. (eds.), *The Epistle of Sālim Ibn Dhakwān*, Oxford, University Press 2001.

Darjīnī [al-], Abū ʾl-ʿAbbās Aḥmad, *Kitāb ṭabaqāt al-mashāyikh bi-ʾl-Maghrib*, ed. I. Ṭallāy, 2 vols., Constantine, Matbaʿt al-Baʿth 1394/1974.

Darwish, A., *Ḥayāt min ajl al-ʿilm*, Cairo 1991.

Ḥārithī [al-], Sālim, *Al-ʿUqūd al-fiḍḍiyya fī uṣūl al-Ibāḍiyya*, Muscat 1403/1983.

Hūd b. Muḥakkam al-Hawwārī, *Tafsīr Kitāb Allāh al-ʿAzīz*, ed. Belhajj Saʿid Sharifi, 4 vols., Beirut, Dār al-Gharb al-Islāmī 1990.

Ibn Baraka, Abū Muḥammad ʿAbd Allāh Ibn Muḥammad, *Kitāb al-Jāmiʿ*, 2 vols., ed. Abū ʾl-Qāsim ʿĪsā Yaḥyā al-Bārūnī, Muscat, Wizārat al-Turāth al-Qawmī wa ʾl-Thaqāfa 1983.

Ibn Jaʿfar, Abū Jābir Muḥammad al-Azkawī, *al-Jāmiʿ*, ed. ʿĀ. ʿAbd al-Munʿim, 3 vols., Muscat, Wizārat al-Turāth al-Qawmī wa ʾl-Thaqāfa, 1981. New edition by Jabr Maḥmūd al-Faḍīlāt and Shaykh Aḥmad b. Ṣālḥ, 10 vols., Muscat, Wizārat al-Turāth al-Qawmī wa ʾl-Thaqāfa 2018.

Ibn Khalfūn, Abū Yaʿqūb Yūsuf Ibn Khalfūn al-Mazzātī, *Ajwibat Ibn Khalfūn*, ed. ʿA. Kh. Ennami, Beirut 1974.

Ibn Khalīfa b. Ḥamd Āl ʿAbd al-Salām, Ṭ. (ed.), *Futyā al-Rabīʿ b. Ḥabīb*, Muscat, Dhākirat ʿUmān 2017.

Ibn Qays, Abū Isḥāq Ibrāhīm al-Ḥaḍramī, *Mukhtaṣar al-khiṣāl*, Muscat 1403/1983.

Ibn Sallām, *Kitāb Ibn Sallām. Eine ibaditisch-maghrebinische Geschichte des Islams aus dem 3.–9. Jahrhundert*, ed. W. Schwartz and Shaykh S. Ibn Yaʿqūb, Wiesbaden, Franz Steiner Verlag 1986.

Jaʿbīrī [al-](Jaabiri), F. (ed.), *Rasāʾil al-imām Jābir bin Zayd al-Azdī*, Sulṭanat ʿUmān, Maktabat al-ḍāmirī 2013.

Jannāwunī [al-], Abū Zakarīyā' Yaḥyā ibn al-Khayr, *Kitāb al-waḍ': mukhtaṣar fī 'l-uṣūl wa 'l-fiqh*, Muscat, Maktabat al-Istiqāma 1990.

Jayṭālī [al-], Abū Ṭāhir Ismā'īl b. Mūsā al-Nafūsī, *Qawā'id al-Islām*, 2 vols., Ghardaya (Algeria) 1976.

Jayṭālī [al-], *Qanāṭir al-khayrāt*, 3 vols., Muscat, Wizārat al-Turāth al-Qawmī wa 'l-Thaqāfa 1983.

Khalīlī [al-], Aḥmad b. Aḥmad *Fatāwā*, 9 vols., Muscat, Wizārat al-Awqāf wa 'l-Shu'ūn al-Diniyya 2013.

Kharūṣī [al-], K. (ed.), *Āthār al-Rabī' b. Ḥabīb: Edition and study*, Wiesbaden, Harrassowitz 2016.

Kharūṣī [al-], Sa'īd b. Khalaf (ed.), *Min jawābāt al-imām Jābir b. Zayd*, Oman 1984.

Kāshif, S.I. (ed.), *al-Siyar wa 'l-jawābāt li-'ulamā' wa a'imma 'Umān*, 2 vols., Muscat, Wizārat al-Turāth al-Qawmī wa 'l-Thaqāfa 1989.

Kindī [al-], Abū Bakr Aḥmad b. 'Abdallāllah, *Muṣannaf*, ed. 'Abd al-Mun'im 'Āmir, 44 vols., Wizārat al-Turāth al-Qawmī wa 'l-Thaqāfa 1979–1984.

Kindī [al-], *al-Takhṣīṣ fī 'l-walāya wa 'l-barā'a*, ed. Ḥamūd b. 'Abd Allāh al-Rāshidī, Muscat, Wizārat al-turāth al-Qawmī wa 'l-Thaqāfa 2011.

Kindī [al-], Muḥammad b. Ibrāhīm, *Bayān al-Shar'*, 71 vols., Muscat, Wizārat al-Turāth al-Qawmī wa 'l-Thaqāfa 1982–1993.

Kudamī [al-], Abū Sa'īd Muḥammad b. Sa'īd, *al-Mu'tabar*, 4 vols., Muscat, Wizārat al-Turāth al-Qawmī wa 'l-Thaqāfa 1984.

Kudamī [al-], *Kitāb al-Istiqāma*, 3 vols., Muscat, Wizārat al-Turāth al-Qawmī wa 'l-Thaqāfa 1985.

Kudamī [al-], *al-Jāmi' al-mufīd min jawābāt Abī Sa'īd*, 2 vols., Muscat, Wizārat al-Turāth al-Qawmī wa 'l-Thaqāfa 1985.

Kudamī [al-], *al-Jāmi' al-mufīd min aḥkām Abī Sa'īd*, Muscat, Wizārat al-Turāth al-Qawmī wa 'l-Thaqāfa 1985.

Malshūṭī [al-], Tibghūrīn b. 'Īsā, *Kitāb uṣūl al-dīn*, ed. 'A. Kh. Ennami, trans. T. Legassik, Paris, Ibadica 2017.

Muṣ'ābī [al-], 'Abd al-'Azīz, *Kitāb al-Nīl wa shifā' al-'alīl*, lit. Cairo 1305/1887. Ed. Gedda, Maktabat al-irshād 1972 (with commentary by Muḥammad b. Yūsuf Aṭfayyish).

Nafūsī [al-], 'Amrūs b. Fatḥ, *al-Daynūna al-ṣāfiya*, ed. Ḥāj Aḥmad Karrūm, Wizārat al-Turāth al-Qawmī wa 'l-thaqāfa, Muscat 1999.

Nāṣir, Muḥammad Ṣāliḥ and Shaybānī, Sulṭān ibn Mubārak, *Mu'jam a'lām al-ibāḍiyya min al-qarn al-awwal al-hijrī ilā al-'aṣr al-ḥāḍir. Qism al-Mashriq al-Islāmī. Dictionnaire des hommes illustres de l'Ibadisme, les hommes du Mashrek*. Beirut, Dār al-Gharb al-Islāmī 2006.

Rabī'[al-] b. Ḥabīb, *al-Jāmi' al-Ṣaḥīḥ* (*Musnad al-Rabī' b. Ḥabīb*), *tartīb Abī Ya'qūb b. Ibrāhīm al-Warjlānī*, ed. 'Abd Allāh b. Ḥumayd al-Sālimī, Damascus 1963. The work has been also edited by Sulṭān b. Mubārak b. Ḥamad al-Shaybānī, 3 vols., Muscat 2003.

Saʿdī, Jumayyil b. Khamīs, *Qāmūs al-sharīʿa al-ḥāwī ṭuruqihā al-wasīʿa*, ed. ʿAbd al-Ḥafīẓ Shalabī, 19 vols., Muscat, Wizārat al-Turāth al-Qawmī wa ʾl-Thaqāfa 1989.

Salimi [al-], A. and Madelung, W. (eds.), *Early Ibāḍī Literature. Abu l-Mundhir Bashīr b. Muḥammad b. Maḥbūb. Kitāb al-Raṣf fi l-Tawḥīd, Kitāb al-Muḥāraba and Sīra*, Wiesbaden, Harrassowitz 2011.

Salimi [al-], A. and Madelung, W. (eds.), *Early Ibāḍī Theology: Six Kalam Texts by ʿAbd Allāh b. Yazīd al-Fazārī*, Leiden – Boston, Brill 2014.

Salimi [al-], A. (ed.), *Early Islamic Law in Basra in the 2nd/8th century. Aqwāl Qatāda b. Diʿāma al-Sadūsī*, Leiden – Boston, Brill 2017.

Salimi [al-], A. (ed.), *Early Ibadi Theology: New Material on Rational Thought in Islam from the Pen of al-Fazārī (2nd/8th Century)*, Leiden – Boston, Brill 2021.

Salimi [al-], A. (ed.), *Ibadi Texts in Oman from the 3rd/9th Century*, Leiden – Boston, Brill 2022.

Salimi [al-], A. (ed.), *Early Islamic Law in Ḥadīth Text from Basra. The Book of Prayer and the Book of Marriage by Jābir b. Zayd (d.c. 93/712–3)*, Leiden – Boston, Brill 2026.

Salimi [al-], A. (ed.), *Early Islamic Law in Kufa. Al-Dīwān al-maʿrūḍ ʿalā al-ʿulamāʾ al-ibāḍiyya*, 2 vols., Leiden, Brill 2027.

Sālimī [al-], Muḥammad, *Nahḍa al-aʿyān bi-ḥurriyyat ʿUmān*, Beirut, Dār al-Jīl 1998.

Sālimī [al-], Nūr al-Dīn, *Ḥāshiyat al-Jāmiʿ al-Ṣaḥīḥ*, 3 vols., lit. Cairo 1326/1908; republ. under the title *Sharḥ al-Jāmiʿ al-Ṣaḥīḥ, Musnad al-Imām al-Rabīʿ b. Ḥabīb al-Farāhīdī*, Oman – Damasco 1963.

Sālimī [al-], *al-Lumʿa al-Murḍiyya min Ashiʿʿat al-Ibāḍiyya*, Wizārat al-Thurāt al-Qawmī wa ʾl-Thaqāfa, Muscat 1983.

Sālimī [al-], *Jawābāt al-imām al-Sālimī*, ed. A. ʿAbd al-Sattār, 6 vols. + index, Sīb (Oman), Maktabat al-Imām Nūr al-Dīn al-Sālimī 1996.

Sālimī [al-], *Tuḥfat al-aʿyān bi-sīrat ahl ʿUmān*, Muscat, Maktabat al-Istiqāma, 1417/1997.

Sālimī [al-], *Sharḥ al-Jāmiʿ al-Ṣaḥīḥ. Musnad al-Imām al-Rabīʿ b. Ḥabīb b. ʿAmr al-Farāhidī al-Azdī*, 3 vols., Sīb (Oman), Maktabat al-Imām Nūr al-Dīn al-Sālimī 1640/2004.

Shammākhī [al-], Abū ʾl-ʿAbbās Aḥmad b. Saʿīd b. ʿAbd al-Wāḥid, *Kitāb al-Siyar*, lit. Cairo 1301/1883. Ed. M. Ḥasan, 2 vols., Beirut-Tripoli (Libya), Dār al-Madar al-Islāmī 2009.

Shammākhī [al-], Abū ʾl-Abbās, *Siyar. Al-juzʾ al-khāṣṣ bi-tarājim ʿulamāʾ al-Maghrib ilā nihāyat al-qarn al-khāmis*, ed. M. Ḥasan, 3 vols., Tunis, Kulliyat al-ʿulūm al-insāniyya wa ʾl-ijtimāʿiyya 1995.

Shammākhī [al-], Abū Sākin ʿĀmir, *Kitāb al-īḍāḥ*, lit. Cairo 1304/1886; 4 vols., Muscat, Maktabat Muscat 2014.

Warjlānī [al-], Abū Yaʿqūb Yūsuf, *al-Dalīl wa ʾl-Burhān*, ed. S. b. Ḥamad al-Ḥārithī, 2 vols., Sulṭanat ʿUmān, Wizārat al-Thurāt al-Qawmī wa ʾl-Thaqāfa 1983/1403.

Warjlānī [al-], *al-ʿAdl wa ʾl-inṣāf fī maʿrifat uṣūl al-fiqh wa ʾl-ikhtilāf*, 2 vols., Muscat, Wizārat al-Turāth al-Qawmī wa ʾl-Thaqāfa 1984.

Warjlānī [al-], *Kitāb al-asmāʾ*, ed. S. b. ʿUmar b. Yaḥyātanī, Paris, Ibadica 2020.

Warjlānī [al-], Abū Zakarīyāʾ, *Kitāb siyar al-aʾimma wa akhbārihim*, ed. I. al-ʿArabī, Algiers 1399/1979 (trans. E. Masqueray, *Cronique d'Abou Zakariya*, Algiers, Aillaud 1878).

Arabic Sources

ʿAbd al-Razzāq, b. Hammām al-Ṣanʿānī, *al-Muṣannaf*, ed. Ḥ. al-Aʿẓamī, 11 vols., Beirut, al-Majlis al-ʿilmī 1970–1972.

Abū Dāwūd, *Sunan*, ed. Kamāl Yūsuf al-Ḥūt, 2 vols., Beirut, Muʾassasat al-Kutub al-Thaqāfiyya 1409/1988.

Abū Ḥanīfa, *Risāla li-ʿUthmān al-Battī*, in M.Z. al-Kawtharī (ed.), Cairo 1368/1948.

Abū Ḥanīfa, *Musnad al-imām Abū Ḥanīfa*, ed. Safwat al-Saqqā, Alep 1382/1962.

Abū Nuʿaym, Aḥmad b. ʿAbd Allāh al-Iṣfahānī, *Ḥilyat al-awliyāʾ wa-ṭabaqāt al-aṣfiyāʾ*, 10 vols., Cairo 1352/1933.

Abū ʾl-Qāsim, Ibn ʿAlī al-Mūsawī, *Muʿjam rijāl al-ḥadīth*, 23 vols., Beirut 1403/1983.

Abū ʿUbayd al-Qāsim b. Sallām, *Kitāb al-amwāl*, ed. Muḥammad Khalīl Harrās, Cairo, Maktabat al-Kulliyāt al-Azhariyya 1968.

Abū Yūsuf, Yaʿqūb b. Ibrāhīm, *Kitāb al-kharāj*, trad. Émile Fagnan, *Livre de l'impot foncier*, Paris, Librairie Orientaliste-Paul Geuthner 1921.

Abū Yūsuf, *Kitāb al-āthār*, Cairo 1355/1936.

Abū ʾl-Walīd al-Bājī al-Andalusī, Sulaymān ibn Khalaf, *Kitāb al-muntaqā. Sharḥ Muwaṭṭaʾ imām Mālik*, 7 vols., Cairo, Maṭbaʿat al-Saʿāda 1332/1914.

Ashʿarī (al-), Abū ʾl-Ḥasan, *Maqālāt al-islāmiyīn*, ed. H. Ritter, 2 vols., Leipzig – Istanbul 1929–1930.

Balādhurī [al-], *Futūḥ al-Buldān*, Cairo 1956.

Bayhaqī [al-], Aḥmad ibn al-Ḥusayn, *Kitāb sunan al-kubrā*, ed. A. ʿAbdallāh ʿAllūsh, Riyāḍ, Maktabat al-Rushd Nāshirūn 2004.

Bayhaqī [al-], *Kitāb sunan al-ṣaghīr*, ed. ʿAbd al-Muʿṭī A. Qalʿajī, 4 vols., Cairo, Maṭābiʿ al-Wafāʾ – Karachi, Jāmiʿat al-Dirāsāt al-Islāmiyya 1990.

Bukhārī [al-], *Ṣaḥīḥ al-Bukhārī*, 9 parts in 4 vols., ed. M.M. al-Dimashqī, Beirut, Irādat al-ṭibāʿia al-munīriyya 1407/1986.

Dāraquṭnī [al-], ʿAlī ibn ʿUmar, *al-Sunan*, ed. M. Shams al-Ḥaqq ʿAẓīmābādī, 2 vols. (4 parts), Beirut 1406/1986.

Dārimī [al-], ʿAbdallāh b. ʿAbd al-Raḥmān, *Sunan*, eds. F.A. Zamralī and Kh. al-Sabʿ al-ʿAlamī, 2 vols., Beirut, Dār al-kutub al-ʿarabī 1407/1987.

Dhahabī [al-], Shams al-Dīn Abū ʿAbd Allāh, *Mīzān al-iʿtidāl fī naqd al-rijāl*, ed. ʿA.b.M. al-Bijāwī, 4 vols., Cairo 1382/1963.

Dhahabī [al-], *Tadhkirat al-ḥuffāẓ fī naqd al-rijāl*, ed. ʿAbd al-Raḥmān b. Yaḥyā al-Yamānī, 2 vols., Haydarābād 1968.

Dhahabī [al-], *Tārīkh al-Islām wa ṭabaqāt al-mashāhīr wa ʾl-aʿlām*, 6 vols., Cairo 1367–69.

Ḥājjī Khalīfa, Muṣṭafā b. ʿAbd Allāh Kātib Çelebī, *Kashf al-ẓunūn ʿan asāmī ʾl-kutub wa ʾl-funūn*, 2 vols., Istanbul, Maarif Matbaasi 1941–1945.

Ḥasan b. Muḥammad b. al-Ḥanafiyya, *Kitāb al-irjāʾ*, ed. J. van Ess, *Arabica* 21 (1974) 20–52.

Ibn ʿAbd al-Ḥakam, ʿAbd Allāh, *Sīrat ʿUmar b. ʿAbd al-ʿAzīz*, ed. A. ʿUbayd, Cairo, al-Maktaba al-ʿArabiyya 1346/1927.

Ibn Abī Shayba, Abū Bakr Alī al-Kūfī, *al-Muṣannaf*, ed. ʿAbd al-Kh. Kh. Afghānī et al., 15 vols., Bombay, al-Dār al-Salafīya 1979–1983.

Ibn Ḥajar, Shihāb al-Dīn Abū ʾl-Faḍl Aḥmad b. ʿAlī al-Asqalānī, *Tahdhīb al-tahdhīb*, ed. Beirut 1968.

Ibn Ḥanbal, Aḥmad, *Kitāb al-ʿilal wa maʿrifat al-rijāl*, 2 vols., Istanbul 1987.

Ibn Ḥazm, Abū Muḥammad ʿAlī al-Andalusī al-Ẓāhirī, *al-Muḥallā*, ed. Aḥmad Muḥammad Shākir, 7 vols., Cairo, Idārat al-Ṭibāʿa al-Munīriyya 1349/1930.

Ibn Māja, *Sunan*, ed. M.F. ʿAbd al-Bāqī, 2 vols., Beirut, Dār iḥyāʾ al-turāth al-ʿarabī 1395/1975.

Ibn Rushd, Abū ʾl-Walīd Muḥammad b. Aḥmad, *Kitāb bidāyat al-mujtahid*, Cairo 1949.

Ibn Saʿd, Abū Aḥmad Muḥammad, *Kitāb al-ṭabaqāt al-kabīr*, ed. E. Sachau, 9 vols., Leiden, Brill 1904–1928.

Ibn al-Ṣaghīr, *Akhbār al-aʾimma al-rustumiyyīn*, ed. M. Nāṣir and I. Baḥāz, Beirut, Dār al-Maʿrif al-Islāmī 1406/1986.

Ibn ʿUmar, ʿAbd Allāh, *Musnad*, vols. 9–10, 1987, in *Musnad Abī Yaʿlā al-Mawṣilī*, ed. Ḥusain Salīm Asad, 16 vols., Beirut, Dār al Maʿmūn li-ʾl-Turāth 1984–1994.

Jāḥiẓ [al-], Abū ʿUthman ʿAmr, *al-Bayān wa ʾl-tabyīn*, ed. Ḥ. Sandūbī, 4 vols., Cairo, al-Maṭbaʿa al-Tijārīya al-Kubrā 1947.

Khaṣṣāf [al-], Abū Bakr Aḥmad, *Kitāb al-ḥiyal wa ʾl-makhārij*, ed. J. Schacht, Hannover 1923.

Kishshī [al-], Muḥammad b. ʿUmar, *Kitāb rijāl al-Kishshī*, Kerbelā *c.*1960.

Malaṭī [al-], *Kitāb al-tanbīh wa ʾl-radd*, ed. Sven Dedering, Staatsdruckerei, Istanbul 1936.

Mālik b. Anas, *Kitāb al-Muwaṭṭaʾ*, 4 vols., ed. Muḥammad Fuʾād Abdalbāqī, Cairo 1373/1954.

Muqātil b. Sulaymān, *Kitāb Tafsīr al-khams miʾat āyah min al-Qurʾān*, ed. I. Goldfeld, Shafār ʿAmrū, Dār al-Mashriq 1980.

Muttaqī [al-], ʿAlāʾ ʾl-Dīn ʿAlī, *Kanz al-ʿummāl fi sunan al-aqwāl wa ʾl-afʿāl*, 8 vols., Haidarābād, Maṭbaʿat Majlis Dāʾirat al-Maʿārif al-ʿUthmāniyya 1312–1314.

Muslim, *Ṣaḥīḥ Muslim*, 5 vols., Beirut, Dār al-Kutub al-ʿilmiyya n.d.

Nawawī [al-], *Sharḥ al-imām al-Nawawī ʿalà matn Ṣaḥīḥ al-imām Muslim*, in the margin of Qasṭallanī, *al-Irshād al-sārī li-sharḥ ṣaḥīḥ al-Bukhārī*, 10 vols., Cairo 1374–5/1957.

Nuʿmān (*al-qāḍī* al-Nuʿmān) Abū Ḥanīfa b. Muḥammad, *Daʿāʾim al-Islām wa-dhikr al-ḥalāl wa ʾl-ḥarām wa ʾl-qaḍāyā wa ʾl-aḥkām ʿan Ahl Bayt Rasūl Allāh*, 2 vols., Cairo 1379/1960.

Qarāḍawī [al-], Yūsuf, *Fiqh al-zakāt*, 2 vols., Beirut, Muʾassasat al-risāla 1997.

Qasṭallanī [al-], Abū Yūsuf Aḥmad b. Muḥammad, *al-Irshād al-sārī li-sharḥ ṣaḥīḥ al-Bukhārī*, 10 vols., Cairo 1374–5/1957.

Riḍā, Muḥammad Rashīd, *Tafsīr al-Manār*, 10 vols., Beirut, Dar al-ma ʿrifa 1973.

Sarakhsī [al-], Abū Bakr Muḥammad b. Abī Sahl, *Kitāb al-Mabsūṭ*, 16 vols., Cairo 1324/1906.

Shāfiʿī [al-], Muḥammad b. Idrīs, *Risāla*, ed. M. Sayyid Kīlānī, Cairo 1388/1969.

Shāfiʿī [al-], *Musnad al-imām al-Shāfiʿī*, ed. S.M. al-Laḥḥām, Beirut, Dār al-Fikr 1417/1996.

Shāfiʿī [al-], *al-Umm*, ed. R.F. ʿAbd al-Muṭṭalib, 11 vols., Beirut, Dār al-wafāʾ li-ʾl-ṭibāʿa 1422/2001.

Shaybānī [al-], Muḥammad b. al-Ḥasan, *Kitāb al-makhārij fī ʾl-ḥiyal*, ed. J. Schacht, Leipzig 1930.

Shaybānī [al-], *Kitāb al-Aṣl*, part i: *Kitāb al-buyūʿ wa ʾl-salam*, ed. Sh. Shihāta (CH. Chehata), Cairo 1954.

Shaybānī [al-], *Muwaṭṭaʾ al-imām Mālik, riwāyat Muḥammad b. al-Ḥasan al-Shaybānī*, ed. ʿAbd al-Wahhāb ʿAbd al-Laṭīf, Cairo 1387/1967.

Ṭabarī [al-], Abū Jaʿfar Muḥammad b. Jarīr, *Annales*, ed. M.J. de Goeje, 11 vols., Leiden 1879–1901.

Ṭabarī [al-], *Ikhtilāf al-fuqahāʾ*, fragment ed. F. Kern, Cairo 1320/1902.

Ṭabarī [al-], *Jāmiʿ al-bayān ʿan taʾwīl āy al-Qurʾān* (*Tafsīr al-Ṭabarī*), 7 vols., Beirut, Muʾassat al-Risāla 1994.

Ṭayālisī [al-], Abū Dāwūd, *Musnad*, Cairo 1952.

Tirmidhī [al-] Abū ʿĪsā Muḥammad ibn ʿĪsā, *al-Jāmiʿ al-Ṣaḥīḥ. Sunan al-Tirmidhī*, ed. Aḥmad Muḥammad Shākir, 6 vols., Beirut, Dār al-Kutub al-ʿilmiyya 1408/1987.

Ṭūsī [al-], Abū Jaʿfar Muḥammad b. al-Ḥasan, *al-Istibṣār*, 3 vols., Najaf 1375–76/1956–57.

Zayd b. ʿAlī, *Musnad Zayd b. ʿAlī*, Beirut, Dār Maktabat al-Ḥayāh 1966.

Zurqānī [al-], Muḥammad b. ʿAbd al-Bāqī, *Sharḥ ʿalā Muwaṭṭaʾ al-Imām Mālik*, 4 vols., Cairo 1373/1954.

Secondary Literature

Abd Rahim, R.A., The Concept of *Ijmāʿ* in Islamic Law: A Comparative Study, *Hamdard Islamicus*, 17 (1994), 91–103, republished in M. Baderin, *Islamic Legal Theory*, Farham, Ashgate Publishing Ltd 2014 (new ed. Routledge, London – New York, 2016), chap. 11.

Abou El Fadl, Kh., *And God Knows the Soldiers. The Authoritative and the Authoritarian in Islamic Discourses. A Contemporary Case Study*, Lanham – New York – Oxford, University Press of America 2001.

Abou El Fadl, Kh., *Speaking in God's Name: Islamic Law, Authority, and Women*, Oxford, Oneworld Publications 2001.

Abu Zahra, N., Adultery and Fornication, in EQ i, 28–29.

Adams, C.C., *Islam and Modernism in Egypt. A Study of the Modern Reform Movement Inaugurated by Muḥammad ʿAbduh*, London, Oxford University Press 1933.

Aillet, C., L'ibâḍisme, une minorité au cœur de l'islam, in C. Aillet (ed.), *L'ibâdisme, une minorité au coeur de l'islam*, a special issue of *Revue du monde musulman et de la Méditerranée* 132 (2012), 13–36.

Aillet, C., *L'archipel ibadite: une histoire des marges du Maghreb médiéval*, Lyon, CIHAM 2021.

Aillet, C. and Hassen, M., The Legal *Responsa* Attributed to Aflaḥ b. ʿAbd al-Wahhāb (208–58/823–72). A Preliminary Study, in B. Michalak-Pikulska and R. Eisener (eds.), *Ibadi Jurisprudence. Origins, Development and Cases*, Hildesheim, Olms 2015, 137–146.

Aillet, C., Cressier, P., Gilotte, S. (eds.), *Sedrata. Histoire et archéologie d'un carrefour du Sahara médiéval à la lumière des archives inédites de Marguerite van Berchem*, Madrid, Casa de Velázquez 2017.

Ali, K., *Marriage and Slavery in Early Islam*, Cambridge, MA, Harvard University Press 2010.

Almamari, A.H., *Oman and Ibadism*, New Dehli, Lancers 1980.

Amara, A., Entre le massif de l'Aurès et les oasis: apparition, évolution et disparition des communautés ibâḍites du Zāb (VIIIe–XIVe siècle), in C. Aillet (ed.), *L'ibâdisme, une minorité au coeur de l'islam*, a special issue of *Revue du monde musulman et de la Méditerrané* 132 (2012), 115–135.

Amara, A., L'ibadisme et la malikisation du Maghreb central: étude d'un processus long et complexe (ive–vi^e/x^e–xiie siècle), in C. Aillet (ed.) *L'ibadisme dans les sociétés de l'Islam médiéval. Modèles et interactions*, Berlin-Boston, De Gruyter 2018, 329–347.

Ansari, H. and Husayn, N., The Concise Book of Doctrines by ʿAbd Al-Kāfī al-Warjalānī', in H. Ansari and N. Husayn (eds.), *Caliphate and Imamate: An Anthology of Medieval Muslim Texts on Political Theology*, Cambridge, Cambridge University Press 2023, 140–147.

Arjomand, S.A., *Sociology of Shiʿite Islam: Collected Essays*, Leiden – Boston, Brill 2016.

Azri [al-], Kh., The 20th Century Islamic Legal Reform of the Family Law with the Focus on Oman's Response to Modernity, *Journal of Middle Eastern and Islamic Studies (in Asia)* 4 (2010), 58–73.

Azri [al-], Kh., Change and Conflict in Contemporary Omani Society: The Case of *Kafāʾa* in Marriage, *British Journal of Middle Eastern Studies* 37 (2010), 121–137.

Azri [al-], Kh., One or Three?: Exploring the Scholarly Conflict over the Question of Triple *Ṭalāq* (Divorce) in Islamic Law with Particular Emphasis on Oman, *Arab Law Quarterly* 25 (2011), 277–296.

Azri [al-], Kh., *Social and Gender Inequality in Oman: The Power of Religious and Political Tradition*, London, Routledge 2012.

Baamara, M., *Ittifāqiyāt al-ʿazzāba*, Ghardaia no date.

Baptiste, E. and Gaiser, A., Early Ibāḍī Historiography: The Case of the Khawārij, in H.L. Hagemann and A.C. Grant (eds.), *Between Rebels and Rulers in the Early Islamicate World. Power, Contention and Identity*, Edinburgh, EUP 2024, 52–70.

Badry, R., A Matter of Limited Female Agency: Oman's Personal Status Law and Ibadi Jurisprudence on *Khulʿ* and Other Forms of Divorce Initiated and/or Consented to by Women, in B. Michalak-Pikulska and R. Eisener (eds.), *Ibadi Jurisprudence: Origins, Developments and Cases*, Hildesheim, Olms 2015, 225–239.

Bashear, S., *Qunūt* in *Tafsīr* and *Ḥadīth* Literature, in S. Bashear (ed.), *Studies in Early Islamic Tradition*, Jerusalem, Hebrew University – The Max Schloessinger Memorial Foundation. Collected studies in Arabic and Islam (previously publ. in *Jerusalem Studies in Arabic and Islam* 19/1995), chap. XIII, 36–65.

Basset, R., *Les manuscrits arabes des bibliothèques des Zaouias de ʿAin Madhi et Temancin, de Ouargla et de ʿAdjadja*, Alger, Impr. de l'association ouvrière P. Fontana 1885.

Baugh, C., *Minor Marriage in Early Islamic Law*, Leiden – Boston, Brill 2017.

Ben Shemesh, A., *Taxation in Islām*, 2 vols., Leiden – London, Brill 1965.

Berjak, R., Injury, in O. Leaman (ed.) *The Qurʾan: An Encyclopedia*, London, Routledge 2006.

Bernardus Papiensis, *Summa Decretalium*, E.A. Laspeyres (ed.), Ratisbon 1860.

Brockopp, J., *Early Mālikī Law. Ibn ʿAbd al-Ḥakam and his Major Compendium of Jurisprudence*, Leiden – Boston, Brill 2000.

Brugnatelli, V., The Original Format of Abū Ghānim's *Mudawwana*: Philological Evidence from a Berber Commentary, in R. Eisener (ed.), *Today's Perspectives on Ibadi History*, Hildesheim, Olms 2017, 125–138.

Bū Larwāḥ, I. ibn ʿAlī, *Musnad al-imām al-Rabīʿ ibn Ḥabīb wa-kitāb al-Jāmiʿ li-Ibn Baraka: dirāsa muqārana*, Beirut, Riyāḍ al-Rayyis li-l-Kutub wa ʾl-Nashr 2013.

Caetani, L., *Annali dell'Islam*, 12 vols., Milano-Roma, U. Hœpli-Fondazione Caetani della Reale Accademia dei Lincei 1905–1926 (repr. Hildesheim, Olms 1972).

Calder, N., *Studies in Early Muslim Jurisprudence*, Oxford, Clarendon Press 1993.

Cherifi, B., La Ḥalqa des *ʿazzāba*: un nouveau regard sur l'histoire d'une institution religieuse ibāḍite, *Bulletin of the Royal Institute for Inter-Faith Studies* 7/1 (2005), 39–68.

Cherifi, B., *Le M'zab*, Paris, Ibadica 2015.

Chikh, S., La délibération des Azzaba de Beni-Isguen, *Annuaire de l'Afrique du Nord*, Paris, ed. CREMS/CNRS 1979, 165–186.

Cilardo, A., *Teorie sulle origini del diritto islamico*, Roma, Istituto per l'Oriente 1990.

Cilardo, A., *Diritto ereditario islamico delle scuole sunnite (ḥanafita, mālikita, shāfiʿita e ḥanbalita) e delle scuole giuridiche zaydita, ẓāhirita e ibāḍita*, Roma-Napoli, Istituto per l'Oriente – Istituto Universitario Orientale 1994.

Cook, M., *Early Muslim Dogma: A Source-Critical Study*, Cambridge, Cambridge University Press 1981.

Cook, M., *Commanding Right and Forbidding Wrong in Islamic Thought*, Cambridge, Cambridge University Press 2000.

Cooperson, M., *Classical Arabic Biography. The Heirs of the Prophets in the Age of al-Maʾmūn*, Cambridge, Cambridge University Press 2000.

Coppola, A.R., Al-Sālimī and the Ibāḍī Theology: The *Mashāriq Anwār al-ʿUqūd*, in E. Francesca (ed.), *Ibadi Theology. Rereading Sources and Scholarly Works*, Hildesheim, Olms 2015, 315–324.

Coulson, N.J., *A History of Islamic Law*, Edinburgh, Edinburgh University Press 1964.

Crone, P., *Roman, Provincial and Islamic law: The Origins of the Islamic Patronate*, New York, Cambridge University Press 1987.

Crone, P., *Slaves on Horses – the Evolution of Islamic Polity*, Cambridge, Cambridge University Press 1980.

Crone, P. and Hinds, M., *God's Caliph: Religious Authority in the First Centuries of Islam*, Cambridge, Cambridge University Press 1986.

Crupi La Rosa, G., I trasmettitori della dottrina ibāḍita, *Annali dell'Istituto Universitario Orientale di Napoli*, N.S. 5 (1954), 123–139.

Cuperly, P., *Introduction à l'étude de l'ibāḍisme et de sa théologie*, Alger, Office des publications universitaires 1984.

Custers, M.H., *Ibāḍī Publishing Activities in the East and in the West c. 1880–1960s: An Attempt to an Inventory, with References to Related Recent Publications*, Maastricht 2006.

Custers, M.H., *Al-Ibāḍiyya, a Bibliography. Second, Revised and Enlarged Edition*, 3 vols., Hildesheim, Olms 2016.

Dennett, D.C., *Conversion and the Poll Tax in Early Islam*, Cambridge, Harvard University Press 1950.

Dostal, W., Tribal Custom Law of Zahran Confederation in Southern Hijaz, in W. Dostal and W. Kraus (eds.), *Shattering Tradition. Custom, Law and the Individual in the Muslim Mediterranean*, London – New York, I.B. Tauris 2005, 122–147.

Dostal, W. and Kraus, W. (eds.), *Shattering Tradition. Custom, Law and the Individual in the Muslim Mediterranean*, London – New York, I.B. Tauris 2005.

Dridi, M., La communauté ibadite entre Orient et Occident musulmans (iiie/ixe–viie/xiiie siècle): une histoire d'échanges et de construction identitaire, in C. Aillet (ed.), *L'ibadisme dans les sociétés de l'islam médiéval. Modèles et interactions*, Berlin-Boston, De Gruyter 2018, 348–366.

Duderija, A., Evolution in the Concept of Sunnah during the First Four Generations of Muslims in Relation to the Development of the Concept of an Authentic Ḥadīth as based on Recent Western Scholarship, *Arab Law Quarterly* 26 (2012), 393–437.

Duderija, A. (ed.), *The Sunna and its Status in Islamic Law. The Search for a Sound Hadith*, New York, Palgrave MacMillan 2015.

Ech-Cheikh, M., Ignored Pages of the History of Ibāḍī Theology in North Africa during the Middle Ages. The *Wājiz* (Summary) of ʿAbd al-Kāfi and the *Dalīl* (Proof and Demonstration) of al-Warjlānī, in E. Francesca (ed.), *Ibadi Theology. Rereading Sources and Scholarly Works*, Hildesheim, Olms 2015, 103–112.

El Shamsy, A., *The Canonization of Islamic Law: A Social and Intellectual History*, Cambridge, Cambridge University Press 2013.

Ennami (Al-Nāmī), ʿA. Kh., A description of new Ibāḍī manuscripts from North Africa, *Journal of Semitic Studies* 15/1 (1970), 63–87.

Ennami, ʿA. Kh., *Studies in Ibāḍism*, Bengasi, Publications of the University of Libya, Faculty of Arts, 1392/1972 (Cambridge 1971, Fitzwilliam College, PhD Dissertation 7538). Available online: studies_in_ibadhism.pdf (wordpress.com)

Esmein, A., *Le mariage en droit canonique*, 2 vols., Paris, éd. L. Larose and Forcel 1891. Online: https://archive.org/details/lemariageendroi01esmegoog.

Fadel, M., The Social Logic of *Taqlīd* and the Rise of the *Mukhataṣar*, *Islamic Law and Society*, 3/2 (1996), 193–233.

Fayer, C., *La familia romana. Aspetti giuridici ed antiquari. Concubinato Divorzio e Adulterio*, Rome, "L'Erma" di Bretschneider 2005.

Fierro, M., Al-Aṣfar, *Studia Islamica* 77 (1993), 169–181.

Fierro, M., Al-Aṣfar again, *Jerusalem Studies in Arabic and Islam* 22 (1998), 196–213.

Francesca, E., Jābir b. Zayd, Encyclopaedia of Islam THREE.

Francesca, E., La fabbricazione degli *isnād* nella scuola ibāḍita: il *Musnad* di ar-Rabīʿ b. Ḥabīb, in U. Vermeulen and J.M.F. van Reeth (eds.), *Law, Christianity and Modernism in Islamic Society, Proceedings of the Eighteenth Congress of held at Katholieke Universiteit Leuven (September 3–September 1996)*, Leuven 1998, 39–59.

Francesca, E., Religious Observance and Market Law in Medieval Islam. The Controversial Application of the Prohibition of Usury according to some Ibādī Sources, *La tradition manuscrite en écriture arabe, Revue des Mondes Musulmans et de la Méditerranée* 99–100 (2002), 191–203.

Francesca, E., The Formation and Early Development in the Ibādī *madhhab*, *Jerusalem Studies in Arabic and Islam* 28 (2003), 260–277.

Francesca, E., Investigating Early Ibāḍī Jurisprudence: Sources and Case Law, *Jerusalem Studies in Arabic and Islam* 30 (2005), 231–263.

Francesca, E., Comparing the Ibāḍī and Sunni Law in Baṣra: The Case of the *zakāt* on Cattle, *Revue des Mondes Musulmans et de la Méditerranée* 132 (2012), 45–61.

Francesca, E., Self-defining through Faith: The *walāya* and *barā'a* Dynamics among the Early Ibādis, in C. Adang, H. Ansari, M. Fierro, S. Schmidtke (eds.), *Accusations of Unbelief in Islam: A Diachronic Perspective on takfir*, Leiden, Brill 2015, 29–41.

Francesca, E., The Concept of Sunna in the Ibāḍī School, in A. Duderija (ed.), *The Sunna and its Status in Islamic Law. The Search for a Sound Hadith*, New York, Palgrave MacMillan 2015, chap. 5, 97–115.

Francesca, E., *Ijtihād* and Ibāḍī Reform Movement in North Africa: Shaykh Muḥammad Aṭfayyish's 'Re'-interpretation of *Kitāb al-Nīl*, in A. Al Salimi and R. Eisener (eds.), *Oman, Ibadism and Modernity*, Hildesheim, Olms, 2017, 69–80.

Francesca, E., Religion and Politics in Contemporary Omani Ibadism, in A. Al Salimi and R. Eisener (eds.), *Oman, Ibadism and Modernity*, Hildesheim, Olms, 2017, 87–95.

Francesca, E., Law and Politics in the Early Ibāḍī Communities: Abū ʿUbayda al-Tamīmī's *Risāla* to Abū ʾl-Khaṭṭāb al-Maʿāfirī, in C. Aillet (ed.), *L'ibadisme dans les sociétés de l'islam médiéval. Modèles et interactions*, Berlin-Boston, De Gruyter 2018, 72–88.

Francesca, E., 'Put the ocean between them': Fornication as Permanent Impediment to Marriage in Early Ibāḍī Islam, *Jerusalem Studies in Arabic and Islam* (50) 2021, 101–137.

Francesca, E., Flogging, Banning, Lapidation: What was the Punishment for Fornication and Adultery in Early Islam?, *Jerusalem Studies in Arabic and Islam* (52) 2022, 165–210.

Gaiser, A., *Muslims, Scholars, Soldiers: The Origin and Elaboration of the Ibāḍī Imāmate Traditions*, New York – Oxford, Oxford University Press 2010.

Gaiser, A., *Shurāt Legends, Ibāḍī Identities: Martyrdom, Asceticism, and the Making of an Early Islamic Community*, Columbia, University of South Carolina Press 2016.

Gaiser, A., *Ballaghanā ʿan an-Nabī*: Early Basran and Omani Ibāḍī Understandings of *sunna* and *siyar*, *āthār* and *nasab*, *Bulletin of the School of Oriental and African Studies* 83 (2020), 437–448.

Gaiser, A., *Sectarianism in Islam. The Umma Divided*, Cambridge, Cambridge University Press 2023.

Gaube, H., *The Ibadis in the Region of the Indian Ocean. Section One: East Africa*, Hildesheim, Olms 2013.

Ghazal, A., Seeking Common Ground: Salafism and Islamic Reform in Modern Ibadi Thought, *The Bulletin for the Royal Institute of Inter-Faith Studies* 7/1 (Spring/Summer 2005), 119–141.

Ghazal, A., The Other 'Andalus': The Omani Elite in Zanzibar and the Making of an Identity, 1880s–1930s, *The MIT electronic Journal of Middle East Studies* 5/5 (2005), 43–58. Online https://dome.mit.edu/bitstream/handle/1721.3/177977/MITEJMES_Vol_5_Fall2005.pdf?sequence=1.

Ghazal, A., *Islamic Reform and Arab Nationalism: Expanding the Crescent from the Mediterranean to the Indian Ocean (1880s–1930s)*, Abingdon, Routledge 2010.

Ghazal, A., An Ottoman Pasha and the End of Empire. Sulayman al-Baruni and the Network of Islamic Reform, in J.L. Gelvin and N. Green (eds.), *Global Muslim in the Age of Steam and Print*, Berkley, University of California Press 2013, 40–58.

Ghazal, A., Politics and Polemics. Ibāḍī Theology in North Africa in the Modern Period, in E. Francesca (ed.), *Ibadi Theology. Rereading Sources and Scholarly Works*, Hildesheim, Olms 2015, 271–281.

Ghazal, A., Tensions of Nationalism: The Mzabi Student Missions in Tunis and the Politics of Anticolonialism, *International Journal of Middle East Studies* 47/1 (2015), 47–63.

Gleave, R., Sectarianism and Integration. Contemporary Categories and the Prospects for Islamic Legal Studies, in S. Siddiqui (ed.), *Locating the Sharīʿa: Legal Fluidity in Theory, History and Practice*, Leiden, Brill 2019, 28–45.

Glick, T., Livesey, S.J., Wallis, F. (eds.), *Medieval Science, Technology, and Medicine: An Encyclopedia*, Routledge Encyclopedias of the Middle Ages, London – New York, Routledge 2005.

Goichon, A.M., *La Vie Féminine au Mzab: Étude de Sociologie Musulmane*, 2 vols., Paris, Geuthner 1927.

Goldziher, I., *Mohammed and Islam*, New Haven, Yale University Press 1917.

Gordon, M.S. and Hain, K.A. (eds.), *Concubines and Courtesans: Women and Slavery in Islamic History*, Oxford, Oxford University Press 2017.

Gouja, H., *Essai d'une lecture patrimoniale d'une source théologique ibāḍite. Le fascicule « Kitāb aṭ-Ṭahārāt » de « Dīwān al-ʿAzzāba ». Etude et traduction fragmentaires*, Paris, L'Harmattan 2015.

Guessous, A., Le rescrit fiscal de ʿUmar b. ʿAbd al-ʿAzīz: une nouvelle appréciation, *Der Islam* 73 (1996), 113–137.

Guggenheimer, H. (ed.), *The Jerusalem Talmud*, Berlin – Boston, De Gruyter 2005.

Haj, S., *Reconfiguring Islamic Tradition: Reform, Rationality, and Modernity*, Stanford (CA), Stanford University Press 2009.

Hallaq, W., Was the Gate of Ijtihād Closed?, *International Journal of Middle East Studies* 16/1 (1984), 3–41.

Hallaq, W., On the Origins of the Controversy about the Existence of Mujtahids and the Gate of Ijtihād, *Studia Islamica* 63 (1986), 129–141.

Hallaq, W., The Use and Abuse of Evidence: The Question of Provincial and Roman Influences on Early Islamic Law, *Journal of American Oriental Society* 110/1 (1990), 79–91.

Hallaq, W., Was al-Shāfiʿī the Master Architect of Islamic Jurisprudence?, *International Journal of Middle East Studies* 18 (1993), 587–605.

Hallaq, W., From Regional to Personal Schools of Law? A Reevaluation, *Islamic Law and Society* 8/1 (2001), 1–26.

Hallaq, W., *Authority, Continuity and Change in Islamic Law*, Cambridge, Cambridge University Press 2001.

Harmūsh, M.M.ʿA., *al-Qawāʿid al-fiqhīya al-ibāḍiyya*, 7 vols., Muscat, Wizārat al-Awqāf wa ʾl-Shuʾūn al-Diniyya 2014.

Hayes, C.E., *Gentile Impurities and Jewish Identities: Intermarriage and Conversion from the Bible to the Talmud*, Oxford, Oxford University Press 2002.

Higgins, A.C., *The Qurʾanic Exchange of the Self in the Poetry of Shurāt (Khārijī) Political Identity, 37–132 AH/657–750 AD*, Diss. University of Chicago, Dept. of Near Eastern Languages and Civilizations 2001.

Hoexter, M., Effects of the Transition from the Turkish to French Regime in Algiers. The case of the Mzābī Ṭalaba (Tolba), *Asian and African Studies* 17 (1983), 121–137.

Hoffman, V.J., The Articulation of Ibādī Identity in Modern Oman and Zanzibar, *The Muslim World* 94/2 (2004), 201–216.

Hoffman, V.J., Ibadi Muslim Scholars and the Confrontation with Sunni Islam in Nineteenth- and Early Twentieth-Century Zanzibar, *Bulletin of the Royal Institute of Inter-Faith Studies* 7/1 (2005), 91–118.

Hoffman, V.J., The Ibadis, in A. Rippin (ed.), *The Islamic World*, New York, Routledge 2008, 235–245.

Hoffman, V.J., Abū ʿAmmār ʿAbd al-Kāfī b. Abī Yaʿqūb, *Encyclopaedia of Islam THREE* 2008.

Hoffman, V.J., Historical Memory and Imagined Communities: Modern Ibadi Writings on Kharijism, in J.E. Lindsay and J. Armajani (eds.), *Historical Dimensions of Islam: Essays in Honor of R. Stephen Humphreys*, Princeton, Darwin Press, 2009, 185–200.

Hoffman, V.J., *The Essentials of Ibāḍī Islam*, Syracuse – New York, Syracuse University Press 2012.

Hoffman, V.J., Ibāḍism: History, Doctrines, and Recent Scholarship, *Religion Compass*, September 2015, 297–307, available at https://doi.org/10.1111/rec3.12164.

Hoffman, V.J., Ibāḍī Scholars on Association and Dissociation from the 10th to the 21st Century, in B. Michalak-Pikulska and R. Eisener (eds.), *Ibadi Jurisprudence. Origins, Development and Cases*, Hildesheim, Olms 2015, 185–193.

Hourani, Albert, *Arabic Thought in the Liberal Age, 1798–1939*, Cambridge, Cambridge University Press 1983.

Hurvitz, N., Schools of Law and Historical Context: Re-Examining the Formation of the Ḥanbalī *Madhhab*, *Islamic Law and Society* 7/1 (2000), 37–64.

Imbert, A., Le droit abadhite chez les musulmans de Zanzibar et de l'Afrique orientale, *Revue Algérienne et Tunisienne de Législation et de Jurisprudence*, Algiers 19 (1903), 5–22.

Ibn Idrīsū, M., *Al-fikr al-ʿaqadī ʿinda al-Ibāḍīyya ḥatta nihāyat al-qarn al-thālith al-hijrī*. Ghardāya 2003.

Ibn Ḥammū Kurrūm, A., *Ishāmāt al-madrasa al-Ibāḍiyya fī khidma al-sunna al-nabawiyya*, El Hamiz (Algeria), Markaz al-manār 1432/2011.

Jaabiri, F., *L'organisation des Azzabas chez les Ibadites de Djerba*, Paris, Ibadica 2016.

Jackson, Sh. A., *Taqlīd*, Legal Scaffolding and the Scope of Legal Injunctions in Post-Formative Theory *Muṭlaq* and *ʿĀmm* in the Jurisprudence of Shihāb Al-Dīn Al-Qarāfī, *Islamic Law and Society* 3/2 (1996), 165–192.

Jackson, Sh. A., Kramer versus Kramer in a Tenth/Sixteenth Century Egyptian Court: Post-Formative Jurisprudence between Exigency and Law, *Islamic Law and Society* 8/1 (2001), 27–51.

Johansen, B., *Contingency in a Sacred Law*, Leiden, Brill 1999.

Jomier, A., *Islam, réforme et colonisation. Une histoire de l'ibadisme en Algérie (1882–1962)*, Paris, Editions de la Sorbonne 2020.

Jomier, A., Muslim Notables, French Colonial Officials, and the Washers of the Dead: Women and Gender Politics in Colonial Algeria, *French Politics, Culture & Society* 39/1 (2021), 9–33.

Jones, J. and Ridout, N., *A History of Modern Oman*, Cambridge, Cambridge University Press, Cambridge 2015.

Juynboll, G.H.A., *Muslim Tradition: Studies in Chronology, Provenance and Authorship of Early Ḥadīth*, Cambridge, Cambridge University Press 1983.

Juynboll, G.H.A., Some New Ideas on the Development of *sunna* as a Technical Term in Early Islam, *Jerusalem Studies in Arabic and Islam* 10 (1987), 97–118.

Juynboll, G.H.A., Some Notes on Islam's First *fuqahāʾ* Distilled from Early *ḥadīth* Literature, *Arabica* 39 (1992), 287–314.

Kamāl al-Dīn al-Imām, Muḥammad, *Sharḥ Kitāb al-Nīl li-l-imām al-ʿalāma Muḥammad b. Yūsuf al-Aṭfayyish. Muṣṭalahāt wa ruʾūs al-masāʾil*, 5 vols., Muscat, Wizārat al-awqāf wa ʾl-shuʾūn al-diniyya 2011.

Kara, S., *Integrity of the Qurʾan. Sunni and Shiʿi Historical Narratives*, Edinburgh University Press, Edinburgh 2024.

Kerr, M.H., *Islamic Reform. The Political and Legal Theories of Muḥammad ʿAbduh and Rashīd Riḍā*, Berkeley, University of California Press 1966.

Kevin, J.R., *Authority, Conflict, and the Transmission of Diversity in Medieval Islamic Law*, Leiden – Boston, Brill 2006.

Khulaifāt (Khleifat), A.M., *Nashʾat al-ḥaraka al-ibāḍiyya*, Amman 1978.

Kister, M.Y., Some Reports Concerning al-Ṭâʾif, *Jerusalem Studies in Arabic and Islam* 1 (1979), 1–18.

Kondo, Y., The Development of Ibāḍī Jurisprudence in Oman in the 3rd/9th and 4th/10th Centuries: A Preliminary Study of Some Marriage Issues, in B. Michalak-Pikulska and R. Eisener (eds.), *Ibadi Jurisprudence. Origins, Development and Cases*, Hildesheim, Olms 2015, 81–91.

Krämer, G. and Schmidtke, S., *Speaking for Islam: Religious Authorities in Muslim Societies*, Leiden, Brill 2006.

Layish, A., *Sharīʿa and Custom in Libyan Tribal Society*, Leiden, Brill 2005.

Leder, S., *Das Corpus Haitham b. ʿAdī (st. 207/822). Herkunft, Überlieferung, Gestalt früher Texte der aḫbār Literatur*, Frankfurt, Klostermann 1991.

Lewicki, T., al-Ibāḍiyya, Encyclopaedia of Islam, Second Edition.

Lewicki, T., Ibn Baraka, Encyclopaedia of Islam, Second Edition.

Lewicki, T., *Études ibāḍites nord-africaines*, Varsaw, Państwowe Wydawnictwo Naukowe 1955.

Lewinstein, K., Making and Unmaking a Sect: The Heresiographers and the Ṣufriyya, *Studia Islamica* 76 (1992), 75–96.

Lewittes, M., *Jewish Marriage. Rabbinic Law, Legend, and Custom*, Northvale (NJ), Jason Aronson Inc. 1994.

Løkkegard, F., *Islamic Taxation in the Classic Period, with Special Reference to Circumstances in Iraq*, Copenhagen, Branner & Korch 1950.

Love, P.M., *Ibadi Muslims of North Africa. Manuscripts, Mobilization, and the Making of a Written Tradition*, Cambridge, Cambridge University Press 2018.

Lucas, S.C., Divorce, *Ḥadīth*-Scholar Style: From al-Dārimī to al-Tirmidhī, *Journal of Islamic Studies* 19/3 (2008), 325–368.

Lydon, G., *On Trans-Saharan Trails: Islamic Law, Trade Networks, and Cross-Cultural Exchange in Nineteenth-Century Western Africa*, Cambridge, Cambridge University Press 2009.

Madelung, W., *Religious Trends in Early Islamic Iran*, Albany, N.Y., Bibliotheca Persica 1988.

Madelung, W., Abd Allāh Ibn Ibāḍ and the Origins of the Ibāḍiyya, in B. Michalak-Pikulska and A. Pikulski (eds.), *Authority, Privacy and Public Order in Islam: Proceedings of the 22nd Congress of l'Union Européenne des Arabisants et Islamisants*, Leuven (Belgium), Peters 2006, 52–57, republished in *Studies in Medieval Muslim Thought and History*, Farnham (UK), Ashgate Variorum 2013, chap. V.

Madelung, W., ʿAbd Allāh Ibn Ibāḍ's Second Letter to ʿAbd al-Malik, in A. Fuʾād Sayyid (ed.), *al-Umma wa ʾl-dawla wa ʾl-tārīkh wa ʾl-maṣāʾir: dirāsāt muhdāh ilā* (*Maulānā*) *Riḍwān al-Sayyid bi-munāsabat bulūghihi al-sittīn*, Beirut, Al-Shabaka al-ʿArabiyya li-l-Abḥāth wa ʾl-Nashr 2011, 7–17, republ. in *Studies in Medieval Muslim Thought and History*, chap. V.

Madelung, W., The Authenticity of the Letter of ʿAbd Allâh b. Ibāḍ to ʿAbd al-Malik, in C. Aillet (ed.), *L'ibāḍisme, une minorité au coeur de l'islam*, special issue of *Revue du monde musulman et de la Méditerranée* 132 (2012), 37–43.

Madelung, W., Ibāḍiyya and Muʿtazila: Two Moderate Opposition Movements in Early Islam, in E. Francesca (ed.), *Ibadi Theology. Rereading Sources and Scholarly Works*, Hildesheim, Olms 2015, 23–28.

Madelung, W., *Aqwāl Qatāda* and the Shuʿaybiyya and Nukkār, in B. Michalak-Pikulska and R. Eisener (eds.), *Ibadi Jurisprudence. Origins, Development and Cases*, Hildesheim, Olms 2015, 25–30.

Maimonides, *Leyes sobre el matrimonio* (*Hilkot ishut*) *del Mishné Torá*. Introducción, traducción y notas por O. Ruiz Morell y A. Salvatierra Ossorio, Estella (Navarra), Editorial Verbo Divino 2010.

Makdisi, G., *The Rise of Colleges: Institutions of Learning in Islam and the West*, Edinburgh, Edinburgh University Press 1981.

Makdisi, G., *Ṭabaqāt*-Biography: Law and Orthodoxy in Classical Islam, *Islamic Studies* 22 (1993), 371–396.

Masqueray, E., *Formation des cités chez les populations sédentaires de l'Algerie. Kabyles du Djurdjura, Chaouïa de l'Aourâs, Beni Mezab*, Aix-en-Provance, Edisud 1983 (réimpression de l'ouvrage publié en 1886 chez l'éditeur Ernest Leroux à Paris. Présentation par Fanny Colonna).

Massignon, L., Islamisme et religions de l'Arabie, *Revue d'Études Islamiques* 4 (1938), 410–411.

Mattson, I., *A Believing Slave is Better than an Unbeliever: Status and Community in Early Islamic Society and Law*, PhD Thesis, University of Chicago, Department of Near Easter Language and Civilization, 1999.

Melchert, C., *The Formation of the Sunni Schools of Law, 9th–10th Centuries C.E.*, Leiden – Boston, Brill 1997.

Melchert, C., How Ḥanafism Came to Originate in Kufa and Traditionalism in Medina, *Islamic Law and Society* 6/3 (1999), 318–347.

Meouak, M., Les communautés ibadites du nord du Sahara au Moyen Âge: espace et société dans la région de l'oued Rīgh, in C. Aillet (ed.), *L'ibadisme dans les sociétés de l'Islam médiéval. Modèles et interactions*, Berlin-Boston, De Gruyter 2018, 244–275.

Mercier, M., *Étude sur le waqf abadhite et ses applications au Mzab*, Algiers 1927.

Milliot, L., *Recueil de délibérations des djemaa du M'zab*, Paris, Librerie Orientaliste Paul Geuthner 1930.

Mirza, Y.Y., Remembering the *Umm al-Walad*: Ibn Kathir's Treatise on Sale of the Concubine, in M.S. Gordon and K.A. Hain (eds.), *Concubines and Courtesans: Women and Slavery in Islamic History*, Oxford, Oxford University Press 2017, 297–323.

Mitter, U., Unconditional Manumission of Slaves in Early Islamic Law: A *Ḥadīth* Analysis, in W. Hallaq (ed.), *The Formation of Islamic Law*, London – New York, Routledge 2004, 115–152.

Modarresi, H., Common Ibāḍī/Shīʿite Legacy: Examples from the Ritual Law, in B. Michalak-Pikulska and R. Eisener (eds.), *Ibadi Jurisprudence. Origins, Development and Cases*, Studies on Ibadism and Oman, vol. 6, Hildesheim, Olms 2015, 111–119.

Morand, M., *Les Kanouns du M'zab*, Algiers, Adolphe Jourdan 1903.

Morand, M., *Études de droit musulman algérien*, Algiers 1910.

Morand, M., *Avant-Projet de Code Présenté à la Commission de Codification du Droit Musulman Algérien*, Algiers 1916.

Motylinski, A. de Calassanti, and Lewicki, T., Abū l-Khaṭṭāb ʿAbd al-Aʿlā al-Maʿāfirī, Encyclopaedia of Islam, Second Edition.

Motylinski, A. de Calassanti, *Le Mobacher*, June 9th, 16th and 23rd 1883.

Motylinski, A. de Calassanti, Bibliographie du Mzab. Les livres de la secte abadhite, *Bulletin de Correspondance Africaine* (Algiers) 4/3 (1885), 15–72 (no. 7, 8, 10, 12, 13, 15, 16).

Motylinski, A. de Calassanti, *Notes historiques sur le Mzab. Guerara depuis sa fondation*, Alger 1885.

Motzki, H., *Wal-muḥṣanātu mina n-nisā'i illā mā malakat aimānukum* (Koran 4:24) und die koranische Sexualethik, *Der Islam* 63/2 (1986), 192–218.

Motzki, H., Der Prophet und die Schuldner. Eine *ḥadīth* Untersuchung auf dem Prüfstand, *Der Islam* 77/1 (2000), 50–61.

Motzki, H., *Die Anfänge der islamischen Jurisprudenz – Ihre Entwicklung in Mekka bis zur Mitte des 2./8. Jahrhunderts*, Stuttgart, Franz Steiner 1991. English trans. by Marion Holmes Katz, *The Origins of Islamic Jurisprudence: Meccan Fiqh before the Classical Schools*, Leiden, Brill 2002.

Mu'ammar, 'A.Y., *Ibāḍīyya bayna firaq al-islāmiyya*, Al-Sīb, Maktabat al-Ḍāmirī li-l-Nashr wa 'l-Tawzī' 2003.

Mu'ammar, 'A.Y., *Ibāḍīyya fī mawkib al-tārīkh*, 2 vols., Cairo, Maktaba Wahba 1964.

Muranyi, M., *The First Compendium of Ibadi Law: The Mudawwana by Abu Ghanim Bishr b. Ghanim al-Khurasani*, Hildesheim, Olms 2018.

Nafi, B.M., *The Rise and Decline of the Arab-Islamic Reform Movement*, London, The Institute of Contemporary Islamic Thought 2000.

Naggar, M., *Fatwā von Jābir an al-Ḥārith b. 'Amr*, unpublished thesis, Ludwigsburg, December 1991.

Neuwirth, A., Sinai, N. and Marx, M. (eds.), *The Quran in Context: Historical and Literary Investigations into the Qur'ānic Milieu*, Leiden, Brill 2010.

Omar, M.A., *Reasoning in Islamic Law*, Cairo, Dār al-Nahḍa al-'Arabiyya 1996.

Ouinten, M., *Ārā' al-shaykh Muḥammad b. Yūsuf Aṭfayyish al-'aqdiyya*, al-Qarāra (Algeria), Jam'iyyat al-Turāth 1996.

Ourghi, A., *Die Reformbewegung in der neuzeitlichen Ibāḍīya: Leben, Werk und Wirken von Muḥammad b. Yūsuf Aṭfaiyaš, 1236–1332 h.q. (1821–1914)*, Würzburg, Ergon Verlag 2008.

Ould-Braham, O., Émile Masqueray au Mzab: à la recherche de livres ibâḍites, *Études et documents berbères* 9/1 (1992), 5–35.

Pavlovitch, P., The Stoning of a Pregnant Adulteress from Juhayna: The Early Evolution of a Muslim Tradition, *Islamic Law and Society* 17/1 (2010), 1–62.

Pavlovitch, P., The Islamic Penalty for Adultery in the Third Century AH and Al-Shāfi'ī's *Risāla*, *Bulletin of the School of Oriental and African Studies* 75/3 (2012), 473–497.

Pellat, Ch., Ḳatāda b. Di'āma, Encyclopaedia of Islam, Second Edition.

Peters, R., Zinā, Encyclopaedia of Islam, Second Edition.

Peters, R., *Crime and Punishment in Islamic law. Theory and Practice from the Sixteenth to the Twenty-first Century*, Cambridge, Cambridge University Press 2005.

Peterson, J.E., The Revival of the Ibāḍī Imāmate in Oman and the Threat to Muscat, 1913–20, *Arabian Studies* 3 (1976), 165–188.

Peterson, J.E., Arab Nationalism and the Idealist Politician: The Career of Sulayman al-Baruni, in J. Piscatori and G.S. Harris (eds.), *Law, Personalities and Politics in the Middle East 1987. Essays in Honor of Majid Khadduri*, Washington, Westview Press 1987, 124–139.

Peterson, J.E., *Oman's Insurgencies. The Sultanate's Struggle for Supremacy*, London, Saqi Books 2007.

Prevost, V., Genèse et développement de la *ḥalqa* chez les ibāḍites maghrébins, *Acta Orientalia Belgica* 19 (2006), 109–124.

Prevost, V., *L'aventure ibāḍite dans le Sud tunisien. Effervescence d'une région méconnue*, Helsinki, Academia Scientifica Fennica 2008.

Prevost, V., ʿAbd al-Raḥmān ibn Rustum al-Fārisī. Une tentative de biographie du premier imām de Tāhart, *Der Islam* 86 (2009), 44–64.

Prevost, V., *Les Ibadites. De Djerba à Oman, la troisième voie de l'Islam*, Turnhout, Brepols 2010.

Prevost, V., La deuxième scission au sein des ibadites. Les descendants de l'imam Abū l-Ḫaṭṭāb al-Maʿāfirī et le schisme ḫalafite, in M. Meouak (ed.) *Biografías magrebíes. Identidades y grupos religiosos, sociales y políticos en el Magreb medieval*, Madrid, CSIC 2012, 29–63.

Prevost, V., Maǧmāǧ et les sept savants: la création du Dīwān al-ʿazzāba, *Acta Orientalia* 73 (2012), 35–58.

Radivilov, D., Rereading Omani Siyar: Khālid b. Qaḥṭān, in E. Francesca (ed.) *Ibadi Theology. Rereading Sources and Scholarly Works*, Hildesheim, Olms 2015, 83–92.

Rebstock, U., *Die Ibāditen im Magrib (2./8.–4/10.Jh.): die Geschichte einer Berberbewegung in Gewand des Islam*, Berlin, Klaus Schwarz Verlag 1983.

Robin (Le Commandant Robin), *Le Mzab et son annexion à la France*, Alger, Adolphe Jourdan 1884 (available online at https://www.fichier-pdf.fr/2014/07/17/le-mzab-robin-1884/preview/page/47/).

Robinson, M., Statistical Approaches to the Rise of Concubinage in Islam, in M.S. Gordon and K.A. Hain (eds.), *Concubines and Courtesans: Women and Slavery in Islamic History*, Oxford, Oxford University Press 2017, 11–26.

Rosen, L., Law and Custom in the Popular Legal Culture of North Africa, *Islamic Law and Society* 2/2 (1995), 194–208.

Rosenthal, F., *Knowledge Triumphant: The Concept of Knowledge in Medieval Islam*, Leiden, Brill 2007.

Rubin, U., *Al-Walad li-l-Firāsh* on the Islamic Campaign against Zinā, *Studia Islamica* 78 (1993), 5–26.

Rubinacci, R., Notizia di alcuni manoscritti ibāḍiti esistenti presso l'Istituto Universitario Orientale di Napoli, *Annali dell'Istituto Universitario Orientale di Napoli*, N.S. 3 (1949), 431–438.

Rubinacci, R., Il Kitāb al-Ǧawāhir di al-Barrādī, *Annali dell'Istituto Universitario Orientale di Napoli*, N.S. 4 (1952), 95–110.

Rubinacci, R., Il califfo ʿAbd al-Malik b. Marwān e gli Ibāḍiti, *Annali dell'Istituto Universitario Orientale di Napoli*, N.S. 5 (1954), 99–121.

Rubinacci, R., La purità rituale secondo gli Ibāḍiti, *Annali dell'Istituto Universitario Orientale di Napoli*, N.S. 4 (1957), 1–41.

Rubinacci, R., Un antico documento di vita cenobitica musulmana. La regola della *ḥalqa* dello *šayḫ* Abū ʿAbd Allāh Muḥammad b. Bakr, *Annali dell'Istituto Orientale di Napoli* 10 (1960), 37–78.

Rubinacci, R., La professione di fede di al-Ǧannāwunī, *Annali dell'Istituto Universitario Orientale di Napoli*, N.S. 14 (1964), 553–595.

Rubinacci, R., L'aḏān presso gl'Ibāḍiti, *Folia Orientalia* 12 (1970), 279–290.

Rumee, A., *Narratives of Islamic Theory*, Oxford, Oxford University Press 2012.

Saad, E., *Social History of Timbuktu: The Role of Muslim Scholars and Notables 1400–1900*, Cambridge, Cambridge University Press 1983.

Sachau, E., Mohammedanisches Erbrecht nach der Lehre der Ibaditischen Araber von Zanzibar und Ostafrika, in *Sitzungsberichte der Königlich Preussischen Akademie der Wissenschaft zu Berlin 15. Feb. 1894*, Berlin 8 (1894), 159–210 (Italian translation by I. Guidi, in *Rivista Coloniale*, 1906).

Sadgrove, P., From Wadi Mizab to Unguja. Zanzibar's Scholarly Links, in S.S. Reese, *The Transmission of Learning in Islamic Africa*, Brill, Leiden 2004, 184–211.

Salaymeh, L., *The Beginnings of Islamic law. Late Antique Islamicate Legal Traditions*, Cambridge, Cambridge University Press 2016.

Sālimī [al-], ʿA., Min maṣādir al-taʾrīkh wa ʾl-thaqāfa: al-siyar al-ʿUmāniyya, *Nizwā* 24 (Oct. 2000), 79–94 (http://nizwa.com/volume24/p79_94.html).

Salimi [al-], A., *The Omani* Siyar *as a Literary Genre and Its Role in the Political Evolution and Doctrinal Development of Eastern Ibadism, with Special Reference to the Epistles of Khwarizm, Khurasan and Mansura*, PhD Thesis, Durham 2001.

Salimi [Al], A., Themes of the Ibāḍī/Omani *Siyar*, *Journal of Semitic Studies* 54/2 (2009), 475–514.

Salimi [Al], A., Identifying the (Ibāḍī/Omani) *Siyar*, *Journal of Semitic Studies* 55/1 (2010), 115–162.

Salimi [al-], A., Early Islamic Theological Influence in Jurisprudence. An Ibāḍī Perspective, in B. Michalak-Pikulska and R. Eisener (eds.), *Ibadi Jurisprudence. Origins, Developments and Cases*, Hildesheim, Olms 2015, 55–71.

Salimi [al-], A., *On the Reception of Early Ibadi Theology. A Commentary on the* "Book on Monotheism" *by ʿAbd Allāh b. Yazīd al-Fazārī (2nd/8th Century)*, Wiesbaden, Harrassowitz Verlag, 2021.

Santillana, D., *Istituzioni di Diritto Musulmano Malichita con riguardo anche al Sistema Sciafiita*, 2 vols., Roma 1926 and 1938.

Savage, E., *A Gateway to Hell, a Gateway to Paradise. The North African Response to the Arab Conquest*, Berlin, Gerlach Press 2021.
Schacht, J., *The Origins of Muhammadan Jurisprudence*, Oxford, Clarendon Press 1950.
Schacht, J., Adultery as an Impediment to Marriage in Islamic and Canon Law, *Archives d'histoire du droit oriental et Revue internationale des droits de l'antiquité* 1 (1952), 105–123.
Schacht, J., The Schools of Law and Later Developments of Jurisprudence, in M. Khadduri and H.J. Liebesny (eds.), *Law in the Middle East*, vol. 1: *Origin and Development of Islamic Law*, Washington D.C., Middle East Institute 1955, 28–84.
Schacht, J., Bibliothèques et manuscripts abadites, *Revue Africaine* (Algiers) 100 (1956), 375–398.
Schacht, J., *An Introduction to Islamic Law*, Oxford, Clarendon Press 1964.
Schneider, I., Imprisonment in Pre-Classical and Classical Islamic Law, *Islamic Law and Society* 2/2 (1995), 157–173.
Schneider, I., *Kinderverkauf und Schuldknechtschaft. Untersuchung zur früher Phase des islamischen Recht*, Stuttgart, Franz Steiner Verlag 1999.
Schwartz, W., *Die Anfänge der Ibaditen in Nordafrika – der Beitrag einer islamischen Minderheit zur Ausbreitung des Islams*, Wiesbaden, Harrassowitz 1983.
Sedgwick, M., *Muhammad Abduh*, Oxford, Oneworld 2010.
Serrano, D., Legal practice in an Andalusī-Maghribi Source from the Twelfth Century CE: The *madhāhib al-hukkām fī nawāzil al-ahkām*, *Islamic Law and Society* 7/2 (2000), 187–234.
Sezgin, F., *Geschichte des Arabischen Schrifttums*, 17 vols., Leiden, Brill, 1967–. Available online https://brill.com/display/serial/GAS.
Siddiqui, S. (ed.), *Locating the Sharīʿa: Legal Fluidity in Theory, History and Practice*, Leiden, Brill 2019.
Simonsen, J.B., *Studies in the Genesis and Early Development of the Caliphal Taxation System*, Copenhagen 1988.
Sinai, N., The Qur'an as Process, in A. Neuwirth, N. Sinai and M. Marx (eds.), *The Quran in Context: Historical and Literary Investigations into the Qur'ānic Milieu*, Leiden, Brill 2010, 407–439.
Skreslet Hernandez, R., *The Legal Thought of Jalāl al-Dīn al-Suyūṭī: Authority and Legacy*, Oxford, Oxford University Press 2017.
Smogorzewski, Z., Essai de bio-bibliographie Ibadite-Wahhabite, Avant-propos, *Rocznik Orjentalistyczny* (Lwów) V (1927) publ. (1929), 45–57.
Spectorsky, S., *Sunnah* in the Responses of Isḥāq b. Rāhwayh, in B.G. Weiss (ed.) *Studies in Islamic Legal Theory*, Leiden, Brill 2002, 51–74.
Stewart, D., *Islamic Legal Orthodoxy*, Salt Lake City, University of Utah Press 1998.
Sulaimi [al-], A.A., The *Iftā'* Office of Oman: Its Objectives and Policy, in ʿA. al-Sālimī and R. Eisener (eds.) *Oman, Ibadism and Modernity*, Hildesheim, Olms 2018, 247–261.

Talbi, M., *Études d'histoire ifriqiyenne et de civilisation musulmane médiévale*, Tunis, Faculté des lettres et sciences humaines 1982.

Ubaydli, A., *Early Islamic Oman and Early Ibāḍism in the Arabic Sources*, PhD thesis, Faculty of Oriental Studies, University of Cambridge, Cambridge 1990 (https://doi.org/10.17863/CAM.20431).

Valeri, M., *Oman: Politics and Society in the Qaboos State*, revised and updated edition, London, Hurst & Company 2017.

van Ess, J., Untersuchungen zu einigen ibāḍitischen Handschriften, *Zeitschrift der Deutschen Morgenländischen Gesellschaft*, 126 (1976), 25–63.

van Ess, J., *Anfänge muslimischer Theologie – Zwei antiqadaritische Traktate aus dem ersten Jahrhundert der Hiğra*, Wiesbaden-Beirut 1977.

van Ess, J., Nachträge, *Zeitschrift der Deutschen Morgenländischen Gesellschaft*, 127 (1977), 1–4.

van Ess, J., *Theologie und Gesellschaft im 2. Und 3. Jahrhundert Hidschra*, 6 vols., Berlin, de Gruyter 1991–1995.

Veccia Vaglieri, L., Il conflitto ʿAlī-Muʿāwiya e la secessione khārijita riesaminati alla luce di fonti ibāḍite, *Annali dell'Istituto Universitario Orientale di Napoli*, N.S. 4 (1952), 1–94.

Vitestam, G., Qatāda b. Diʿāma as-Sadūsī et la science du *ḥadīth*, in *Actes du Vᵉ Congrès International d'Arabisants et d'Islamisants*, Bruxelles, Publications du Centre pour l'étude des problèmes du monde musulman contemporain 1970, 489–498.

Warscheid, I., *Droit musulman et société au Sahara prémoderne. La justice islamique dans les oasis du Grand Touat (Algérie) aux XVIIᵉ–XIXᵉ siècles*, Leiden, Brill 2017.

Weiss, B. (ed.), *Studies in Islamic Legal Theory*, Leiden, Brill 2002.

Weitz, L.E., *Between Christ and Caliph: Law, Marriage, and Christian Community in Early Islam*, Philadelphia, University of Pennsylvania Press 2018.

Welchman, L., *Women and Muslim Family Laws in Arab States. Comparative Overview of Textual Development and Advocacy*, Amsterdam, Amsterdam University Press 2007.

Wensinck, A.J., Ḳunūt, Encyclopaedia of Islam, Second Edition.

Wilkinson, J.C., Bio-bibliographical Background to the Crisis Period in the Ibāḍī Imāmate of Oman, *Arabian Studies*, 3 (1976), 137–164.

Wilkinson, J.C., The Omani Manuscript Collection at Muscat – Part II – The Early Ibāḍī *fiqh* Works, *Arabian Studies*, 4 (1978), 191–208.

Wilkinson, J.C., Ṣuḥar (Sohar) in the Early Islamic Period: The Written Evidence, in M. Taddei (ed.), *South-Asian Archaeology, 1977*, 2 vols., Naples 1979, ii, 889–905.

Wilkinson, J.C., The Early Development of the Ibāḍī Movement in Baṣra, in G.H.A. Juynboll (ed.), *Studies in the First Century of Islamic Society*, Carbondale, Southern Illinois University Press 1982, 125–144.

Wilkinson, J.C., Ibāḍi *Ḥadīth*: An Essay on Normalization, *Der Islam* 62 (1985), 231–259.

Wilkinson, J.C., *The Imamate Tradition of Oman*, Cambridge, Cambridge University Press 1987.

Wilkinson, J.C., Ibāḍī Theological Literature, in M.G.L. Young, J.D. Latham and R.B. Serjeant (eds.), *Religion, Learning and Science in the ʿAbbasid Period*, Cambridge, Cambridge University Press 1990, 33–39.

Wilkinson, J.C., *Ibâḍism: Origins and Early Development in Oman*, Oxford, Oxford University Press 2010.

Wilkinson, J.C., Contextualizing the Development of Ibadi Fiqh, in B. Michalak-Pikulska and R. Eisener (eds.), *Ibadi Jurisprudence. Origins, Development and Cases*, Hildesheim, Olms 2015, 15–23.

Yanagihashi, H., *A History of the Early Islamic Law of Property. Reconstructing the Legal Development, 7th–9th Centuries*, Leiden – Boston, Brill 2004.

Yanagihashi, H., *Studies in Legal Hadith*, Leiden – Boston, Brill 2019.

Zellentin, H.M., (ed.), *The Qur'an's Reformation of Judaism and Christianity: Return to the Origins*, Abingdon, Routledge 2019.

Zeys, E., *Droit mozabite – le Nīl. Du mariage et de sa dissolution*, Algiers 1891.

Zeys, E., *Législation mozabite, son origine, ses sources, son présent, son avenir*, Algiers 1886.

Ziaka, A., The Roots of the Uṣūl al-Fiqh in the Ibāḍī Madhhab: A Comparison Between Abū Saʿīd al-Kudamī and Ibn Baraka, in B. Michalak-Pikulska and R. Eisener (eds.), *Ibadi Jurisprudence. Origins, Developments and Cases*, Hildesheim, Olms 2015, 93–100.

Zorgati, R.J., *Pluralism in the Middle Ages. Hybrid Identities, Conversion, and Mixed Marriages in Medieval Iberia*, New York – London, Routledge 2012.

Zysow, A., *The Economy of Certainty. An Introduction to the Typology of Islamic Legal Theory*, Atlanta (Georgia), Lockwood Press 2013.

Index of Names and Authors

Index of Arabic Terms

 | HTTPS://DOI.ORG/10.1163/9789004765764-014

Index of Places

www.ingramcontent.com/pod-product-compliance
Lightning Source LLC
LaVergne TN
LVHW082059151026
850117LV00004B/25